Women in European History

THE MAKING OF EUROPE

Series Editor: Jacques Le Goff

The *Making of Europe* series is the result of a unique collaboration between five European publishers – Beck in Germany, Blackwell in Great Britain and the United States, Critica in Spain, Laterza in Italy and le Seuil in France. Each book will be published in all five languages. The scope of the series is broad, encompassing the history of ideas as well as of societies, nations and states to produce informative, readable and provocative treatments of central themes in the history of the European peoples and their cultures.

* OP

Women in European History

Gisela Bock

Translated by Allison Brown

First published 2002

2 4 6 8 10 9 7 5 3 1

Blackwell Publishers Ltd
108 Cowley Road
Oxford OX4 1JF
UK

Blackwell Publishers Inc.
350 Main Street
Malden, Massachusetts 02148
USA

British Library Cataloguing in Publication Data

A CIP catalogue record for this book is available from the British Library.

Library of Congress Cataloging-in-Publication Data

Bock, Gisela.
    Women in European history / Gisela Bock.
       p.   cm. — (The Making of Europe)
    Includes bibliographical references and index.
    ISBN 0-631-19145-3 (pbk.: acid-free paper) — ISBN 0-631-23191-9 (hdbk.: acid-free paper)
      1. Women—Europe—History. 2. Feminism—Europe—History. I. Title. II. Series.

HQ1587 .B63 2001
305.4′094—dc21

                                  2001002364

Typeset in 10.5 on 12 pt Sabon
by Ace Filmsetting Ltd, Frome, Somerset

This book is printed on acid-free paper.

Contents

Series Editor's Preface

Europe is in the making. This is both a great challenge and one that can be met only by taking the past into account – a Europe without history would be orphaned and unhappy. Yesterday conditions today; today's actions will be felt tomorrow. The memory of the past should not paralyse the present: when based on understanding it can help us to forge new friendships, and guide us towards progress

Europe is bordered by the Atlantic, Asia and Africa, its history and geography inextricably entwined, and its past comprehensible only within the context of the world at large. The territory retains the name given it by the ancient Greeks, and the roots of its heritage may be traced far into prehistory. It is on this foundation – rich and creative, united yet diverse – that Europe's future will be built.

The Making of Europe is the joint initiative of five publishers of different languages and nationalities: Beck in Munich; Blackwell in Oxford; Critica in Barcelona; Laterza in Rome; and le Seuil in Paris. Its aim is to describe the evolution of Europe, presenting the triumphs but not concealing the difficulties. In their efforts to achieve accord and unity the nations of Europe have faced discord, division and conflict. It is no purpose of this series to conceal these problems: those committed to the European enterprise will not succeed if their view of the future is unencumbered by an understanding of the past.

The title of the series is thus an active one: the time is yet to come when a synthetic history of Europe will be possible. The books we shall publish will be the work of leading historians, by no means all European. They will address crucial aspects of European history in every field – political, economic, social religious and cultural. They will draw on that long historiographical tradition which stretches back to Herodotus, as well as on those conceptions and ideas which have transformed historical enquiry in the late and early twenty-first centuries. They will write readably for a wide public.

Our aim is to consider the key questions confronting those involved in Europe's making, and at the same time to satisfy the curiosity of the world at large: in short, who are the Europeans? where have they come from? whither are they bound?

Jacques Le Goff

Preface

I don't see why we are always concerned with the men, or even with their battles; the history of women is usually much more interesting.
Theodor Fontane, *Beyond Recall*, 1891

While Europa was playing with her female companions at the water's edge, Zeus approached her in the form of a bull and abducted her. Illustrations of the myth show Europa fearfully sitting on the back of the bull; she waves to her friends, looking back wistfully. Fear and wistfulness were natural reactions, since Zeus did not take her with a shower of gold, as he did with Danaë, he raped her. Europa's progeny have laid claim to peace and freedom. But are they free today? Judaeo-Christian tradition has proved even more important for her progeny than the imagery of ancient Greece and Rome: not so much Europa and Zeus, but Eve and Adam. Gender relations have often been debated using the language of the Bible, especially the Book of Genesis. Maria Deraismes, who in 1870 was one of the founders of the first lasting association of the French women's movement, entitled her 1868 book *Eve dans l'humanité* (it has been reprinted several times, including a recent edition). The title alludes not only to biblical imagery but to a situation that any history of women needs to confront: if the subject is women, then it is about humankind, and thus also about men. It was in this sense that Helene Lange opened her journal *Die Frau* in 1893, writing 'the woman question is also a man question'. In her time, it was not only women who were interested in the history of women but also some men, and even (albeit seldom) some professional historians. In his work *Grundriss der Historik* (Foundations of Historiography, 1858), Johann Gustav Droysen argued that the 'status of woman' and the 'patriarchal order' are important subjects of the historian's work; yet in a later edition he modified this to 'family' and the 'so-called patriarchal order'. Today there is greater and more widespread awareness of the urgency of such historical work. A history ignoring half of humankind is less than half of history, for without women, a history would not do justice to men either, and vice versa.

The *Making of Europe* series heeds this new awareness by including the 'second' sex as a major subject in European history. I was reluctant to take on the heavy burden of treating the topic in a limited number of pages, because of the time period spanning many centuries and because this small book, too, would have to deal with not half but all of European humankind. The task was to write an essay; this form has been defined as 'the genre of human finitude' and a 'departure from fixed categories'. I departed from the infinite and the categorical by focusing not on 'the' women and 'the' men – which do not exist anyway – but on a phenomenon that characterized European history: a *querelle des femmes* or *querelle des sexes*, a debate on the question of what are women, men, the sexes and humanity. So readers should not be surprised if this essay raises more questions than it answers.

The concept of the *Making of Europe* series, to present major topics in European history in a concise form, made it necessary to omit most discussions by historians and to neglect or just hint at certain issues, including the links between the history of European and non-European women. Only the United States has been included to a greater extent in some chapters. With respect to certain subjects, comparisons among European countries are made, but the central focus is on common, transnational developments. The gender debate did not take place only within national borders but was a transnational one. Many statements were read and discussed across borders within Europe and on both sides of the Atlantic. The question regarding continuity and change over the course of centuries is always apparent; and the judgement on whether tradition or innovation has greater weight over centuries (this is presently a subject of debate) can vary depending on the respective level under discussion, whether social or political, law, language or symbols. The fact that this volume is centred around a querelle has made it useful to include many voices from the past. I think it is important that today's readers become acquainted with these voices, their arguments and vocabulary, including the paradoxes; that is, the notions that contemporaries encountered and used, or reshaped. They are not always speaking directly to us and thus need to be read within their own historical context. The voices of the protagonists who appear in this book should not only illustrate the querelle they were a part of, but facilitate a dialogue over the centuries.

1

Querelle des femmes: *A European Gender Dispute*

Quid est mulier?
> Tertullian, around 200 CE

What are Women?
> Christine de Pizan, 1402

European history is rich in evidence of how differently the sexes, their peculiarities and their relationships can be perceived and interpreted. In the *querelle des sexes* these differences were debated for centuries, often in the form of complaints and accusations (this was the meaning of the French term *querelle* in the fifteenth century, which later came to mean battle or dispute) about what or how women and men are, should be, could be. More and more voices were raised during the early Renaissance, particularly in Italy, France and Spain, and the debate moved quickly to other parts of Europe. The growing significance of writing, and especially the development of writing in the European vernaculars, helped spread the discussion. Additional momentum came with the printing of books, reproduction of pictures and countless pamphlets. Both male and female authors participated in the querelle. Men wrote misogynistic (attacks and defamatory diatribes) as well as supportive, philogynous texts (in defence or praise of women). Most extant writings by women were philogynous. What was considered pro- or anti-women, however, depended on the respective context. Of all the views that have been passed down, only a minority had been voiced by women, but these comprised a large share of the total works written by women from that time. The origins of the dispute trace back to the Middle Ages. It developed during the Renaissance, especially under the influence of humanism and religious reform, and continued on into the Age of Enlightenment.

The Dignity of Man and the Dignity of Woman

Are women human?

In the late Middle Ages – or the Early Renaissance in Italy – the question as to human nature was raised and answered anew. In his epochal work *On the Dignity of Man* (*De dignitate hominis*, 1486), Giovanni Pico della Mirandola spoke of men. God was speaking to Adam alone; man was to determine his own nature according to his own free will and live in his preferred form. The postulate of the dignity of man was directed against the old doctrine of *miseria humanae conditionis* (Pope Innocent III expressed this in *On the Misery of Human Life*). Women were particularly affected by the *miseria*. The Church fathers had made Eve responsible for the Fall, and identified women with sexuality and sin. To Tertullian they were 'the devil's gateway' (*janua diaboli*), and Augustine regarded both extramarital and marital sexuality as sinful. Sin could only be avoided, according to St Jerome, through chaste living, since a man's love for a woman, who embodies evil and temptation, could not be reconciled with love of God and threatened the salvation of man. Salvation-seeking men had to protect themselves from women; salvation-seeking women, from themselves. Tertullian and Chrysostomos had answered their question 'What is a woman?' with a long series of vices ('enemy of friendship, necessary evil, temptation by nature, threat to the house, delightful misfortune, nature of evil'). The sexes had usually been depicted as dichotomous opposites. The scholastic synthesis of Aristotle and the Bible served to weaken the virtually Manichaean dualism (active/passive, form/matter, spirit/flesh, good/evil, merit/vice, etc.), but, like Aristotle's 'error of nature', even for Thomas Aquinas, woman remained a 'deficient' or 'misbegotten male' (*mas occasionatus*). Thomas and Aristotle both assigned women an important role in the household (and Thomas insisted that both sexes were made in God's image and thus both could be redeemed), but only under male dominion. It did not follow from the fact that women were indispensable that they had equal status. The *mas occasionatus* would long retain its – however disputed – position.

By no means did all people (or even all men) in medieval and early modern Europe think this way about mankind and women. In some sermons that did not remain inaccessible to most women – as Latin writings did – but were addressing a female audience as well, female vices were sometimes played down, and male vices were also criticized. Occasionally, this was the preacher's response to open protests by women who felt they had been defamed.[1] Furthermore, women could be viewed not only as gateways of the devil but – in the case of a virtuous, virginal woman – as the 'bride of Christ'. Both of these were abstractions that had little to do with real women, but served instead to present 'the woman' as a question that could be resolved only with a paradox. Starting in the twelfth century in southern France, the paradox assumed a new form – in the minnesong of the chivalrous troubadours. They dreamed of a gentlewoman whose physical distance and virginity represented the *sine qua non* of love. Nevertheless, as removed as this literature was from reality, it would have a wide and lasting effect in Europe, helping to establish new standards of deportment and cultural models.

The process of replacing the imagery of paradoxes and polar opposites was long and full of conflict, tied in many ways to actual conditions and social change. The *querelle des sexes*, which shaped early modern culture more than any other subject, dealt with the dignity and virtue of the 'other' sex, with its inferiority, superiority, equivalence or equality *vis-à-vis* its male counterpart. Galeazzo Flavio Capra's 1525 work *Della eccellenza e dignità delle donne* (On the Excellence and Dignity of Women) was one of the first querelle writings in a vernacular, thus meant for and accessible to women. It was republished a short time later in Capra's *Antropologia*, juxtaposed with a chapter on *The Dignity of Man*. Heinrich Cornelius Agrippa von Nettesheim, also a defender of the dignity of man (*De homine*), wrote a treatise *Of the Nobilitie and excellency of woman kynde* in 1509. First published in Latin in 1529, it was soon translated into six European languages and reprinted many times, becoming a fundamental resource in the gender debate (English 1542). In 1595, a *Disputatio nova contra mulieres qua probatur eas homines non esse* (A new disputation against women, in which it is proved that they are not human beings) was first published in Germany, anonymously and in Latin. The work caused quite a furore since it answered the question, whether women are human, in the negative. It too appeared in several languages and was reprinted, copied and excerpted into the eighteenth century. The responses it provoked ranged from indignation to amusement to agreement.

In 1440 in France, Martin Le Franc had already written *Le Champion des Dames*, a lengthy defence of the female sex, and dedicated it to Duke Philip the Good of Burgundy, a defender of women. It is the story of Franc Vouloir (Free Will) going to battle against the slanderous Malebouche (Vicious Tongue) in the *querelle des dames*. Later French writings included *Le débat de l'homme et de la femme* (1520), *Apologie du sexe féminin* (1522), *Controverses des sexes masculin et féminin* (1534) and, somewhat more belligerent, *La guerre des mâles contre les femelles* (The War of the Males against the Females, 1588). In Germany, Wilhelm Ignatius Schütz (*Ehren-Preiß Deß Hochlöblichen Frauen-Zimmers*, 1663) wrote to the 'European woman' and Johannes Gorgias (*Gestürzter Ehren-Preiß*, 1666), to the 'very praiseworthy European male sex'; Christiana Mariana von Ziegler wrote a satirical ode to 'the male sex, sung in the name of some women' (1639).

In fifteenth- and sixteenth-century Italy, Jewish scholars and poets also joined the debate. Venetian rabbi Leon Modena translated *Fior di Virtù*, a popular Italian work, into Hebrew (*Tzemah tzadik*). While *Fior di Virtù* was a dialogue on female virtues and vices, Leon Modena selected only the misogynistic passages and omitted the philogynous ones. The debate was especially heated in Mantua. Abraham Sarteano composed fifty tercets called *The Misogynist*, and Jacob Fano wrote *Defender of Men*, wherein he asserted not only that men were created in God's image, but also that this physical image was further completed by circumcision. Fano also felt that Jewish men should follow Christian men's practice of avoiding the company of women. Elijah Ish Genazzano supported Abraham Sarteano. Both were challenged by the praise of women (*Shevah Ha-Nashim*) written by the pious and learned rabbi and cabbalist David Messer Leon. A Jewish woman named Sarah was so taken with the piece that she requested Messer Leon to write a larger work on the theme. He responded with a commentary to the final chapter of Proverbs, praising the deeds and virtues of women based on the Talmud, Midrashim, and ancient Roman and more recent Italian literature, such as Dante. Gedaliah ibn Yahya showed similar enthusiasm in the sixteenth century as a defender of women. He expounded the theory that women were more worthy than men, justifying his claim on the basis that Adam was created from dust, whereas Eve came from Adam's rib. Gedaliah also argued that women were just as rational as men, and had great strength, as demonstrated by the pains of childbirth they endured.[2]

Roughly a thousand such works were written in the fifteenth and sixteenth centuries, even more including translations and reprints. There were thousands if we also take into account other works that took a stand in the querelle, such as the French *Bibliothèque bleue* in the seventeenth and eighteenth centuries. Much earlier, in the thirteenth century, Jean de Meun had composed the *Roman de la rose* ('All of you are, were, or will be whores by action or intention'); Ernst Robert Curtius called it a manifesto of 'erotic communism' (1948). *The Romance of the Rose* was the most-read work of the French Middle Ages, a 'cult book of the intellectuals', whether aristocratic or bourgeois. Geoffrey Chaucer's *Canterbury Tales* followed in the fourteenth century with 'The Wife of Bath'; Giovanni Boccaccio's *Concerning Famous Women* (based on Plutarch's *Virtues of Women* and Petrarch's biographies of men); Boccaccio's *Decameron*, his misogynistic satire *Il Corbaccio*, which conjured up the old image of female insatiability and insatiable femininity, and his *Fates*

of Illustrious Men ('A sweet and deadly evil is the woman'). Ludovico
Ariosto's *Orlando Furioso* appeared in the early sixteenth century, and
in 1528 Baldesar Castiglione's *Il libro del Cortegiano* (The Book of the
Courtier), the Renaissance book par excellence, whose influential dialogue form allowed the verbal duel to become the standard literary structure for such works. Castiglione called Boccaccio a misogynist outright
and let his major characters, the Aristotelian Gasparo Pallavicino and
the Platonist Giuliano de' Medici, argue with each other. Women, according to Gasparo, are an error of nature, useful at most for bearing
children; that's why they are so flawed and are less virtuous than men,
though admittedly (in deference to the women present), not through any
fault of their own. Another character mentioned the possibility of teaching women 'some good qualities through force'. Gasparo responded that
women themselves thought men were more worthy, since 'every woman
would like to be a man'. Giuliano countered that they did not want to be
men for the sake of being more perfect, but 'to have freedom' and to
avoid male domination. Femininity – according to the Platonic element
in the debate – was just as perfect as masculinity, irrespective of gender
differences, which were 'nothing essential'. Women, so Platonists claimed,
were just as capable of having virtue, reason, and even of governing states
as men were. Gasparo, however, mobilized (male) form versus (female)
matter and feared the worst: should 'the men be relegated to the kitchen
and the spinning wheel'?

Some writings used the debate as a chance to declare its having been
concluded, by attempting to define firm norms. *De institutione foeminae
christianae* by Spanish arch-humanist Juan Luis Vives (1523) had been
commissioned by the English queen Catherine of Aragon to teach her
daughter Mary Tudor; it was soon translated into several European vernaculars (*Instruction of a Christian Woman*, 1540; in German, 1544).
Further standards were set by Fray Luis de León of Spain (1583) in his
La perfecta casada (The Perfect Housewife) and by Gervase Markham's
The English Housewife (1615). Finally, there was the vast world of pictures, 'the layman's book' (*liber laicorum*) of high art and popular graph-
ics, where the conflict of and about the sexes was one of the most popular
subjects. Michelangelo's *David* was to be displayed in 1504 in Florence,
two years after the Florentine electorate had voted Piero Soderini
Gonfaloniere, or chief magistrate, for life. Politicians, artists and artisans
debated on the proper location. The politicians were able to assert their
choice of the highly symbolic site where it still stands today (now as a
replica): in front of the Palazzo della Signoria. Their suggestion also served
to unseat Donatello's sculpture *Judith and Holofernes*, which had been
displayed at the site in 1495 by the supporters of the radical republic of
Savonarola as a symbol of liberation from (Medici) tyranny. The moder-

ate republic removed *Judith*, since they considered her 'a symbol of death', and it 'was not proper that the woman kill the man'.[3]

Some scholars today have considered this battle of the sexes merely a literary phenomenon without thematic significance, little more than an exercise for the display of scholastic or Platonic logic, irony and sarcasm, and parody and paradox. But of course satire and irony do not rule out a deeper meaning, and at the time, different people interpreted the words and images differently. The anonymous *Disputatio nova* on whether women are human emerged as a satire on the Polish Anabaptists, whose hair-splitting was seen to be as absurd as the claim that women were not human. The German version of 1618 still had a philogynous Jesuit arguing with a misogynistic Benedictine: 'The word *homo* comes from *humus*, the stuff of which only man was made. Woman was merely formed from a rib of man. Because she was not originally created from *humus*, she could not be human.' And to the notion 'that women wish to consider themselves human' because they give birth, 'the answer already exists, namely, that beasts also give birth with pain, but that does not make them human. . . . In summary, no beast is so poisonous; women are much more poisonous, yes, more diabolical and evil than the devil himself'. But readers were not concerned with ironic or religious intentions, and the broad resonance of the work came solely from its position in the debate on the sexes. Incensed women tormented a man they thought had written the text and did not stop until he conceded that they were not human, but angels. The text was refuted in three Protestant reports the year it was published, including *Verteidigung des weiblichen Geschlechts* (Defence of the Female Sex), by Simon Gediccus, professor of Hebrew in Leipzig and a pastor in Halle. He argued 'that in the kingdom of Christ it is truly no longer justified to make distinctions, neither those of nation, nor status, nor sex'.[4] Another defence of women appeared in the Netherlands in 1639, a year after the *Disputatio nova* had appeared in The Hague. The Catholic Church reacted as well. When the *Disputatio nova* of 1595 appeared in Italian in 1647 (*Che le donne non siano della specie degli uomini*), it was immediately placed on the Roman Catholic Index (though it took more than three hundred years before a papal letter was issued about *Mulieris dignitatem*, the dignity of woman, in 1988).

The ironic side of the debate came from the fact that female subordination was accepted as a matter of course and irrefutable, and – if it was doubted – as coming from the paradox of a topsy-turvy world. It was no coincidence that a number of woman-friendly voices presented themselves precisely as paradoxical; for example, Charles Etienne's *Paradoxes, ce sont propos contre la commune opinion* (an imitation of Ortensio Landi's *Paradossi* and reprinted seven times between 1553 and 1638) praised women for their pre-eminence; or *Paradoxe apologétique* (1594) by Alexandre de Pontayméri. Furthermore, the paradox was derived from the double meaning of *homo* – human being or man, whereas man in the strict sense could be expressed by the Latin *vir*. (Since Cicero it had been believed that *virtus* was derived from *vir*, but this has meanwhile been refuted.) But in most European languages there was no third option (as in the German *Mensch* or the Dutch *mens*, which theoretically but not always in practice referred to both sexes), and even the Latin *homo* gradually lost its gender-encompassing meaning. Madame d'Épinay, *femme de lettres* and *salonnière* who corresponded with Catherine the Great and Frederick the Great, wrestled with the problem in 1776 – that is, in the Age of Enlightenment. She was referring not to grammar but to education when she wrote: 'When I say man (*l'homme*), I mean all human creatures; when I say a man (*un homme*), I am designating only a human creature of the masculine gender (*genre masculin*), and when I say a woman (*une femme*), I am designating a human creature of the feminine gender (*genre féminin*).'[5] The question 'Are women human?' thus also meant: 'Are women (like) men?' The puzzle caused (and still causes) quite a lasting stir. The wide diffusion of the early modern dispute shows that it was an integral part of how the world was perceived at the time, its *imaginaire* (Jacques Le Goff). Opposition to traditional polemics against women became virtually a cultural code for opponents of scholasticism. In the sixteenth century, the *querelle des femmes* joined ranks with the *Querelle de l'amye*, the dispute over friendship (Are women capable of friendship?), and in the seventeenth century with the *Querelle des anciens et des modernes*. Those who claimed that more recent literature and scholarship took precedence over the ancient works were generally in favour of changing the image, status and value of women. Around the same time, Molière's satirical comedies ridiculed *Learned Ladies* (*Les Femmes savantes*, 1672) and the salons of the famous *précieuses* (in his *Les Précieuses ridicules*, 1659) and Lope de Vega conjured up the man-hating woman in *La vengadora de las mujeres* and *Diablos son las mujeres*.

Women participated in the debate from early on. Starting around the twelfth century, female theologians and mystics used biblical and spiritual language to express themselves and question the hierarchy of the sexes. Among them were Hildegard of Bingen, Elisabeth of Schönau, Beatrice of Nazareth, Mechthild of Magdeburg, Marie d'Oignies, Marguerite Porète, the Italian Angela of Foligno, the Englishwoman Juliana of Norwich, and Margery Kempe. In her vision of the Trinity and the incarnation of God's word, Hildegard saw 'that motherly love of God's embrace entered the world that nourished us to life'.[6] Around 1400, theological differences and suspicion of heresy (Marguerite Porète was burned in Paris in 1310) were replaced by a veritable controversy. It broke out because male words were challenged for the first time by a woman, the early humanist Christine de Pizan. Born in Venice, Christine moved to Paris with her husband. She lived at the court of Charles V, and later as a widow she supported herself and her two children, often with difficulty, by transcribing and writing. For years she argued publicly with prominent French scholars about the image of women and men that the *Romance of the Rose* had created. Its author had taken up numerous misogynistic sayings – old and new, clerical and secular, scholarly and vernacular. 'What are women?' asked Christine. 'Are they serpents, wolves, lions, dragons' or 'enemies of human nature, that are to be deceived and overcome?' The first major literary debate in France was on the question of what constitutes women, as well as on the moral tasks of literary writing. This was also the first of many individual *querelles des femmes*. Christine ironically referred to her own voice as 'a tiny cricket that flaps its little wings frantically all the livelong day, chirping loudly'. And she too expressed a paradox. Because of her unusual life and writing, she saw herself becoming a man (*'devenir homme'*). Jean Gerson, chancellor of the University of Paris, supported her and characterized her as *insignis femina, virilis femina* (remarkable woman, virile woman). Her adversaries – also including other learned early humanists – branded the courage, acumen and wit of the cricket as unfeminine arrogance. It was said of 'this woman who calls herself Christine and makes her writings public, . . . oh foolish presumption! . . . Beware, that you do not share the fate of the crow, who began to sing more loudly than usual when its song was praised and let fall the food it had in its beak'.[7]

Christine's protest to the *Romance of the Rose* expressed numerous grievances of women: the 'heartrending grievances' of the 'ladies and noble girls, distinguished women, citizens and virgins and women in general', their complaints 'about the brutal assaults, reprimands and slanders, and about infidelities, hurtful insults, lies and all sorts of other offenses'. The *Romance of the Rose*, clearly dissociating itself from the troubadour tradition, had proclaimed that women are fickle and gullible, deceptive and conniving, evil and insatiable, unfaithful and jealous. They had no conscience and stole money from men's pockets. And love served only to satisfy male instincts, as shown by 'nature'; one only had to look at 'the cows and bulls, or the sheep and rams'. 'My God, what a windbag', sighed Christine in view of this licence for 'indecency and vice': it is by no means 'folly, arrogance, or presumption' if 'as a woman I dare to reprimand such a sensitive author and contradict him, after he as a man has dared to defame and reprimand an entire sex without exception!' She found de Meun's rude vocabulary for male and female genitalia to be especially repulsive, as well as the postulate that 'in the war of love it is better to betray than to be betrayed'. Christine was of the exact opposite opinion. Moreover, the depraved comment of the author, that nature created 'all women for all men, and all men for all women' and that is why men unceasingly pester women, contradicted his own suggestion: 'Dear gentlemen, beware of the women, if you love your bodies and your souls. . . . Flee, flee, flee, flee, flee, children, such a creature . . . , for it destroys, poisons and contaminates every man who approaches her, . . . the evil, cold serpent.' The peak of Christine's controversy with the misogynistic tradition was her *Livre de la Cité des Dames* (*Book of the City of Ladies*, 1404–5). Here she reversed de Meun's admonishment: 'Remember, dear ladies, how these men call you frail, unserious, and easily influenced but yet try hard, using all kinds of strange and deceptive tricks, to catch you, just as one lays traps for wild animals. Flee, flee, my ladies', namely, from the sinful, boundless 'foolish love [the men] urge on you!' For in the end it is 'always to your detriment'.

Even back then, misogyny was downplayed by claims that it was art or convention. But complaints by women clearly show that more was at stake. Christine knew that apparent humour or unrealistic satire could very well serve to shape the relationship between the sexes. She knew of a husband who viewed the *Romance of the Rose* 'as a kind of gospel' and who referred to the work when beating his wife: 'You are just as the *Romance* says. . . . This wise master Jean de Meun knew all of women's tricks!' At the beginning of *The Book of the City of Ladies*, Christine presents herself as a victim of such literature. Distraught, she asked herself why so many different men, learned ones among them, 'all concur in one conclusion: that the behavior of women is inclined to and full of every vice'. Her examination of her 'character and . . . conduct as a natural woman' and her conversations with other women convinced her that such judgements were groundless, but she could not fathom how so many famous men could spread such lies. She doubted herself, felt that all of the female sex were indeed 'monstrosities in nature' and she wrangled with God: 'Why did You not let me be born in the world as a male, so that . . . I would be as perfect as a male is said to be?' But she is given counsel: 'Come back to yourself, recover your senses, and do not trouble yourself anymore over such absurdities.' With the 'pick of your understanding' may she build a city that is a haven and protection for all women of all social strata. The allegorical *City of Ladies* presents an alternative to the misogynistic tradition and historiography, and creates a new world. Even male authors at this time occasionally indicated (usually in an ironic, ambivalent style) that history written by women – if they could write – would be different from history written by men. Chaucer, for instance, did so in *The Wife of Bath*; as did Johann Nider (through the voice of a nun) in his *Formicarius* (1437), although he otherwise attributed diabolical powers to women; and Luther ('if women wrote books, they would write of men the same that men wrote of them'). Agostino Strozzi, on the other hand, took it very seriously around 1500: 'If women, like men, had been allowed to write about the past, how radiant and shining they would have been in the stories.' And a century earlier, Christine meant it just as seriously: 'If women had written the books we read, they would have handled things differently, for women know they have been falsely accused.'[8]

The Book of the City of Ladies, today a best-seller, raised questions that would continue to influence the gender debate for a long time. Christine claimed that the female soul is equivalent to the male soul. The female body, even though it was created weaker than the male, is still just as perfect. In accordance with a God-given division of labour, statesmanship was a task ascribed not to women but to men. But not only did men often fail to fulfil this obligation adequately (peace was a main subject in Christine's works, including a guide for a prince, and one for a princess, on how to rule ethically and effectively), women have a natural sense for government and had, in fact, often assumed such tasks successfully. They did not lack intelligence. If their knowledge is more limited than that of men, it is because 'they are not involved in many different things, but stay at home, where it is enough for them to run the household'. If it were 'customary to send daughters to school like sons, and if they were then taught the sciences, they would learn as thoroughly and understand the subtleties of all the arts and sciences as well as sons'. When men refuse to let their wives and daughters experience 'the sweet taste of knowledge acquired through study' because 'their mores would be ruined as a result', this merely proves that there are 'many foolish men' who are unhappy that women know more than they do. Irrespective of her love for her husband and her loneliness after his death ('I am alone, I want to remain alone, my tender friend left me all alone'), Christine saw a connection between solitude and intellectuality. She said to a woman, if your husband 'were still alive, you certainly would not have been able to devote yourself to your studies to the extent that you now do; keeping house would have prevented it'. Her standard self-reference, 'I, Christine', was an expression of her awareness of her dignity as a woman and individual.

Soon the number of women voicing their opinions in the querelle increased – mocking, outraged, angry – even if they would remain isolated for a long time and were known to varying degrees in their own time. Well known were the 'three stars in the Venetian sky'. Moderata Fonte, 'a virgin, well-educated in the sciences', presented a conversation among seven women in *Il merito delle donne* (The Merits of Women, 1600): 'A free heart lives in my breast; I serve no one, belong to no one but *myself*.'[9] Lucrezia Marinella wrote *Le nobiltà et eccellenze delle donne et I diffetti, e mancamenti de gli huomini* (On the Nobility and Excellency of Women and the Deficiencies and Faults of Men, 1600) in response to a defamation of women composed by Giovanni Passi in 1599 (*I donneschi diffetti*) that was itself a reaction to earlier writings. The final work by Arcangela Tarabotti (*Che le donne siano della specie degli homini: Difesa delle donne*, 1651) was a polemical riposte to the Italian translation (1647) of the *Disputatio nova* on whether women are human. Although – or perhaps because – Tarabotti was a nun, she was not satisfied that the Church officially condemned the treatise. Here and in other writings she went above and beyond a mere response, conceiving a vision of female liberty.

In England a woman entered the debate for the first time in 1589 (under the pseudonym Jane Anger). In *Her Protection for Women*, the author inveighed against 'the falsehood of men', and man's wish 'to show his true vein in writing' and thus especially 'to write of us women'. She stressed that men could not survive at all if women did not do the housework. Anger challenged the assertion that 'the man is the head of the woman', claiming 'some sovereignty in us women'. Polemics, pamphlets and pseudonyms characterized the English querelle in the sixteenth and seventeenth centuries. In *The Women's Sharp Revenge* (1640), Mary Tattlewell and Joan Hit-him-home addressed 'the Male Gender' that has so little compassion for 'the Female Gender'. The authors complained that if women are weak by 'Nature', men strive to make them even weaker by 'Nurture', since women were not allowed to learn anything but 'to please and content [men's] licentious appetites'. The Benedictine Benito Feijóo, father of the Spanish Enlightenment, published a *Defence of Women* in 1739 (it was translated into English in 1778). Also in 1739, a learned woman in England writing anonymously under the pseudonym Sophia presented her arguments in *Woman Not Inferior to Man*, a pamphlet that provoked others in response. Sophia asserted that there is no 'essential' sexual difference that could grant legitimacy to men's superiority over women (the physical difference would tend more to legitimate the opposite). She perceived 'no other difference than what their tyranny has created'. There was 'perfect equality' between the sexes, even if that seemed 'as great a paradox' as, until recently, the notion that people on the other side of the globe stood on their heads. Only lack of education, which had to be rectified, put women in their present inferior position. In 1762, Madame de Beaumer opposed unnamed male critics, writing in the *Journal des Dames* that 'I love this sex and am jealous to uphold its honour and its rights'.[10] It was a time when significant women had become active in public (though they were excluded from the academies of the Enlightenment): the *salonnières* in France, the circle of the Bluestockings in England, and some painters who gained international fame, such as Angelika Kauffmann of Switzerland, who lived in England and Italy, and Elisabeth Vigée-Lebrun in France.

The authors involved in the querelle dealt not with women alone but with men as well (whereas much more numerous works of the time dealt exclusively with men). The words and images spanned a wide range of subject areas: marriage and adultery, sex and chastity, beauty and shame, virtue and vice, work and children, money and violence (within and outside marriage), intellect and domination (within and outside marriage), heaven and hell (usually their worldly variants), and God and the world. In the context of the witch hunts, there were also controversies from the very beginning whether or not witches existed, where they got their powers from, and who should be regarded as a witch. Though female writers were a minority in the *querelle des femmes*, women comprised a majority of the victims of the witch debate. The debate came to a deadly conclusion for around 100,000 people, more than two-thirds of whom were women (there were also many women among the accusers). Even at the time, there was discussion as to why 'so many more women become bewitched than do men'. In 1576 in Germany, there were frequent references to women's gullibility and curiosity – Eve's legacy – and to women's vindictiveness and greed. In England, too, Eve and the characterization of women as 'a tool of the devil' were conjured up in 1627. It was argued that women's inclination to gossip led to exposure of their witchcraft more easily than in the case of men, and that women were more domineering than men and therefore more likely to become witches.[11]

In general, the Bible, especially Genesis, played an important role in the debate: did God create 'man in his own image' and 'as male and female' in a single act of creation (Gen. 1:27)? Or was woman – referred to as *virago* in the Vulgate, parallel to *vir*, which gave rise to the term 'she-man' – taken from man (Gen. 2:20–3)? And if so, was that a symbol of her inferiority or rather of her superiority, since she was made out of a more noble material than was man, who was formed from the dust of the earth? And what is the meaning of 'they shall be one flesh' (Gen. 2:24)? And which one of them bore more or less blame for the Fall and original sin? It was not only in Luther's eyes that Genesis was written 'for us'. It was also a battleground of the querelle, especially since many men and women could not read the Bible until its translations into the vernacular circulated in the sixteenth century. In 1536 Jean Bouchet even argued that 'la querelle de l'homme contre la femme' had begun with Adam and Eve themselves.[12]

Moreover, it was not always so easy to determine what a man was, as Parsifal's mother once thought (Eschenbach's *Parzival* was first printed in 1477). 'With other women', she watched the baby eagerly and when she 'joyfully realized that it was male, she gave it the caressing it was due'. A man could also be recognized by way of his trousers, and the trousers became a symbolic site of the battle of the sexes (in the traditional and richly illustrated 'fight for the breeches'); the scholar Joseph Glanvill maintained in 1661 that truth had no chance if 'the *Affections* wear the breeches and the *Female* rules'. Furthermore, the beard was a symbol of male superiority (as seen in early Christian writings). In his *École des femmes* (*School for Wives*, 1662), Molière had Arnolphe say: 'Du côté de la barbe est la toute-puissance.' A rebellious or masculinized woman was occasionally called *mulier barbata*, a bearded woman. Marie de Gournay argued in her treatise *Egalité des hommes et des femmes* (1622) that women resemble men as a female cat resembles a tomcat; that women could be priestesses; that Christ came into the world as a man only because in view of misogynistic Jewish tradition he would never have achieved anything as a woman; and that women are denied having been created in the image of God because God – unjustly – is thought to have a beard. In 1792, Theodor Gottlieb von Hippel, a supporter of women, published *Über die bürgerliche Verbesserung der Weiber* (On the Civic Improvement of Women). He criticized the view that male American Indians were unmasculine because they did not have beards, and that for the same reason women were not created in the image of God. Thus the former were considered 'a much lower class of human beings', and the latter – 'O the beardless conclusion!' – were considered to have an inferior mind.[13] The image of man, as characterized in querelle literature, was indeed often less flattering than the depiction in Pico della Mirandola's *De dignitate hominis*. It was an image that women (as well as some men) did not always want to resemble. Although the voices in support of women always insisted that both sexes had the same capacity for reason and virtue, the debate was not about equality in the sense of sameness, but the relative superiority or inferiority of the sexes in everyday life.

The question whether or not women are human caused a stir, especially after the publication of the *Disputatio nova* in 1595. But the issue had been brewing even earlier. Christine de Pizan saw reason to argue 'that women belong to the . . . human race as much as men' and are by no means 'another species or dissimilar race'. Erasmus of Rotterdam was one of the few male dialogue authors who allowed women to speak themselves. In his *Senatulus sive conciliabulum muliercularum*, a circle of women complained that men 'use us only for their pleasure and barely deem us worthy of the name *human*'. The influential French legal scholar Jacques Cuias denied women's humanity in 1587, as did the German jurist Scipio Gentilis a year later. Some regarded the entire issue as a joke; others took it seriously, and in the major encyclopedias – from

Pierre Bayle (1697) to the German Zedler (1747) – the question was debated in earnest. Pietistic librarian and court poet Georg Christian Lehms wrote in 1715 in *Teutschlands Galante Poetinnen* that the judgement that 'womenfolk are not human' contradicted 'both divine and secular rights, and all honourable souls of honoured men who respect this noble sex'. The question remained controversial, since depending on how 'man' was defined – through soul or reason, bodily strength or virtue, freedom or dominion – its meaning also changed. Zedler's *Grosses vollständiges Universallexikon* found the opinion that 'women are not human' simply 'foolish'. But by no means did the Zedler encyclopedia find some concrete aspects of the question foolish. 'Do women become blessed through childbirth?' was answered somewhat reluctantly in the affirmative. 'Are women capable of acquiring academic honorary degrees?' ('Why not?'); 'Should women be allowed to teach in public?' (no); and a 'women's regiment' was out of the question, since 'leaving the breeches' to the women in the house meant to attack the divine order. It was thus not surprising that Mary Wollstonecraft argued in 1790 and 1792 against the assumption that 'one half of the human species, at least, have no souls' and that females counted 'rather as women than human creatures'. At the same time, Hippel also wondered, 'Humanity? Are not women human beings as well? . . . Why should women not be considered as persons?' And in 1833, the Swiss Jakob Leuthy, in *Das Recht der Weiber* (The Rights of Women), asked 'Have human beings the right to be free? Are woman not human?'[14] Three decades later John Stuart Mill urged the House of Commons to replace the word *man* with *person* in the new suffrage law in order to include women, but the motion was rejected.

Misogamy and Misogyny; Philogamy and Philogyny

> Every hour we judge things differently, and we should not be ashamed of correcting our errors. Change is natural, for men as well as women. . . . And so all things change: men, women, and the times.
>
> João de Barros, 1540[15]

The debate on marriage, celibacy, sexuality and the Bible quotation 'It is not good that the man should be alone' (Gen. 2:18) was known as the *querelle du mariage*. It became an integral aspect of the gender debate. Christine de Pizan was also familiar with this subject and viewed it from various perspectives. Her adversaries accused her of being anti-love, but she countered their reproach by asserting that 'perfect love' does not necessarily imply sexuality and certainly not promiscuity. She responded harshly to Jean de Meun's claim that women enjoy being raped. She attacked the traditional male view that marriage is so unbearable because women are unbearable and the source of all evil. She offered a critique of marriage from a woman's perspective, at the same time praising marriage. On the one hand, 'there are many women greatly mistreated by their husbands', and because of their husbands' harshness they lead weary lives, they suffer more 'than if they were slaves among the Saracens' and in fact 'men are masters over their wives, and not the wives mistresses over their husbands'. Before marrying, it is less important 'to warn men about women's ruses' than to warn women 'against men's traps'. On the other hand, Christine also presented numerous arguments and evidence in favour of marriage that proved that women are not as bad as men assume. She also stressed that not all women are good, just as not all men are bad; that 'not all marriages are conducted with such spite'; and that God should be thanked for 'giving them so much happiness'. In the case of conflicts, she comforted the wives, 'Don't be sad that you are so greatly subjugated by your husbands . . . since often the state of liberty is not advantageous', and advised them to be patient with their 'difficult' husbands. Christine's praise of marriage was a means to praise women, and her critique of marriage was a means to criticize men.

In Christine's time, marriage had gone through considerable changes. In works that attempted to do justice to the different situations of women, they were not only generally treated on the basis of three categories – the triad of virgins, widows and wives – but their actual status was defined primarily by their position within the family and the larger kinship. In many places during the eleventh and twelfth centuries marriage was considered an alliance and peace treaty between families (often enemies), particularly among the dynasties, aristocratic circles and the cities, whereas virtually nothing is known about the rest of the population. The bride was a pledge and an instrument for a harmonious union. Family alliances were based on the exchange of women. Only gradually was emphasis placed on the married couple and the 'good wife'. Three main factors were significant in this regard.

First, starting in the late eleventh century the Church was increasingly successful in insisting that both spouses entered matrimony of their own free will. The bride's freedom to say 'I do' (or to say no) was especially explosive with respect to the family's interests. Free choice of spouse gained acceptance at least in theory and by the Church, though not in practice (silence on the part of the woman was usually regarded as consent). In the same period, marriage assumed a sacramental character, and thus became fundamentally indissoluble. Women throughout Europe around 1200 were likely to marry very young (nobility and urban patriciate at around thirteen years of age; in rural areas around seventeen), and their husbands were usually considerably older. Power relations were therefore based not only on gender but on age. After the Black Death in the mid-fourteenth century, when Europe lost approximately one-third of its population, the female marriage age rose and the 'western European marriage pattern' developed – a relatively high marriage age for women (the poorer and more rural the woman, the later she married) and a large number of women who never married. Leon Battista Alberti insisted in his treatise *I libri della famiglia* (1432–41) that women should marry young 'so they do not fall prey to vices while waiting for what is demanded by nature'.[16] Married women spent most of their adult life dealing with pregnancy and childbirth (an average of ten children in Florence, nine for the French peasantry); barely two of the offspring survived their parents in Florence of the late Middle Ages. About one in seven mothers (of all social strata) died in or as a result of childbirth, and many more suffered permanent damage to their health. Most nursed their children themselves, but well-to-do women often sought the services of a wet-nurse (roughly one in four of these babies died). Among a wife's obligations (before and after the great changes in marriage) were fertility, fidelity in marriage, domesticity and responsibility for the chastity of the daughters. The main duty of the husband was to support the wife, but within the family he was also the master and had the right to use corporal punishment. (This does not mean that women did not also scold and occasionally hit their husbands.)

Second, marriage meant a crucial transfer of money and property. Many – perhaps most – women, from those of royal rank in the eleventh and twelfth centuries to the middle class of the fourteenth and fifteenth centuries, married below the status or property of their birth family (this is sometimes used to explain the theme of the bitter and thus quarrelsome wife, which abounded in the gender querelle). In the early Middle Ages it was common for families to exchange gifts: the husband (or his family) gave a gift to his bride (or her family) after the wedding day and, in the other direction, the bride's family paid a dowry. From the twelfth to the fifteenth centuries, the husband's gift gradually fell out of practice (later in northern than in southern Europe). Complaints by women as a result are hardly surprising, since this meant a lessening of her value, even an expropriation. The dowry became the crucial transfer of the marital exchange; its value was subjected to centuries of inflation (efforts to slow down the increase were as numerous as they were unsuccessful), and it became more and more expensive for fathers to marry off their daughters. Dante Alighieri mourned the good old days 'when a daughter's coming of age did not frighten her father'. Almost everywhere women lost their rights to administer their own dowry, which had originally served as a substitute for the paternal inheritance. They retained – even as widows – at most usufructuary rights. Girls whose fathers could afford only a small dowry, or none at all, did wage labour to save enough for one (usually in the textile industry, such as sewing or spinning, or in girls' institutions during the Renaissance by embroidering precious robes and tapestries). Other than that, a poor woman's 'sole capital is her chastity',[17] according to one Italian author in 1674 in retrospect. Sometimes a pious foundation paid the dowry for her to get married.

Third, it became increasingly important for women to marry. Those living outside a family setting suffered a life of bitter impoverishment, and even resorted to begging. Most importantly, a new pattern in the relationship between work and family life had developed in the twelfth century. In the cities and in those rural regions where people worked in bondage, options for marriage increased and the married couple became a working couple. Liberation from bondage was not possible individually, but only as a couple that worked for the market. Women retained responsibility for the housework, but only married couples – together with the other family members – could assure their subsistence.[18] In the late Middle Ages and early modern times, this laid the foundation for the modern family as the 'nucleus of the new organization of the economy'.

It is not surprising that in this period of radical change in many other areas as well, marriage became a pressing social, political and moral issue. The *querelle du mariage* took place at the interface between tradition (ancient as well as Christian) and innovation (humanism as well as religious reform). One reason why many humanists felt the dignity of man excluded the dignity of woman was because they rejected marriage. Humanist opponents of marriage answered the old male question *An uxor sit ducenda* (Should a man marry?) with an attack against women and by reverting to the ancients (Juvenal had advised a bridegroom, 'Are you mad? Or hunted by the Furies? Taking a wife! Would you not rather take a rope and hang yourself?'). The *suasio* or *dissuasio nubendi* was a popular theme. Hatred of marriage, or misogamy, became a vehicle for expressing misogyny, and vice versa. The earnest Petrarch complained about marriage in a letter, as did the mocking Boccaccio in the *Decameron* and the satirical *Il Corbaccio*. In his biography of Dante, Boccaccio criticized the poet, saying that Dante's creativity suffered as a result of his marriage. The celibate Pico della Mirandola, who 'fled both marriage and worldly service', was less severe. In response to the question which of the two burdens – solitariness or coupledom – is easier, Pico preferred marriage 'with a slight smile'. Marriage was for him 'less servitude and not as dangerous. For he loved freedom above all else', as Thomas More reported in his biography of Pico.[19] Pico's learned friend Ermolao Barbaro was less willing to compromise in *De coelibatu* (around 1472), claiming that nothing was so harmful to scholarship as matrimonial 'chains', the *iugum uxoris et cura puerorum*, the marital yoke, caring for children and listening to their crying. In Rabelais's *Third Book* (*Tiers Livre*, 1546) the question *Me dois-je marier?* (Should I marry?) was examined from all conceivable angles – Panurge fears that a wife would cuckold him – and Bernardo Trotto harshly condemned marriage in *Dialoghi del matrimonio e vita vedovile* (1578), calling it 'a waste of time, money and the brain'. Ercole Tasso, a married scholar, composed a treatise against wives, which provoked an apologia for marriage and wives by Torquato Tasso, a confirmed (and homosexual) bachelor. Giovanni della Casa, cleric and author of a classical Renaissance essay on male virtues and social etiquette (*Galateo*), wrote *An uxor sit ducenda* (1537). In it, he asserted that the survival of mankind is not threatened by celibacy. As we have seen from the animal kingdom and times before 'legitimate marriage' existed, he expounded, procreation is amply secured through naturally occurring promiscuity. Uneducated rather than noble or aristocratic men should take responsibility for reproduction. Woman is closer to animals than to man; her body and character make marriage unbearable, and since she is hardly seen prior to the wedding, it is like buying a pig in a poke. Della Casa continued that almost all women are ugly; and even if a woman did happen to be attractive, one would tire of her in six months and 'only the appeal of a new one would help ease the boredom'. After having borne children, 'you would not want to look at her anymore; her breasts hang, her limbs feel limp and flabby'. She menstruates and is perpetually ill, gluttonous and foul-smelling. Once she gets old she is toothless and 'her entire body is alarmingly ugly'. Women are weak, his diatribe went on, lazy, incapable of holding public office and 'not useful even in war', since their office is 'one for peace and quiet'. They are only suited for one 'certain duty', but that is hardly gratifying with one's own wife.[20]

Not only the humanists but clerics as well made a smooth transition from misogyny to misogamy and vice versa. They based their thoughts not on classical but on Christian tradition, and enjoyed turning around the female virtues of the Old Testament (Prov. 31:10–29). These include the *Alphabet* written around 1400 by the Archbishop of Florence, which was printed in the sixteenth century and later published in Latin, Spanish, French, English and Dutch, and the *Alphabet de l'imperfection et malice des femmes* (1617) by the Franciscan Alexis Trousset, which in turn provoked a whole series of counter-alphabets and treatises in defence of women. In the late fourteenth and early fifteenth centuries, misogynistic and misogamous satires such as *Le Miroir du Mariage* and *Les quinze joyes de mariage*, which complained of the loss of freedom that men suffered in marriage, became widespread in France. Jurists also got involved in the debate. André Tiraqueau's *De legibus connubialibus*

(1513) was reprinted and expanded many times. It was an encyclopedia of quotes and commonplace adages that aimed to prove the inferiority of women within and outside marriage.

Misogyny and misogamy were, aside from satire, a serious matter and they were earnestly criticized, especially by two groups of men, the civic humanists and religious reformers. Both these groups sought to upgrade marriage and therefore, even though it was not their primary thrust, they tended to revise the tradition of misogyny. The civic humanists charged their leisure-loving colleagues with lacking a sense of *res publica* and its social foundations. Leonardo Bruni, Florentine chancellor, censured Boccaccio for his criticism of Dante's marriage. He referred to the many great philosophers who were married ('What great philosopher was married?' was a question still being posed by Nietzsche), and railed against the ignorance of those 'who hide themselves in solitude and idleness' and 'do not even know three letters', for 'Man is an *animal civile*', and 'the primary union, from whose multiplication a society emerges, is that between man and woman, and without it there is no perfection'. Giannozzo Manetti praised Socrates not only as a philosopher and citizen but as a father; and he vindicated not only man but woman as well. In *On the Dignity and Excellence of Man* (*De dignitate et excellentia hominis*, 1452), Manetti rejected the teachings of human *miseria* and its presumed root, having been born of a woman. He criticized Pope Innocent III who, because he did not know Hebrew, had wrongly concluded from Genesis that women, the body and love are inferior dimensions of life. In 1472 in Germany, Albrecht von Eyb asked whether or not a man should take a wife (*Ob einem manne sey zu nemen ein eelichs wib oder nit*). He discussed the pros and cons of marriage for a man and in the end answered affirmatively. Even the Platonic ascetic Marsilio Ficino attacked the Abelard complex. Since man was created in God's image, Ficino believed man should also propagate this gift. Also, for a man, marriage is a 'domestic *res publica*', and he must direct 'all prudence and virtue to rule over it'. 'By governing the family with great care, you form yourselves, gather experience and honour in the earthly kingdom, and make yourselves worthy of the Kingdom of Heaven.' Such humanists saw the true problem with marriage as lying not in the general badness of women but in making the correct – and difficult – choice of a spouse. Francesco Barbaro, grandfather of the misogamist Ermolao, dedicated his treatise in praise of marriage to this subject (*De re uxoria, On Wifely Duties*, 1415–16). Around the mid–sixteenth century, another Venetian patrician impressed upon the prospective father 'to choose with utmost care the terrain upon which he thinks to spread his seed'.[21]

The second criticism of misogamous and misogynistic tradition evolved from the desire for religious reform. Christian celibacy had long since ceased to mean sexual abstinence. 'Many are celibate, but few are chaste', bemoaned Erasmus of Rotterdam. Secular clerics were living in concubinage; popes had mistresses and children. In Venice alone there were approximately thirty convents involved in court cases on sexual relations in the fifteenth century, and pregnant nuns were not unusual. Erasmus was especially critical of religious vows, albeit more so for monks than for nuns. In his dialogue on the misogamous virgin (*Virgo misogamos*, 1523), he claimed that many nuns 'follow Sappho's example', although that was not their genuine inclination. In the end the virgin was compelled by love to decide to marry. Here and in other writings Erasmus expressed a new marriage ideal. In contrast to others, he discussed it not only from the man's perspective but from a woman's as well. On the one hand, more and more voices admonished a return to the virginal ideal for clergy and nuns; on the other hand, an increasing number made reference to Paul (1 Cor. 7:9, 'it is better to marry than to burn') in demanding that sexual relations be legitimized and the ban on marriage eliminated for secular priests.

From 1519 to 1523, Martin Luther denounced the priestly celibacy with increasing stridency as the work of the devil. He was far from alone in doing so, and was not even a spokesman. Years earlier, Reformation clerics had already dared to take the sensational step of marrying in public. They thus risked being charged with concubinage, and they attacked celibacy as an 'abominable murder of the soul'. Luther went beyond the common criticism of priestly vows of celibacy, inveighing against monasteries 'as morasses and whorehouses of the devil'. He condemned the doctrine of the monastic 'state of perfection', thereby rejecting a lifestyle that had been recognized for well over a millennium. After the marriage epidemic had struck, Luther also became active with respect to nuns. He organized the liberation of nine nuns who had come to him for advice, freeing them 'from the prison of human tyranny' and justifying his intervention in his treatise *Ursache und Antwort, daß Jungfrauen Klöster göttlich verlassen dürfen* (1523, Reason and answer to the question whether virgins are allowed by God to leave the convent). A woman, he argued, 'is not created to be a virgin, but to bear children', as 'proven by the fact that God created her body to serve this purpose'.[22] In 1525, at the age of forty-two, Luther married one of the freed nuns, Katharina von Bora.

The controversies over priests marrying and virginity were a focus of Protestant as well as Catholic reform, for both men and women. The issues were not resolved once and for all until the final session of the Council of Trent in 1563. Their repercussions for the general population were greater than that of Luther's Ninety-five Theses and they brought widespread support for the Reformation. The image of the Reformation, especially in its scandalous early phase, was marked by the public marriages of priests, monks and nuns; the suppression of monasteries; and an epidemic of marriages in Germany – the destination of French reformers in haste to get married. An essential element of the European *querelle des femmes* was not only the secular *querelle du mariage* but its religious counterpart as well. Luther railed against the popular misogamy and intervened in the dispute with his *Vom ehelichen Leben* (*On Married Life*, 1522). It is 'a hue and cry of writing about women and matrimony', he declared, that 'has such a generally deplorable reputation. There are many heathen books that describe nothing but the vices of women and the offensiveness of matrimony', and even Christians claimed (recalling Tertullian) 'that a woman is a necessary evil and there is no house that does without such evil'. For Luther the conflict was not literature but life: 'This is why the young men should be wary if they read the heathen books and hear the general complaint, making sure they do not draw up poison. For the devil is not happy with married life, since it is God's work and goodwill. That is why he let there be so much called out and written against it in the world', such as 'fleeting joy and lasting woe'. In view of the daily routines of matrimony, 'natural reason, a clever whore', might turn up the 'nose and say, "Oh, should I rock the child, wash the nappies, make the beds, smell the stench, watch the night, care for it when it cries, heal its rash and sore, and then care for the woman, feed her, work" . . . and what more does matrimony teach of dispassion and toil'. Faith, however, according to Luther, argued that the burdens of matrimony are nothing but 'external dispassion and toil', while the important thing is the 'spiritual, inner desire', 'that man and wife love each other, are one, and care for each other'. Faith even seemed to suggest a change in roles. 'If a man went and washed the nappies and did otherwise despicable chores for the child', all might jest, but 'God laughs and is pleased with all the angels and creatures, not that he washes nappies, but that he does it out of faith'. Yet Luther merely used the ironic querelle paradox of the topsy-turvy world to underline his teachings that faith is more important than deed. He too considered sexuality within marriage to be sinful, but a sin no greater than other sins. Other than that (regarding the man), it was a matter of nature and 'natural fluids': 'To say it crudely but honestly, if it doesn't go into a woman, it goes into your shirt.'[23]

Although the subject of the heated debates was indeed religion, Protestant philogamy was also perceived as a question of gender and sexuality. In France as well as Germany, Catholics turned around the Protestant attacks on clerical fornication and accused the Protestants of propagating marriage for the sake of carnal lust and of taking the side of women. Calvin saw cause to reject the presumption: 'The papists want the world to believe that all the discord and debate between us and them is a kind of Trojan War that we are waging *for the women*.' German Reformers, on the other hand, emphasized that they did not marry because of sensual desire; instead, they bore the 'Cross of Christ' out of brotherly love as a duty and sacrifice, in order to fight the 'false, diabolical chastity'.[24]

Irrespective of their theological and political differences, however, Protestants and Catholics were soon reunited in their ideas on the status of married women. First of all, the enhanced status and reform of marriage that the Protestants introduced, which also served to promote a new image of women, was not nearly as new as it seemed to many contemporaries. In fact, it advanced previous Church and secular movements towards reform that were now also taken up again by the Catholic Church. Second, Catholic reform adopted essential initiatives of the Protestant marriage ideal. In both camps, marriage had a threefold meaning – procreation, avoidance of extramarital sin and mutual companionship. Differences often existed only in the respective prioritization. Catholics such as Juan Luis Vives, as well as Reformers such as Calvin, stressed companionship over procreation. Protestants and Catholics alike produced countless treatises, sermons and homily readings from the pulpit praising marriage as a God-given lifestyle and the foundation of both the spiritual and worldly orders. Among the best known was the work on Christian matrimony by Heinrich Bullinger, successor to Zwingli, which appeared in 1540 in Switzerland but was especially popular in England, describing the 'marital yoke'; Thomas Becon's *The Book of Matrimony* (1562) and the homily on matrimony which was read at weddings in Tudor England ('True it is, that [women] must specially feel the griefs and pains of their matrimony, in that they relinquish the liberty of their own rule, in the pain of their travailing, in the bringing up of their own children, in which offices they be in great perils, and be grieved with many afflictions, which they might be without if they lived out of matrimony'); Johann Freder's *Dialogus dem Ehestand zu ehren* (Dialogue in Honour of Matrimony), which appeared in 1545 with a foreword by Luther and which refuted misogynistic and anti-matrimonial sayings in the form of a debate; the *Philosophisch Ehzuchtbüchlein* (Philosophical Treatise on Conjugal Discipline) by Johann Fischart of Strasbourg; and Catholic authors such as Vives, Erasmus and preachers such as the Portuguese João de Barros. Catholics no longer promoted celibacy by strenuously insisting that women were fundamentally bad; instead, they used other means. Third, there was confusion among both Protestants and Catholics regarding the relationship between faith and deed with respect to the sexual obligations of wives. It was not only Catholics, such as Vives, who maintained that a wife's sexual deed for her husband was a deed for God. Protestants, too, believed that in bed she should 'rather be Catholic than Lutheran, keeping more to the deed than to faith'.[25] Fourth, Reformers viewed marriage as a secular arrangement, whereas for Catholics it was a sacrament. In practice, however, it was virtually indissoluble, not only for Catholics but for Protestants as well. Fifth, Protestantism changed considerably after its rebellious beginnings. Behind the new disciplinary order in Protestant cities and the elimination of the 'women's houses', the houses for urban prostitutes, stood the old picture of the sexually insatiable and domineering woman. In the end the Reformation, which at first had propagated the same sexual ethics for both sexes and the dignity of the married woman, suspected all women, single or married, of being ever ready to surrender themselves to their lust for debauchery.

Despite many similarities across confessional lines, there was a dramatic difference between Protestant and Catholic regions in Europe, and it constituted the only genuine and institutional innovation of Protestantism: the elimination of celibacy and the introduction of marriage for pastors. The debates that took place on the issue revealed deep fears regarding masculinity and femininity and a search for a new identity for men and women. For women, the change had several consequences. First, it meant losing the chance to live with women and not under direct male custody. Some convents were dissolved peaceably, others by force, and many nuns put up powerful resistance. Caritas Pirckheimer argued cleverly with the new doctrine of *sola fide*: 'We know that the convent cannot make us blessed, but it also cannot make us wretched.' Whoever thinks 'that that could make her blessed is just as wrong as someone who thinks that merely leaving the convent is enough to make one blessed; there is more to it than that'. Even though Luther took sides against the peasants in the Peasants' War, he and peasant women were agreed on one thing that concerned not faith but a woman's task. A crowd of angry peasant women stormed a nunnery, complaining about their hard work and the good life in the convent and demanding that the nuns also be part of the 'ordinary masses' and 'have to have children and suffer the same pains as they did'. Pastor Erasmus Alber was happy that 'there were so many thousands of married women who used to be (if you please) vain whores'; and married life is 'a magnificent state'. In Protestantism, the new-old marriage ideal became binding for all women. In 1522 Luther had still emphasized that it was legitimate for women, truly and of their own free will, to feel a calling to virginity and 'cloistering', though 'of a thousand, certainly hardly one' would be found. And one should not 'make a commandment out of a liberty'.[26] But it was not long before the new conjugal freedom became a conjugal duty.

Second, the Reformation created a new figure – the pastor's wife. She became the new model for man's 'companion' or 'helpmeet' (Gen. 2:18), an exemplary house mother and exceptional church mother. Katharina

Zell, who had married in 1523 (her two children died young), took this companionship very seriously. In a pamphlet (*Defence of her husband, who is a pastor and servant in the word of God in Strasbourg*), she publicly justified the spectacular marriage of her Reformer husband Matthew, and in doing so she made reference to a paradox that was often used in the *querelle des femmes*: 'God has chosen that which is weak in the world to ruin that which is strong.' She offered her home as a refuge to hunted Lutherans, took care of them, even gave a public speech after the death of her husband, and argued that marriage was a means of saving souls – one's own as well as others'. Third, there were many concubines who were abandoned by their priestly friend if he ultimately chose Catholicism and once again took his vows seriously. Many of them suffered and complained, especially if they had children by him. Fourth, there were many nuns for whom the convent had truly been a prison and who were glad to be able to leave and seek a husband. Fifth, especially among women who were not nuns, there were many who highly respected the new dignity of matrimony, wife and companionship. Among them was Marguerite d'Angoulême, sister of Francis I of France and queen of Navarre. In her *Heptameron*, a kind of *comédie humaine* which circulated from 1549, the year of her death, she allowed women and men to argue about love, marriage and sexuality, coming to the conclusion that men and women were equal with regard to both vice and virtue. She argued that priests should marry rather than living a false, chaste life, and that celibacy was made for man, but man was not made for celibacy. But she never went so far – especially with an eye to women – as to value marriage higher than an unmarried life.

But what exactly was the relationship – for Protestants as well as Catholics – between companionship and domination, obedience and autonomy, freedom and domesticity, or among superiority, inferiority and equality? This was a controversial issue, especially in actual married life, and would remain so for centuries. In Protestant historiography as well as in the secularized world of the nineteenth and twentieth centuries, the concept of 'companionship' gave way to that of 'complementarity'. In any case, raising the status of the wife contributed to the formation of the married couple as a working couple. And new tasks became legitimate for wives and mothers, especially the early education (including religious education) of sons and daughters. For Protestant women there was no longer a cult of the Virgin Mary or the saints, which had been so important for Catholics since the twelfth century. And for all women the old legal rule from the Justinian *Corpus Iuris Civilis* still held, that the dignity of women was less than that of men (*major dignitas est in sexu virili*). In English common law it assumed the form of coverture for married women, according to which man and woman were *one* person – as in Genesis *one* flesh – and the person of the flesh was the man. In serious conflicts it was not vague values that mattered, after all, but rigid law.

Raising the status of women by raising the status of marriage was a balancing act filled with tension. Help was found once again in the Book of Genesis. Since Eve did not come from Adam's head, she was not superior to him. Since she did not come from his foot, she was not inferior to him. The rib implied equality. Luther wrestled with the problem of overcoming the old polarity of inferiority versus superiority by constructing a new one. Eve was not solely responsible for the Fall and she was also not a deficient man. According to Luther, the fact that Genesis spoke of two sexes demonstrates, on the one hand, that both are equally capable of salvation; on the other hand, it also shows that woman not only has a different body from that of man, but also a weaker spirit (*ingenium longe infirmius*). Although both Eve and Adam were created as *praestantissima creatura* (pre-eminent creations) and resemble each other with respect to *iusticia, sapientia, et salus* (justice, wisdom and salvation), Eve remains nevertheless a woman (*tamen fuit mulier*) and thus inferior (*inferior masculino sexu*). Luther illustrated the difficult relationship using the image of the sun and the moon: 'As the sun is more splendid than the moon' – hastily underscoring the tension: 'although the moon is also a most splendid body' – woman is inferior to man in dignity (*tamen non aequabat gloriam et dignitatem masculi*). As companions they shine together among the stars (the household, children and livestock), *et tamen magna differentia est sexus*. Sun and moon were perfectly suited to continue the *querelle des femmes*, which was supposed to come to an end. In contrast to Luther, Johann Fischart, a Strasbourg Protestant, did not see any contradiction in woman being man's companion and man nevertheless being the head of woman: just 'as the sun does not destroy the light of the moon, . . . a just man should do his woman honour', since the two cannot exist without 'such community'. François Rabelais, humanist, physician and cleric, had let the physician Rondibilis in the *Third Book* explain that woman resembles the moon in that she appears in her best light when the husband-sun is absent, especially at night. Rabelais's theologian Hippothadeus thought that the light of female virtue was at most a reflection of her husband's light. According to another French author, she resembled the moon to the extent that 'all dignity of the woman comes solely from her husband'. In contrast to the moon, however, she should never be seen in the absence of her sun, 'she must live in stillness and watch over the house'.[27] Such an image was not new. Even Plutarch had used it, and in the early Christian period the moon was merely a reflector in contrast to having a true existence.

Does that mean there was nothing new under the sun? Most doctrines on matrimony were now agreed that physical violence by the husband was only legitimate if the wife 'truly' deserved it. Open 'tyranny' was – at least in theory – no longer acceptable. Misogyny still existed, especially in Luther's blunt language, but even husbands were seriously reprimanded by pastors. Like theology, actual married life also remained a balancing act that required constant renegotiating, and a querelle. 'Women love to rule and dominate by nature', Luther asserted, and Cyriacus Spangenberg complained that only very few 'are obedient and subservient to their husbands. They do not let themselves be governed; instead, they always want to be Doctor She-man'. They claim that the Bible calls women 'she-man' and therefore they deserve to 'rule and govern as much as does the man'. The early Enlightenment thinker, Samuel Pufendorf, postulated in 1673 'that by nature all individuals have equal rights' and that is why man does not rule by nature: 'Whatever right a man has over a woman, inasmuch as she is his equal, will have to be secured by her consent, or by a just war.'[28] According to Luther as well as Mary Tattlewell and Joan Hit-him-home, women did not marry for their husbands' sake but – despite all the pain – to have children.

Instead of the old, male form of misogamy, a new female form emerged. Mary Astell, a scholar and writer who never married, asserted that men married only to obtain a practical housekeeper, one 'who may breed his Children, taking all the care and trouble of their Education, to preserve his Name'; and 'one whom he can intirely Govern', a 'necessary evil' (she used the early Christian expression). Freedom of choice as regards one's spouse was a farce, Astell emphasized, and the only true choice was between such a marriage and remaining single. She thought it was 'not good for a woman to marry' and that is why women should 'never consent to be a wife'. The *Précieuses* of the French *Âge classique* considered marriage a plague: 'One marries only in order to hate and suffer.' They discussed whether or not, and how, power could be divided up among the partners, such as by taking turns. In Germany, Hermann von Weinberg's parents tried just that. They were supposed to alternate each week; sometimes they forgot whose turn it was, and when the wife insisted, her husband said, '"True, it is your turn today and this week; I will be in charge next week", making fun of the arrangement'.[29] The *Précieuses* also considered living together without being married, or negotiating a marriage for a limited time; if the woman did not choose to extend the agreement, then the child would stay with the father and the mother would receive a severance payment and her freedom.

New ideas of philogamy did not lead to philogyny, much less female liberty, but they did lay the groundwork for future debate. The new Europa still had to choose between Zeus and her female companions. Protestantism, too, could not totally do without offering a way of life for women void of men; consequently, numerous Protestant women's homes were set up. In her *Serious Proposal to the Ladies* (1694), Mary Astell demanded Protestant convents in England where women could devote themselves to religion, scholarship, teaching and contemplation. Astell found support for her proposal from other women. In the rest of Europe, women's congregations became widespread, taking on a broad spectrum of religious and social missions. Arcangela Tarabotti, who had written a defence maintaining that women were indeed human, wrote a work on the *condizione femminile*, complementing Dante's work on the *condizione umana*. After attacking the constraints of the convent in *Inferno monacale* (Nuns' Hell), Tarabotti also spoke out against the *ragion di stato*, the 'reason of state', of dowries, declaring that it would be more just if the men paid instead of the 'women having to buy themselves a husband'; and she opposed the maltreatment of women in marriage (*Il purgatoria delle malmaritate*). Finally, in *Il Paradiso monacale*, she envisioned what freedom was possible within the convent if one chose freely to be a nun.

The Power of Fathers, the Power of Men, the Power of Women

> If all men are born free, how is it that all women are born slaves?
> Mary Astell, 1706

Christine de Pizan had argued that women as well as men had a capacity for political power and – as was common in the querelle – she provided many biblical, mythological and historical examples. In *Senatulus*, Erasmus of Rotterdam had his character Cornelia demand a *respublica foeminea* with a *reipublicae disciplina*: a women's parliament, like the bishops' and monks' councils, that would consult on 'our dignity and our interests'. Contrary to this vision, political power in Europe was given legitimacy through paternal, patriarchal authority by linking the 'father of the house', 'father of the country' and 'God the father' in both theology and politics. The ruling head of the household became the model for all power relations, and vice versa. Authority – secular and religious – was considered patriarchal. In the emergence of the modern state, matrimonial jurisdiction gradually shifted from the Church to the state and from local to central authorities. This was true especially in Protestant areas, but also to some extent in Catholic regions, in particular in France. Laws and jurisprudence developed a close pact between family and state structures from the sixteenth century, strictly regulating marriage, marital conditions and inheritance issues and subjecting them to royal authority. The new central state was based on male authority in both the family and the state. In England, the doctrine of divine right and the 'natural' right of kings was given legitimacy through God the father and the 'natural' rule of the father over wife and children. This doctrine was taken to extremes at the same time as it was disputed. In *The Necessity of the Absolute Power of all Kings* (1648) and *Patriarcha* (1680), the 'flagship of Royalism', Robert Filmer justified royal authority on the basis of the authority of Adam over Eve and his children.

John Locke protested in his *Two Treatises on Government* (1689), claiming that legitimate political power originated from the voluntary association and consent of the subjects. Family relations, according to Locke, were pre-political and natural, not part of civil society. The father has no political power over his children – 'we are born free' – rather, he has only the duty to raise them properly. If paternal and political power were of the same kind, nonsense would result. All fathers would be kings and the king himself would reign only over his own children. But what of Eve? Although Locke collaborated with his learned companion, theologian Damaris Cudworth Masham, his conclusions on this issue were entirely his own, and, once again, a balancing act was called for. Locke insisted that conjugal society was a contract, that wives also had a right to own property (in sharp contrast to common law), and that divorce must be possible. But above all, God did not give Adam any real power over Eve, and certainly not political power. If that had been the case, more nonsense would result, since there would be 'as many Monarchs as there are Husbands'. Mother and father have equal authority over their children (the mother even more so since she was more involved in procreation than the man, who in contrast to her thinks only of the pleasures of sex). Their authority is not 'paternal' but 'parental'. If authority over children were confused with political power, a third kind of nonsense would result: women would have to have political power. Even for John Locke that would have been a topsy-turvy world, and his argument was made powerful by virtue of the paradox. The subordination of the woman is not political but 'conjugal', and thus natural: 'that Subjection they should ordinarily be in to their Husbands'. But how does that conform to the idea of marriage as a contract? And what happens in the event of a conflict over the 'common Interest and Property'? In such a case, there must be a 'last Determination' and some sort of 'Rule', which 'naturally falls to the Man's share, as the abler and the stronger'. This view would be widely shared in the future, as would the view of the relationship between family and political government. Locke's successful disavowal of patriarchal rule was based on a strict separation of political and gender relations, of civil society and the family. From this point on, the issue would no longer be the power of fathers but the power of men.

A response came promptly from Mary Astell. Attacking Locke, she argued in 1706 in the third edition of her *Reflections upon Marriage* (1700) against the supposed 'natural inferiority of our Sex'. In a way, she agreed with Filmer when she claimed that power is power, whether in politics or in the family. But she also set Filmer straight, wanting to apply the new liberalism in politics to the family. If 'absolute sovereignty' was not necessary in the state and considered an evil, why should it exist in the family? It is even more unnecessary in the family, since man and woman – unlike government and subject – chose each other freely, or should do so. If 'Arbitrary Power is evil in itself, and an improper method of governing rational and free agents, it ought not to be practis'd anywhere'. In her view, absolute power was even more problematic within the family, since '100,000 tyrants are worse than one', and 'If all men are born free, how is it that all women are born slaves?'

Ninety years later, a growing number of women had further contemplated, both in writing and in public, the relationship between the sexes. It was then that the writer and governess Mary Wollstonecraft, like Astell, questioned the double standard for the political and the private (it was not Locke but Wollstonecraft who referred to the family as 'private'). 'Public virtue is only an aggregate of private', she argued, and 'every family might also be called a state.' She held reason to be especially important for women, in order for them to satisfy their private duties and take advantage of their rights. For their 'private virtue' to be 'a public benefit', women – whether married or not – needed a 'civil existence in the State'. Like many women of her time, Wollstonecraft admired Rousseau and his political doctrine. But also like others, she rejected his theory on gender, his postulate that women existed only to obey and delight men ('what nonsense'!), harshly inveighing against the notion that women had no reason and thus no virtue. This, she said, was women's main problem – not that they had no power. They had enough of that, but in an irrational way. Women used their supposed weakness, sensuality and sexuality in order to obtain privileges and illegitimate power: 'Women, in general, as well as the rich of both sexes, have acquired all the follies and vices of civilization.' Women are slaves – 'in a political and civil sense' – precisely because 'indirectly they obtain too much power and are debased by their exertions to obtain illicit sway'. This applied to all women, according to Wollstonecraft, since all women were raised to exploit their sexual power, but particularly to the ladies of the court and the salons, who influenced cultural life especially in France and played an important role in the wrangling for power and career, both in and out of the royal court. The power of women was virtually a characteristic of the *ancien régime*, according to Wollstonecraft, in which they 'illicitly had great sway' – although, or perhaps because, they had 'no political existence' – 'corrupting themselves and the men with whose passions they played'. Women, 'as well as despots, have now, perhaps, more power than they would have if the world, divided and subdivided into kingdoms and families, were governed by laws deduced from the exercise of reason'; but in obtaining such power, 'their character is degraded, and licentiousness spread through the whole aggregate of society'. Then Wollstonecraft became more specific. 'This is the very point I aim at: I do not wish them to have power over men; but over themselves', and 'It is not empire, – but equality, that they should contend for.'[30]

Of course, in the *ancien régime* women also had power – based not on the nature of their gender but on that of their 'blood'. The prominent humanist Sir Thomas Smith clearly distinguished between family duties in the eleventh and sixteenth chapters of his work *De Republica Anglorum* (1583). The husband has the task of earning and spending money, the wife is responsible for saving and 'nurtriture' of the family, and 'each dothe governe' in their respective spheres. In politics, however, women could not rule except 'by right of blood'; that is, 'in such cases as the authoritie is annexed to the bloud and progenie, as the crowne, a dutchie, or an erledome for there the blood is respected, not the age nor the sexe'.

Nevertheless, gender did indeed play an important role. Queen Elizabeth (1533–1603) presented herself as a strong virgin – without husband or children – and, where a man was needed, as a man. When in 1588 the Spanish Armada set sail and the English troops were assembled in Tilbury, she appeared in armour. Although her body was weak, she told the men, she had 'the heart and stomach of a king and a king of England too'; she 'will take up arms, I myself will be your general, judge, and rewarder of every one of your virtues in the field'. Against the parliament, which wanted a successor, she insisted that as 'your natural mother . . . unto you all', she was more essential. Women reigned as queens in their own right, as queens at the side of their husbands, as sovereigns or as – often politically powerful – 'mistresses' in unofficial marriages. In France, where the Salic law of succession excluded from the throne all females and those males whose claim to rule was based on descent through a female (the rank of king could only be passed down through men), there was nonetheless an almost unbroken line of female regents from Louise of Savoy (1476–1531) to Anne of Austria (1601–66). Catherine de' Medici (1519–89) initially presented herself as a dutiful wife and later, always dressed in black, as a dutiful widow. Spain's rule of the Netherlands was traditionally put in the hands of a woman. Margaret of Parma (1522–86) was known for her tolerant regime. A female line of succession was introduced in England in 1688 in order to avoid the threat of Catholicism, which was embodied in the male succession to the throne. Empress Maria Theresa (1717–80) had ten children (and numerous miscarriages) and demonstrated her ability to rule by presenting herself as the ideal wife and mother. It had not been easy to find recognition for the female succession in the Hapsburg dynasty by all the European states (in the

Pragmatic Sanction of 1713). Catherine the Great (1729–96), empress of Russia, initially also presented herself as a dutiful wife of the heir to the throne; then she took power into her own hands and had many lovers. Christina of Sweden (1626–89) was designated from the outset to be queen and she therefore enjoyed a masculine upbringing, supervised by Count Axel Oxenstierna, who observed 'with satisfaction . . . that Her Majesty is not like other members of her sex', and thus 'raises the highest hopes'.[31] She was fascinated by Cartesian thought, and corresponded with Descartes. In opposition to pressure by parliament, she resolutely refused to marry. She wanted to be an Amazon queen with a male mind in a female body. She wore men's clothing and acted like a man. But she loved her autonomy more than her power and abdicated when she was twenty-nine years old, spending the rest of her life in freedom in Rome. The end of the eighteenth century was also the end of the epoch of powerful ruling women, even if Queen Victoria was able to continue the tradition.

Rousseau had foreseen this end in his republican project – both modern and anti-modern – in his *Lettre à d'Alembert* of 1758. 'Whether a monarch governs men or women ought to be rather indifferent to him, provided that he be obeyed; but in a republic, men are needed.' Rousseau was also a protagonist in the *querelle des sexes* and responded to that tradition in his writings. Rule by women was one of the main subjects of that querelle, not as a question of 'blood' but of gender. In England, John Knox wrote *The First Blast of the Trumpet against the Monstrous Regiment of Women* (1558) on the occasion of the coronation of Mary Tudor and her half-sister Elizabeth. His concern was more with religion than sex, but the treatise was received and responded to as a statement in the battle of the sexes. The 'justness, usefulness, and necessity of sexual difference in succession to the throne', which was the rule in Germany, Italy, France and Spain, was presented in Germany as the result of a struggle between men and women (*Certamen masculo-foemineum*, 1602 and 1606). Marie de Gournay offered harsh criticism of Salic law in 1622 and was joined by many women. When the German poet Joseph von Eichendorff wrote of the 'old as well as remarkable battle' in 1847, it had long since entered a new stage.

2
The French Revolution:
The Dispute is Resumed

Femme. Bientôt ce nom n'existera plus: les femmes veulent l'abolir, et faire le nom d'homme des deux genres, comme en latin. Si les hommes veulent conserver le nom de femme, ils le prendront pour eux.

Anon., 1788, 1826

The age of revolution – the period that began in 1776 in the British colonies and ended with the European revolutions of 1848 – shook not only the political order but the gender order as well. The anonymous author of an entry in a French encyclopedia complained in 1788, and again in 1826, that the word 'woman' would soon cease to exist, supposedly because 'women wish to abolish it'.[1] Things would not go that far. Instead, the French Revolution laid the groundwork for modernity in France and throughout Europe. The revolution was significant for women; the way they thought, spoke and acted was closely related to the dramatic changes from 1789 to 1795 and beyond to Napoleon's rule and subsequent defeat. And women were significant for the revolution, even if the radical changes were largely shaped by men. As male efforts continued to develop and escalate, women's hopes, demands and visions also changed. Traditional views mingled with unprecedented ones, anti-modern with modern, patriotic pathos and visions of peace and happiness with hate and violence – among women as well as men. Visions of female *citoyenneté*, citizenship, took their place next to their male counterpart. Developments in Paris differed in many ways from those in the rest of France. Women spoke out and acted on all sides of the controversies and conflicts. There were impressive movements by women, but no autonomous women's movement. In 1776 Abigail Adams had advised her husband John, a signatory of the Declaration of Independence who later became the second president of the United States, to 'remember the ladies' and that 'all men would be tyrants if they could'. Nevertheless, a few years later such admonitions were expressed with greater severity and furore in revolutionary Europe. The images of women – images of heroism and defeat, of commitment and silence, of revolutionary home-making and revolutionary violence, of counter-revolutionary religion and subversion – that emerged in the course of the revolution circulated throughout Europe and would have a lasting impact.

Hopes

Ne pourrions-nous pas vous opposer un corps d'États aussi Généraux, formé de notre sexe? Cessez d'être surpris.

Dames françoises, 1789

When will there be bread?

Parisian market women, 1789

The revolution was ushered in by an event that was as unprecedented for France as it was for the rest of Europe: King Louis XVI called upon all his subjects to voice their complaints freely. And they did so extensively, recording them in *cahiers de doléances*, registers of grievances and expectations, that they entrusted to their deputies for the assembly of the Estates-General summoned on 5 May 1789 in Versailles. It had been convened for the first time since 1614, forced by the impending financial bankruptcy of the state and coming at a time of great inflation and wide-spread destitution. The *cahiers* expressed hunger and anger, hopes for bread and liberty, and economic and political reform. Proposals for pol-itical modernization, mostly in a constitutional sense, appeared side by side with everyday worries about taxes and sheer survival. Here, as in the course of the revolution in general, women played an active role, and in some of the roughly thirty thousand extant *cahiers de doléances* their voices can be heard.

On 1 January 1789, before the election procedures for the Estates-General were even made known (that occurred on 24 January), 'women of the third estate' submitted a petition to the king that captured the reform-oriented spirit of the times: 'Women, eternal object of admira-tion and contempt by men, should they not also let their voices be heard amidst this general turmoil?' The authors held the laws excluding women from the National Assembly to be 'deeply rooted' and they doubted that the pending elections and the future deputies would be chosen without bias. Thus they refrained from requesting to be allowed to 'send their own representatives to the Estates-General', though not without explicitly mentioning their hope. Instead they cited wrongs that were characteristic for the *cahiers* submitted by women: 'Almost all the women of the third estate are born destitute.' They continued that their education was deplorably pathetic; even at a young age 'they are taught to work', and by fifteen they were obliged to earn their keep, receiving the poorest of wages. If they were pretty they were preyed upon by seducers. They would then flee to Paris, where their 'shame' was easier to hide and where they fell victim to prostitution owing to their 'difficulty in earning their bread in a decent manner' and men's incessant demands. Proscription of prostitution was proposed as an antidote. Daughters born out of wedlock, ostracized even by their parents, had an especially hard time. For this reason, it was proposed, men should be banned from all professions open to women and above all 'we demand to have a say in our education and career'. Instruction should include 'the virtues that are befitting our sex, gentleness, modesty, patience and charity'; women learned the fine arts on their own, and strict science would lead only to 'foolish arrogance' and 'pedantry' instead of to 'faithful wives and mothers of a family'.[2]

Education and social issues took pride of place among women's grievances. An obviously educated woman took up the cause of the poor and argued from a religious as well as anti-clerical perspective. 'If my sex, which daily faces all the great wrongs of society, can contribute to the good order to be established in the kingdom of the best of all kings, then I demand that the unfortunate poor children who are found in a frail and invalid state . . . should find a retreat befitting their social standing and thus be removed from horrible misery. They should be taken in by the monks; *le sexe* [the girls] by the nuns, who like the monks spend their days idly.' The author demanded a reduction in the price of bread and political reform that provided for officials to be elected rather than appointed. In early May, the market women in Paris had their complaints recorded by the man who had informed them that the king, 'notre bourgeois de Versailles', had allowed all the world to present their grievances. They railed against the rich and their luxury, the exorbitant price of bread and the 'screaming injustice' of the licence to levy taxes which, they claimed, raised the price of meat and especially the wine that was needed to endure the cold of the *Halles*, the major Paris food market, and the outdoor markets. They complained that a baptism now cost as much as a good wine and a wedding was even more expensive. The 'poor mothers who have nothing more to bite than their misery' were forced to turn their daughters into prostitutes in order to obtain some money.[3]

Some *Dames françoises* even entered the political arena and proposed convening an assembly in addition to the Estates-General, composed 'of our sex' and nevertheless just as 'general' as the other. Madame B. B. of

Caux made reference to the Enlightenment, the imminent liberation of black slaves (this would take until 1793 and only last for a few years) and demanded freedom for women as well. In earlier, ignorant, times the rule for women had been 'work, obedience and silence'; thus they were 'the Third Estate of the Third Estate'. She then raised the question of political participation for women: 'It is not at all to the honours of government . . . that we aspire but we believe that it is entirely fair to allow wives, widows or daughters possessing lands or other properties to lay their grievances at the feet of the throne; that it is equally just to let them vote, since they are obliged, like men, to pay royal taxes and to satisfy the demands of commerce.' Such women could only take advantage of their right to vote through male proxy, but B. B. countered by saying that 'since it has been shown, with reason, that a nobleman cannot represent a commoner, nor the latter a nobleman, in the same way and with more justice, a man cannot represent a woman, since representatives must have absolutely the same interests as those represented: women, therefore, can only be represented by women'.[4] This argument was doubly revolutionary since it demanded modern parliamentarianism and wanted women to participate *as women*. This remained the justification for political participation by women into the twentieth century. It corresponded to the theory of representation postulated by Abbé Sieyès, that the third estate could not be represented by the nobility. At the same time it stood in contrast to the influential and disputed doctrine of Jean-Jacques Rousseau, who strictly rejected parliamentary representation, supporting instead a direct democracy of the *volonté générale*.

These and other women's voices express a peculiar combination of tradition and modernity. Education as a means to perfect both personality and society, often also with respect to women, had been a subject of discussion since the Enlightenment. Complaints about women's lack of liberty, their poverty and abuse had been part of the earlier querelle, as was male ridicule of women's aspirations. Such ridicule circulated in the summer of 1789 in a satirical version of the Declaration of the Rights of Man and Citizen that was then passed on 26 August: 'If men are free to go to women, then the women must be free to receive them. . . . Having freedom in her own person, she can sell or give herself unto the one who pleases or pays her most.' A *Declaration of the Rights of Woman* from Lyon (1791) declared that 'the art of talking nonsense is an inherent and imprescriptible right of women'.[5] More numerous, however, were the male – as well as a few female – voices blaming women for bringing France to the brink of ruin, especially Queen Marie Antoinette, the *salonnières*, and the court mistresses. Allegations of sexual debauchery were widely used by the broad-based press campaign to symbolize the political corruption of the absolute monarchy. In the trial that led to her execution in 1793, the queen was charged by radical revolutionaries with emasculating her husband, taking up with ministers, having lesbian relations, neglecting her duties as a mother and having incestuous relations with her son. Meanwhile the old arguments used to legitimate female rulers within the framework of the courtly state disappeared and – long before kingship suffered the same fate – queenship was rejected. In March 1791 the National Assembly discussed whether or not Salic law should remain in force. It was approved in the new constitution in September: the kingship had to be 'passed down by inheritance from man to man according to primogeniture, to the perpetual exclusion of women and their descendants'.

We do not know how many women shared the grievances expressed by some, but the active participation of women in the various stages of the revolution suggests that the *cahiers* of women were by no means isolated utterances. Moreover, gender relations were an important aspect of the controversies among the different factions of revolutionaries – whether republicans, constitutional monarchists or social revolutionaries – and finally, there was a growing number of women among the 'counter-revolutionaries' and those who were 'suspect', as well as those who denounced others to prove their own *citoyenneté*, and those who were themselves denounced.

A form of active citizenship for women, which in the sense of Rousseau – who was then very popular – implied directly exercising the sovereignty of the people, was the involvement of lower-class women, especially in Paris and in the revolutionary *journées*. Here they expressed their own *doléances* and hopes. Within only a few years their activism linked them to the revolutionary terror that broke out in autumn 1792 and was declared the official principle of the revolutionary government on 5 September 1793. Earlier, however, on 5–6 October 1789, the march of the Parisian women to Versailles played a decisive role in implementing liberty and constitutional order. For contemporaries – and up to the present day – the march became a symbol of the early revolutionary phase. Whereas the storming of the Bastille on 14 July was largely a male action, the October revolt was predominantly a female enterprise.

Tradition played an important role. Women had long taken the initiative in popular uprisings, though they tended to leave the use of open violence to men. Their turning directly to the monarch was also nothing new. In the harsh winter of 1708–9, women had marched to Versailles to demand that the Sun King, Louis XIV, alleviate the mass famine and end the war. The Parisian *poissardes* (fishwives) and other market women had direct access to the court of Louis XV through his wife Maria Leczinska, one of the most popular French queens. Marie Antoinette always received the Parisian market women on 25 August, the feast day of St Louis, and did so again in 1789, when roughly one thousand women together with the newly formed National Guard moved out to Versailles under Lafayette to pay traditional tribute to the king and queen (although the very same fishwives had been making nasty remarks that Marie Antoinette had not been pregnant in a long time). The language of the market, *poissard*, had always been irreverent. In autumn 1789 the lack of respect turned into open aggression, when food for the capital was in short supply despite a good harvest (presumably because the peasants were no longer in a hurry to sell their harvest, since the seigneurial taxes had been abolished in August). In September the Parisian women had blocked grain transports several times, redirecting them to the Hôtel de Ville (town hall). On 4 October they almost lynched a baker who was suspected of selling underweight loaves of bread. The famous saying attributed to Marie Antoinette was repeated again and again: 'If they have no bread, let them eat cake.' At the top of her lungs, a market woman blamed the queen for the general impoverishment, pressing the crowd to march to Versailles to demand a supply of bread for the capital. It had also become known that the king refused to unconditionally approve the decree to abolish feudal privileges, the Declaration of the Rights of Man and the articles of the constitution of 9–10 September that stripped him of his power. Rumour spread that officers of the loyalist Flanders Regiment had trampled the tricolour cockade of the revolution at an orgy in Versailles and had distributed black cockades to ladies-in-waiting to honour the queen and white ones for the king, thus offending the nation. To the Parisian masses, the efforts of the deputies in Versailles to give the country a constitution meant filling their empty stomachs. Hunger joined forces with anger, bread (wine as well, for the market women) with politics, and the sovereignty of the people – the definition, introduction and parliamentary institutionalization of which was at the time the subject of endless debates – was understood as imminent prosperity, the *bienfaits de la révolution*, in other words, paradise on earth.

In the early hours of 5 October, more than a thousand market women, traders and artisans assembled in front of the town hall yelling 'When will there be bread?' (This was the title of a well-known pamphlet.) As had been common in popular revolts since time immemorial, the women prodded the men to action by accusing them of being fearful: 'The men are reluctant and cowardly; we'll take things into our own hands.' With the help of some men they broke open the gate to the town hall, then sent the men away, presumably to underscore their non-violence – in spite of the brooms, spits and muskets that represented more symbolic than actual violence. They stormed the building and only Stanislas Maillard, one of the most respected *vainqueurs de la Bastille* and a National Guardsman, was able to keep them from burning the files. With Maillard leading the way and two cannon (albeit without ammunition), the women made their way in heavy rain to Versailles, singing in their ironic *poissard* that they were seeking *le bon papa* Louis. The woman who supposedly rode the cannon became legendary. Later the rumour started that the rioters were actually men disguised as women, but this was no march of transvestites. Along the six-hour march, the women occasionally took bread and wine from local merchants. Shortly before noon Lafayette managed to make his way through the crowd to the town hall, only to learn that the women had already left and that the men of his National Guard were about to follow them to guard the king instead of the Flanders Regiment. Under pressure from his rebelling guards, Lafayette also decided to follow the women in order to give the march some semblance of legitimacy.

The women, whose number had more than doubled along the way, arrived at Versailles late that afternoon and were received with speeches and wine by the commander of the Versailles National Guard. Maillard explained the purpose of the event to the National Assembly convened in Versailles: 'The aristocrats want us to die of hunger', and it was necessary to put a stop to the actions of the grain speculators. The women were carefully kept out of the palace, but they stormed the gallery of the National Assembly clamouring against the clergy and nobility. However, they were not interested in the current debates on abolishing feudal obligations and demanded to speak to the king. A delegation of twelve was eventually admitted and Louis promised them that all available grain stores would be brought to Paris immediately. Many of the women who had been waiting outside in the rain were not satisfied with a verbal promise; they argued amongst themselves and then dispersed. Pressured by the crowd and the National Assembly, the king finally accepted the Declaration of the Rights of Man and the other decrees. When it became known that the Parisian National Guard was on the way (15,000 men arrived around midnight), tension reached crisis point, since the Guard not only wanted to match themselves against the royal bodyguards, they also refused to return to Paris until the king agreed to come with them and take up residence amidst his people (there had been talk of this in Paris since September). The king hesitated. At 5:30 in the morning an armed crowd entered the palace. A woman shouted that they should 'tear out the heart of the *coquine* [Marie Antoinette], cut off her head, fricassee her liver and even then it would not be all over'. There was bloodshed and two soldiers were killed (by men); the guards outside Marie Antoinette's chamber were run down. At this point only a few women were still actively rioting. The queen saved herself by a hair's breadth, and then appeared with the king and Lafayette before the crowd, who called out 'Long live the queen!' Hours later the royal family and twenty thousand people made their way in the rain to Paris. Soldiers and women carried loaves of bread on their pikes, along with the heads of the two casualties, and sang that they were bringing 'the baker, the baker's wife, and the baker's lad to Paris'. The next day Louis's title was changed from 'King of France and Navarre' to 'King of the French'. And the *poissardes* sang: 'To Versailles like bragging lads / We brought with us all our guns. / Though we were but women we had to show / A courage that no one can reproach us for. / Now we won't have to go so far / When we want to see our king.'

Soon everyone was talking about these October Women. Supporters of the *ancien régime* were harshly critical of them, at the time and later on. Irish politician and philosopher Edmund Burke, who had adamantly defended the American Revolution, referred to the women's march to emphasize his repugnance towards the events in France. Others, such as historian Jules Michelet in 1854, praised them. In late 1789, the mayor of Paris gave many of the *bonnes citoyennes* a medal and at the same time tried to find those responsible for the 'misdeeds' of 6 October to punish them. Reine Audu, who was supposed to have ridden the cannon, was arrested and charged; she was not released until September 1791 and was decorated with a rapier 'for her courage and patriotism'. The 'heroines of the revolution' were publicly honoured, songs were written about them, they marched at republican festivals alongside the male 'vanquishers of the Bastille', and on 10 August 1793 a triumphal arch was built in their honour. Two years earlier, after the flight of the royal family, the October Women declared with others that 'the women brought the king back to Paris and the men let him get away'.[6] Although they had gone to Versailles not with the intention of bringing the king to Paris but because of the food shortage, it was owing to them that the National Guard took advantage of the opportunity, that the king ultimately agreed to move his residence, and that there were only isolated instances of violence.

In subsequent years, however, there would be real violence in Paris. Women of the lower classes – washerwomen, shopkeepers, workers, unemployed women, wives of artisans or traders – were part of the masses in the capital that had grown more and more radical over the course of time in demanding political rights even for passive citizens, proclaiming social egalitarianism and impatiently waiting for the true *bienfaits* of the revolution. The female sans-culottes (or *sans-jupons*) took part in the revolutionary assemblies and festivals, especially the funeral of the murdered Jean Paul Marat, in awareness of their patriotic duty to defend the revolution and the Jacobins against the 'enemy within', to secure food for their families and 'to strangle and kill all the rich'. They gauged the constitution by the price of bread, practised *taxation populaire* and favoured the use of terror as a means to fight excessive prices. The 'legal' terror that grew into *grande terreur* in the summer of 1794 and cost the lives of about 16,000 people throughout the country largely served to secure food for the capital. The sans-culotte women articulated hatred and violence in their language, gestures and emotions. They were called 'furies of the guillotine' and soon they were referred to as *tricoteuses*, or knitter women – the word evokes the contrast between domestic activity, on the one hand, and aggression, blood and violence, on the other: women of the people sat knitting in the spectator stands of the National Assembly or the Revolutionary Tribunal and applauded the 'cult of the guillotine' as a symbol of the people's sovereignty.

From 1792 the food supply for the capital worsened again, especially as a result of the civil and foreign wars. In spring 1793 food riots again broke out. France was now run by a dictatorial revolutionary government, without a constitution; the new constitution of June 1793 was postponed until the end of the war and would never come into effect. Under pressure from the sans-culottes, and in order to feed the army, maximum prices for grain were introduced in May 1793. In September came the General Maximum that applied to wages as well as food, which led to resistance by wage-earning consumers as well as wholesalers and retailers. After Robespierre was overthrown in July 1794, the end of the terror and the suspension of the Maximum in December, the food supply for the Parisian lower classes collapsed completely during the winter. Mothers could no longer nurse their infants, women suffered from starvation-induced amenorrhoea, and sans-culottes standing in long queues for bread expressed their anger and bitterness in dramatic threats. In their view, the revolution had not kept its promises. On 1 April and 20 May 1795 (12 *Germinal* and 1 *Prairial* of Year III) there were violent uprisings in Paris and, like October 1789, these *journées* were women's days. Primarily female sans-culottes from the working-class suburbs stormed the National Convention, unarmed but boisterous, demanding 'bread and the constitution of 1793!' Bread was promised, the women plundered and scuffled with gangs of young men. But on this occasion the revolt led to a defeat. The National Guard was not on the side of the women this time and the *Prairial* uprising, also started by the sans-culotte women, was as harsh and bitter as it was unsuccessful. Armed troops were called in against the male sans-culottes hurrying to their aid, and there was bloodshed. It was the defeat of a vision of politics, popular sovereignty and *citoyenneté* that was meant to bring bread and – at least in Paris – had succeeded for a time in doing just that.

Rights of Man and Rights of Woman

From the beginning the paradox involved in the declaration of inalienable human rights was that it reckoned with an 'abstract' human being who seemed to exist nowhere . . . since we know 'men' only in the form of men and women; that is, the concept of man, if it is to be usable in a political sense, must always inherently include the plurality of the human being.
Hannah Arendt, *Origins of Totalitarianism*, 1955[7]

The sans-culotte women practised political participation, but they did not demand this in the long term for themselves by any means. Their call for the constitution of 1793, which, like that of 1791, did not grant suffrage or access to political office for women, must be understood literally: the sans-culotte women as well as their husbands supported the widespread idea that women and the entire family were represented by the father or husband, at local and national levels. This concept was both traditional and modern. But to the same extent that parliamentarianism and representation were at the core of innovative political theories and became the concrete manifestation of the sovereignty of the people – by no means only in France – the exclusion of women became a key aspect of modern republican, democratic theory and practice, without any distinction being made between a direct or representational sovereignty of the people.

Measured against the novelty of the new political ideas – in the Enlightenment suffrage had not even been demanded for all men – and the even greater novelty of women criticizing them, the number of those who were not content to allow the 'other' sex to speak for women appears considerable. Some male revolutionaries shared this critique, first and foremost the Marquis de Condorcet. He was one of the most influential intellectuals before and during the revolution, an opponent of slavery, and was married to Sophie de Grouchy, a brilliant woman who shared, if not inspired, his opinions. Condorcet saw the radicalization in 1792 in Paris as a threat to a republic based on reason, responsibility and representation. He had already proposed equal suffrage for women and men in 1787. His essay 'Sur l'admission des femmes au droit de cité' (On the Admission of Women to the Rights of Citizenship, 1790) appeared in the *Journal de la Société de 1789*, which he founded, and caused quite a stir. To him it was an 'act of tyranny' to exclude women from 'natural rights', since women as well as men were 'sentient beings, capable of acquiring moral ideas and of reasoning concerning these ideas'. And since that was precisely the foundation of the rights of man, 'either no individual of the human species has any true rights, or all have the same. And he who votes against the rights of another, of whatever religion, colour or sex, has thereby abjured his own'. Women too loved freedom, he argued, and were very capable of political activity; Britain would have fared better if the historian Catherine Macaulay had been a member of the House of Commons. Furthermore, 'Why should individuals exposed to pregnancies and other passing indispositions be unable to exercise rights which no one has dreamed of withholding from persons who have the gout all winter or catch cold quickly?' Of course it was women who gave birth, but 'it is unnecessary to believe that because women could become members of national assemblies, they would immediately abandon their children, their homes and their needles'; on the contrary, this would make them more capable 'of rearing human beings'. The difference between women and men was not an argument opposing equal rights, since 'it is not nature but education and social existence that cause this difference'.[8]

Two further arguments by Condorcet would remain important for the gender debate until into the twentieth century. First, he criticized the view that 'women, in spite of much ability, sagacity and a power of reasoning carried to a degree equalling that of subtle dialecticians, are never governed by what is called reason'. It was true, he argued, that women did not always follow 'the reason of men. But they are governed by their own reason'. Condorcet believed such a female sense of reason (this was also a point of criticism of the Enlightenment concept of reason) was highly legitimate, since 'their interests not being the same as those of men through the fault of the laws, the same things not having the same importance for them as for us, they can, without lacking reason, govern themselves by different principles and seek a different goal'. Condorcet linked 'reason' with 'interests' and their political representation as a 'natural right'. Second, he rejected a principle of classical liberalism according to which only individuals who were intellectually and materially autonomous could exercise political rights, and this excluded women since they were considered uneducated and were legally dependent on their husbands. Condorcet interpreted this as an irrational circular argument: the dependence of wives upon their husbands could not be alleged 'against their claims, since it would be possible at the same time to destroy this tyranny imposed by civil law. The existence of one injustice can never be grounds for committing another'.

The *individu absolu* conceived by moderate as well as radical revolutionaries was male. According to the law to elect the legislature (December 1789) and the constitution of 1791, 'active' citizens had to belong to the National Guard; the war further masculinized the *citoyenneté* through the 1793 *levée en masse*, the mobilization for the war effort, which was celebrated by the sans-culottes as an expression of their belonging to the nation. Women were not considered 'true individuals' owing to their dependence, and thus their responsibility for the family (the fact that men were dependent on the domestic activities of the women was not perceived as a restriction of their autonomy). There were two sides to the new rights: civil (or human) rights that guaranteed freedom *from* the state, and political rights that guaranteed participation *in* the state – negative and positive liberty. The relationship between the two was one of great tension. Abbé Sieyès, who had declared the third estate to be the *nation* (on 17 June it proclaimed itself to be a National Assembly), also defined the distinction between 'active citizens', entitled to political participation, and 'passive citizens', who had only the 'natural' (or social) rights of liberty, property, security and resistance. The 'active citizen' also appeared in the constitution of 1791. In addition to children, foreigners, servants and non-taxpayers, Sieyès defined all women as 'passive citizens', at least 'in the present stage'. When the radical Camille Desmoulins (and later Robespierre) protested in 1791 against the limitation of suffrage and thus against 'passive' citizenship – 'the active citizens are those who took the Bastille' – he was thinking of the men of 14 July, not the women of 5 October. And when on 11 August 1792 a decree announced that 'the differentiation of the French into active and passive citizens shall be abolished', this too applied only to the men.[9]

In mid-1789, in the period leading up to the Declaration of the Rights of Man and Citizen, the fine distinctions within the *citoyenneté* were a subject of heated debate among the 1,200 men in the National Assembly. Did rights come from nature and were thus inherent in the *homme*, or were they granted by society in the form of a social contract and thus apply (only) to the *citoyen*? Do *hommes* and *citoyens* have different rights? Does man, by nature, have only rights or, as a citizen, duties as well? And finally – a point of contention in the National Convention in spring 1793 – the age-old question, do *hommes* include *femmes*, are women human? Pierre Guyomar, a deputy who sympathized with the Girondins, answered the question in the affirmative, citing classical Latin: '*Homo* comprises both words commonly used today – *man* and *woman*. Thus I will use that word, and if I used the word *individual*, it is because it appears most suitable in characterizing men regardless of their sex or age, who are, in my view, all part of one big family populating the earth.' In the end, the Declaration of the Rights of Man and Citizen did not speak of women, and with respect to nature and social contract – many declared the question to be mere metaphysics – a compromise was found: gone were the days of a detour via what seemed an 'original' or 'natural' condition, and the declaration became a balancing act, a symbol for the 'ambiguities of 1789'.[10]

Pierre Guyomar represented a minority opinion, and the Cercle Social was also a minority – but didn't this apply to all the factions that followed in rapid succession in Paris? The Cercle Social was founded in

1790 and its membership quickly grew to over 5,000. Condorcet and Brissot (later the leading figure of the Girondins) were among the Cercle's main activists. The Cercle Social was the first club that admitted women as members. The Confédération des Amis de la Vérité (Confederation of the Friends of Truth) was established as a section of it; the Amies de la Vérité, its female counterpart, was formed in March 1791. The Cercle Social was the only male-led club in Paris that set up a women's section to speak out in support of women. It was also a general lobby for women's rights and made its press available for that purpose. In December 1790 Etta Palm d'Aelders, a Dutch woman who would soon become president of the Amies de la Vérité, announced in a major speech to the male and female 'friends of truth' that the rights of man and citizen had to apply to women as well. Moreover, a cultural revolution (*régénération des mœurs*) would be necessary for women.[11] It was not political but civil rights that were most important for the Cercle. Aelders's principle was that 'the powers of husband and wife must be equal and separate'. Political rights, she declared, were useless without civil rights. Equality within marriage (she considered marriage a civil contract and a means to hold the father responsible for maintaining his children) and the option to divorce (which was discussed as a women's issue, as a 'natural' right to liberty) should be the basis of a democracy within the family, which was in turn the foundation and guarantor of political democracy. Everyday problems were closely connected to this idea, and the Amies de la Vérité worked on the following issues: protection from domestic violence and poverty; support for hospitals and childcare facilities (they were supposed to be free of charge for poor women from the countryside who became pregnant in Paris); paid work and education for women; reform of the inheritance law, which had favoured sons over wives and daughters; and a new adultery law (a 1791 draft of which allowed only the man to report adultery, and in the case of adultery by the wife, her dowry went to her husband). The high membership fees for the Amies de la Vérité club showed that its members were more well-to-do women who were fighting not only for their own rights but for those of their needy sisters.

It was largely due to the efforts of the Cercle, the Amies de la Vérité and supporters of both groups that women were granted equality in the inheritance law of April 1791 (primogeniture had already been abolished). They also succeeded in having marriage laid down in the constitution of September 1791 as a civil contract. On 20 September 1792, the day of the famous battle of Valmy, the women enjoyed their own 'Valmy des citoyennes': in its final session, the legislature passed a divorce law that was unique in Europe, legalizing divorce on the basis of mutual consent by the spouses. The number of divorces rose dramatically and two-thirds of the petitions were filed by women who were taking advantage of this form of civil individuality. Yet only one in four was dissolved on grounds of *consentement mutuel*; in all other cases the reason was abuse of the woman, desertion by the husband and 'incompatibility of humour or character'. Most of the cases that were heard before the newly created *tribunal de famille*, however, dealt with inheritance law. There was a 'war between brothers and sisters'; daughters sued their fathers for their share of the inheritance, care and benefits; and widows brought the families of their deceased husbands to court for seizing the dowry. Many referred to the 'natural and inalienable rights of the female sex', insisting that the 'man' of the Declaration of the Rights of Man included women and girls.[12] Especially if the women's petitions were successful, these trials seriously impinged on the traditional family structure based on maintaining the family property and unity. Yet most women did not just use the revolutionary language of overly individualistic rights but fused it with a moral vision of justice and a family structure in which mutual affection was more important than traditional property and male domination. There were hopes that the same values of justice and morality that should apply in the family would now predominate in the public sphere and the state as well. This vision would remain significant far into the next century.

After the Massacre on the Champs de Mars (17 July 1791) the Cercle Social was banned, but its leadership later reappeared in the national arena as the core of the Girondins (or Brissotins). From early 1793 they had to fight for survival in the face of embittered faction wars; the woman question was tabled – not even Condorcet could risk taking it up in the draft constitution of February 1793. The issue was closed once and for all when the Girondins were stripped of power in June 1793 by the Montagnards and a popular revolt in Paris, and many of them were executed. Condorcet was denounced in 1794 by a patriotic woman: she recognized him in a pub as an 'aristocrat' because he ordered an omelette made with twelve eggs. He died a short time later in prison, perhaps by his own hand. Etta Palm d'Aelders then became 'suspect' – during the Reign of Terror, people who were considered suspect were likely to be executed. She escaped to Holland and was never allowed to return.

Olympe de Gouges also worked with several revolutionary clubs and attended their assemblies, and she too frequented meetings of the Cercle Social. Today a classic, to most contemporaries de Gouges was an odd character, an outsider as pugnacious as she was tenacious, by no means a 'typical' woman (what woman is typical of all others, anyway?). She grew up in the provinces in a modest and uneducated environment, and later claimed to be the out-of-wedlock child of a nobleman. Some biographers believe her claim; others do not. Still others see this and other

mysteries in her life – during which she published much autobiographi-
cal material – as a manifestation of de Gouges's attempt not merely to
live her life in her own way, but to fashion her own identity. She gave
herself the name by which she became known (her mother's name was
Anne-Olympe Gouze). At sixteen she was married to a man she did not
love, had a son – there may have been more children – whom she did love
and financially supported until her death. Her son, however, publicly
dissociated himself from de Gouges in the turbulent times of her later
political activism and especially after she was executed in 1793. Around
1770, at twenty-two, de Gouges left southern France for Paris and was
initially one of the many *femmes galantes* – albeit outside the noble and
scholarly salons. She was supported by a long-term companion and ultimately became, despite her modest education (she dictated most of her
roughly 140 writings), a *femme de lettres*, which is how she was referred
to in the protocol of her trial and execution. It was her passion to compose provocative texts. She considered writing to be political action, in-
vesting a great deal personally and risking scandal for the sake of
publicizing her works – as pamphlets, of which 1,000–2,000 copies were
printed, or as posters plastered on building facades in Paris. Towards the
end of her life there was not much left of her worldly goods. Starting in
the 1780s she moved in the circles of reform-oriented publicists and wrote
on political subjects, such as her play *Zamora et Mirza, ou l'heureux
naufrage* (1784), a critique of the economy of privilege of the *ancien
régime*, with its misogyny, colonialism and slavery. It was performed for
the first time in 1789 under the title *L'Esclavage des nègres* and sparked
a theatre scandal. French colonial lords saw that it was soon taken off
the programme. In 1788 de Gouges also published her *Réflexions sur les
hommes nègres* ('Men are the same the world over'). She thus placed
herself on the side of those who had founded the Société des Amis des
Noirs in 1788: her friend Brissot, the Abbé Grégoire, who also spoke out
for the civil equality of the Jews, as well as Sieyès, Mirabeau and
Condorcet.

De Gouges passionately admired Rousseau and viewed him as her spiritual mentor, whereby she did not have Sophie from *Émile* in mind but
nature and the social contract. In 1788 she drafted her own design of a
society in its natural state in *Le bonheur primitif de l'homme*, based on
Rousseau's model and earlier doctrines of natural law. A dying father
admonishes his children to follow his wise legislation: the path to happiness involves cooperation, equality and respect for 'brothers, neighbours
and friends'. The children's mother is virtually absent, but marriage as a
union between lovers with equal rights is mentioned. Here de Gouges
expressed a paradox that had great impact on her life and works: 'If I go
any further in this matter, I will go too far and attract the enmity of the

newly rich, who, without reflecting on my good ideas or appreciating my good intentions, will condemn me pitilessly as a woman who has only paradoxes to offer and not problems easy to resolve.' Three years later, in the postamble to her *Déclaration des droits de la femme et de la citoyenne* (Declaration of the Rights of Woman and Female Citizen), de Gouges again took up the paradox and applied it to gender relations: 'If my attempt to give my sex an honorable and just stability is now considered a paradox on my part, an attempt at the impossible, I must leave to men yet to come the glory of discussing this matter, but meanwhile, the way can be prepared through national education, the restoration of morals, and by conjugal conventions.' It was both a new way of putting old paradoxes, those of the *querelle des sexes*, as well as the anticipation of new ones as they would later be formulated by John Stuart and Harriet Taylor Mill and, even a century later, by Hannah Arendt.[13]

De Gouges wrote the *Declaration of the Rights of Woman and Female Citizen* (including a dedication to the queen, a prologue, a preamble, seventeen articles, a postamble, and a *contrat social*) two years after the Declaration of the Rights of Man and Citizen was drafted; she completed it only a few days before 13 September 1791, when Louis XVI sanctioned the constitution that defined active citizens as definitively excluding women. The modern aspects of de Gouges's text clearly outweigh the traditional, albeit at the expense of containing paradoxes. She understood that in the vocabulary of the revolutionaries and in the *Déclaration* of 1789 – in spite of some opposition – *homme* did not mean human but male. At times she played with the ambiguity of linguistic gender assignment. She referred to herself in *Le cri du sage: Par une femme* (1789) as an 'homme d'État', and at other times she simply wanted to disregard her sex: 'Leave aside my sex: heroism and generosity are also women's portion, and the Revolution offers more than one example of it.' However, her prologue to the *Déclaration* clearly begins with: 'Man, are you capable of being just? It is a woman who asks the question. At least this right you cannot take away from her. What has given you the sovereign authority to oppress my sex?' And in the postamble to the declaration – which begins with 'Woman, wake up! The tocsin of reason is sounding throughout the Universe; know your rights' – *hommes* also means human beings. The reason for this is made clear in the *Déclaration* itself. The prologue makes reference to nature, understood to mean animals, plants and minerals: 'Look, search, and distinguish if you can, the sexes in the administration of nature. Everywhere you will find them mixed up, everywhere they co-operate harmoniously in this immortal masterpiece.' Man, however, claims to be an exception to this harmony and 'wishes to command as a despot over a sex that has received every intellectual faculty; that claims to enjoy the revolution and asserts its rights to equality'. In the postamble, she admonished women not to let themselves be intimidated when the legislators claimed (she used and modified Jesus's provocative question to his mother in the Gospel of St John): 'Women, what do we have in common with you?' Her answer was the same as Sieyès's to the question, 'What is the third estate?': 'Everything!'

De Gouges's Declaration follows the seventeen articles of the male Declaration exactly and is as much a balancing act as the original. Despite the title, her Declaration does not pertain only to women, but to men as well: 'Woman is born free and remains equal in rights to man' (Article 1); 'the goal of every political association is the preservation of the natural and imprescriptible rights of Woman and Man', and they are liberty, property, security and the right to resistance (Article 2); 'the source of all sovereignty resides essentially in the Nation, which is none other than the union of Woman and Man' (Article 3). The same applies for the right to political participation, since 'the law must be the expression of the general will; all female and male citizens must participate in its elaboration personally or through their representatives. It must be the same for all; all female and male citizens, being equal in the eyes of the law, must be equally admissible to all public honours, positions, and employments, according to their capacities and with no distinctions other than those of their virtues and talents' (Article 6). The 'citizenesses and citizens' should determine taxes or administrative expenses directly or through their representatives (Articles 13, 14). Rights always also include duties. Since women are to be treated the same as men in criminal law (Articles 7 and 9), de Gouges put forward an idea in Article 10 (which in the male Declaration had dealt with freedom of religion and had been particularly controversial) that was especially significant for her as a writer and which, in the future, would be the sentence of hers most often cited: 'Woman has the right to mount the scaffold, she must equally have the right to mount the rostrum.' In the postamble she appealed for a more effective separation of powers (in her view the executive branch had too much power compared with the legislature) and she drew a parallel to the necessary separation of power between husband and wife, 'who must be united, but equal in force and virtue, in order to make a good household'. Here the bearer of rights is pluralized by including women and naming men. At the same time, use of the word *homme* in a male sense questions the presumed universality of the Declaration of 1789, and de Gouges contrasted this with true universality. The 'individual' now was beyond gender: 'The constitution is null and void if the majority of the individuals who compose the Nation have not participated in its framing' (Article 16). At times de Gouges deviated somewhat from her model. She juxtaposed liberty with justice, which should also secure natural rights against the 'perpetual tyranny' of men, and changed 'the law', which was invoked with highly exaggerated importance in the 1789 document and which could again be used to restrict all basic rights, into 'laws of nature and reason' (Article 4).

Yet de Gouges did not assume all the postulates of 1789. Only to a certain extent, in her view, were the rights of men and women identical. True equality only made sense if it were applicable also for different individuals. This is demonstrated in her preamble. Appearing to draw a parallel to 1789 – 'The representatives of the French people, constituted as National Assembly, . . . have resolved' – she inserted a vision not of the sameness of 'absolute individuals' but of sexual difference: 'The mothers, daughters and sisters, representatives of the Nation, demand to be constituted as National Assembly.' De Gouges turned around the common tirades, according to which women had to be excluded from politics because of the female role: women represented the nation not *although* they were mothers, daughters and sisters but *because* they were. Together with the female 'intellectual faculties' referred to in the prologue, the argument resembles that of Condorcet, who attributed to women a sense of reason that is different but just as legitimate as that attributed to men. With her claim that women too were individuals, de Gouges did not reject sexual difference; instead, she made it the basis of the rights of man that also applied to women. Gender was thus very important and at the same time irrelevant: a paradox that emerged from the one-sidedness of the male Declaration. Moreover, de Gouges conceived of a National Assembly that – alongside the male institution – was made up entirely of women. Perhaps a women's senate, as Cornelia in Erasmus's *Senatulus* had proposed, or women's representation in the sense of the petition of the *dames françoises* of 1789? Did de Gouges doubt that women could assert their interests *vis-à-vis* the male representatives in a joint assembly? Or was it meant as a provocation – if the male half of the third estate claimed to represent the entire nation, why then couldn't the women?

At the end of the preamble, the balancing act between equal rights and sexual difference brings to mind the earlier *querelle des femmes* and the political thought of the women's movement that was yet to come: 'The sex that is superior in beauty as in courage during childbirth, recognizes and declares, in the presence and under the auspices of the Supreme Being, the following rights of woman and citizen.' In Article 11 (which in the male Declaration dealt with freedom of speech), de Gouges abandoned the model for a totally new idea – gender relations with respect to maternity, paternity and sexuality: 'Free communication of thoughts and opinions is one of the most precious rights of woman, since this liberty guarantees that fathers will acknowledge their children. Any female citizen can therefore freely say: "I am the mother of your child", without a barbarous prejudice forcing her to hide the truth'; she is also obliged to speak the truth. In view of gender difference here, and its special significance for women, Olympe de Gouges could not be content simply with admitting women to the rights of man. Without freedom of speech women would have neither the option nor the power to bind fathers to their duties towards their children. Once again, motherhood – a reason commonly used to exclude women from rights – is presented virtually to grant legitimacy to female citizenship: female citizens not *despite* but *because of* their sex. Paternity should not be determined merely on the basis of conjugal union or the statement of the man but a statement by the mother, which would guarantee a greater degree of truth. Maternity is therefore understood not only as a physical problem but a social one; and not as a female-specific and thus particular problem, but as a universal category. De Gouges felt that maternity had a legitimate place among basic rights that are claimed to be universal. Women were human *because* and not *although* they were women.

But why did de Gouges use motherhood outside marriage, of all things, to illustrate such a challenge to the relationship between the particular and the universal? Her own history of being born out of wedlock might have played some role, but more important was the social and political context. The issue had been discussed in France – and all over Europe – for a long time, and it would remain current in the future as well. It had been common practice for centuries in many parts of France that unmarried pregnant women had to submit a *déclaration de grossesse* (pregnancy declaration) and were obliged to name the father of the child in order to force him to pay for the child's maintenance – the *recherche de la paternité*, which was so influential in French history. If there was more than one man who could have been the father, all of them had to pay (though in reality this was extremely rare). The question of truth and falsehood from the mouth of a woman, especially with respect to pregnancy, was as crucial as it was controversial. In pre-revolutionary jurisprudence, paternal maintenance payments were gradually rejected and, along with them, the woman's right to file a paternity charge. Since the late 1780s Olympe de Gouges had been speaking out for improved conditions for single and poor mothers. She was enraged by the agony they endured in inadequate maternity facilities and demanded public assistance for these women and the restoration of the *recherche de la paternité*. A decree of 28 June–8 July 1793 provided for the establishment of a facility in each district where unmarried pregnant women could give birth at no charge and anonymously, and leave their child there as an *enfant de la patrie*. At the same time, single mothers were encouraged to nurse their children themselves and were given support. Eventually, even foundlings were granted the same rights as other children. On 12 *Brumaire* in

Year II (2 November 1793), the same day that de Gouges appeared before the Revolutionary Tribunal, another wish of hers came true: children born out of wedlock would receive their father's name and in certain cases they were able to claim their parents' inheritance.

De Gouges was equally concerned with marriage itself. Her list of rights culminated in a model social contract. She transferred Rousseau's or Locke's model of a political contract to marital relations in her *Forme du Contrat social de l'Homme et de la Femme*. Because the affluence of a woman in the upper classes was dependent on her husband (or other men in her life) and did not give her any security when she became old and was no longer attractive, and because women in the lower classes did not in any case have any options to earn their own livelihood de Gouges believed that traditional marriage was 'the tomb of trust and love'. For this reason she proposed that in future the property of both spouses would belong to both of them; and the children – whether or not they were conceived within wedlock – would have the right to inherit that property. The children should be able to choose either the mother's or the father's name. In the event of divorce the property should be divided, and on the death of one spouse half should go to the children (a year earlier, Olympe de Gouges had already dealt with the rights of children in the event of divorce). If a rich man fathered a child with his poor neighbour, he should adopt the child so that the mother would not need to seek refuge in a pitiful maternity home. If a man broke a marriage promise, he should pay the woman compensation commensurate with his fortune. In the reverse situation, the woman should also be penalized. Prostitutes should go about their business in designated districts only; in any case, de Gouges asserted, it was not prostitutes who perverted morals but the 'women of society'. And 'a foolproof way to elevate the soul of women' was to 'join them to all the activities of man'. That would make prejudice disappear and 'nature' would regain its rights. In closing, de Gouges coupled her commitment to women and children with a commitment to black people. In the colonies, which were 'closest to Nature' and where 'reason and humanity' were most needed, the 'blood [of the colonial lords] flows in the veins' of the children, which their fathers deliberately spread by indulging in their lust for black women without assuming the responsibilities of paternity. With her social contract de Gouges juxtaposed political rights with the civil rights of the married female individual, and transferred the debate on the difficult relationship between political and civil rights and between 'active' and 'passive' citizenship to gender relations within marriage.

The *Déclaration* was, despite all the efforts of its author, hardly known in its time. De Gouges knew that it was appreciated only by a few and she herself referred to the *Déclaration* as 'bizarre'. But half a century later she was to become a symbol that 'the history of our first revolution is ringed by a shining halo of great women who honored their sex and their country', according to Jeanne Deroin and Eugénie Niboyet, who in 1848 once again demanded women's suffrage and rejected the model of the *tricoteuses*.[14] De Gouges became a symbol because of her writings and her death. She was considered a martyr, like Charlotte Corday and Manon Roland. Corday had killed Jean Paul Marat in July 1793 for political motives (in her view his appeal for the Terror, which he had been equating with freedom since 1789, was treasonous to the revolution), and for that reason she courageously mounted the guillotine. Roland had hardly appeared in public, but behind the scenes she had actively supported her husband's revolutionary career, written his speeches, run a political salon for him and his friends, and stood up for civil rather than political rights, and especially for the education of women. The execution of twenty-one Girondin men on 30 October 1793 also brought some prominent women to the guillotine. The queen was guillotined on 16 October, Olympe de Gouges – as the first woman after the queen – on 3 November, at the age of forty-five, and Manon Roland five days later. That was 18 *Brumaire*, a day immortalized in the annals of history by the coups d'état of the two Napoleons.

All four women were executed as women, and the *Moniteur Universel* of 19 November announced the reason to the *Républicaines*: Marie Antoinette was, in the eyes of her prosecutors, a 'bad mother' and 'spouse with a debauched lifestyle'; Manon Roland was 'a monster in every sense'. Although she was a mother, she had betrayed 'nature' by wanting to rise above it: 'Her desire to be wise led her to forget the virtues of her sex, and this dangerous failure of memory meant her ruin at the guillotine.' The *Moniteur* also reported on Olympe de Gouges from the trial and execution protocol (the verdict was also reported by other newspapers): she had, so it was written, mistaken the 'delirium' of her 'exalted imagination' for an 'inspiration of nature'; she wanted to be a 'man of state' and, in her want of reason, divide France. She was punished for 'having forgotten the virtues that belong to her sex'. At that time, alongside the 'liberty trees' that had been planted everywhere in 1790, symbolic or actual guillotines were set up. After the end of the Terror, a flyer was circulated entitled 'Here lies all of France'. It pictured Robespierre, standing on the constitutions of 1791 and 1793 and guillotining the last remaining hangman. Next to him is an obelisk with smoke rising from the liberty cap at the top. He is surrounded by a forest of guillotines marked with the names of their victims. One of them is labelled 'Old men, Women and Children'.[15]

Why was Olympe de Gouges executed? She was a vehement opponent of Robespierre and in various pamphlets she criticized him so harshly –

at the height of his power – that he took up the challenge. She had no illusions about the outcome and on 4 July 1793, more than two weeks before she was arrested, she sent out her *Political Testament:* 'I have foreseen everything. I know that my death is inevitable.' She bequeathed her heart to her country, her honesty to the men ('they need it'), her *esprit* to the fanatics, her religion to the atheists, her soul to the women and her cheerfulness to women in menopause. A few days later her pamphlet, *The Three Urns or The Good of the Nation, by a Traveller of the Air*, provided the final grounds for her execution. She demanded a referendum in which all French men and women would decide by secret ballot whether they wanted a republic (*une et indivisible*), a constitutional monarchy or a Federation. The last named was especially considered reprehensible Girondism. Her proposal, however – provocative as it was – was an attempt to give the sovereignty of the people a chance.

Was Olympe de Gouges radical, moderate or conservative? In order to answer the question, we need to take into account that these classifications are anything but clear cut, especially since each label is used as an honour or a reproach depending on the author. In a literal sense she was radical, since she tackled problems at their roots, especially with respect to women and black people. She was also radical in terms of the historical development of the concept, since the word first appeared as a political term in 1830s England to refer to the philosophic radicals, including John Stuart Mill. He too spoke out for women's rights, though he did not believe in the language of 'origins' and 'natural' rights. If radicalness is identified with mass movements of the lower classes, then de Gouges was not radical. Even though she was active and often spent her days on the streets of Paris and in the galleries of the parliament, she was neither one of the October Women nor among those who applauded the guillotine. Her actions were the spoken and written word. In this she was more radical than Mary Wollstonecraft, whose *Vindication of the Rights of Woman* (1792) revealed not even a trace of the French women of those turbulent times. If de Gouges is judged by whether she demanded active and passive suffrage, then she was more radical and modern than her contemporaries, including the Parisian sans-culotte women and Mary Wollstonecraft, since de Gouges claimed for women the same suffrage as that enjoyed by men.

If de Gouges is classified as moderate or conservative, it is because she did not join the Jacobins or the movements further to the 'left', because her sympathies were with the Girondins, and because she dedicated her Declaration of the Rights of Woman to the queen and expected her to support the female sex. In addition, de Gouges spoke out in favour of the royal veto, defended Louis XVI during his trial and agitated against his execution. The fact is that she supported the Girondins because many of them – unlike the Jacobins – spoke out for women's rights. She welcomed the constitution of 1791 because it abolished absolute monarchy and created a parliamentary system of representation in which she wanted women to be represented as well. She was well aware of where the exercise of a direct revolutionary sovereignty of the people might lead – after Robespierre, that was clearly demonstrated by the two Napoleons. And yet she spoke out in *The Three Urns* for direct democracy on the most important issue – the constitution. She despised Robespierre and pamphleteers like Marat for two reasons: because they identified freedom and virtue with terror, and because the quickly fluctuating parties of the men and their bitter faction wars were mere power plays: 'Mountain, Plain, Rolandins, Brissotins, Girondins, Robespierrists, Maratists, disappear – shameful names!' She would never have argued in the same way as Madame Roland – 'There must be blood to cement the revolution' – who like other Girondins was defeated by the logical application of her enthusiasm. Instead, de Gouges claimed that 'it is not blood that can cement the revolution'. She demonstrated historical far-sightedness, albeit without much political adaptability, in arguing that a murdered king continues to live for a long time; politically, he is 'only really dead if he survives his overthrow'.

Her calls to women to unite and articulate their own interests, such as in the treatise *Lettre au Roi, lettre à la Reine* (1792), went unheard: 'Women, is it not time that a revolution also take place among us? Or should women remain forever isolated from each other and form a whole with society only in order to slander their own sex and arouse pity in others?'[16] Most of the active women were caught up in the political interests of the men, whereas de Gouges's autonomous thinking – at least within the spectrum of male politics – made her walk a tightrope of paradoxes. It was women who applauded her execution without any signs of sympathy. But the historical significance of Olympe de Gouges and the other voices that were raised for female citizenship resides not in the fact that they failed but that they existed at all. The revolution gave them space, and the revolution silenced them. De Gouges raised almost all the questions that would affect the future of women. Her quotation from Jesus in the *Déclaration* can be carried further: 'My hour has not yet come.'

Amazons and Counter-revolutionaries

Mothers teach their children early on to speak the male language of liberty.

A Jacobin in Orléans, 1792

When God was there, we had bread.

A woman in Bayeux[17]

The new culture of citizenship, including artistically celebrated national festivities (with highly masculinized images of the nation as 'mother') and soon also a cult of violence, had not only social and political dimensions, but also a symbolic one. The forms of address 'Monsieur' and 'Madame' were abandoned in favour of *citoyen* and *citoyenne*. What was actually meant by *citoyenne* remained enigmatic and controversial. The women who were involved in revolutionary, republican or Jacobin clubs from 1791 to 1793 identified themselves explicitly as *citoyennes*. The example set by the Parisian Amies de la Vérite was followed by women in Bordeaux, Creil, Caen and Arles, and there were women's clubs, with memberships ranging from twenty to eight hundred, in some sixty cities and even small towns and villages. In Grasse, Pau and Montcenis the women's clubs referred to themselves as Amazons or 'constitutional Amazons'. To them, *citoyenne* meant getting involved for the *patrie*, the revolutionary nation. They asserted that the Declaration of the Rights of Man applied to women, and many of them participated in the referendum on the Jacobin constitution of 1793 and in the patriotic oath; they even sometimes claimed, 'We are the sovereign'. In view of the traditional connotation of *femmes*, they almost never referred to themselves as women's clubs. On the contrary, it was their male critics who chastised them as *femmes* or a *club de femmes*, since their activities were a thorn in the side of the men. To these polemicists – such as the Jacobin Louis-Marie Prudhomme in a dispute with women from Dijon and Lyon – true *citoyennes* were only those who better served the republic 'by staying home, not making a spectacle of themselves, not exposing themselves to ridicule' and instead 'letting the men make the revolution'.[18] At the end of the revolutionary decade *citoyenne* had acquired the connotation of 'rabble' and was used to refer to maids in well-to-do society, whose employers once again became *madames*. The term disappeared entirely in the Consulate under Napoleon.

The women in the provincial clubs were usually middle-class wives or daughters of members of the men's clubs. They read political literature together, voted in their clubs, decorated city festivals, lauded their role as republican mothers and supported their revolutionary men or swore not to marry 'aristocrats'. They also drafted programmes for educating their children in a patriotic way and read with them the Declaration of the Rights of Man or the seventh chapter of Rousseau's *Social Contract*, dealing with the sovereignty of the people. A section leader in Orléans commended the fact that children thus learned 'the male language of liberty' at an early age. Club women found work for needy women, sewed clothing and blankets for soldiers, sat in the galleries of their local *assemblées*, wrote petitions to the National Assembly, supported price controls and the expulsion of nuns from their convents – some clubs then assumed the nuns' charitable tasks – and upheld the new state religion. As of 27 November 1790, clerics had to swear an oath to the nation, the law, the king and the new civil status of the clergy. A short time later a number of other civil oaths were added (anyone refusing to become a *prêtre constitutionnel*, a constitutional priest, was considered suspect). A few clubs demanded in 1793 that women's suffrage be incorporated into the new constitution, and a few also demanded weapons for women, since citizenship was closely connected to bearing arms in revolutionary symbolism. Elisabeth Lafaurie held a 'Discourse on the State of Nothingness *[nullité]* in which Women are Held, Relative to Politics' at the Jacobin men's club of Saint-Sever-Cap. 'It is time to bring about a revolution in the customs of women', argued another woman in Dijon. The aim of such a revolution was first and foremost to politicize the family in the patriotic, revolutionary sense. Most of these clubs identified themselves as Jacobin, but some – especially the largest one, in Bordeaux – protested against the flood of pamphlets from Marat and condemned the factionary struggles: 'We are women and do not turn like some men do at the mercy of their passions and their interests, basely sacrificing the interests of the country.'[19] The debate on female *citoyenneté* came to a head in 1793 in Paris. Consequently, the provincial clubs got caught in the polemical crossfire and, inversely, the activities of the provincial women encouraged the escalation in Paris.

The event that spurred the debate was the founding of the Société des Citoyennes Républicaines Révolutionnaires (Society of Revolutionary Republican Citizenesses) on 10 May 1793 by Claire Lacombe, a former actress, and Pauline Léon, the daughter of a chocolate manufacturer. The club's active core comprised about one hundred women, most of whom came from the lower classes. Their goal was to combat the 'enemies of the republic' and the 'enemies within'; to 'exterminate all scoundrels' and lock up all suspect citizens; and 'to annihilate the aristocrats'. To this end they wanted to arm themselves as Amazon companies – Pauline Léon and Théroigne de Méricourt, a former participant in the march on Versailles who dressed as an Amazon, had already attempted this in 1792 – and take over the leadership of the sans-culotte women. One of the first actions of these radical revolutionaries took place on 15 May when they attempted to prevent ticket-holders from attending a session of the National Convention. In the process the no less revolutionary Théroigne de Méricourt, who was mistaken for a Girondin since she had a ticket to the Convention, was subjected to a frenzied beating from which she never recovered. Her family brought her to an insane asylum, and finally to the notorious Salpêtrière, where rare visitors heard de Méricourt mumbling revolutionary slogans. Her insanity, it was said, symbolized the logical conclusion to compulsive revolutionary idealism.

The ruling Montagnards praised and supported the revolutionary republican women as long as they served their interests; that is, as long as the women assumed the language and politics of the Jacobins (who did not demand equal rights for women). But in the context of the conflicting male factions and the radicalization of the masses they sided with the Cordeliers and then the Enragés. After the Convention had resolved in spring 1793 to make it mandatory for men to wear the tricolour *cocarde*, or cockade – symbol of the Jacobins – the revolutionary women of the Société were very enthusiastic. Not only did they want to wear the cockade themselves, they wanted it to be compulsory for all women. A war of the cockade ensued, and the revolutionary women and some of the *tricoteuses* picked a fight with the *poissardes* and the 'heroines of 5–6 October'. The latter group rejected a *citoyenneté* that forced them to bear arms and serve in the military; they viewed it not as a right but as an unpleasant duty. On 18 September the revolutionaries battered an old woman who was not wearing a cockade in the name of the nation. Then the *marchandes* tore the cockades off their adversaries. In an effort to end the rioting, the police asked the National Convention to make it mandatory for women, too, to wear the cockade. The Convention agreed, but the quarrelling continued and on 28 October the *marchandes* attacked the revolutionaries; they also received a positive response to their petition requesting that it not be made compulsory to wear a cockade. What did this symbolic politics stand for? Some think the men watched in scornful amusement as the battle between the Robespierrists and the Enragés was carried on by the women. It is more likely, however, that in the context of inflation and the setting of a maximum price for food, the opposing interests of housewives and shopowners (who often had nothing left to sell), of customers and saleswomen, came into conflict.

The Montagnards had no further use for the revolutionary women and on 30 October, the day the Girondins were guillotined and three days before Olympe de Gouges's execution, the National Convention banned all women's organizations after thorough consultation on the female *citoyenneté*. Far-reaching and fundamental decisions were proclaimed on this occasion. Jean-Baptiste Amar, an advocate of the Terror, announced that 'it is not possible for women to exercise political rights' and was seconded by the ultra-radical Pierre Chaumette, one of the prime inciters of the Terror (especially against homosexuals and prostitutes), who referred to Sophie, Rousseau's creation in *Émile*: 'Nature ... has spoken to woman: "Be a woman! Your business is the tender care of the children, the small domestic tasks, the sweet pains of motherhood."' According to Prudhomme, men were the 'natural representatives' of women.[20] But it was still possible for women to be politically active in mixed-sex organizations. All that changed on 23 May 1795 in reaction to the bloody women's revolts of 20 May (the Jacobin clubs were also banned that year). Pauline Léon, who had been arrested in October 1793, was now released. The revolutionary women were spared the guillotine.

Olympe de Gouges had publicly turned around the discourse on the revolution; Madame Roland talked revolution behind the scenes; and the revolutionary republican women accepted it along with the language of the Terror. Théroigne de Méricourt took the revolutionary discourse with her in her derangement. All these versions of female citizenship failed. Meanwhile a growing number of women, especially in provincial regions, towns, villages and rural areas, sought a different form of political participation and chose the (only) alternative universalistic discourse – the Christian religion. Like the October Women, these women took up the tradition of popular riots, including forms of female violence. At the same time they paved the way for the nineteenth century. In the openly counter-revolutionary revolts they dramatically fought for crown and altar in the Lyonnais and Vendée, where roughly 40,000 men and women were killed by the revolutionary military and many women were raped in the civil war in 1793–4, and in Brittany, where the Chouans of the bocage fought a drawn-out battle against the centralist republic.

As crucial as these counter-revolutionary movements in the west and south were for the fate of the revolution, the battle of countless communities in northern and central France had consequences that were more far-reaching. They were by no means opponents of the republic and would in fact have welcomed the social and political changes, but they were not prepared to accept the Parisian cultural revolution. The critical turning point in their stance regarding the revolution was not the Civil Constitution of the Clergy (July 1790) that made priests into civil servants but the institution of a civil oath for the clergy. Starting in early 1791 this led to heated conflict, not only between many clerics and the revolutionary men (as of 1792 *réfractaires*, priests who refused to swear the oath, could choose only between going underground or fleeing the country) but also within the lay population. The battle of the oath among the laity often lined up as a veritable battle of the sexes, cutting across all social divisions. The guerrilla war that women were waging against the wild men of Paris, the new civil servants and the *représentants en mission* escalated to the same extent as the dechristianization campaign that attempted to replace Catholic 'superstition' with revolutionary 'reason', which in some ways resembled a genuine witch hunt. In quick succession traditional cults were replaced by the cult of liberty, the cult of reason and in June 1793 the cult of the Supreme Being. The new cult was itself a type of religion.

Monastic vows were abolished in October 1789 and religious congregations in April and August 1792. This included especially the women's congregations with their 55,000 members, who had long performed a large share of the care for the poor and the sick. The former nuns and congregationists were supposed to marry former monks, live happily in idyllic families and put their 'barren breasts' – republican imagery was obsessed with the female breast – in the service of the nation. The new calendar replaced the seven-day week of the Judaeo-Christian calendar with a 'rational' ten-day variant. Not only were the number of holidays reduced, but local Sunday rituals were eliminated. The ringing of church bells, which had played a significant role in patterning daily and weekly routines and the rituals surrounding life and death, was banned and churches were closed (in November 1793 in Paris as well). Life was to be ensured not by bells and prayer but by republic and rationality. An official statement declared that 'Under a good constitution and a pure sky the parturient mother thinks of the constitution and feels no pain'.[21] Worship of saints and the Virgin Mary was abolished, and with it the traditional rhythm of the year. Religious objects were confiscated and Christian rituals of birth and death were replaced by civil alternatives. Husbands were required to teach their wives civil reason. In Arles the heads of families had to bring their wives to a ceremony at which they were to spit on the host together, to demonstrate their being patriots and thus masters of the house. Some Parisian *marchandes* disrobed and publicly whipped the Sœurs de la Charité. From early 1794 it was even difficult for constitutional priests to read the mass; and confessions were no longer heard.

It was primarily women who doggedly resisted the cultural revolution in collective actions. Although they often acted together with their husbands, women usually assumed the leadership. They came from all social classes, and their revolts, ruses and collective violence – in contrast to the revolutionary *émeutes*, or riots, in Paris – were by no means a protest of the poor against the local elite. The French nuns held on to their vows with more conviction than did the monks. Lay women hid priests and clandestine 'white' masses (celebrated by laypeople and without communion) were held in private homes, barns or illegal chapels. Women marched together to the mayor to take church keys away from him. They occupied and forcefully opened locked churches; defended sacred rooms, bells, statues and rituals; and they prevented the destruction of crosses. They stole onions, cabbage, lettuce and peas from the new republican teacher's garden, which they still considered the property of the deposed *curé*. Hundreds of women came to sing in front of the locked village churches and refused to stop when a municipal officer tried to get them to disperse. Although female participation was not class-specific, hunger crises and poverty played an important role. Whereas the Parisian sans-culotte women demanded 'bread and the constitution of 1793', their religiously motivated sisters called out, 'When God was there, we had bread'. They were maligned by revolutionary adversaries as *fanatiques*, *dévotes* and *béguines*, but it became increasingly impossible to challenge this everyday guerrilla war. In view of the massive pressure in the provinces, the Thermidorians made some concessions in 1795 – *nonante cinq* was the year of republican disillusionment – that gave a powerful thrust to the religious revival (parallel to Protestant revivalist movements in Britain and Germany). This revival gained strength under the government from 1797 to 1799, which was more left wing and thus closed the churches once again.

Women buried the dead at night. Occasionally they stole a corpse to give it a Christian rather than a civil burial. They illegally rang the angelus-bell, sometimes sending their children with cowbells, and celebrated the festivals of the saints and especially the Virgin Mary; they said rosary, led processions and threw ash and stones at their adversaries, as in traditional *émeutes*. They laid a picture of Mary on the bellies of women in childbirth, gave their children biblical and saints' names instead of naming them after Marat, and taught them to pray. They celebrated Sundays and some of them gave their maids a day off on Sundays instead of *décadi*. Even women of the Parisian lower classes sometimes raised their voices in protest at the guillotine, using biblical language, or they defended the baptistery of Saint Eustache (in the middle of the major Parisian market) from being desecrated. In Saint Germain de Laval (in the Mâconnais) Jacobins had erected a statue of a naked woman on the square where a cross had previously been displayed; they painted the statue in the colours of the tricolour and declared it to be the Goddess of Liberty. When it rained, the paint ran and they cheered the miracle of a menstruating goddess. The enraged women in the village carried the statue to the river, washed it and restored her honour as a woman. Former congregationists were supposed to take a civil oath as *citoyennes de secours* before a town official, in order to be able to continue to care for the sick. At the public ceremony in Montpigié they declared that they preferred the guillotine to the oath; the assembled women from the village applauded and were quickly arrested. Their husbands demanded their release, since there was no one to tend to the housekeeping and the children. A jail revolt ensued and in the end the women locked up the official. In Saint Vincent near Lavoûte-sur-Loire, the Supreme Being was supposed to be honoured on a *décadi* in the Temple of Reason and in the presence of the village dignitaries. The female audience rose during the patriotic speech and turned around, lifted their skirts and exposed their bare buttocks to the new deity. The dignitaries disappeared in unseemly haste, and *montrer le cul aux gens* became a common expression.[22] To the same extent that Catholicism was besieged, the faith was feminized and – in view of the central role of the Virgin Mary – also Marianized.

Like other women in the French Revolution, these 'counter-revolutionaries' – as they were seen from a Parisian perspective – were at a sort of interface between tradition and innovation. Obviously they seized upon the traditional role of women who usually acted collectively in the popular riots in early modern Europe (in France as elsewhere) to defend the interests of their children, family and community. The issue here was material as well as spiritual nourishment. Their collective and public insubordination was based on informal social relationships within the village. Furthermore, women were generally considered naturally hysterical and easily duped, and thus less responsible for their actions. Consequently, they received fewer or lighter punishments than men did. They took advantage of this situation (some men even disguised themselves as women for this reason). 'We are only women; they don't do anything to women', they said in their own defence in Toucy against charges of having forcefully broken down a church door. The fact that women believed they had a traditional right to riot was nevertheless only one side of the story. The other side was the revolutionary context, the ideology of which reinforced traditional convictions. The Catholic women in the countryside were well informed about the new doctrines of religious freedom and sovereignty of the people. 'Since everyone had the freedom of opinion, we desired our religion and thought we were authorized to demand it', said the women of Vaux. A woman named Marie Rémy argued, 'one heard that we had religious liberty'. A fearless woman named Suzanne hung a notice on a fallen liberty tree with the words, 'We are enchained to the point where we are not allowed to pray on Sundays. . . . After this, are we sovereign? Isn't this playing with people?' These women defined revolutionary freedom according to their own needs, which included religious practices as a context for expressing emotions, for community relations, for the cycle of life and death and a spiritual sense of the fragility of life, and for life crises that could not be mastered with revolutionary reason: 'Religion alone can give us the courage to withstand the calamities of a long revolution.'[23]

There was yet another way in which the activities of the religiously motivated women were advanced by the revolution. Whereas for men it opened up new political spheres of action, women remained – as was the case in the *ancien régime* – excluded from them. Only in isolated instances in the early phase of the female cultural struggle were they concerned with observing prohibited rituals in secret and in private. Later, the primary goal was to gain public recognition and political significance. It was of the utmost political significance, for example, to bury a husband publicly in accordance with Catholic rites or to collectively demand a church key from a mayor, or to organize a procession without a priest. For women, there was twofold significance to both public and subversive religious practice. First of all, it granted legitimacy to the spiritual dignity of those excluded from earthly power and demonstrated that earthly power was not the greatest good. Second, in view of the collapse of clerical leadership and hierarchy, Catholicism became a sphere in which women could speak publicly, act autonomously and expand their liturgical and community roles. In the religious revolts of the revolutionary period women laid the groundwork for the gradual feminization of religion in the nineteenth century. This feminization was not merely a result of the female role in the family and an increasing dichotomization of public and private space. Its roots lay also in women's experience of the revolution.

Napoleon and the Revolution in Europe

Or that it is not the good son, the good husband, the good father who makes a good citizen!

Jean-Jacques Rousseau, *Émile*, 1762

With his coup of 18 *Brumaire* (1799), Napoleon secured merely what many republicans had long since viewed as the defeat of their ideas. When the Constitution of the Year XII entrusted Napoleon as emperor with 'the government of the republic', the revolution had led to a powerful military, technocratic state that appealed to the emotional solidarity of the French people. At the same time, however, the political culture of the revolution – the ideals of liberty and equality – persisted and spread through all of Europe. Napoleon did not think much of female citizenship and he expressed the logic of the male revolutionaries succinctly: 'Since women do not exercise any political rights whatsoever, it is inappropriate to refer to them as *citoyenne.*' It was not public law but civil or private law that would express the basic values of the new civil society. Napoleon's attempt to unify continental Europe politically had far-reaching consequences (especially for the countries conquered, revolutionized, annexed, occupied or converted into satellite states by Napoleon's armies; that is, Italy, not including the islands; Germany, except for Prussia; and Belgium, Spain, the Netherlands, Switzerland and the Grand Duchy of Warsaw). To this end the *Code civil*, completed in 1804 after years of work, was renamed the *Code Napoléon* three years later. It was definitely not reactionary, since it retained the abolition of feudal privilege and the separation of Church and state, guaranteed – at least for men – the right to property, and sought to negotiate between natural law and tradition. This mixture was especially explosive for women. Jean-Étienne-Marie Portalis, theoretician of the *Code Napoléon*, worded the new-old gender relations in precisely the same way as Rousseau and the *Déclaration des droits et devoirs de l'homme et du citoyen* of 1795 had done earlier. Most of the revolutionaries and all the sans-culottes had adhered to this formulation and it was also incorporated into some non-French revolutionary constitutions, such as that of the Ligurian Republic (1797). 'Private virtue alone can guarantee public virtues; it is through the small fatherland, which is the family, that we attach ourselves to the great fatherland; it is the good father, the good husband, the good son, who makes the good citizen.'[24] The requirement of masculinity to receive political and full civil rights would remain valid throughout Europe for over a century, even if it was only rarely mentioned explicitly in later constitutions and other legal corpora.

Napoleon's *Code civil* declared *puissance maritale*, the husband's authority, to be the constitutive principle of the family, and these articles (212–216) were publicly recited during civil marriage ceremonies, usually by the mayor: 'A husband owes protection to his wife; a wife obedience to her husband.' Portalis justified this article (213) as an attempt to put an end to the old *querelle des sexes:* 'These are the entire morals of spouses. There was a long debate on the precedence or equality of the two sexes. Nothing is more futile than such a dispute. . . . Nature made them so different only in order to unite them. This difference in their very essence is the basis for their respective rights and obligations.' It is not merely nature, however, but society as well that requires the inequality of the sexes. And like John Locke, Portalis too found that 'the authority of the husband is based on the necessity that, in a society of two individuals, the decisive voice is to be given to one of them, and on the precedence of that sex that has been assigned this priority'.[25]

Accordingly, the man determined the common place of residence, and the wife assumed his citizenship. Community of property was the standard and it was administered by the husband. Even in the case of a separate contract for property the wife brought to the marriage, she did not have any rights of disposal over that property. She could undertake no legal transactions without her husband's authorization, nor could she appear in court. *Recherche de la paternité*, the right to a paternity suit which then obliged the father to pay support for a child conceived out of wedlock, was abolished once and for all, and according to the new penal code of 1810 female adultery was punished severely, male adultery only – and less harshly in any case – if the man had indulged his passion in the couple's joint residence. As was common, traditionally and internationally, married women engaged in business were excepted from the *puissance maritale* in order not to hinder the economy, but her civil freedom to enter into contracts applied only to her business and not to intramarital transactions.

Through these regulations the *Code Napoléon* distinguished, first of all, between two types of private spheres, male private business transactions, for which the man had full civil rights, and the female private sphere of the family. Within the family the woman did not have authority, nor was she viewed as a contractual partner; instead, *le mari est le chef* (the husband is the boss) and *puissance paternelle*, paternal authority over the children prevailed. Second, the Code strictly separated the female private sphere from the male public sphere. Third, it obligated the women to a republican, private virtue that was distinguished from male republican virtue through its sexual connotations. 'The more kindly sex must also be more virtuous, for the sake of the happiness of humanity.' Only one important achievement of the revolution with respect to family law remained intact: the same inheritance law applied to sons and daughters. Marriage remained a civil contract, even though it was very important to Portalis that it be considered a contract *sui generis*: marriage should be a 'sacred' union like a sacrament, and although the right to divorce was retained for the time being, this definition opened the door to its being abolished again in 1816.

In contrast to the lack of opposition to the ban on women's clubs in 1793 and 1795, some critical voices were raised with respect to the gender relations laid down in the *Code Napoléon*, in France as well as in countries to which the Code was exported. The opinion circulated that 'from the way the Code treats women, you can tell it was written by men'.[26] The demand to eliminate *puissance maritale, pouvoir paternel* and the ban on *recherche de la paternité* would later become the most important issue for the French women's movement. Nevertheless, marital law in France was not treated with hostility at the time but celebrated as a national achievement. The reason was that, first of all, there was a long tradition to the subordination of women in marriage; also, it was primarily the matrimonial order that was intended to guarantee the envisioned balance between tradition and new civil liberties. Second, the new family code was considered a legitimate reaction to the preceding dramatic politicization of the private sphere. The excessive intervention of revolutionary politics into matters of privacy contributed to the collective tendency to protect the private sphere from politics, keeping the two radically separate. And, finally, the new codification of conjugal hierarchy became a modern variant of an old political postulate. In traditional patriarchalism, the head of the household represented the entire family (including male family members) in public and politics. But as Charles Théremin, a confidant of Abbé Sieyès, had already stressed in 1797, according to the new republican gender relations the husband represented his wife: 'The vote of one counts for both; that of the wife is virtually included in that of the husband. . . . Husband and wife form a single political person.'[27]

This political vision also applied throughout the nineteenth century in countries where a wife's conjugal dependence was treated more liberally than it was in France. Two other codes of natural law emerged at that time and showed traces of the Enlightenment thinking – liberty, equality, property – that influenced their development: the Prussian General Code (*Allgemeines Preussisches Landrecht*), which came into force in 1794 and would remain valid until 1900 (in the parts of Prussia west of the Rhine, in Hesse-Darmstadt and in Baden, however, it was the *Code civil* that predominated until 1900), and the General Civil Code in the Hapsburg Empire (*Allgemeines Bürgerliches Gesetzbuch*, 1811). Both of these were based (especially in the early discussion stages) on the principle that the two sexes had the same birthrights. Thus it was necessary specifically to justify sexual inequality if it was to continue. The two postulates were artfully linked, though not always logically. All codes retained the man as the head of the family (conjugal authority and *cura maritalis*), but in the Prussian code the contractual element outweighed the French emphasis on exclusive authority. Similar to the practice in the *Code Napoléon*, several different justifications for male domination were brought into play: woman's 'nature' (weakness, sensuality and lack of reason); tradition; the need for a final deciding will in the case of marital dissent; the construction of a contract according to which a woman subordinated herself voluntarily; the need to regulate human procreation; and above all man's 'nature', which was equated with reason. Children born out of wedlock and their mothers were disadvantaged – their treatment was best under the Prussian code – and male authority over children born within marriage was not disputed whatsoever (the same was true for children born out of wedlock for whom a male guardian had to be appointed). In contrast to the *Code Napoléon*, the two German-language codes allowed married women to appear independently in court under certain conditions. The Austrian code treated separation of property as the standard, but the woman could only in rare instances autonomously administer the property she brought to the marriage. Divorce was legal in Austria only for Protestants and Jews; in Prussia it was handled liberally, but in mid-century a simple trick was employed there: costs were raised to such an extent as to prevent many petitions for divorce from being filed in the first place, since most of the women petitioning belonged to the 'lowest social class'. These petitions were often filed on grounds of 'brutality by the husband', although all three legal codes prohibited corporal punishment by the man. Married and unmarried women, as well as widows, were affected by the wrangling over traditional gender tutelage, or *cura sexus*, by which a man represented the interests of the woman in court and was supposed to protect her even against the husband if necessary. All three codes abolished *cura sexus* and the husband alone retained authority over his wife. The difference in legal status between married and unmarried women was thus intensified. Germany, with its many sovereign states, had many different regulations and there were some regions in which *cura sexus* applied but not *cura maritalis*, and others in which both forms of legal tutelage continued to exist. Throughout almost all of Europe, liberty, equality and property were now guaranteed by civil law essentially to the male sex only. This was already expressed in 1800 by Germaine de Staël: 'Women's existence in society is still uncertain. . . . In the present state of affairs, most are neither part of the natural order nor part of the social order.'[28]

The revolution, and especially its excesses, which were seen as an overstatement of the law of nature and of reason, played a major role in the drafting of the three consequential legal codes. The early phase of the revolution served as an inspiration; the later phase as a deterrent. Not only legislators but also other people outside France had reacted to French events, perceiving them in a number of ways. The revolution as well as its failure and the counter-revolution had an impact far beyond the borders of France and were a common topic of discussion in neighbouring countries. Later, the *Code Napoléon* became a model for the civil codes in Italy (1865), Portugal (1867) and Spain (1889), and influenced some in Swiss cantons as well.

The revolutionary ideas had resonance in Germany, mostly because the way had been paved for them in the late Enlightenment starting around 1770. There were some movements (more revolutionary than republican), extensive support among intellectuals, and many women and men welcomed the abolition of privileges and the constitutionalization of the monarchy. The entire family of the wholesale merchant Sieveking in Hamburg held a huge celebration on the first anniversary of the storming of the Bastille. But women and men turned away from the revolution as it moved towards regicide and terror; and the invasion of the French army and the plundering of the conquered territories served to discredit the early enthusiasm all the more. Painter Ludovike Simanowiz, who lived in

Paris during the turbulence of 1792, wrote a short time later to her friend, Christophine Reinwald, sister of Friedrich Schiller: 'How wonderful and great the revolution seemed to me in the beginning, and how often my enthusiasm for it brought tears to my eyes. I was a warm democrat with all of my heart, but that is no longer the case. When this great, powerful nation with so many good heads let a handful of raging people become the masters, it lost the respect of all its neighbours.' Some women were active in the sensational Jacobin club in Mainz; and here and in France and elsewhere, they expressed their republican leanings by supplying the men with warm clothing and by organizing festivals, and some demanded equal rights for women. The citizen Morlok of Mainz addressed her co-citizens: 'How much we must love a constitution that restores our original dignity! We are no longer the plaything of your private life to which despotism has degraded us. . . . The republic has authorized this expectation for us. . . . But do men think the same?' The answer was the same as for most Jacobins: 'Do you not already possess the most precious of privileges? Are you not the man's recreation after a long day's work – his happiness?'[29]

More significant for Germany was a veritable *querelle des femmes* that started even before the revolution, was intensified by it, and continued until into the nineteenth century. In letters, pamphlets and books, in the press and in philosophy, men as well as women spoke out. Emilie von Berlepsch complained about the 'misogynistic tone' of contemporary journalism and in 1791 she emphasized that a woman was 'no longer merely the homemaker of the husband and bearer of his children' but also had to 'act independently'. For that reason, she must 'be able to think freely and independently; that is, not to be a machine, dependent on the will of the man. . . . We must learn to stand alone!' Ernst Georg Brandes's misogynistic diatribe *Ueber die Weiber* (On Women, 1787) was a special bone of contention ('Woman was not made to govern herself. Man's vocation, however, is to rule'). Whether or not 'women are human' became a common question. Internationally, female 'nothingness' (*Nullen, nullité, nullità*) was again set against 'the dignity of woman' and sometimes the beard was still considered a symbol of the 'sexual insignia' of the man.[30] Theodor Gottlieb von Hippel's writings were drafted in the context of this querelle, especially his extensive treatise *Über die bürgerliche Verbesserung der Weiber* (On the Civic Improvement of Women, 1792), the title of which was borrowed from Christian Wilhelm Dohm's *Über die bürgerliche Verbesserung der Juden* (On the Civic Improvement of Jews, 1781–83). It drew considerable reactions, both positive and negative, from contemporaries as well as later readers.

In pointed, ironic and cheerful tones Hippel criticized the tirades that were circulating about female nature, Rousseau and the French constitution 'that thought it good to forget one half of the nation', even though 'women had carried the banners of the revolution'. He took up old topics of the querelle, the story of creation and the questions 'Are we not the ones who deny them a soul and reduce them to mere body?' and 'Why should a woman not be allowed to pronounce the word *I*?' Hippel also construed a natural state and assumed that women had been subjugated even prior to civil society. That had led to a 'leaden time' for the female sex, in which male 'fears that the other sex would rule us have laid the foundations for our domination over them'. Moreover, 'the oppression of women has caused oppression in the world in general'. This had to be stopped, Hippel argued, referring to the categorical imperative defined by his friend Immanuel Kant (who meant it differently, however): 'The rules by which you act must be such that they could be universal laws.' The 'gallant Bastilles, the domestic wards and the bourgeois dungeons' must be eliminated and whoever is given 'the necessary aptitude to be a citizen of heaven' must also be given the right 'to be a citizen of the state'. Women had even 'a divine calling to civil office', which 'most of the good-for-nothings among high-level civil servants lack'. That which was considered the nature of woman – pregnancy and childbirth, nursing and raising children – did not rule out his appeal, Hippel stressed, but gave it legitimacy: 'The bearing of children, generally considered among the main proof of their weakness to which the law has condescended to assign an extraordinarily high value, is none other than a natural proof of the strength of this fair sex. I should not like to see this business handed over to the men', and 'Who can claim *that the peculiarity of the sex is not crucial for civil society?*' The 'great vocation of nature', to be the 'wife of her husband and the mother of her children', demands that she be 'a member, a citizen, and not merely an object of protection by the state'; she did not owe 'her worth only to the man'. Here he quoted from a letter a French woman had addressed to the National Assembly (she 'dared to voice her indignation'); perhaps he was referring to Olympe de Gouges's *Déclaration*. She had complained, he continued, that 'the constitution totally omitted women, although mothers ought to be citizens of the state'. He put forward the hypothesis that if French women had been made 'active voters' from the outset the violence would have remained limited. According to Hippel, nature granted 'equal rights to both women and men'. Natural equality, understood as civil rights, might be compatible with 'political inequality', since political participation required independence. But by no means could 'an entire sex be proclaimed unworthy which includes as a rule more independent persons than the male sex'.

In the Weimar *Journal des Luxus und der Moden* (Journal of Luxury and Fashion) an obviously ironic complaint by the 'fair sex to the current

French parliament' appeared in 1789: since the men were so busy lately ('whom can we play with?') and liberty and the nation were the 'terrible rivals' that 'steal the heart of every young man from us', they asserted 'that our sex also makes up half of humankind and the nation', and should be granted access to legislature and 'better education'; otherwise they would refuse to do the housework. In December 1793, the *Journal* printed a polemical treatise against Mary Wollstonecraft's gospel of equality and liberty from the oppression and tyranny of men (her *Vindication of the Rights of Woman* had appeared exactly one year earlier), as well as the National Convention speech held by 'Saint Amar' on 30 October, after the conflict between the 'revolutionary women' and the fishwives: 'We believe that a woman should never be allowed to leave the circle of her family to get involved in the business of administering the state.' In 1797 a woman named Aspasia introduced 'proof that the most zealous defenders of liberty and equality are the greatest despots'. It had been virtually raining down 'natural law and universal rights', she mused, and in particular 'a man who stands there like a giant among pygmies' and 'whom I would love if I did not need to hate' audaciously claimed (and here she correctly cites Immanuel Kant, albeit without naming him explicitly) 'that in order to be an independent being, a citizen, one may not be a woman or a child!!' He could not have meant it so badly, she thought, since 'if we had no liberty, we would also not be human. If we were not human, there would be no rights of man, but *rights of males*. If there were no rights of man, then all liberty and equality would be buried under the rubble along with us'. Johann Adam Bergk, a Kant scholar, agreed with Aspasia, also in 1797: 'Thus I do not know how one could legally deny women rights of citizenship, as long as they are considered in good faith to be human. . . . What does the state have to do with the natural destiny of each sex, since it should treat both of them as *equal, free, and independent.*' If Aspasia had already read Johann Gottlieb Fichte's *Grundlage des Naturrechts* (Foundations of Natural Right, 1796), she would have felt not a mixture of love and hate, as she did for Kant, but pure hatred. In it Fichte declared, 'The second sex is at a lower level than the first, according to the order of nature', especially by virtue of its position during the sexual act, and 'only a few confused heads among men' demand rights for women. In 1798 Leipzig women protested against being 'nothings in political society', borrowing Hippel's reference to 'citizens of heaven' and 'citizens of the state': 'What a contradiction!' The anonymous author of *Über die politische Würde der Weiber* (On the Political Dignity of Women, 1799) commented on Hippel's work in the classical querelle style of a dialogue between a man and a woman. 'In truth', claimed the woman, 'I cannot say that all the declarations one hears presently on the *rights of man* truly deserve this name. I would rather tend to call them declarations of *male rights.*' But 'nature, my dear friend!' responded the man, and then 'reason instead of nature. But then you will fare even more poorly. For you know that in the last century doubt was raised as to whether women were human'. The woman referred to the 'rib of man' that was given to the woman as an honour, to which the man countered, 'Oh! Forget about that crass myth of a coarse nomadic Hebrew, invented totally without vigour and spirit'. The man concluded that 'women, my dear friend, are not men', and because of man's intellectual strength it was up to him 'to implement the bonds of society'.[31]

The mixture of irony, satire and profound meaning, of sense and (especially male) nonsense, clearly shows that the early modern *querelle* had reappeared in more modern attire. It also demonstrates that in the course of revolutionizing France, both the civil and political liberation of women became seriously conceivable, and was indeed conceived. However, the long-standing and deep-rooted gender hierarchy made this seem paradoxical. And, in particular, it was opposed by men as vehemently as it was supported by women and other men. The woman-friendly demands were in the minority – though many such texts have recently been discovered – and when, for example, the influence of the revolution led to the old patrician constitution being replaced in 1796 in Nuremberg by an elective parliament, no voices appear to have been raised demanding that women be included. However, the oppositional liberal Wilhelm Joseph Behr, who became a member of the first Bavarian parliament in 1819, argued candidly in 1804 and again in 1810 that 'those of the female sex, too, are capable of holding and directly exercising citizenship rights'.[32]

What eventually won out had been suggested by some of the pamphlets of the time: If political participation by women was not acceptable to the male decision- and law-makers, and did not seem attractive to many women, then priority had to be given to the civil right to education, employment and liberties within and outside marriage. Amalia Holst, unmarried by choice 'as Kant is, and Leibnitz was' (and Hippel too), and just as dedicated to scholarship, warmly recommended to the readers of her 1802 treatise *Über die Bestimmung des Weibes zur höheren Geistesbildung* (On Women's Vocation for Higher Education) that they should read Hippel's work, though with respect to women holding public office she thought 'that such a total upheaval in civil relations might bring forth considerable confusion'; she felt the issue of education was more realistic and useful. This was a way, after the revolutionary turmoil, to demand independence and legal rights, as Sieyès, Kant and many other advocates of revolution, parliamentarianism and constitutionalism had proclaimed. In order to be a citizen it was necessary, according to Kant – to the indignation of Aspasia – 'that he be his own

master (*sui juris*), and therefore own some property (to which . . . scholarship can also be counted), which nourishes him'. Even though Kant
was referring only to himself and other men, this idea would shape the
rocky road travelled by the nineteenth-century European women's movement.

Education seemed to mark the road to freedom for Jews as well. Michel
Berr of Nancy was the son of Berr Isaac Berr, the great champion of
citizenship for the Jews of eastern France. The younger Berr appealed in
1801 for the Peace of Lunéville to advance the emancipation of all of
European Jewry, as had been resolved for France after heated debate in
September 1791. Among the arguments he used to demonstrate the human and civic dignity of the Jews was the education of Jewish women.
'Not only among our sex are there Jews who are useful to their fatherland and who are called upon to delight a small circle of educated and
enlightened friends.' The Jewish women he was referring to lived in Germany; above all he named Esther Mandel in Hamburg, who was seen as
the Sévigné of her nation, as 'virtuous and intelligent', and who combined 'all the wonderful gifts of her own sex with the solid features of
ours'.[33] These women doubtless held the revolution in high regard for
the sake of Jewish emancipation. Other German Jewish women had already spoken out more clearly. When Esther Gad of Breslau referred to
the rights of man in 1791, it was first and foremost for the sake of the
Jews and then also for women. At a time when most Jewish women –
whether in Alsace, Breslau or Berlin – laboured hard both in and outside
the home, Gad's polemics harshly attacked Joachim Heinrich Campe,
who had been acclaimed throughout Europe for warning women against
scholarship in his 1789 *Väterlicher Rath für meine Tochter* (Fatherly
Advice for My Daughter). With reference to Condorcet, she countered
with comments that in 1801 would bring her the title of a 'German
Wollstonecraft': 'No matter what sex, the soul has no sex', and 'Who is
more destined for loneliness through physical, moral and political laws
than woman? How shall she shield herself against the inevitable suffering caused directly and indirectly by nature and civil society; what should
make her strong . . . if not the acquisition of good, useful knowledge that
creates a world within us that *no* turmoil can overturn?' After the revolutionary turmoil in Europe, she dismissed violent coups and 'politicizing
women'.[34] She lived out her life in Britain, and admired its constitutional
monarchy. In 1814 she defended the Germans against the judgements of
Madame de Staël, which caused her childhood friend, Rahel Levin
Varnhagen, to call her the 'German Staël'.

Michel Berr had referred neither to Esther Gad nor to Rahel Levin.
Rahel Levin of Berlin knew next to nothing about the revolution or
contemporary politics, despite her trip to Paris around 1800, when she

brilliantly gathered together a circle of unorthodox people for the first time. As a woman and a Jew – of all the Jewish women in Berlin who hosted such social gatherings, she was the only one who was not married – she had no access to public space, and she sought 'purely human' contact in the private and personal spheres. 'The more strength and depth the personality can win and the more freedom reason can acquire, the more world we can grasp. Where these two qualities come together, a human being will combine the highest degree of independence and liberty with the greatest richness of being', rather than 'losing oneself to the world'. Rahel's 'salon' ended in 1806 with the war and the Prussian defeat, and anti-Jewish sentiments grew. When in 1812 Napoleon returned to Berlin on the Russian campaign, she read Spinoza to calm herself; she also dealt with the liberal Prussian edict pertaining to the Jews, and the Battle of the Nations at Leipzig stirred her feelings of patriotism. But she rejected the prevailing 'patriotic rage'. Now Rahel dreamed that all European women would speak out against war and 'together help all those in suffering': 'I want peace and that every son be with his mother.' In her 'charity office' in Prague she found a satisfying mission, her happiness in fact, taking care of German as well as French wounded. In 1819, the year she founded her second salon, she condemned the opinion that 'our mind is different' from that of men. The reason for the alleged frivolity of women was their dependence. They had 'no room for their own feet', and 'every attempt, every wish to free themselves from this unnatural condition is called frivolity'. She wrote this – as Abigail Adams wrote her 'remember the ladies' – in letters and diaries that were not published until much later. By 1820 she had long since developed an interest in political life, and months before the July Revolution she predicted with fascination that the French had 'the republic in their bones' and 'they will become a republic'. 'Republic is as *inevitable* for the French, who are always a step ahead of us, as constitution is for us'; there is 'no other way for the future'. This revolution gave her a zest for life, 'because the "world" truly, in reality, moved'.[35] Rahel's path contrasted with that of many women of the 1790s. In her early phase she sought, with continually wavering self-esteem, contentment in intellectuality. The Great Revolution meant nothing to her; she honoured Friedrich Wilhelm III. It was not until later that she took an interest in politics, declared her commitment to the republic and participated in the gender debate. Irrespective of Rahel's uniqueness, this path would later be more characteristic for women than the activities of the former revolutionary women.

Aside from Germany, the revolution had the greatest echo in the Netherlands and Italy. In the Batavian Republic, the gender issue was raised in modern terminology starting in 1795 by, among others, Etta Palm d'Aelders, who aimed to promote the formation of women's clubs based on her experience in Paris. Other women and men also supported women's political rights, but in particular they advocated better education as a first step. After Napoleon annexed the Dutch provinces and after his defeat in 1813, women played an important role in the anti-French revolts.

In Italy female commentary on the revolution came from the *Triennio* (1796–9), when Napoleon's troops, with active support from Italian revolutionaries, introduced constitutions based on the French model. Eleonora Fonseca Pimentel, of noble origin though a radical adversary of noble privilege, was a Jacobin in the short-lived Parthenopean Republic, and writer, editor and publisher of the *Monitore napoletano*, one of the numerous revolutionary journals. In August 1799 she was hanged together with a hundred other insurgents. Pimentel is representative of the sort of revolutionary women who said almost nothing about the gender issue, but she by no means corresponded to the image of the republican described in the Turin journal *La vera repubblicana*: 'A republican woman should never speak out, unless she wishes to express feelings reserved for a sex that is part of the sovereignty.' Other republican women also failed to comply with this instruction and took the floor within and outside the political clubs – not least in *La vera repubblicana* – and they did so in support of their sex. A protest was signed by 2,550 *cittadine* against their *nullità assoluta* and *egoismo mascolino*. Italian women justified their *cittadinanza*, their citizenship, on the basis of liberty and equality, of their virtue and independent dignity as mothers and child-rearers – not only 'relative with respect to men' – and of their service for the 'preservation of the species' as a contribution to the 'common good' and 'general happiness'. An anonymous 'advocate of her own rights' explained that with respect to political rights, women 'think differently' than men do: 'If the right to representation is natural, universal and inalienable, how can women be robbed of it?' They at least had to have a vote in matters 'that concern them', since 'we are not free until the laws by which we are governed are ones we drafted or approved of ourselves'. 'Monarchic or aristocratic despotism is no more illegitimate than despotism exercised by one sex over the other.' Another woman stressed that 'the difference between woman and man is a wonderful balance': 'We are different as regards our sex, but similar or the same as regards nature.'[36] Time and again education for women was demanded, either as a goal in and of itself or as a prerequisite for active citizenship. Only a few voices explicitly demanded suffrage, but they were loud enough for the *circolo costituzionale* of Milan to issue a formal decision opposing the matter. The role of the woman in the family, it declared, is irreconcilable with the exercise of political power. In Italy, as in France, women played a considerable role in the counter-revolutionary uprisings against the new republics.

There were two contradictory versions of what in the last two decades of historical research has been termed 'republican motherhood'. (The phrase was originally coined for the American Revolution and the early republic.) One supported citizenship for women on the grounds of motherhood; the other rejected it on precisely the same grounds. Mary Wollstonecraft is the best-known advocate of the first version. She was politically active at a time when the last waves of the traditional bread riots were passing over England, and her friends, the radical Dissenters ('true Whigs', 'English Jacobins'), demanded political reform and found additional inspiration in France. Wollstonecraft's vocabulary came from the Enlightenment, the Dissenter tradition and old European republicanism, in which corruption of society and politics was attributed to a lack of civic virtue: luxury and idleness, weakness and injustice, egoism and frivolity had emasculated and feminized society. But virtue required liberty, reason, independent judgement and true masculinity. This was Wollstonecraft's language in *A Vindication of the Rights of Men* (1790), where she harshly criticized Edmund Burke's *Reflections on the Revolution in France* (1790). The fame she found with this riposte was soon overshadowed by Thomas Paine's *The Rights of Man* (1791–2). She railed against the rich and powerful, who, because they 'supinely exist without exercising mind or body, have ceased to be men'. Instead, she argued, the important thing was to 'unfold the mind, and inspire a manly spirit of independence'. She reproached Burke for portraying women as 'little, smooth, delicate, fair creatures, never designed that they should exercise their reason to acquire the virtues'. This is also the main theme of Wollstonecraft's *Vindication of the Rights of Woman*, a 'treatise on female rights and manners' (1792). She settled the score with Rousseau and English ideologues, who believed women should live for domesticity, obedience and the pleasure of their husband. But equally she settled up with women and demanded a 'revolution in female manners'. She saw education as being responsible for female frailty and sensuality because it clearly distinguished between the sexes and convinced women to adapt to the image men had of them. Women were taught, Wollstonecraft maintained, to crave admiration and to be conniving and flirtatious. They were made 'systematically voluptuous' in order ultimately to be degraded by being made 'contentedly the slaves of casual lust'. In France, Italy and England, female 'modesty, the fairest garb of virtue', was denounced as prudishness. However, Wollstonecraft did not think virtue and modesty should be understood only in a sexual sense but in the sense of rational and natural perfection; soul, mind and virtue had no sex, she declared.

Along the entire spectrum of women who spoke out at that time, Wollstonecraft was perhaps the only one who clearly – and in a shockingly direct manner for her contemporaries – traced the 'enslavement' of women to sexuality. She argued that Rousseau's Sophie was a product of his sexual fantasies ('voluptuous reveries') and that his was a 'philosophy of lasciviousness'. It was absurd to suppose 'that a girl is naturally a coquette'. Women, she argued, are 'confined then in cages like the feathered race, they have nothing to do but to plume themselves, and stalk with mock majesty from perch to perch'. Although they were fed and did not need to toil for it, they sacrificed health, liberty and virtue. She criticized the fact that girls were educated to lying, falsehood and hypocrisy; that they were taught, on the one hand, to make a splendid catch and, on the other hand, to repress their natural feelings. Wollstonecraft harshly condemned the tricks women had to resort to out of powerlessness and especially Rousseau's notorious idea that the male was a sexual being only at times, but the female was one forever. She retorted that 'women would not always be women, if they were allowed to acquire greater understanding', and 'This desire of being always women, is the very consciousness that degrades the sex'. The *Vindication of the Rights of Woman* is an appeal to revolutionize education for girls and for equal education of boys and girls. She dedicated the treatise to Talleyrand, a member of the French National Assembly, who had submitted a programme for a national educational system in 1791 and whom Wollstonecraft met in England at that time. Public virtue, she argued, could only grow upon private virtue, and no sexual distinctions should be permitted here. 'Unless virtue be nursed by liberty, it will never attain true strength' and what is being said 'of man I extend to mankind'. Since 'those virtues and talents, the exercise of which ennobles the human character', are limited to men, she wished that women 'may every day grow more and more masculine' and 'rational men will excuse me for endeavouring to persuade [women] to become more masculine and respectable'. The sexual side of virtue – chastity within and outside marriage – applied not only to women but also to men. In the dedication, she suggested that Talleyrand implement her ideas in France; later in the text she formulated a utopia: 'A wild wish has just flown from my heart to my head, and I will not stifle it though it may excite a horse-laugh. I do earnestly wish to see the distinction of sex confounded in society, unless where love animates the behaviour.' This vision was to be achieved through child-rearing and education.

Wollstonecraft's vision of education also contains a concept of female citizenship, including both rights and duties. The 'only method of leading women to fulfil their peculiar duties is to free them from all restraint by allowing them to participate in the inherent rights of mankind'. Reason and judgement could only be developed in freedom, for women as well as men. It was not obedience, she declared, but the fulfilment of natural and social duties that constitutes citizenship. Only 'the being who discharges the duties of its station is independent; and, speaking of women at large, their first duty is to themselves as rational creatures, and the next, in point of importance, as citizens, is that, which includes so many, of a mother'. Rights and duties are mutually dependent and inextricably linked. Among the 'natural' and 'peculiar duties' of the woman was motherhood practised according to nature and reason, as well as nursing one's own children; the practice of wet-nursing and foundling homes should be abolished. Whereas the man satisfied his civic duty in war (Wollstonecraft, as a pacifist, supported at most a defensive war) and in civic life; 'his wife, also an active citizen, should be equally intent to manage her family, educate her children and assist her neighbours'.

Wollstonecraft's concept of sexual difference in no way contradicted her wish for 'masculine' women and gender equality. She saw women and men as having 'different duties to fulfil; but they are *human* duties'; they have to follow the same principles. The 'femininity' that she reprehended was not motherhood but irrationality and coquetry. She saw motherhood not as a weakness but as a strength. For her, the terrible contrast was 'the patient drudge, who fulfils her task, like a blind horse in a mill' and is 'defrauded of her just reward; for the wages due to her are the caresses of her husband'. Instead, in order 'to be a good mother, a woman must have sense, and that independence of mind which few women possess who are taught to depend entirely on their husbands'. Furthermore, Wollstonecraft demanded, 'make women rational creatures and free citizens, and they will quickly become good wives and mothers'. Men, too, should satisfy their duties of fatherhood. Finally, she argued, women should not be limited to domestic duties or even coerced to perform them. Gainful employment was the foundation for economic independence and duties of another kind: women could be doctors, midwives and teachers, and new professions needed to be opened to them. They could 'study politics', and thus create a solid basis for their charitable activities. Independence would save them from slipping into prostitution.

Duties also implied rights. In her dedication to Talleyrand, Wollstonecraft criticized the French constitution, which forced women, 'by denying them civil and political rights, to remain immured in their families groping in the dark'. She gave highest priority to civil rights for women, who were presently 'cyphers'. 'To render [woman] really virtuous and useful, she must not, if she discharge her civil duties, want individually the protection of civil laws; she must not be dependent on her husband's bounty for her subsistence during his life, or support after his death.' Man and woman 'were made for each other, though not to become one being'.

Her comments were more succinct and cautious with respect to political participation, which she still viewed as utopian. 'I may excite laughter, by dropping a hint, which I mean to pursue, some future time, for really I think that women ought to have representatives, instead of being arbitrarily governed without having any direct share allowed them in the deliberations of government.' Enlightenment thinker Christian Gotthilf Salzmann, publisher of the German edition of Wollstonecraft's treatise in 1793–4, expressed dismay in his commentary on this passage: 'Oh, a woman who satisfies her duties as a mother and educates a couple of good citizens, both men and women, has rendered sufficient services to the state, and has so many things to do, that there could hardly be much time left for her to participate in the government.'[37] For a quite different reason – with an eye to the English constitution – Wollstonecraft herself had serious reservations about political participation. 'As the whole system of representation is now, in this country, only a convenient handle for despotism, [women] need not complain, for they are as well represented as a numerous class of hard-working mechanics. . . . How are they represented whose very sweat supports the splendid stud of an heir-apparent, or varnishes the chariot of some female favourite who looks down on shame?' The 'emancipation' of women did not lie first and foremost in the political sphere, according to Wollstonecraft, but in their liberation from traditional manners in favour of morals. 'Would men but generously snap our chains, and be content with rational fellowship instead of slavish obedience, they would find us more observant daughters, more affectionate sisters, more faithful wives, more reasonable mothers – in a word, better *citizens*.' Like Olympe de Gouges, Hippel and many other philogynists of the time, Wollstonecraft did not feel motherhood and citizenship were mutually exclusive. On the contrary, motherhood was seen as granting legitimacy to equality, rather than hierarchy, of the sexes and to equality between married and unmarried women.

Not only were the Parisian revolutionaries referred to as 'women turned hyena' (Friedrich Schiller), but Wollstonecraft, too, was called a 'hyena in petticoats' (Horace Walpole). Nevertheless, both of her *Vindications* enjoyed considerable support. The second was immediately translated into French and German. Emilie von Berlepsch – who was hesitant to read it at first since she feared a female Thomas Paine – saw her own ideas on cultural autonomy confirmed by Wollstonecraft: 'How my soul flew out to my sister soul! . . . What a pure, determined, non-exaggerated concept of female dignity and destiny! What a profound look into the depravity of society! . . . It pleases me greatly that these words can be understood in Germany much earlier than in Britain, and it feels as though I am not using the word "freedom" in an ominous, political sense, nor to express an impudent lack of restraint. No, I wish to denote solely the moral strength, its autonomy and power over human thought, desire and actions.'[38] Wollstonecraft died in childbirth in 1797 at the age of forty-four. Her daughter Mary later married the poet Percy Shelley and wrote the novel *Frankenstein*. In 1798 the Dissenter William Godwin, Mary's father, published his memoirs, in which he revealed that Wollstonecraft had had premarital affairs and was already pregnant with Mary before she married him. He claimed that she had previously given birth to a child out of wedlock, who had died, and that she had attempted suicide twice. This was enough to ruin Wollstonecraft's reputation. But the debate on a cultural revolution of gender relations that she had started continued in Britain after most English Jacobins had rejected the Terror in France. When Millicent Fawcett republished Wollstonecraft's book on the occasion of its centennial, she thought that women owed Wollstonecraft as much 'as modern Political Economy owes to her famous contemporary, Adam Smith'. Bertha Pappenheim translated the book into German seven years later, shortly before she founded the League of Jewish Women (Jüdische Frauenbund).

Nocturnal Intrigues

> For centuries, the government of France in particular has depended on the nocturnal administration of women.
>
> Olympe de Gouges, *Déclaration*, Postamble

Why did the revolution fail? Why for men? Why for women? Did it really fail at all?

Of all French women, it was the Catholics who influenced the fate of the revolution the most, whether they were republican, 'counter-revolutionary' or really counter-revolutionary. A myth developed in the nineteenth century, furthered by Jules Michelet in *Du prêtre, de la femme, de la famille* (1845), that these women had betrayed the revolution. But if the revolution and the republic failed, it was not the fault of the Catholic women. It was due, first of all, to the religious ignorance of the revolutionaries. Germaine de Staël, who wrote the first history of the French Revolution – a short time earlier Catherine Macaulay had written a history of the English Revolution and Mercy Otis Warren wrote one of the American Revolution – believed that one reason 'why the revolution so quickly diverted from its original path' lay in the deplorable situation 'that the French revolutionaries did not know how to reconcile religion and liberty'.[39] Second, there were crucial reasons outside religion. Whereas the revolutionary notables wanted to create a modern state, a segment of the people had actually been hoping for an anti-modern paradise (the 'universal happiness' of the constitution of 1793). The revolution failed because it could not supply the daily bread it had promised the poor in sufficient quantity. It was not able to replace the traditional poor relief by a state-sponsored one, and the largely destroyed family economy by a functioning new form of economy. It failed due to poor harvests, a costly and never-ending war, the destruction of its own currency and, last but not least, the contempt for human life, general demoralization, the decline in industriousness and deep chasms in society. The revolution failed with respect to the hopes of the male revolutionaries. But for good reason the Napoleonic period was and still is viewed not merely as a revision but also as the climax of the revolution. In any event, in the long run the revolution did not fail. But it would take a century before its main goals were to be realized – for men only, that is. For women, it would take another century; for them it was indeed the longest revolution.

A considerable number of female voices, and some male ones, had been raised early in the revolution and had expected that women as well as men would profit from the *bienfaits*, whether in the form of 'bread' or rights or cultural renewal. The number of statements that have survived and their circulation throughout Europe are all the more remarkable considering that women were not at all used to intervening in political matters at all, and certainly not on behalf of their sex. When the transition from a constitutional monarchy to a republic brought with it regicide and civil and European wars, most European women – and men – withdrew their sympathy for the revolution. The private had become far too radically political. Mothers, daughters, sisters and wives became casualties of the civil war by the thousands and over a million of them lost their menfolk in the European wars. But the failure of the revolution for women was more than a by-product of these developments. There have been many explanations why this was so. So many, in fact, that the opposite question must be raised: was it even realistic to expect that the revolution would liberate women? Hippel's hypothesis is also legitimate here: might the revolution have been more successful if women had been made 'active voters' early on?

When the revolution began, the hopes of women might truly have seemed realistic precisely because of the pronouncedly universalistic discourse of the revolution and its hitherto inestimable thrust. The failure was primarily due to the rigid attitudes of the Montagnards. Female commitment was welcome as long as it served their purposes, as could be read in the *Révolutions de Paris* journal of 1791: '*Citoyennes* of all ages, all ranks! Leave your homes, all of you at once; rally from door to door and march towards the town hall. . . . You are called upon to save the honour of your sex, which has been compromised by one of you. Armed with incendiary torches, stand before the gates of the palace of your tyrants.' Once the need had passed, a different message came: '*Citoyennes*! we would want to see you return to your homes and once again take up the accustomed yoke of domestic duties; . . . reign sweetly inside your households, teach the rights of man to the stuttering child . . . but do not compete with us.'[40] Did the desire to use women, on the one hand, and exclude them, on the other, derive from *egoismo mascolino*, as the Italian *cittadine* believed, or from a 'basic misogyny' or 'hatred' and the contempt of men towards women?[41] Yet it turned out to be possible to overcome the hatred and contempt for other groups that were ultimately part of the sovereignty – the men among the poor, the Jews and the slaves. There are three explanations for this.

Most weight must be given to, first and foremost, the traditional subordination of the female sex. Not even the most radical of women – whether Olympe de Gouges with her paradox or Mary Wollstonecraft with her wild wish – could avoid defining the admission of women to the *droit de cité* as a vision for the future only; and the overwhelming majority of politically active women did not act autonomously but within male political factions. It was for good reason that Olympe de Gouges appealed in her *Déclaration*: 'Oh women! Women! when will you cease to be blind? What advantages have you gained from the revolution? A more marked scorn, a more signal disdain . . . what then remains for you? The proof of man's injustice.' Tradition carried greater weight relative to innovation. In the new order, which appeared to make men into individuals, they now represented 'their' women. The 'virtual representation' that some viewed precisely as the inclusion of women in the polity – a core element of both the *ancien régime* and the project of modernity – meant exclusion to others, who wanted women, too, to be understood as individuals. Second, classical republicanism, whose tradition was carried by many revolutionaries, had always been clearly man's business. The attack by women and supporters of women might have contributed to challenging its masculinity even further. And the 'male spectacle' of revolutionary violence – as Prudhomme referred to it – might have furthered the need felt by its activists, who also crusaded most vehemently against female *citoyenneté*, for an ideal domestic world for which the women were held responsible.

A third and perhaps most serious reason is that virtually all of the revolutionaries, republicans, constitutional monarchists, women and men alike, whether or not they spoke out for the liberation of women, were all agreed on one point. Women and their power – which included their 'frivolity' – were considered the cause and symbol of the *ancien régime* and its corruption. 'The rule of the courtiers accelerated the decline of the nation; the rule of the queens brought it finally to an end' was to be read in the journal *Révolutions de Paris* in 1791; and virtually all women

– except for the poor who applauded the 'male spectacle' – were 'aristocrats'. Wollstonecraft equated aristocratic vices with female vices, and saw a close relationship between the sexual subordination of women and their just as traditional, albeit illegitimate, power; that was why they were 'slaves'. De Gouges saw things in a similar way: 'During centuries of corruption, you reigned only over the weakness of men. . . . Women have done more evil than good' and the *ancien régime* depended on 'the nocturnal administration of women'; they 'want to be women and yet they are their own worst enemy'. In Italy, a republican voice asked 'How much misfortune, how much destruction have the chatter, irrationality and ambitions of women already brought forth?' And the Italian *cittadine* condemned – as in the eighteenth-century *querelle des femmes* – luxury, inflationary dowries and debauchery. One exception was Hippel, who, also in the querelle tradition, praised female rulers and believed that they exercised their power far better than male 'good-for-nothings'. And de Gouges had dedicated her *Déclaration* to the queen in hopes that she – and consequently the other women of courtly society – would speak out *as women* for her sex. But revolutionary men and women, philogynists as well as misogynists, were agreed that women were to be feared as 'secret agents of the past'.[42] For the friends of women, the 'new' woman had to be the opposite of the 'old' one: masculine, a strong mother, *sui juris* instead of an intriguer who dominated men with borrowed power. Compared to this antithesis, the antithesis of republican motherhood – obedient wife of a republican, or *cittadina madre* in her own right – was pushed into the background. In the foreground remained what Olympe de Gouges referred to as the genuine and effective paradox, or *antithèse*, in her *Déclaration*: 'this sex, which was formerly contemptible and respected but, since the revolution, is respectable and yet contemptible'. It was not least the political language used to criticize the *ancien régime* – femininity as a symbol of corruption; masculinity as a symbol of virtue – that limited the revolutionary innovation to men. Thus it became necessary to ask the questions 'What are women? What is human?' anew, beyond the old paradoxes. Nevertheless, the universalistic language of the revolution also continued to work for and on women. But they had to develop a new vocabulary: on the one hand, as a consequence of the fact that this language had been realized in a male-specific way; and on the other hand, owing to the far-reaching social change that the nineteenth century was to bring.

3
Challenging Boundaries: A Third Gender Dispute

The women's movement – that remarkable social revolution now going on
in old Europe as well as in young America. . . .

Theodore Stanton, 1884

The history of women in the nineteenth century cannot be separated from
the history of the women's movement; they were inextricably intertwined.
When some feminists published a volume analysing the present status of
their movements in 1901, they sought to acknowledge their historical
beginnings. Ersilia Majno Bronzini, who had just co-founded the Unione
femminile in Milan, named 'pioneers' such as Isotta Nogarola in the fifteenth century; others made reference to Christine de Pizan, Agrippa von
Nettesheim or the French salons of the seventeenth century. Nonetheless, they agreed with Isabella Moszezenska of Poland that 'even though
there are sporadic examples in every century of women striving to liberate themselves from their oppressed situation . . . the true women's movement in all countries is a consequence of the century now past'. The
Greek physician Maria Kalopokathès gave a definition: 'The women's
movement' was understood as 'the conscious demand by women for their
rights and the systematic efforts to obtain them'. Even earlier, in 1884,
Theodore Stanton, son of the leading American feminist Elizabeth Cady
Stanton, compiled a volume on the European women's movements. In it,
Millicent Garrett Fawcett of Britain sought out the beginnings of this
'great social movement', in which she would remain active until into the
twentieth century, and emphasized that it is 'essentially modern'. The
authors of the two works (including two men) agreed that the source and
cause would be found in that 'upheaval of the human mind' which had
also been at the roots of the French Revolution and women's criticism of

it. Gertrud Bäumer, still early in her career in the German women's movement, underscored Rousseau's merit in having posed the correct question – whether or not prevailing gender relations were in fact determined by nature. But she asserted that the answer he had offered in *Émile*, 'that woman is specially made for man's delight', was erroneous. The grounds for the classical women's movement were also expressed in other terms, both at its beginning and its end. William Thompson and Anna Wheeler, Irish supporters of Robert Owen, saw the cause in 1825 as lying in the 'eternal prison-house of the wife' (in their *Appeal of One Half the Human Race, Women, Against the Pretensions of the Other Half, Men*), while Ray Strachey, who published the first history of the British women's movement in 1928, saw it in the 'prison-house of home'. The problem that was called the 'woman question' in the nineteenth century was a modern variant of the question whether or not 'women are human'. It concerned the relationship between women and men, and the nature of the family as women's primary focus. Some of the almost fifty contributors to these two works saw the situation faced by women in their respective countries as a story of success; others painted a dismal picture, such as Concepción Arenal, who as a Spanish patriot wanted 'history, not romance' to speak.[1] While the national differences were great, the problems were largely the same.

In the 1901 book the term 'feminism' makes a sporadic appearance. It was coined only a short time earlier in France and would become widespread internationally in the twentieth century. But its meaning was already relevant in the nineteenth century. It was about women's right to determine autonomously their own place in society and to freely develop their personalities; thus, as was often insisted, it also advanced the common good. The historical reflections of these protagonists clearly reveal their awareness that the woman question was age-old, yet marked just as clearly by changes during their time; and it was about economic and social issues as well as cultural ones. Today the classical women's movement is again viewed as a 'cultural apprenticeship' interacting with the gradual or revolutionary upheavals of the century. Women acted and reacted in this apprenticeship, as well as *vis-à-vis* other movements and loyalties such as religion, class, nation or empire. And they dealt with many single issues. This is not surprising in view of the countless areas affected by the hierarchical gender order. Old and new ways of talking about gender collided, and also merged.

Changing Debates and Languages

The only difficulty is in deciding what that true and natural sphere is.
                                                  Marion Kirkland Reid, 1843

It has become commonplace to attribute to the Victorian age (Queen
Victoria reigned from 1837 to 1901) or to civil society a specific, clear-
cut and unambiguous image of gender relations: a strict separation of
man's and woman's spheres, a sharp division between the female private
sphere and the male public sphere, a polarization of 'ontologically' based
features of the sexes that are seen as both contrasting and complementary. Work and 'the world' are seen to have been the responsibility of
men; and home and domesticity that of women, according to a saying at
the time: 'To the man, the state; to the woman, the family.'[2] This vision is
often illustrated (both then and now) with the glorified image of woman
as the 'angel in the house'. The image came from the poem 'The Angel in
the House' by Coventry Patmore (1855) and was popular in Britain, the
United States and continental Europe (though less so in Germany). It
joined forces with talk of the dignity of woman, her 'vocation as homemaker, wife and mother' and her role as protector of morals, culture and
religion. Moreover, it is often claimed today that the image was conceived and reinforced by the natural sciences. Around 1800 anatomy,
gynaecology and anthropology are seen to have broken with the long-
standing Aristotelian tradition, according to which woman was viewed
as 'a lesser man' (or *homme manqué*). The new model would no longer
consider women as 'inferior' but as essentially 'different' and complementary to the man, that is, separate but equal. The earlier 'one-sex model'
is said to have been replaced by a 'two-sex model', and social relations
between the sexes also corresponded to such a 'biological' concept. These
gender assignments and the actual relationship between the sexes are
often seen from a long-term perspective as a low point in the history of
women. In the course of social and political modernization, the early
modern age – as a golden age of gender mixing, gender equality and the
rule of women – was to be replaced during the Victorian age by a radical
separation and division of labour between the sexes that would remain
in effect until far into the twentieth century.

However, the nineteenth century was not dominated by a model, much
less by one single model; it was dominated instead by a debate that would
last throughout the entire century, and it was anything but a secondary
issue. Men as well as women argued and negotiated about the relationship between the current gender order and a reasonable, natural, God-
given, just or desired one. The situation was new in that there were just

about as many women as men involved in the debate, since women now had easier access to the printing press and thus to the public sphere. The 'woman question' was a real – that is, open – question. Answers were marked not by certainty but uncertainty. The century started with the deep sigh of Ruth Courtauld, the wife of a man who failed in his career as a silk-throwster and mother of a man who founded a silk factory: 'Oh did we but all know our proper stations and could but be content with acting properly in them, what a world of pain it would save us.' Over a century later, when Sigmund Freud showed an interest in the 'dark continent', the question had yet to be answered: 'What does woman want?'[3] The answers varied and were as controversial as they were contradictory. There was not merely a bass or tenor solo but a many-voiced chorus in which the available linguistic material was processed, exchanged and answered; and soprano and alto could clearly be perceived and at times even set the tone. The prevailing form of recitative was not pronouncement but question and debate; it was not a monologue but a dialogue.

German liberal Carl Welcker may serve here as basso continuo. His entry on 'Gender Relations' in the influential *Staats-Lexikon* of 1838 started by stating that the problem was 'the most difficult for a legal and political theory', and that the 'voice of nature' did not speak 'quite understandably for all'; Welcker continued with six major questions on the 'subordination of the woman under the man'. It was necessary to consider the questions, he explained, because subordination was recently questioned by 'revolutionary women' and some men – Welcker was well informed about such voices in Europe and the United States – and because state theory, especially for him as a liberal, used 'the rights of man as the basis for civil law' and 'equality in the latter is based on equality in the former'. Therefore, Welcker asserted, 'new grounds for justification' needed to be found for female subordination, which continued to be essential. The result of this difficulty is a clearly over-determined argumentation. Welcker did not only draw upon nature – in the form of Karl Friedrich Burdach's anthropological work, which had luckily just been published and which projected social relations onto nature. He also consulted reason, habit, society and history for a construction that peaked in 'Christian and German family life', the 'greatest and most hopeful aspect of progress in the entire history of mankind'. And finally, male common sense – anything but innovative – referred to the old traditions, including that of natural law: men were given reason, women weakness. Like Locke and Portalis, Welcker argued that with respect to marriage, there could never be a society 'in which the participants always wish to stand side by side with equal voice, without any final decision-making authority in cases of differences of opinion about their common concerns'. The more rational man would have to decide. However, Welcker concluded, man did not only have reason, he was also haunted by 'uncontrollable desires' for which – 'as hidden as possible, yet under good police control' – prostitutes should be made available. The theory of physical drives plaguing male nature would play just as important a role in nineteenth-century gender images (and not only those of men) as that of male reason.

Welcker's constructions (and also those derived primarily from the natural sciences) were by no means a two-sex model of equivalent complementarity but a vision of women's inferiority and men's superiority. It was not by chance that John Stuart Mill chose the title *The Subjection of Women* for his epochal work of 1869; or that Maria Deraismes opened *Eve dans l'humanité* with an attack on the postulate that declared the 'inferiorité des femmes'; or that Freud's female critics contested, in the early twentieth century, the assumption that woman was 'un homme manqué'. The 'woman question' was not about difference; it was about the hierarchy of the sexes. In the words of a critic of Mill in the *Saturday Review*, 'When two people ride a horse, one must sit behind'.[4] Despite the (not totally) new vocabulary, the new image of women differed from the older one in that it responded to social and political change, and especially to voices that continued to speak out since the querelle of the 1790s.

So much ink was spent writing about the woman question and its resolution in the nineteenth century that Victorian gender relations might today appear as a 'model'. Yet this is not so much the result of the 'model's' undisputed validity as of the fact that its hegemony was uncertain and as often defended as it was challenged, either by opponents or by social change itself. This is why the precise point in time when it became a social and mental reality is highly disputed today. Was it since Rousseau and the late eighteenth century? Or since the French Revolution? Or starting in 1830, after the first phase of industrialization in Britain? Or after the European revolutions of 1848 and their failure? Or not until the end of the century, when the women's movement and other critical voices could no longer be ignored and their adversaries wanted to turn back the wheels of history, while the post-Victorians needed a handy tendentious travesty to use against their parents?[5] Indeed, there was much talk on nature, but as always nature could be used to validate different, even opposite, opinions. The term 'biology' had been used with respect to the sexes since mid-century in France (by August Comte, as a result of which John Stuart Mill broke with him). Elsewhere it was not used in this sense until the late nineteenth century, when evolutionary biology replaced anatomy as the leading science and transformed anthropology. Since Herbert Spencer and Charles Darwin, however, evolutionary biology declared that the relationship between the sexes was based not on complementarity but on predominance and subordination. Thus in 1870 the publisher of an English edition of Condorcet's famous text on women's rights could explain traditional male supremacy by pointing to 'Natural Selection'. Parallels were often made between women and ethnic groups; Professor Carl Vogt of Geneva, for example, whose *Lectures on Man* were originally published in Germany in 1863 and were received in Europe and the United States, argued that 'The grown up Negro partakes, as regards his intellectual faculties, of the nature of the child, the female, and the senile White'. The natural and social sciences continued to refer to the *mas occasionatus*, the misbegotten male, and – despite or because of the glorification of 'woman's dignity' – the social conclusions were obvious. When John Stuart Mill demanded women's suffrage in the House of Commons on 20 May 1867, a representative countered, unfazed by any two-sex model: 'How did the hon. Gentleman propose to deal with these differences of opinion [with respect to voting] between the head of the family and her whom the poet called "the lesser man"?'[6]

As in Welcker's language, images of women were often – albeit usually in isolated instances – introduced into the vocabulary of the nation and nation-state, which on the surface had only male connotations. Although the discourse on gender relations was remarkably similar beyond national borders – the German variant of the English 'lofty pine and slender vine' was an oak or 'elm for the faltering ivy' – the ideal woman often had a nationally specific connotation. 'No housewives are more perfect than the French', wrote the former German revolutionary Karl Hillebrand, whose work appeared in German and French: 'Without boasting of their housekeeping skills as the Germans do', many of them 'even take the husband's place in business' (which is why, he believed, things did not go as well as in Germany). The idle English lady was contrasted with the hard-working Dutch housewife, and the 'English girl' was said to be 'something franker than a Frenchwoman, more to be trusted than an Italian, as brave as an American but more refined, as domestic as a German and more graceful'.[7] Moreover, the discourse was not 'middle class' but clearly crossed class lines. It did not 'trickle down from above' (even if maids who married a working-class man after working in a middle-class household brought various skills they had learned to their marriage). Instead, it was an integral component of working-class discourse. Chartists, both men and women, were agreed that the ideal husband worked for the family's income and the ideal wife worked for the family. Reginald John Richardson was one of the handful of male Chartists who, contrary to the People's Charter of 1838, supported civil and political rights for women. In his writings and speeches, such as when he addressed a group of female calico printers who congenially listened to his appeal on *The Rights of Women*, Richardson underscored the point that 'your places are in your homes: your labours are your domestic duties . . . and not in slaving thus for the accumulation of the wealth of others, whose slaves you seem willing to be'.[8] It was an image of the domestic working-class wife as a comrade-in-arms fighting against exploitation. The workers' movement regularly called for men to be breadwinners and to reduce or even eliminate factory work for women.

In Britain and elsewhere, any public statement bearing on the woman question was likely to generate responses, and expressing norms or dissent was part of a common, argumentative public sphere. Numerous 'models' circulated, coexisted, competed and overlapped with each other. In addition to the 'natural law' model of Welcker, Balzac's vision took up old paradoxes: 'The woman is, strictly speaking, only an annex of the man. She is a slave whom we must know how to place on a pedestal.' There was also the notion of the angel in her 'sphere' of domestic duties at the side and in the service of her husband (this was the message of the widely read books of etiquette by Sarah Ellis, according to which women were 'relative' creatures, dependent on the man); and the minority view of absolute gender equality (according to John Stuart Mill, who assumed nevertheless that most women would continue of their own free will to work for the family). Another notion was that of the angel outside the home, who extended the female sphere into the public space through social work that was philanthropically or religiously inspired; Florence Nightingale became the popular icon. A radical variant of the angel, sometimes referred to today as utopian or apocalyptic feminism, took the much-avowed moral superiority of women literally, claiming for the female peculiarity a leading role on the road to a new era of community and love (such as supporters of Saint-Simon, Fourier or Owen). Giuseppe Mazzini – many Italian feminists were also Mazzinians – proclaimed his variant in *Dei doveri dell'uomo* (1860): 'The angel of the house is the woman. . . . This is why she should be your equal in civil and political life.'[9]And finally, starting in the 1860s, there were the lasting, organized women's movements.

The internal contradictions in the discourse on 'women's place is in the home', *la femme au foyer*, *l'angelo focolare*, *angel de hogar*, *die Frau gehört ins Haus*, and 'To the man, the state; to the woman, the family' were patently obvious. The theory and the laws, according to which the man was the decision-maker in cases of marital dissent, contradicted the notion that the house was the woman's domain and that of a clear-cut separation of male and female spheres. 'Even in the family the woman is a nullity', criticized the Saint-Simonian Élisabeth Celnart in 1832. Others also condemned their *état de nullité*. One Swiss woman signed her 1831 complaint about 'our nothingness up to now' with a '0' instead of her name.[10] The new doctrine that at least natural (if not political) rights should apply for all human beings was as contradictory as was that of woman's maternal, moral, cultural and civilizing 'mission' and her role as a bearer of the culture. Not only did the latter contrast with the just as often asserted dichotomy of the female realm of nature and the male realm of culture, but when women took the mission seriously, they quickly confronted the limits to their mental and social agency. These contradictions – what exactly comprised the 'female sphere', what was the meaning of equivalence, complementarity, female mission? – led to new discourses, some of which became very popular, although – or because – they agreed to some extent with the restrictive vocabulary. Sarah Lewis's *Woman's Mission* (1839) became a best-seller, with seventeen British and five American editions up to 1854. Lewis took up arguments from Louis-Aimé Martin's *De l'éducation des mères de famille, ou la civilisation du genre humain par les femmes* (1834; English: *The Education of Mothers; or, The Civilization of Mankind by Women*, 1843). Martin's treatise had gone to eleven printings in French by 1883, three in English, and it was also translated into Swedish, German and Italian. Most of the arguments were discussed internationally.

Lewis rejected – as Wollstonecraft had earlier done – both the assumption that women were 'mere objects of sensual passion' and the notion of female inferiority (except with respect to physical strength) and countered that with their 'moral and intellectual equality'. It was 'paradoxical', irrational and 'inconsistent' that women were proposed 'at the same time expansion of views and contraction of operation'. Though she thought nothing of transferring male rights and offices to women and accepted 'the principle of divided labour' as God-given, Lewis viewed the 'mission' and the 'dignity and value' of women as residing in the mobilization of their 'family affection' and especially their 'maternal affection' against materialism and capitalism and for the 'regeneration of mankind', for which God declared women to be the 'prime agents'. Women's task, she declared, was the responsible education of girls and boys and intelligent advising of men, including in public affairs, since 'good mothers make good men' and the family virtues should also apply to the state. 'Governments will never be perfect till all distinction between private and public virtue . . . be done away!' In France, Martin was also praised by the radical *Journal des femmes*. In Britain, Lewis was fondly recommended to married women by the popular novelist George Eliot (who was still unmarried at the time); the Scottish writer Marion Kirkland Reid, in *A Plea for Woman* (1843), combined reluctant praise for Lewis's criticism of prejudices with a clear critique. She asserted that there were so many contradictory sentiments on the 'woman's sphere' and 'mission', whether narrow and bigoted or extended and liberal, that there was 'as yet no definite, precise and unmistakable meaning': 'The only difficulty is in deciding what that true and natural sphere is.' Reid supported 'a more enlarged view of those duties and a more active discharge of them', and saw 'no good ground for the assumption that the possession and exercise of political privileges are incompatible with the right performance of the home duties of the sex'. Reid felt that a woman could only be a good companion to her husband if she were free and had equal rights to develop her abilities outside the home as well.[11]

With a moral mission and the metaphors of spheres, gender characters, social and spiritual motherhood and social housekeeping, the opposite of domesticity, that is, female vocational and other activities outside the home, gained increasing legitimacy. In the second half of the century, however, there was dispute about whether such activities could encompass charity only or whether nursing or even the profession of physician could be included. Admission to the profession and thus to the study of medicine was the subject of vehement argument on all sides. Queen Victoria harshly opposed it and the conflicts continued until into the twentieth century. Jurisprudence was the most rigid bastion of the male sphere. John Ruskin's 'Of Queens' Gardens' (in *Sesame and Lilies*, 1865), reprinted more than thirty-five times in the nineteenth century and even read in schools, was a classical statement on the Victorian separation of spheres, but it was just as much an appeal for women to get involved in the pressing questions of social reform. In his exalted rhetoric of 'peculiar qualities' and 'separate spheres', Ruskin virtually turned the image on its head: 'Home is yet wherever she is; and for a noble woman it stretches far round her.' A woman needed physical exercise, he maintained, she should learn everywhere ('let her loose in the library') and her 'queenly power' was absolutely essential 'with respect to the state'. Just as men's public duties were nothing more than an expansion of their personal work and family duties, the same was true with respect to the public tasks of women: on the battlefields (the professionalization of nursing by Florence Nightingale created a sensation ever since the Crimean War from 1853 to 1856), in the slums, among the poor, uneducated and prostitutes. Women's sphere and power seemed to Ruskin to be virtually boundless. Meanwhile, John Stuart Mill was of a different opinion. He had completed *The Subjection of Women* in 1861, three years after the death of his co-author, Harriet Taylor Mill. Their vocabulary was not about power but liberty, the elimination of male 'tyranny' in marriage, the best possible development of the personality with full equal rights for men and women, access for women to social competition, and the resulting advancement of the common good. These were the same ideals he had formulated in his most famous work, *On Liberty* (1859), which he also co-wrote with Harriet; it was largely, albeit by no means exclusively, gender-neutral. *The Subjection of Women* went into fourteen printings by the turn of the century (three times together with *On Liberty*) and was quickly translated into all European languages. It became, regardless of the controversy surrounding it, obligatory reading for the educated, both men and women, including the Russian intelligentsia. The debate began as soon as it was published.

It was equally true for France that 'with so much talk about "the woman", one can no longer be sure what she is', and the *Encyclopédie Nouvelle* of 1843 emphasized that 'this is not about a debate among scholars' but 'the fate of the present-day woman'.[12] In the early phase of the debate, utopias of sexual liberation were in the forefront, creating a stir throughout Europe. Saint-Simonism (which for Welcker was a nightmare) proclaimed a female Messiah, the union of the sexes in a 'priestly couple', the 'rehabilitation of the flesh' and regulated sexual mores in a way that some considered promiscuity. Saint-Simonian women broke with this religion in 1832 and started to formulate their own meaning of *La Femme libre* (the title of their journal). Many became revolutionaries in 1848. They identified the common ground of women, beyond class and party boundaries, in the *nullité* of their social existence as well as in motherhood. They saw motherhood not merely as a peculiarity of female otherness but as a universal category. In the words of Jeanne-Désirée Véret, 'The banner of women is universal, for are they not, as our sister Suzanne [Voilquin] has said, all united by the same bond of *motherhood*.' The notion of sexual difference was thus not necessarily retrogressive; it could serve to grant legitimacy to the demand for change. It could even legitimize a more utopian demand than the notion of sexual similarity. That was how Eugénie Niboyet argued for women's suffrage in 1848, when French men – in the language of the times – were given *suffrage universel*. 'We do not aspire to be good male *citoyens*, we aspire simply to be good *citoyennes*, and if we demand our rights it is as women and not as men. . . . We are claiming our rights only in the name of our duties.' Her journal *La Voix des femmes* went even further in April 1848, demanding a transformation of the men: 'Woman should not emancipate herself by making herself a man; she must emancipate the man, by making him a woman.' A decade later Jenny d'Héricourt, a midwife who had completed medical school (not until the 1870s was a woman officially allowed to study medicine in France) and had once also contributed to *La Voix des femmes*, preferred to argue on the grounds of gender sameness or gender neutrality: 'Woman must not claim her rights as woman but only *as a human person and a member of the social body*.'[13] But precisely for that reason she thought it was premature to demand suffrage for women, since in their present situation women would merely vote the same as the men. The prerequisite for even demanding the right to vote, she argued, was equality for women in marriage, the right to divorce and access to education.

Yet the arguments diverge only on the surface, since public discourse on gender relations was shaped by its appeal and historical context. Niboyet's statement was addressed to Ledru-Rollin, interior minister of the new republic, and in early 1848 many things still seemed possible. D'Héricourt, on the other hand, had experienced how manhood suffrage led to the rise of Napoleon III and thus to the defeat of the revolution. Her voice was one among many in the dispute, which created a sensation internationally over the misogynistic remarks made by the socialist Pierre-Joseph Proudhon, and the somewhat more gallant ones made by the republican and historian Jules Michelet. Both men pointed to racial difference as the basis for the hierarchy of the sexes, which placed 'a barrier between them like the difference of race between animals'. According to Proudhon, who once again reiterated Aristotle, 'Woman is a diminutive of man in whom one organ is missing that would permit her to become adult', and 'the preponderance is acquired by the stronger sex in the proportion of three to two, which means that man will be the master and that woman will obey. *Dura lex, sed lex*'.

Juliette Lambert Adam, later to become the 'Grand Dame of *lettres françaises*', retorted that physical strength does not legitimize power. 'Woman supplies society with other elements than supplied by man, but that are no less indispensable.' For 'it is the agreement between feminine elements and masculine elements that provides social harmony, and it is their blending that determines humanity's progress'. Equality did not mean sameness (*identité*), but equal value (*équivalence*). Everyone had particular abilities, some were more male and others more female, but 'it would, however, be very dangerous to freedom to try to determine in advance the respective roles of men and women and to imprison either in occupations by their respective sex'. D'Héricourt, too, who emigrated to the United States in 1863 and whose treatise appeared in English in 1864, rejected the male mania for superiority and classification. Gender and class ('le genre, la classe!') were nothing but mental constructions. She emphasized that housework was also a form of work. In view of the 'insane utopias' that men had 'invented on the nature of women', she insisted that we cannot know: 'We shall never have a certain answer until we allow arbitrary restrictions to cease. . . . I know not, and you know no better than I, what are the true characteristics arising from the distinction of the sexes, and I believe that they can be revealed only by liberty in equality, parity of instruction and of education.' But most of all she insisted that 'you have no right to think and to wish in my place.'[14] Proudhon presumed to know better: 'No, Madame, you know nothing about your sex.'

No Angels in the House: Ideals and Realities

Je décline l'honneur d'être un ange.

Maria Deraismes, 1868[15]

Preached ideals and lived realities could diverge and be played off against one another. Queen Victoria, who sometimes served as an example of women's capacity to rule, thought nothing of women's rights. With her nine births, her wish to designate her German husband Albert 'Prince Consort' and to share the throne with him (he then received only the title 'His Royal Highness'), and her self-presentation after his death as a mourning widow in black dress, she appeared to be a symbol of Victorianism. But Queen Victoria did not quite fit that image; she was anything but demure and well-mannered, devoid of passion or prepared to endure the painful task of maintaining her dynasty without complaint. She used chloroform when she gave birth – it was partly due to her example that anaesthesia became widespread during childbirth – and she certainly did not praise motherhood as a lofty female destiny. When her eldest daughter Victoria married the Prussian crown prince (as of 1888 she was called 'Empress Friedrich' and sympathized with the women's movement) and became pregnant in 1858 with the future Wilhelm II, Queen Victoria wrote to her daughter, 'What you say of the pride of giving life to an immortal soul is very fine'. But the queen could not relate to such feelings and giving birth made her 'think much more of our being like a cow or a dog at such moments; when our poor nature becomes so very animal and unecstatic. . . . I think our sex a most unenviable one'. When she was discouraged from further pregnancies, she complained, 'Oh Doctor, can I have no more fun in bed?'[16]

Throughout the century opinions praising or criticizing the domestic confinement and social subordination of women were juxtaposed with those demonstrating the fulfilling, sociable, educated and satisfying existence of women within and beyond the family. Such were the stories of three generations of the middle-class Merkel and Roth families in Nuremberg and Munich (1780–1850), or that of the middle-class Paget family in Britain (1780–1950). Here, in harmonious if not always conflict-free community, women and men mingled with each other and the 'world'. Women (as well as men) often did not live according to the contemporary ideal and present-day stereotype of female passivity, emotionality and ignorance, and male activity, harshness and reason. Men, whether married or unmarried, also dedicated themselves to domestic sociability (John Stuart Mill thought they had become more domestic than they used to be); married and increasingly more unmarried women shaped their lives autonomously and diversely, and the 'angel in the house' rarely existed in practice. It has been long since refuted that 'Victorian' or 'puritan' passionlessness and sexual passivity of women – regardless of class – was the rule. No different than in early modern times, though social circumstances had changed dramatically, (good) marital relations corresponded to the old metaphors of sun and moon.[17] Florence Nightingale and many other women of the late nineteenth century, who complained about their youthful years spent in idle boredom or waiting for a bridegroom, nevertheless used those years to acquire a well-grounded education, albeit not in the conventional male education system.

Women participated in the economic changes in many ways. They contributed to smaller or larger accumulations of capital through inheritance and marriage. Also, it was not true that only men 'worked' and women only 'cared for the family'; Jenny d'Héricourt and Juliette Lambert Adam were not the only ones to draw attention to that fact. Domestic work by women was indispensable, no matter what social class they belonged to. It took on a number of forms, including housekeeping, child-rearing, thrifty administration of the husband's income, estate management, social representation, hosting family gatherings and keeping up contact among family members who were separated geographically, as was often the case among Jews. The more modest the husband's income, the more difficult the wife's job, and male leisure time usually implied work for the wives. This is why the angel in the house, who knew nothing of hard work and financial worries, was – as has been shown for Britain – more of a dream of middle- and lower-class housewives who had to make do with at most two hundred pounds per year. In late nineteenth-century Berlin 'the comedy of housework' for middle-class women also meant giving an outward impression of leisure, elegance and conspicuous consumption. Silverware for the second course of a meal had to be washed quickly and secretly, with time to let it cool, so guests would not notice that there was not enough for both courses. Cultural provisions also included 'handicrafts' such as knitting, embroidering, crocheting and sewing a variety of objects. These skills were often done not in isolation but in the circle of the women in the family and their female friends. The (economically) useless products, mostly gifts, helped to shape and maintain family relations. German Protestant reformer Amalie Sieveking dismissed such knick-knacks around 1850, yet generations later the German Jewish reformer Bertha Pappenheim produced delicate lace chains throughout her life as a 'symbol that even the plainest of materials can be given a spiritual meaning'.[18]

The work-filled domestic balancing act of the lower and middle classes, the education and freedom of women in families of the upper classes, and efforts to satisfactorily organize women's lives and especially married life and profit from the social prestige of a housewife or lady of the house caused many people to become sceptical of radical analyses and reform proposals. Although many were fascinated by John Stuart Mill's critical statements – in 1869 Fanny Lewald, a converted Jew, saw 'joyful and understanding agreement' among her countrywomen in Germany – it was precisely women who also contradicted Mill's assumption of male 'tyranny', female subjection and his ideal of perfect moral, intellectual and legal equality. Anne Mozley reproached him in her review of his book: 'Woman, as she is, is his enemy.' His ideal is abstract, superficial and attractive only for a minority of exceptional women, she argued. Most women, when following his call 'to act as if they were men', would have more to lose than to gain; namely, their 'feminine element' and the breadwinner of the family. Mozley was angered by Mill's insinuation that women who wrote for and about women (as she herself did) did so only in the service of men. Margaret Oliphant, an early widowed mother of three whom she supported herself (also as a writer), and hostile to British marriage law, reproached Mill for viewing women both in the past and present merely as victims of their husbands and even claiming they had internalized their slavery. The common law according to which husband and wife were 'one person' expressed a truth whose roots went far deeper than law itself. It was misleading, she asserted, to justify equal rights on the basis that the sexes were identical in all respects. That was relevant at most, Oliphant maintained, for 'highly cultivated, able, mature, unmarried women' of the upper classes and (once again opposing the nineteenth-century reiteration of Aristotle), 'A woman is a woman and not a lesser edition of man'. Moreover, far removed from the status of a tyrant, many men suffered almost as much as women did under the hardships of the world. In the everyday lives of the 'common mass of humanity which toils along the weary ways of the world two by two', 'common sacrifice, common self-denials, mutual aids', interchange and sympathy were more significant than the merely philosophical concept of women's subjection.[19] Oliphant contrasted the life of the lower classes with what she considered Mill's bourgeois attitudes.

The conservative Mozley and the more progressive Oliphant certainly had some good arguments on their side. Did women really live in an inhuman domestic prison? Or were male 'tyranny' and female 'slavery' words taken from traditional political discourse whose relevance to the complex realities of gender relations was at most metaphorical? As far as concerned real life and human experience with respect to and in dealing with relations between the sexes and the generations, diverse realities, happiness and unhappiness, continued to coexist in the nineteenth century within all social classes. But when an irreconcilable conflict eventually developed – between husband and wife, or between the experience and expectations of women – then female subordination became all too obvious. Conflict and disparity between experience and expectation ultimately provided the basis for the women's movement.

The pathos of the purely female domestic mission, across all class lines, contrasted dramatically with the lives of a large portion of the 'common mass of humanity' on the issue of motherhood as well. In *Women's Mission and Women's Position* (1843), Anna Jameson criticized the contradiction and pointed to the situation of working-class women: '"Woman's mission", of which people can talk so well and write so prettily, is irreconcileable with woman's position, of which no one dares to think, much less to speak.'[20] While the English queen suffered from her traditional duty of securing an heir to the throne, the lower classes faced new conditions with respect to motherhood. Female workers in the expanding industrial city of Manchester had to work between twelve and sixteen hours a day in the 1830s in order to earn a minimal subsistence. Even in pain, the women worked until the day or even the hour they gave birth. Once they delivered, they could stay out of the factory for two weeks at most before returning; due to lack of time or under-nourishment, many women were unable to breastfeed their babies. There were a number of options regarding care of the infants. Mothers could put them in the care of older siblings, relatives or neighbours, although that often cost them a portion of their meagre wages. Or they gave the babies opium or laudanum to keep them quiet; they then either left the babies at home or, in the case of new-born infants, they held them on their laps while working at the looms. Baby-farming was widespread in Britain. New-born babies of impoverished women who could not afford to pay for childcare were given up to homes, where treatment was so poor and the mortality rate so high that a public scandal ensued around 1870, leading to legislative reforms. Long after 'general' living standards had improved, working women still reported catastrophic conditions regarding pregnancy and giving birth, exhaustion and self-sacrifice, miscarriages, abortion and, time and again, uterine prolapse as a result of insufficient pre- or postnatal care. Now women workers began writing their accounts themselves (half a century earlier most had their reports written for them), in letters, for example, which the Women's Cooperative Guild encouraged them to send and which were published in 1915 as a collection entitled *Maternity*. Founded in 1883, the Women's Cooperative Guild was the most significant organization by and for lower-class women in Britain. In 1903, female textile workers went on strike in Crimmitschau, a small town in Saxony. Despite its failure, their strike had a far-reaching impact and became a symbol of both the women's desolate situation and their self-esteem. In 1925, an impressive protest gathering of pregnant workers in Crimmitschau led to the publication of their reports –

Erwerbsarbeit, Schwangerschaft, Frauenleid (Employment, Pregnancy, Women's Woe). Thousands of German and Austrian women workers described their full seven-day working week of domestic and outside work, with expressive titles such as *Mein Arbeitstag, mein Wochenende* (My Workday, My Weekend, Berlin, 1930) and *So leben wir*. . . (How we live . . . , Vienna, 1932). The Women's Cooperative Guild published another collection of personal accounts in 1931 (*Life as We Have Known It*), with an introduction by Virginia Woolf. Living conditions had improved since the nineteenth century, but they were still deplorable and the auto-biographical memoirs demonstrate the meagre existence of women in the early phase of industrialization.

In England, only London could boast of an institution that was widespread in continental Europe: a foundling home. The London Foundling Home was established in 1741; initially it admitted about one hundred abandoned children annually. This figure rose drastically to several thousand when it was announced that the hospital would accept all children up to two months of age that were brought there. During this General Reception period (June 1756 to September 1760), almost 15,000 babies were put into the hospital's care. The persons responsible for this experiment (including the members of parliament who had approved funding to support the children) were amazed and shocked to see how many poor mothers and fathers were willing to burden the community with the costs of rearing their children, whether they were born out of wedlock or within marriage. Consequently, the earlier more restrictive admission conditions were reinstituted, and in the nineteenth century only several dozen children annually enjoyed the privilege of growing up as a ward in the sole English foundling home.

On the continent, foundling homes were more common. Wherever they opened with generous admission regulations, hundreds or even thousands of children streamed in each year. On the eve of the Revolution, when in France alone almost 25,000 *enfants trouvés* were taken in annually, the ever-increasing number was interpreted as follows: 'Mothers today believe that their children will be treated at least as well in a foundling home as in their dark hovels. They are assured they may reclaim the child whenever they wish; and they hope to do just that, if fate remains merciful, at a time when they can afford it financially.'[21] This was the idea that had led Jean-Jacques Rousseau to give up his five children, thoughtlessly acting against the will of the mother. And in the decades after Napoleon's defeat, at a time when the word 'pauperism' was coined and the impoverished population of Europe grew to immeasurable proportions, at least one hundred thousand single mothers or even married parents each year could not help but consider this option. Around mid-century there were about half a million children in the care of European foundling homes; in the nineteenth century altogether, the figure was about ten million. The number of foundlings grew rapidly only where special homes were established for them, whether this was a long-established tradition or a recent development. In Italy, Portugal and Spain this had been in practice since the Renaissance; in Paris since the *Roi-Soleil*, and in the rest of French territory since Napoleon's decree of 19 January 1811 (to compensate for the prohibition of paternity suits – *recherche de la paternité*); in Moscow and St Petersburg since Catherine the Great; in Vienna, Prague, Brussels and other Hapsburg cities since Joseph II. The temptation not to raise one's own children was greatest where a mother or midwife could anonymously place the child in a turning cradle, or where the process was simple in some other way. (Turning cradles were built into the outer wall of the home; a new-born baby could be placed in the cradle from the street and the cradle could be rotated on its axis so that the child was shifted into the foundling home, without the person dropping off the child being recognized.)

In Portugal a law made the establishment of *rodas* – the word for the turning cradles, which came to refer to the foundling homes themselves – mandatory in all cities and towns of the kingdom in 1783, which led to a constant increase in abandoned children. There were 15,000 yearly around mid-century, which was – relative to the total population – a European record. The *rodas* were regarded by contemporaries as one of the most important institutions of public welfare; this continued until 1879, when the number of children admitted was drastically limited. In Lombardy, the large number and long-standing toleration of foundling homes encouraged parents in dire straits to give up their children. Around 1850 in the capital Milan the mothers of impoverished families deposited almost half of their babies in the Pia Casa degli Esposti and usually used the turning cradle, or *torno*; sometimes midwives did it for them (and some babies were handed over directly, without the cradle). The *beneficienza del torno* was the most important branch of public welfare for Milan's poor mothers and fathers, since the Pia Casa offered free wet-nurse services and general care for the children left there for the first few years of their lives. Yet only on very rare occasions did parents intend to be permanently separated from the child, as emphasized by a Milan physician for the poor: the mothers, with whom he was in daily contact, all assured him that their children 'were not left in the Pia Casa indefinitely; rather, they wanted to pick up their children as soon as they were in a position to care for them themselves and when the children no longer needed constant attention. They did this in order to devote themselves entirely to the kind of work they did in order to survive'.[22]

His words touched the core of the modern foundling question. From the mid-eighteenth to the late nineteenth centuries, the number of abandoned new-born babies reached unprecedented heights almost all over Europe, especially in the larger cities, which had foundling homes with liberal admission regulations. This was because the facilities answered the needs of mothers whose poverty forced them to work for pay without any interruption. These women were more often married than single and working in traditional jobs rather than as factory workers. They could leave their children when caring for them would be difficult or impossible to combine with the absolute necessity to contribute to the family income or even support the family entirely. Thus abandoning a child usually did not result from a mother's indifference towards her baby but the wish to save its life. Even if this wish did not come true, due to the overcrowding of the foundling homes and the resulting high mortality rate among the babies, many of the parents who abandoned their infants either were not aware of this or they more or less consciously repressed their awareness. Hence free wet-nursing of infants and free care of small children were to allow mothers to continue their wage labour without interruption. This was clearly among the most important tasks of foundling homes, as shown by measures taken in the second half of the nineteenth century to stem the flood of child abandonments. Wherever a turning cradle was closed or it was otherwise made more difficult to give up new-borns to the care of a hospital, other ways were sought to help mothers who now had to nurse and rear their children themselves, such as breastfeeding allowances, day nurseries or other material benefits. Such benefits were not able (nor meant) to compensate entirely for the services of the foundling hospitals; but the fact that these services were offered in the first place meant acknowledging the principle that assistance for needy mothers and families was the responsibility of state welfare. This principle would have great consequences for the future. Furthermore, the women's movement in the second half of the century was to offer its own vision of motherhood that contrasted especially with that of the foundling institutions.

Old and New Labour

Always toil, toil . . . incessant labour is the sole condition of existence.
                                                          Anna Jameson, 1843[23]

Meanwhile, the groundwork had long since been laid for European – and soon global – industrialization. The Industrial Revolution in Britain from 1780 to 1830 was so dramatic that contemporaries responded with 'wonder and astonishment' (Patrick Colquhoun in 1814). The nineteenth century was also 'the century of the woman worker'.[24] Within the context of industrialization, urbanization and migration, women's 'spheres' – employment and domesticity, paid and unpaid work, private and public domains – were not separate but closely tied to one another and overlapping. Yet at the same time gender relations corresponded exactly with the core of the 'sphere' ideal; that is, the traditional and (through industrialization) redefined postulate of female inferiority.

Calculations made by today's historians are problematic with respect to the history of women. On the basis of aggregate national data, they tend to conclude gradual growth, especially in view of the rise in wages and living standards. But on the one hand, the censuses of the nineteenth century, based on individual occupations, did not register the numerous informal activities by which women acquired either money or food, such as domestic work for boarders, babysitting or sewing, some forms of cottage work, helping out in the husband's business, grain gleaning after the harvest, laundering for other households, frequently changing casual jobs – precisely those activities that had characterized the economy of expedients, or 'makeshift economy', of early modern times and continued into the nineteenth century. On the other hand, the categories of the occupational censuses changed. Initially, unpaid family labour by housewives or by daughters who worked as domestic servants in relatives' households was counted, then it was disregarded towards the end of the century. Consequently, the German women's movement demanded in 1901 that the Imperial Statistics Office include housework as a 'productive occupation' in the census and that housewives be included in the category of 'provider' instead of 'dependant'. Norwegian women demanded the same thing, with the support in 1912 of Anders N. Kiær, director of the Central Office of Statistics.

Today, in calculating the total wage development curve, only the men's income is used as a basis.[25] But an essential – perhaps the most important – foundation for the 'revolution' was the use of the cheapest possible labour, and that was primarily the labour of women and children. In Britain around 1800 the textile industry was the leading sector; in the wool industry women and children, both boys and girls, made up 75 per cent of the workforce. The proportion was only slightly less in the cotton, silk and lace industries, and somewhat higher in the Birmingham metal manufactures. Cultural factors also played an important role. Women and children were considered better suited than men for technological and organizational experiments owing to their dexterity and co-operativeness. It was nothing new that women's and child labour was cheaper than that of men; unprecedented was the extent to which they were systematically incorporated into the technologically innovative, rapidly expanding and labour-intensive sectors of factory and outwork. Where both men and women worked in a factory, there were two different hierarchies of tasks and wages, one for men and one for women; all women's wages were lower than all men's wages. This was the case, for instance, around 1860 in the Courtauld silk mill in Halstead, Essex, where women earned less than those in other textile centres but more than those in other available jobs in Halstead, and where they were paid different wages for weaving, spooling, shearing and twisting.

It was also new that the political economy substantiated these conditions at a theoretical level. In 1835 Scottish economist Andrew Ure argued that it was 'the constant aim and tendency of every improvement in machinery to supersede human labour altogether or to diminish its cost, by substituting the industry of women and children for that of men'. In justifying the low level of women's wages despite the hard work and, particularly in the textile and sewing sectors, the often high qualifications of the women workers, the *mas occasionatus* was brought into play, by Eugène Buret, for example, who in 1840 remarked with regard to France and Britain: 'From the point of view of industry, woman is an imperfect worker.' The language of political economy corresponded to the topos of female inferiority, as it had also been expressed by anthropologists, gynaecologists and evolutionary biologists. In 1891, the Fabian reformer Sidney Webb identified the cause for the value hierarchy of women's and men's work: 'Where the inferiority of earnings exists, it is almost always coexistent with an inferiority of work. And the general inferiority of women's work seems to influence their wages in industries in which no such inferiority exists.' Even though a majority of female – as well as male – workers performed unskilled tasks, gender was the primary factor in wage calculation, whether for skilled or unskilled work. Max Weber perceived this clearly (and with mild criticism) when he defined, in 1909, the wage differential as a special 'sex bonus' for men.[26] In her doctoral dissertation on the causes of unequal pay for male and female labour (*Über die Ursachen der ungleichen Entlohnung von Männer- und Frauenarbeit*, 1906), Alice Salomon traced the pay differential to the 'unequal standard', according to which women received individual wages and men received a family wage.

British women certainly contributed to the Industrial Revolution and its success to a greater extent than French women did to the French Revolution, either to its initial success or later failure. In both cases women helped pave the way for modernity and in both they paid a high price. But industrialization did manage to bring women an income for factory and homework, in the cities and the countryside. Many women were highly mobile and migrated among a number of jobs and between their job and their family. Sofia Budde, for example, was on the permanent workforce of the Mechanical Weaving Mill in Bielefeld, Germany (only a minority of women had such a position). Between 1890 and 1925, starting at the age of fourteen, she worked as a weaver for twenty-nine years, interrupting her work three times to give birth. The first time she took two months off; the second and third times, seven and nine, respectively. For a long time most of the women in the expanding sectors did not work in factories but at home, where they could combine gainful employment with work for the family; but at the same time they often suffered boundless exploitation. In the 1840s Henry Mayhew had already studied and denounced the sweating system, named after the intermediary boss, or sweater, who exploited homeworkers for deplorable wages. At the end of the century in France and Germany, both male and female social scientists published many hundreds of critical surveys on the 'hell of domestic industry'.[27] Domestic industry followed the pattern of the pre-industrial putting-out system, creating a transition from old to modern times – including the same hardship of piecework – that often seemed more of a continuity than a change. In all phases of industrialization, as had previously also been the case, most women adapted their paid work to the demands of the family and not vice versa.

Old and new ways of making an income coexisted. Women worked underground in British, German, French and Belgian mines, usually wearing trousers and stripped to the waist. Émile Zola's novel *Germinal* (1885), Camille Lemonnier's *Happe-Chair* (1886) and the early paintings of Vincent van Gogh denounce their working conditions. Of all women workers, the miners were often the most self-confident, and despite the public outrage about their exploitation and supposed immorality – which in many countries led to the prohibition of this type of female employment – women continued to work in mines until well into the twentieth century. Generally, however, mining work had become a man's job. The wife took care of the household and, wherever possible, a vegetable garden to supplement the husband's income. In the early nineteenth century the governess – in addition to the 'factory girl' – became a symbol of the employed single woman. Usually poorly paid, this occupation was, for middle-class women, almost the only alternative to needlework. Governesses circulated internationally. The 'French *mamselles*', often Huguenot or Swiss women from Neuchâtel, were very popular (sometimes notoriously so) in Germany, and German governesses worked in Britain or Russia or even Latin America. Some agreed with Charlotte Brontë, author of *Jane Eyre* (1847), that 'a private governess has no existence, is not considered as a living and rational being except as connected with the wearisome duties she has to fulfil', but her famous novel helped to revise this image.[28] Julie Daubié was a governess who went on to become the first French woman to obtain the *baccalauréat* and the *license en lettres* (in 1861 and 1871, respectively). Her treatise *La femme pauvre au XIXe siècle* (1866) received honours from the Academy of Lyon. Beyond the turn of the century, the most common and rapidly expanding women's occupation throughout had meanwhile become domestic service, either as daily help or living-in servants. Over the nineteenth century domestic service came to be feminized, and for young women migrating to the city it was a transition from rural to urban life that often ended in the factory, with its more regulated working hours and wages. Even though in Britain craftsmen and skilled workers, too, and in Germany modest civil servants as well, hired maids, having domestic servants became a status symbol, a result of the rising standard of living of the middle class. For many women, prostitution offered a way out of destitution (Welcker had suggested their services especially to migrating men). Julie Daubié attacked the promotion and spread of prostitution and Marion Reid used prostitution to demonstrate the instability of pathetic images of women. Prostitutes were forced, she argued, to 'leave their only proper sphere, and work for their subsistence – to starvation'.[29]

The reason for the availability and mobility of female – and male – labour power in the process of industrialization was twofold: the preceding and continuing agrarian and demographic revolution. In Britain agricultural productivity had been growing since the eighteenth century, for example, through the replacement of the sickle, which women also used, by the male scythe, and many workers migrated from agriculture to manufacture. For centuries western European women did not marry until they were twenty-five or older, and a large proportion remained single, since marriage was postponed until a stable household could be set up. In Britain the average age at marriage had been dropping since the late eighteenth century, as had the proportion of those women who remained single – 'marriage had never been so popular' – and consequently, the birth rate rose. In the lower classes, the frequent common law marriages contributed to this trend. Among France's poor, concubinage (living together without being married) was common. Julie Daubié condemned men's irresponsibility towards their children and the children's mothers as a result of concubinage, as well as the ban on paternity suits. She believed that families were more stable in Britain and Germany. Yet in many parts of Germany, local citizenship was a pre-requisite for getting married (the local communities thus protected themselves from the costs of caring for the poor). This is why, here too, unmarried cohabitation was widespread among the lower classes; when the restrictions were lifted around mid-century, a veritable 'marriage surge' ensued.[30] Outside Britain the average marriage age for women remained as high as previously and the population explosion was – as was the case in Britain too – mainly a result of the decline in infant and child mortality (though this was not true in France and Ireland). People certainly married for reasons of affection, but mostly because they hoped for a tolerable future which could be better mastered as a twosome than alone. In the early industrialization period, men and particularly fathers of families could hardly survive on their income alone; the meagre income of the women, whether wives or daughters, was absolutely essential. Low wages for men seem to have more greatly affected the extent of employment for women (by increasing it) than attractive wages for women.[31] The married couple once again became – or remained – a working couple, but this time it was in an expanding economy and with increasing income for men across all class lines.

The later phase of industrialization was characterized by a different kind of married and working couple and was expressed in the political economy of the family wage. This was no longer the family earnings to which all family members contributed according to their individual abilities and which, if they all worked for the same company, was usually paid to the father. It was a new version, one that would also mark economic, political and cultural gender relations in the twentieth century: the income of the father was not only to be higher than a women's wage but it was to be sufficient to support the entire family. The new family wage (also called 'social wage' in Germany) was propagated by economists, politicians, Catholics, trade unions and the workers, especially for those male employment groups in which it was as yet more of an ideal than a reality due to the very slow rise in wages. The 'non-working' wives and homemakers, whose work was to serve the family, were supposed to manage the man's income thriftily in order to help raise the level of consumption and, especially with the development of a mass consumer culture, to guarantee a standard of living that rose along with the rise in male demands for domestic care and comfort and demands on child-rearing. Thus working-class men were supposed to be kept out of their pub culture and their drinking habit, which often led them to harass and beat their wives (these being in Germany the most common grounds for divorce). Women and particularly wives increasingly turned into 'consumption workers' in their homes. Originating in the United States, numerous consumer's leagues and associations started emerging in Europe in which women became involved. They defined the work of the modern woman as 'the systematic organization of consumption' and saw their power in their 'purchasing power', or 'basket power' as it was called by the Women's Guild Cooperative, while Anna Lampérière and Augusta Moll-Weiss in France called it *pouvoir d'achat* around 1910.[32] Not only production but consumption was also perceived as a process in which value was created.

Even if statisticians and many others overlooked female housework, it was by no means invisible. Lorenz von Stein, in his 1874 work *Die Frau auf dem Gebiete der Nationalökonomie* (Woman in the Field of Political Economy), praised the 'labour of love' that the wife did for her husband, who could only devote himself to his own 'enthusiastic work' through her. According to von Stein, she cared for 'consumption', which was 'woman's work': 'Cooking is first and foremost calculating; secondly it is calculating, and thirdly it is calculating,' and one must 'be either very wealthy or very poor in order not to understand that'. The woman was in charge of 'creating the order of time and space in his house'; when he returned home 'her soft hand wipes my brow', and now 'work has no right to me any longer'. Housework, which von Stein assumed encompassed twenty-four hours a day, was the 'value of all values', which was incalculable and invaluable, but otherwise, from an economics perspective, 'in ten years it would amount to hundreds of millions added to our wealth, if the woman of the house is a housewife in an economical sense. . . . Are you smiling?' Gustav Schmoller, author of a work on political economy (*Allgemeine Volkswirtschaftslehre*, 1900) and the teacher of some feminist political economists, did not smile at all when he wrote that the woman 'administers in the kitchen, basement and closets, she cleans and mends, restores order throughout the house, wages a small battle against dust and decay and ensures that all the property, all the tools, all furniture last much, much longer; with the same income, she can accomplish double if she distributes her budget correctly, if she shops with knowledge of the merchandise and of people'. The 'health and lives of all family members depend' on her. 'What makes the work that is presently done in the family economical and good? That it is done with love for husband and child and for most personal interests; that it is not paid and recorded, that it is not calculated.' This was still known much later when John Kenneth Galbraith emphasized in *Economics and the Public Purpose* (1973) the crucial role played by women with respect to consumption. 'The conversion of women into a crypto-servant class was an economic accomplishment of the first importance.' Women were now 'available, democratically, to almost the entire present male population'.

In the late nineteenth century, and also much later, it was by no means only men who recommended the coupling of the male family wage and female housework for the lower and middle classes. Especially in view of the rising standard of living, many women also saw this ideal as a liberation from the hardships of early industrialism as expressed by Thomas Hood in 1843 in *The Song of the Shirt*: 'Stitch! stitch! stitch! . . . Work! work! work!' French schoolgirls were recommended to read the poem instead of Rousseau's *Émile*, and it also appeared in the German press. Charlotte Elizabeth Tonna, the publisher of *Christian Ladies Magazine*, protested against such 'deplorable wretchedness', demanding in *The Wrongs of Women* (1844) the right of women to have a household of their own in terms reminiscent of those of Chartist Reginald John Richardson: 'We assert the inalienable right of woman to preside over her own home, and to promote the welfare of her own family; we cry out against the grievous wrong that drags her thence to minister to the coveting selfishness of men who will be rich.'[33] The Austrian Adelheid Popp argued in a similar way in her 1909 autobiography, which went into multiple editions. Even the best of her many employers 'still got rich through the productive work' of his subordinates, and she escaped her own grind in poorly paid jobs through a happy marriage, domestic and maternal tasks and ultimately through her work for the Social Democratic Party. Most workers' wives saw it as the husband's responsibility to bring home the necessary money in exchange for the wife's domestic work. If he could not or would not do that, it could easily come to open matrimonial conflict.

During the later phase of industrialization in Britain, the rate of women's employment, especially that of married women, did actually drop. The women's employment rate (the proportion of employed women among all women able to work) went down from 42 per cent in the period from 1851 to 1871 to 32 per cent from 1881 to 1921. In France, however, the rate rose from 40 per cent in the 1880s to 53 per cent in 1921; in Germany it increased from 38 per cent in 1882 to 49 per cent in 1925. In Russia, women made up one-third of the industrial workforce in 1914, and in the Russian part of Poland women comprised 41 per cent of the industrial workforce in 1885; in Italy around 1900, about half of the industrial workforce were women. In late nineteenth- and early twentieth-century Europe, the share of women in the workforce, except for the Netherlands and Spain, was considerably higher than it was in the United States. However, it would be rash to explain the causes of temporary, long-term or sector-specific declines by saying that women had now finally fallen into the trap of the prevailing image of women, or even that they had become accomplices in their own subjection or were forced from the labour market against their will owing to the gradual implementation of factory legislation (ban on female underground mining work and night work, shortening of the workday, maternity leave). The factory laws, which were usually enacted against resistance from most employers, were regularly ignored by them owing to their interest in cheap labour. The general exclusion of women from industrial work or even from any gainful employment was seriously supported only by Catholics and trade unions. The latter's attack on women as wage-cutters was all the harsher since it targeted precisely women's function for industrialization – their cheap labour. However, the unions succeeded only on isolated points, when they joined forces with employers. When trade unions around the turn of the century gradually took on women's demands for 'equal pay for equal work', it was often with the intention of excluding women since they actually did not receive 'equal' pay. Domestic work, even hard work, alongside a husband with sufficient earnings seemed to many women to be an attractive alternative to the industrial day-and-night shifts, the makeshift economy or even, in Britain, to the work-house, where according to the Poor Law Amendment Act of 1834, women and children were separated from the men and had to work under miser-able conditions. Moreover, many housewives of all social classes were well aware of their value.

Nineteenth-century women were not merely victims of social change. Irrespective of the fact that women had to pay the high price of earning low wages or performing unpaid housework, the real problem was not the lack of work but poverty and dependence. The idealized image of woman, regardless of class, did not correspond to social reality and women had diverse spheres of agency. Material and cultural differences resulted from personal life circumstances, different economic sectors, the chang-ing relationship between poverty and wealth and – for women as well as men – affiliation to the emerging social classes. Nevertheless, similar to the situation in the old estates society, women's lives differed clearly from those of the men in the respective social class and women's own class status was determined by virtue of 'their' men, either fathers or hus-bands, that is, as daughters or wives.

In the later phase of industrialization, as the economic and cultural vision of the male 'breadwinner' and the woman as 'worker of love' (who actually made, bought, prepared and served the 'bread') was increasingly questioned, the ironical German topos of the three Ks, *'Kinder, Küche, Kirche'* (Children, Kitchen, Church), emerged as a summary of the do-mestic model. Schmoller's earnest variant of *'Küche, Keller und Kammer'* (Kitchen, Cellar and Pantry) would soon lose its relevance, since house-holds in the cities rarely had an actual storage cellar. The women's move-ment criticized and internationalized the topos and treated it ironically. It became a symbol of a type of domesticity that non-German feminists saw as particularly widespread in Germany, as Käthe Schirmacher re-ported from what she had heard at the conference of the International Council of Women in London in 1899. Clara Zetkin quoted a news-paper in 1904, according to which the traditionalist German empress (in contrast to her mother-in-law, Empress Friedrich) had suggested 'four Ks': *'Kirche, Kinder, Küche und Kleider'* (Church, Children, Kitchen and Clothing); there was also talk of *'Kinder, Küche, Kaiser'* (Children, Kitchen, Emperor). Henriette Fürth, German Jewish feminist who had studied political economy and – highly unusual at the time – was the mother of eight children, described in 1914 the transformation of woman into a 'house slave' as a product of the nineteenth century. She demanded a change and reassessment of her work, scoffing at 'the trinity of *Kinder, Küche und Konversation*' (Children, Kitchen and Conversation). The same year, American historian Mary Beard dealt with the topos with respect to the United States, where she considered 'women's old spheres, the three Ks', to be long since outdated.[34] Female poverty, dependence – material as well as intellectual – and the three or even seven Ks had come under attack by the international women's movement.

Pre-Pioneers and Pioneers of the Women's Movement

The pre-pioneer stage of the Movement was in some ways more entertaining than the Movement itself.

Ray Strachey, 1928[35]

The women's movement did not emerge as an organized or even mass movement. But many women moved individually or together with other women (and some men). It was possible to cross the border between private and public because of its fluidity, and even those who strove to define the boundary rigidly were not agreed about precisely where it should be set.

In the generation before the formation of lasting feminist associations, a literary and journalistic feminism emerged in many places whose main themes were criticism of marriage and female (as well as male) poverty. George Sand, who like Olympe de Gouges chose her own name, set female passion against conventional marriage in her immensely popular novels *Indiana* (1832) and *Lélia* (1833). In Germany, women's novels flourished in which the protagonist attempted to break out of her role – usually involving the drama of enduring dependence and grief in arranged or convenience marriages – sometimes accepting an early death in exchange. This was the case in *Clementine* and *Jenny* (both 1843), novels by Fanny Lewald, who also vehemently supported the emancipation of the Jews. Johanna Goldschmidt, a Hamburg Jew who had refused to marry a Christian, wrote *Rebekka und Amalia* (1847) in the form of a correspondence with a noble woman. She condemned the 'frivolous activities' of women who did not devote any time to their children. She saw the 'holy mission' of mothers in their responsibility for their children, whom they should help to advance, at worst, like an 'angel with a fiery sword'. For Goldschmidt, 'the shadow side of female life' was primarily affected by the treatment of Jews, whose liberation she demanded.[36] Luise Mühlbach's *Aphra Behn* (1849), about the life of the famous English author of the novel *Oroonoko* (1688), was conceived as the story of breaking out of a hated marriage. Subsequently Behn married Oroonoko, the black king of the slaves, who died on the funeral pyre – at the right time, so to speak – so that Aphra Behn finally belonged only to herself.

In Louise Otto's fourth of over two dozen novels, *Schloß und Fabrik* (Castle and Factory, 1846), the female protagonists represented the conflicting worlds of nobility, capitalists and workers; of wealth and need. Passages that Otto had taken from Karl Marx were censored. A few years earlier Bettina von Arnim had described and denounced the hardship of the poor in *Dies Buch gehört dem König* (This Book Belongs to the King, 1843). At the time, it was praised as 'an event, a deed, that flies far beyond the concept of a book'.[37] In the future, books would continue to be events and shape the consciousness of readers.

Many such works appeared; and large numbers of copies were printed, in the original language as well as in translation. In Britain – as in France – female novelists had long ceased to be a rarity and even earlier they had begun making an issue of women's condition. So many women took up their pen (Jane Austen and the three Brontë sisters are merely the most famous) that writer and literary critic George Henry Lewes said in 1850, with only a trace of irony, that 'it's a melancholy fact, and against all Political Economy, that the group of female authors is becoming every year more multitudinous and more successful. Women write the best novels, the best travels, the best reviews, the best leaders, and the best cookery-books ... – they are ruining our profession. Wherever we carry our skilful pens, we find the place preoccupied by a woman. . . . How many of us can place our prose beside the glowing rhetoric and daring utterance of social wrong in the[ir] learned romances and powerful articles?'[38] Grace Aguilar, the most prominent Anglo-Jewish poet of her time, wrote *The Spirit of Judaism* (1842) and *Woman's Friendship* (1851, German 1857). In *The Vale of Cedars, or The Martyr* (1850, Swedish 1855, German 1860, Spanish 1920), Aguilar told the moving story of love and sorrow of Marie, an apparently Catholic but really Jewish woman in Spain of the early Inquisition. Queen Isabella supported her despite the royal couple's expulsion of the Jews, stating that even though Marie was the 'offspring of a race which every true Catholic must hold in abhorrence, she is yet a *woman*' and 'only a woman can give to woman this perfect sympathy'. In 1855 in Norway, Camilla Collet published her novel *Amtmandens Døttre* about the degradation of women married to men they did not love. In Poland Eliza Orzeszkowa's *Marta* (1873) caused a sensation and became the Polish women's novel of the century. The memoirs of Nadezda Durova, who had joined the Russian army in 1807 disguised as a cavalryman, were published in 1836 originally by Alexander Pushkin; *The Cavalry Maiden* was translated into many languages. In Russia as well as, for example, Hungary, several women wrote in the early nineteenth century in support of reforming gender relations. In Greece, literary feminism was characterized by metaphors such as 'slavery', 'prison', 'cage' and 'harem'. In 1844 twenty-five-year-old Louise Otto, who had just published her first two novels, wrote with respect to Germany what applied to all of Europe: 'a new spirit has come into force among the female sex too. . . . Political poetry has awakened German women'.[39]

The new spirit sought to create space at a social and political level and the European revolutions of 1848 were decisive in this regard. Female Italian patriots took part in the revolts. Fanny Lewald hurried to revolutionary Paris and reported on women workers who presented petitions at the Hôtel de Ville demanding higher wages; her report was also translated into Italian. The committed democrat Louise Otto demanded the full participation of women in the newly developing political life. An anonymous woman from Vienna did not doubt that 'the divine spark of liberty also shines in female hearts', that there was 'no high-minded woman who would not be a bit of George Sand' and she claimed 'equality of political rights. Why should women not be elected to the parliament?'[40] George Sand was a symbol of radicalism because of her male clothing and cigars. Louise Otto, however, clearly dissociated herself from such manners, for which Louise Aston was the representative in Germany; Aston was banished from the country in 1846 by the Prussian authorities. Yet George Sand viewed the issue of political participation differently from the Viennese woman who incorrectly alluded to her. The moving conflict among Parisian republican women highlights not only the options that were open to early feminists internationally but also those of the later women's movements. George Sand wrote and anonymously edited the *Bulletins de la République* of the revolutionary government. Feminist revolutionaries and former Saint-Simonians – who published the journal *La Voix des femmes* – sought to use her authority to advance the cause of women's suffrage. Publicly they suggested George Sand as a candidate for the National Assembly elections, but Sand declined. She had considered the manhood suffrage of 1848 as premature, which the conservative election results and the rise of Louis Bonaparte were to confirm. She declined because she had not been consulted in advance, because she believed the struggle against female (and male) poverty to be more urgent than the political claims of educated women and because she felt *égalité* should not be confused with presuming that the sexes were identical (*identité*) (on this point she was in full agreement with the *La Voix des femmes*). Most of all, however, she felt that women's personal autonomy – through education and rights within marriage – was a prerequisite for the autonomous exercise of the franchise and must therefore take priority. Doing it the other way around was putting the cart before the horse and would be detrimental to the cause of women in public.[41] In keeping with the logic of marital law, women's suffrage as motioned by Deputy Victor Considérant in 1849 (as was also the case with John Stuart Mill's 1867 motion) referred only to unmarried and thus legally independent women. The dividing line between married and unmarried women in nineteenth-century Europe was at least as trenchant as the class barrier.

For many women of the middle and upper classes, however, actions to aid the poor and oppressed, whom George Sand believed should be given priority, became the preliminary step and vehicle for their engagement on behalf of their own sex. Marion Kirkland Reid participated in the 1840 World Anti-Slavery Congress in London, which, although women were not allowed to speak – or rather, precisely for that reason – became a milestone for the women's movement, including the movement in the United States. Reid presented her *Plea for Women* (1843) under the motto 'Can man be free, if woman be a slave?' She compared the situation facing women with that of the black slaves and pointed to the British anti-slavery movement, in which many white women had become involved since the end of the eighteenth century, as inspiration for the struggle for their own rights. She did not explicitly mention black women, but both black and white women were involved in abolitionism in the United States. There, the voice of a former slave could be heard, answering the old question 'What is a woman?' in her own way. Sojourner Truth, moving preacher and courageous advocate of women's suffrage, spoke out against the old male postulate of female weakness at one of the first women's rights conventions, in 1851 in Akron, Ohio. 'I have ploughed, and planted, and gathered into barns, and no man could head me! And ar'n't I a woman? I could work as much and eat as much as a man – when I could get it – and bear de lash as well! And ar'n't I a woman? I have borne thirteen children, and seen 'em mos' all sold off to slavery and when I cried out with my mother's grief, none but Jesus heard me! And ar'n't I a woman?' She directed attention to women who were not only poor but also black, and therefore lived under even more desolate circumstances than the European poor. Most importantly, however, she drew attention to the fact that they were not perceived as women. Against those who viewed her as a 'non-woman' (nor yet a man either) she set an 'and yet a woman'. In Europe, too, it was not unusual to hear similar statements, such as that of French deputy Jules Simon, whose treatise *L'Ouvrière* (1860) placed the 'woman question' at the centre of industrial modernization; he claimed that 'a woman who becomes a worker is no longer a woman'.[42]

Female *caritas*, acts of charity or love for the poor, especially women and children, demanded great personal strength that collided with the image of female weakness and restraint and which was a point of departure of the women's movement all over Europe. In 1813 in Britain, the Quaker Elizabeth Fry began visiting female prisoners in jail. To this end she founded the Newgate Association in 1817, and in 1836 the British

Ladies' Society at a national level. She became a key figure in prison reform, in Britain and internationally, and her writings were translated into many languages. She demanded separate spaces for male and female prisoners, and female guards to care for the latter. Fry and many others very quickly discovered the limitations which opposed their efforts with what a contemporary called 'masculine officialism'.[43] Female philanthropists sought entry into the British poorhouses to devote their energies to the women and children there. Louisa Twining, secretary of the Workhouse Visiting Society, founded in 1858, would soon also speak out in favour of women's suffrage. An impressive network of charitable women's organizations was starting to cover Britain – schools, children's food programmes, job referrals, care for incarcerated and released prisoners, for mothers, prostitutes and impoverished girls. The energy of these women also impressed many on the continent, including Helene Lange, who, after having travelled through Britain, clearly distinguished between British 'ladies' and German *'Damen'*. In the course of the century organized poor relief in Britain became largely feminized, partly despite resistance from men and partly with their support. Roughly 800,000 women in 1893 viewed this kind of work as their profession, or rather their calling, since such work, which required not only a great deal of energy but also financial resources, was considered an honorary civil office and not a paid profession. The women broadened their horizons, travelled, raised funds, learned about institutions, administration and politics, gained self-esteem and independence and often became painfully aware of their own lack of a grounded education. Lower-class women were not always pleased with the assistance, especially since it could hardly guarantee any lasting improvement in their situation, but also because of the cultural rift between the benefactors and the beneficiaries. Feminists – in Britain as well as on the continent – tried all the more to develop new strategies which would question the limitations of their own class status and replace 'benevolence' with 'social work'.

Concepción Arenal was a radical liberal jurist who was also dedicated to prison reform, and she too became known internationally. Her manifold commitments aimed to reform society at large, both morally and socially, and her voice was one of the first in Spain to speak out for women's liberation. Joséphine Mallet and Madame d'Abbadie d'Arrast worked for prison and other social reforms in France around the mid-nineteenth century. Laura Solera Mantegazza established an infant crèche in 1850 in Milan that served as a model for many others, and in 1862 she started a self-help organization for women workers and the first women's trade school. In the Prussian part of Poland the first women's club was started in 1831 to do welfare work. In numerous countries the 1832 cholera epidemic moved many women to become involved in welfare work and in France it had particular significance in raising the consciousness of Saint-Simonian women. At the time of the wars of liberation in Germany, women's clubs emerged to help the wounded, and later cholera patients; during the Polish uprising in the 1830s Polish wounded were cared for. In the *Vormärz*, the period leading up to the March Revolution of 1848, women went to battle against pauperism and supported political refugees after the 1848 revolution. Some founded industrial schools to provide training for gainful employment, or maternity clubs. The kindergarten movement based on Friedrich Fröbel's education methods combined innovative child-rearing with a new perception of women's tasks in social and political life. In Germany, Jewish women especially were leaders in this area (as well as in Italy, Britain and the United States). Johanna Goldschmidt of Hamburg established a non-denominational women's club in the 1840s that propagated Fröbel's ideas. Henriette Goldschmidt of Leipzig opened various kindergartens for lower-class children from 1872 on, so that mothers could more easily take on paid employment, as well as the Association for Family and People's Education (Verein für Familien- und Volkserziehung). Lina Morgenstern of Berlin founded soup kitchens (as did Helene Mercier in Holland), Jeannette Schwerin started the Girls' and Women's Groups for Social Assistance (Mädchen- und Frauengruppen für soziale Hilfstätigkeit) in 1893, for which Alice Salomon later provided a professional foundation. And Bertha Pappenheim created the Women's Care Club (Verein Weibliche Fürsorge) in 1902. In the Netherlands, Betsy Park founded the first women's club in 1872; its goal was to develop sewing into a source of income for women. In Norway women's missions and temperance clubs emerged in mid-century, and also in Finland – as in the United States – the revivalist and temperance movements played an important role in paving the way for the women's movement. Agitation by the international temperance movement (which in Germany and Italy, however, were not dominated by women) against male alcohol consumption was not least a protest against sexual harassment and violence against women.

The 'maternal' or 'female mission' emerged also – sometimes primarily – within a religious context. Catherine Booth, 'mother of the Salvation Army', was one of the most influential British women of the nineteenth century; men and women were admitted equally to this 'army'. In Britain, female philanthropy was based on a Christian-inspired faith in love's ability to transform society. Jewish philanthropists grounded their work on their faith (one of the prayers Bertha Pappenheim wrote was a 'Prayer of a Chairman before a Meeting'). Religion could but did not necessarily stand in the way of women's growing self-awareness, at least not when it was mobilized precisely to demonstrate the meaning and value of social intervention by women. Religiousness was attributed to women to a far greater degree than to men; within the context of social 'labours of love', religion was feminized in many countries. There was no denomination in which women did not mobilize in this sense, whether within the scope of conventional churches, the new revivalist movements or the non-conformists and Dissenters. Anglican and Protestant deaconesses started appearing in the 1830s in Germany and Britain. They were often accused of borrowing from the virginal ideal of the Catholics. Amalie Sieveking created the Women's Union for Poor and Sick Relief (Weiblichen Verein für Armen- und Krankenpflege) in 1832 in Hamburg. Originating in the 'Motherhouse' in Kaiserswerth, a women's diaconate was formed which was subject to strict male supervision. But the Bethanien home for deaconesses in Berlin was operated differently. Mariane von Rantzau, of aristocratic heritage, assumed her position in 1847 after she had visited similar homes in Britain, France, Belgium, Switzerland and the German states, and she insisted on 'liberty and independence'; Theodor Fliedner, the founder of Kaiserswerth, criticized this as 'sovereign women's regiment'.[44] After the French Concordat of 1801, the number and size of Catholic women's congregations rose sharply in France as well as in Germany – at first based primarily on the model of the Sœurs de la Charité – especially since the Prussian constitution of 1850 guaranteed the freedom of religious assembly. The consciousness of acting on God's behalf, 'the hand at work, the heart with God', gave their actions combating pauperism particular tenacity. Irrespective of the male clerical hierarchy, they were more autonomous than most deaconesses; Catholic congregationists had the right to elect their Mother Superior. They worked as teachers, cared for the poor and became pioneers of modern nursing. On the initiative of Ellen Ranyard, the Bible Women's movement emerged in Britain in 1857. The members belonged to the working class and visited the very poorest, carrying the Bible into their homes where they would be welcomed as 'a motherly woman, of their own class'. They provided the 'missing link' (in the words of Ranyard) between rich and poor.

In Risorgimento Italy and in France, welfare workers inspired by Catholicism less often found a direct connection to the emerging women's movement, since the front between state and Church also affected social life. On the other hand, the feminism of the French Saint-Simonian women was shaped as much by religion as by criticism of religion. For two other religiously motivated women's groups, the English and the German Dissenters, the interface between religious reform and women's movement had clear contours. The union of religious reform, criticism of religion, democratic ideas and the emancipation of women was a constituting element for the emergence of the German women's movement from 1845 to 1852. Religious Dissenters, including Louise Otto, were at the centre of the feminist associations formed in the 1860s. Quaker and Unitarian women were among those who founded the organized women's movement in Britain in the 1850s and 1860s.

The 'labours of love' were based on the notion of a specifically female mission: that women were called upon to overcome class confrontation and to reform society materially and culturally. Although they often appealed to the assumption that caring for the poor was a traditionally female activity, they also knew that, in view of the profound social changes, tradition alone did not suffice. Julie Daubié in France protested against the 'male monopoly on the most maternal offices of public welfare' and the fact that, except for men, only the perfumed *'dames patronesses'* and Catholic nuns were permitted to perform public care for the poor, but secular women of the middle and lower classes were not. She countered that 'to woman belongs the great mission of regenerating charity: it is she who will reconcile the suffering class and the idle class'. The German women's magazine *Kränzchen* protested in 1849–50 against the 'moralists' who 'wish to see women of all nations only in the practical sphere assigned to them', and demanded that they be admitted 'with greater liberty to social life' and that 'a national guard of poor relief' be formed from among the female population. 'Some degree of breaking out from the house by the woman is imperative, and only woman can form the necessary foundation of political life, a truly civil society. Up to now we have had only family and state.' The *English Women's Journal* declared the goal to be 'not so much a change in practical duties' as a 'change in the public estimate of the value of those duties, so that they may be henceforth accomplished in freedom and under the sanction of better laws'.[45] The freedom they demanded also meant that women wished to assume leadership positions from which they had hitherto been excluded.

The ideas and practice of the American settlement movement greatly influenced the new female social work in Europe, especially turn-of-the-century Germany. This applied in particular to its founder (and later Nobel peace prizewinner) Jane Addams, even though the European – especially the continental – variants did not enjoy the same public recognition and influence on the emerging welfare state as their American counterpart. But in Europe as well, pioneers such as Alice Salomon integrated philanthropy with science, practical approaches with theoretical ones – sociology, political economy and politics – and were supported in their efforts by experts such as Max Weber and Gustav Schmoller. Italian Sibilla Aleramo's statement in 1910 might apply to many countries: 'The most significant figures among female intellectuals are the philanthropists.'[46] On the one hand, the social commitment of the philanthropists was an attempt to contribute to the common good; they drafted an alternative to solving the 'class question' through class struggle and thereby discovered their own intellectuality and subjectivity. On the other hand, the organized women's movement strove for self-development as a solution to the 'woman question' and was certain that 'women's good' (*Frauenwohl*, the name of several German groups) also contributed to the – correctly interpreted – common good.

A Social Movement

One cannot find a formula for women's emancipation, because the idea of emancipation encompasses too much, and is too encroaching, to be defined in a few words.

Cécile Goekoop-de Jong van Been en Donk, 1897[47]

The classical women's movement of the nineteenth and early twentieth centuries was a movement by women (albeit not all women, and also including some men) and for women. They sought fundamental change in gender relations by improving women's condition from economic, social, political and cultural perspectives, both in comparison with their traditional situation and in comparison with and relation to men. Their goal was not to switch gender roles or make them the same but liberation from subordination by virtue of their sex. The women's movement stressed not individualism in the sense of an *individu absolu* but individuality as self-development, the search for their own subjectivity and independence or – as it was often called – autonomy. Their model was not the life of men, even less so since most men did not lead autonomous lives. Instead, they wished freely to develop their own strengths and eliminate barriers erected by tradition and law. The women's movement was a social movement because it intervened in the 'social question' of pauperism, understood the 'woman question' also as a social question and, like other social movements of the time, adopted the form of a 'movement'. In the second half of the nineteenth century the old *querelle des sexes* was taken up by an organized and growing movement that attempted to resolve it. This was a historical innovation. Yet even though this movement sought fundamental change and was inspired by the revolutions since 1776 and 1789, first of all in its hopes that change could indeed be implemented, it was not, and did not claim to be, revolutionary. For one thing, women lacked the power needed for a revolution in their own interest precisely because of their gender-based situation; and second, from the age of revolution they had learned that while revolution could open up new spheres of action for them temporarily, it could not guarantee lasting improvement or equality. Often just the opposite was the case. Not only the great French Revolution but also the 1848 revolutions in France, Austria and many German states ended with a ban on women's participation in political associations. As Jenny d'Héricourt put it in her statement to Proudhon in 1860, 'The woman is like the people; she does not want to hear any more of your revolutions. She wants liberty and equality for all women and men, or she will see to it that no one shall have it.'[48]

The women's movement did not emerge solely – or even primarily – as a totally degraded sex breaking out of its 'prison-house of home'. Instead it appeared in the wake of the 'widening sphere' which women claimed in the nineteenth century and which they conquered, often laboriously and step by step. Elise van Calcar of the Netherlands described the process in 1884: 'The definition of the term *womanly* broadens every day, and when society hesitates to give us what it is our right to have, our women associate and establish for themselves organizations similar to those from which they are excluded.'[49] The movement was carried by escalating claims and the growing awareness of a 'relative deprivation', whether in comparison with contemporary men or with women of past times. Some believed the women of the past used to have smaller spheres of action; others tended to view the past through rose-coloured glasses. Diverse historical constructions were used to grant legitimacy to the aspirations of the women's movement. John Stuart and Harriet Taylor Mill, and many others, conjured up a perpetual and unbroken male despotism that the forward-looking and enlightened modernity would finally do away with. Conversely, American feminist and historian Mary Beard saw *woman as a force in history* (which was the title of her 1946 book) from time immemorial. Friedrich Engels, on the other hand, and some early historians of women's history viewed the nineteenth century as a low point after a long descent from the good old days – whether primeval matriarchy, the Middle Ages or early modern times – from the golden age to the golden cage, from which the women's movement was expected to rise like a phoenix out of the ashes. The *Journal des femmes* criticized in 1838 that 'women are more deprived of all rights than under the *ancien régime*'. In Germany Gertrud Bäumer and Lily Braun pointed to industrialization, which, on the one hand, brought women workers unbearable living conditions and, on the other hand, let the older 'homemaking skills decline in value' through the 'advancing socialization of life'. While women were offered no economic or intellectual compensation for the loss, it raised their expectations to have a share in the progress.[50] Not only today but also at that time women's history was investigated and often served as a 'usable past'; and most of the views on tradition and innovation of gender relations over centuries have remained both current and controversial. In any case, nineteenth-century public communication – which advanced rapidly through the development of print media – made it possible for women to present their grievances to themselves, to other women and to men, comparable to the *doléances* that were raised at the beginning of the French Revolution and had inspired high expectations.

Women's grievances were varied and a common denominator could not always be found. Accordingly, the women's movement was by no means homogeneous. As with other social movements, there was often disagreement with respect to priorities, programmes, alliances and adversaries, friendships and animosities, styles and strategies, colliding or complementary loyalties with other groups with which the women were involved and which were dominated by men. Jewish women, such as Fanny Lewald or the Jewish Women's League (Jüdischer Frauenbund) that Bertha Pappenheim founded in 1904, compared women's emancipation with emancipation of the Jews, and sought to combine the two. Around the turn of the century Catholic women's organizations appeared in France, Italy and Germany. They integrated some of the feminist efforts – usually in heated debate with the men of their denomination – and led to divisions in the movement. Whereas Protestants in Anglo-American countries, especially the Dissenters, supported women's efforts, German Protestantism served as a conservative braking mechanism, including the League of Protestant Women established in 1899. All the women's movements acted and reacted within their respective national contexts, especially when democratization was on the national agenda and with regard to legal status and political participation, as well as colonialism and imperialism. The latter enabled a number of women of all social strata – at one time Spanish, in the nineteenth century especially British, and since the turn of the century German – to expand their religious or secular sphere of activity or even to lead an independent life beyond the borders of Europe. Some worked to improve the situation of indigenous women; others participated in their subjection. Wherever slavery existed, there were some women among the slaveholders. Some feminists, too, used a condescending vocabulary according to which indigenous women were seen as backward and needing to be 'raised' to the status of European civilization. The British women's movement was not in agreement with respect to Irish Home Rule. Irish women, in turn, were divided between the priority of national and women's liberation, while the Austrian, Czech and Hungarian women's movements were also closely tied to issues of nationality in the Hapsburg monarchy.

The question of priority, competition or parallelism of women's and men's liberation manifested itself especially, and with clear national differences, in the relationship between the women's and the workers' movements. In the revolutions of 1848–9 the two movements seemed, if only for a short time, to merge in the utopia of universal human liberation. Most Italian feminists were still in close contact with Italian socialism around 1900. In Russia, women's efforts to achieve personal autonomy came together with the elimination of serfdom and the Great Reforms under Alexander II, who wanted to retain the autocratic system yet in a more modern form, thus opening Russia towards the west. But the connection between the women's and the workers' movements dissolved as the latter gained strength. The stronger or more revolutionary it became – this was the case especially in Germany – the more it dissociated itself from the women's movement, which it referred to towards the end of the nineteenth century as *bürgerlich*, or bourgeois. And French socialists, too, spoke of *féminisme bourgeois*. Consequently, most women's movements felt more drawn to liberalism, although they insisted everywhere on their non-partisanship and did so to the same degree that they grasped the woman question as one cutting across class lines. When in the 1890s a socialist women's movement emerged, Clara Zetkin stressed that it was 'not at all a women's movement but a socialist workers' movement', since it fought for the proletariat and not for 'bourgeois' women. According to Zetkin these women were part of the class enemy and were, as she argued using a biblical reference, 'bone of the bones and flesh of the flesh of the propertied class'; hence, the 'woman question' was a 'secondary matter'. August Bebel, however, who had written the internationally influential *Die Frau und der Sozialismus* (1879; English: *Women under Socialism*, 1883) did not share Zetkin's view. And Zetkin's remarks did not prevent Helene Lange and Gertrud Bäumer from declaring in 1901 that in addition to the movement of women workers (which was not always socialist), the socialist women were also part of the women's movement. When in 1899 German Jewish social reformer Alice Salomon spoke in English at the International Council of Women in London on the women's movement in Germany, she resolved the ambivalence of the German word *bürgerlich* (which refers to citizenship as well as bourgeoisie) in the spirit of the women's movement. She spoke neither of the 'middle class' nor the 'bourgeoisie' but of the 'civic women's movement'.[51]

The women's movements needed to expend a considerable amount of energy to overcome divisions and diverging loyalties. These resulted from the simple fact that women were not an isolated group but were (and are) present within all social groups. Hence an organized 'movement' – at a national level, but especially also at a local level – was necessary in order to formulate the common interests of the female sex and raise women's awareness of them. Sometimes the diverse currents were closer to each other than public polemics on colliding loyalties made it seem. In large parts of Europe the lasting, organized women's movement emerged in the 1860s when political life became liberalized in many places; the national movements influenced each other from the very beginning. British women organized around the *English Women's Journal*, established in 1858. In Germany the Allgemeiner Deutscher Frauenverein (General German Women's Association) was formed in 1865; at the inaugural meeting (which August Bebel attended) it had yet to be decided if men would be allowed to join, but then the women did decide to focus on 'self-help'. Over the next fifty years the association, primarily under the leadership of Louise Otto, together with the Women Teachers' Union initiated by Helene Lange, made up the core of the German women's movement. The Lette-Verein ('for the advancement of the female sex') was founded in 1866, modelled after the influential London Society for Promoting the Employment of Women. The aim of the Lette-Verein was to promote training and employment opportunities for women of the middle and lower classes; it also included men. Its leadership was quickly transferred to Anna Schepeler-Lette, daughter of the founder. The Jewish feminist Jenny Hirsch, who managed the Lette-Verein's headquarters, translated Mill's *The Subjection of Women* into German in 1869, shortly after it appeared in English.

The Association pour le droit des femmes (Association for Women's Rights) followed in 1870 in France, presided over by Maria Deraismes and Léon Richer. The association's charter made references to associations in the United States, Britain, Germany, Italy, Holland and Switzerland; it proclaimed for women 'equality in dissimilarity', 'equality in diversity' and 'equality in morality'. In the Netherlands the Vrije Vrouwenvereeniging (Free Women's Union) was established in 1889. In Italy, many women were involved in the 1860s in the struggle for national unification; in the 1880s a number of women's leagues emerged, including the umbrella organization Unione femminile (as of 1905 the word 'nazionale' was added). In Spain too the *Sexenio democratico* (1868–74) expressed uncommon opinions on the woman question, and around the turn of the century the Asociación para la enseñanza de la mujer (Association for Women's Education) was founded. New projects followed starting around 1910, especially through connections to Catholic social reform and Basque and Catalonian national movements. The 1880s were decisive in northern Europe. The Kvindesamfund in Denmark, the Norwegian Union for Women's Rights in 1884, the Fredrika Bremer League in Sweden and the Finnish Women's League came into being. Between 1892 and 1918 feminist associations joined forces in national umbrella organizations, usually following the model of the National Council of Women launched in 1888 in the United States. National organizations were formed in the following countries, in chronological order: Finland, Germany, Britain, Sweden, the Netherlands, Denmark, Switzerland, France, Austria, Italy, Hungary, Norway, Belgium, Russia, Bulgaria, Greece, Serbia, Portugal, Spain. These umbrella organizations then usually joined the International Council of Women, also founded in

1888 in the United States. (In 1868 Marie Goegg of Geneva had attempted to create such an organization, but it quickly failed.) Since the turn of the century, Jewish women, especially in the United States, Britain and Germany, collaborated beyond national borders with each other and the international organizations. Shortly after World War I the World Council of Jewish Women was formed, and women from seventy countries attended its first conference in 1923 in Vienna.

Irrespective of some national differences between these movements (they included many women who were not official members of associations), they dealt with three core issues that were closely related to previous and continuing commitment for social and moral reforms. The first was the centuries-old question of women's education, whether higher or elementary level (in Italy, Spain and Portugal an important problem was female illiteracy, which was not only higher than the respective male rate but also far higher than the female illiteracy rate in the rest of Europe); second, the creation and expansion of employment opportunities and increased wages for women; and third, reform of civil law with respect to relations between wife and husband, including married women's right to earn income and own property, and between mothers and their children. Whereas in the nineteenth century lower-class women were equal to men as regards political rights – that is, both were excluded – with respect to civil rights virtually all wives were treated as equals with children, servants and the mentally handicapped. Even before the turn of the century two further issues emerged, initially in Britain: first, the issue of sexuality or 'moral purity' – this was the sexual double standard that required women to be chaste and monogamous, while granting men sexual freedom – and thus also the state regulation of prostitution; and second, the question of political participation.

Education, employment and civil code reform were issues everywhere at the time the organizations were being formed. The public outcry of Caroline Norton in Britain, whose husband had taken her three sons away from her, caught the public attention and led to a modest reform of custody law in 1839. In 1878 Harriet Martineau saw this as 'the first blow struck at the oppression of English legislation in relation to women'. But maternal authority was only hesitatingly – in 1873, 1886 and ultimately in 1925 – set on a par with paternal authority. Organized pressure by British women was also necessary to introduce civil divorce in 1857. The petition to the House of Commons had been signed by 26,000 people, including the writer George Eliot. A series of half-hearted laws followed, until finally in 1882 married women were granted the right to property and income. Some friction had arisen earlier, when John Stuart Mill insisted – against the majority of organized women – that suffrage should be given higher priority than legal and moral equality of husband

and wife; and also when for reasons of respectability the suffragists avoided the major campaign initiated by Josephine Butler in the 1870s. Butler opposed the newly passed prostitution laws (which punished the prostitutes and threatened other women as well, but not the male clients). It was a sensation when she made a public issue of male and female sexuality. It was the first genuine mass campaign of the European women's movement; 250,000 people gathered in 1885 in Hyde Park for a morality demonstration to combat 'vice' and speak out for 'purity'. In 1875 Butler launched the International Abolitionist Federation (for the purpose of abolishing the state regulation of 'vice'). Bertha Pappenheim also dedicated her life to fighting the 'white slave trade', the big business of prostitution, extending far beyond the borders of Europe and blossoming in the wake of major waves of international migration. Among the victims – since the Jewish exodus from Russia starting in the 1880s – there were also many Jewish women. Ersilia Majno established the Asilo Mariuccia in 1902 in Milan, which took in young prostitutes and was part of the Italian committee against the 'white slave trade'.

Efforts in France focused on abolishing *autorité paternelle*, *autorité maritale*, and allowing paternity suits; other issues were schools for girls, women's wages and admission to the professions. The right to divorce was considered the first step on the way to women's citizenship. Adolphe Crémieux, Minister of Justice in the Second Republic and a pioneer for the emancipation of the Jews, had petitioned to no avail in 1848 for a divorce law; divorce was not permitted until 1884. Married women were not allowed to dispose of their own income until 1907. After German unification in 1871, a national civil code was drafted (which would then take effect in 1900). All wings of the women's movement had been active since 1877 against 'paternal authority' and the mandatory obedience of the wife towards the husband, but their success was minimal. Marianne Weber, wife of sociologist Max Weber, demanded further reforms in her (still) classic work of 1907 *Ehefrau und Mutter in der Rechtsentwicklung* (Wife and Mother in the History of Law). The stipulation under which a woman was not permitted to take up employment if her husband objected was not abolished until 1957. And it was not until the early twentieth century that the German women's struggle for education led to serious reforms in public education of girls and the admission of female teachers to girls' high schools. To this end Helene Lange's *Gelbe Broschüre* (Yellow Brochure, 1887) was very influential, with its ironic attack on the widespread notion that educating women served only to keep the husbands from getting bored. In Germany education was the key catchword of the upper middle class, but women were not regularly admitted to universities until between 1900 and 1913, later than in other countries (the liberal southwestern states were the first to do so, and Prussia was a late-comer). In Italy, where women were not officially prohibited from attending universities, 'istruzione e educazione' and the elimination of *autorizzazione maritale* were the main issues of the women's movement after national unification. The debate on the woman question in the Netherlands emerged in the 1860s as a struggle for changes in marriage law and the right to education. Aletta Jacobs, who was soon to take on a leading role in the Dutch and international suffrage movements, joined the women's movement in answer to the difficulties women faced in studying at the university level (in her case, medicine). Since 1870 Geesje Feddes, and later the Free Women's Union, fought for reforms in family law. In Spain the debate subsequent to Concepción Arenal's claim for education as a social right and key to social reform was supported especially by republican women in Catalonia, Andalusia and Madrid, as well as by men in the *Krausismo* education movement. Other important issues were employment and the civil code. Similar priorities were set by women's rights associations in Norway and Sweden, while in Finland education was considered the 'road to work and equality'.[52] Irrespective of Poland's special political situation – foreign rule and struggle for national liberation – the same subjects were on the agenda when women started organizing there in the 1880s, namely, family law and education (owing to political oppression, schools were operated underground). In Russia, too, the women's movement began in the 1860s with great debates on female education; similarly, the women's movement got started in Hungary in 1867 by focusing on education and social work. In Greece, schooling for girls was a major subject and there – as everywhere – female teachers were among the major protagonists of the movement.

Demands were expressed and proclaimed in various ways, whether to women or to men, in local clubs, in public or closed meetings, in exhibitions or national and international conferences. Since the first international conference was held in 1878 in Paris, such conferences took place in rapid succession, and since the 1892 conference in Paris they occasionally referred to themselves as 'feminist'. At times they also worked in cooperation with well-meaning male politicians (in France, for instance). They sent petitions to local administrations and governments (the most signatures were gathered in Britain) and, where possible, appealed to queens as representatives of the female sex. Numerous regional, national and international networks and friendships evolved which were supported through travel, whether for the purpose of public speaking or to expand their horizons.

The priority of education, employment and marriage reform, coupled with actions to combat female poverty, indicate essential characteristics of the classical women's movement. First, the issue was economic, intellectual and moral autonomy and self-assertion, for their own sake.

Second, such independence was viewed early on, and then with increasing frequency, as a prerequisite for political participation. This corresponded to nineteenth-century political thought – from liberal conservatives to radical liberals, from Immanuel Kant to John Stuart Mill – which tied suffrage to independence. Wherever the suffrage issue was raised, whether early or later, the demand was derived not from the need of a few privileged, property-owning or tax-paying women (although 'no taxation without representation' was also a popular slogan) but from the decades-long commitment of women for a 'femminismo pratico' or 'femminismo sociale' – as it was called in Italy – and the bitter recognition that reforms that demanded legislative intervention failed because of the male legislators' lack of insight.

Third, where the women's movements raised legal issues, they were about the moral, political and cultural dimensions of gender relations. John Stuart and Harriet Mill's radicalness went much further than the ideas of most women, but the women's movement nevertheless agreed in one point with the Mills' thesis in *The Subjection of Women*: marriage was 'the most fundamental of the social relations', it was asserted, and that was why it had to be a relationship of individuals who were free and equal. The women's movement questioned not marriage and the family, but the marital subordination, restrictions and obligatory obedience of the wife. This was one of the connotations of the metaphor of breaking out of the 'prison-house of the wife'. According to the entry under 'woman' in the 1830 German encyclopedia *Damen Conversations Lexikon*, 'If a woman is to become a good housewife, she must be free, respected, equal to the man'. Malwida von Meysenbug, who had emigrated to London (and then on to Rome) after the failure of the German 1848 revolution, theorized that democratic marriage was the foundation of democracy in society at large. Léon Richer argued along similar lines in 1877 in *La Femme libre* ('It is an inevitable fact that tyranny in the family gives birth to tyranny in the state'), and in 1868 Maria Deraismes claimed in *Eve dans l'humanité* that the inequality of the sexes disrupted the harmony of the family; under such conditions 'the family, which should be the best school for consciences, starts out by warping them because it depicts the perpetual violation of rights as legitimate' and 'the theory of the double standard gets taught in a setting where good morals and justice in relationships should instead be the law'. This vision of female independence, not only outwardly but especially within the marriage, was a break with age-old traditions and was thus more radical and – especially for the everyday lives of women of all social classes – more important than the lifestyle of 'free love' and extramarital motherhood, which was often proclaimed starting around 1900 – in Germany by Helene Stöcker and the mixed-sex League for Maternity Protection (Bund für

Mutterschutz); in France by Nelly Roussell; and in Britain by Marie Stopes. The provocative power of this minority position resulted, most of all, from the fact that efforts to democratize marriage – that is, independence not only *from* but *in* marriage – had so little success and did not lead to a broad-based cultural transformation of marital relations. Yet a considerable number of women preferred 'single' life to marriage or 'free love', often within their kinship or a family of choice, with adoptive children or in a long-term relationship with another woman. Correspondingly clear was feminist criticism of marriage. Its flip side was an almost utopian vision of a 'happy marriage', that is, one with liberty of women.

The classical women's movement opposed the notion that women were merely 'sexual beings'; both sexes were seen as human. It did not sweepingly deny sexual difference but rejected the specific assignments made on that basis, the gender hierarchy and thus the core of misogynistic discourse: female inferiority and male superiority. According to this movement, women did not show less reason than men did. They demanded dignity and freedom for women (and often also for men), regardless of whether or not they were the 'same' or 'different', even from a metahistorical perspective. The women's movement assumed that women had common interests, whether by virtue of their shared inequality (to which the generalization and codification of their legal inequality in the nineteenth century also contributed), their responsibility for the family, their work or their presumed moral qualities. The criticism was aimed not at bearing children and motherhood but at the subordination of mothers *vis-à-vis* the fathers. Feminists firmly opposed domestic drudgery and the squandering of energy, but they did not categorically reject a gender-based division of labour and, in view of the generally poor employment conditions at the time, they could hardly suggest the modern double burden of family and employment as a universal means of liberating women. Among all feminists, only a handful spoke out in favour of sharing childrearing and housework with the husbands or even transferring these tasks to them entirely. However, with the same dedication as today's feminists question the sexual division of labour, the classical women's movement raised the question of sexuality: the elimination of a gender-based double standard, to be replaced by moral equality and thus a moral reform of men. To the same extent, the majority of feminists condemned abortion. They saw it more as giving men free rein for irresponsible conduct than as a solution to women's problems. But around the turn of the century, more and more feminist voices also started demanding contraception.

The women's movement assumed – both realistically and utopistically – that the world of women was not identical to the world of men, even if the two could and should overlap in many ways. For these women, the often-cited complementarity meant equal rights and equal worth.

Neither sun and moon nor pine and vine were the ideal; and neither was making men and women the same. They sought what Catherine Barmby claimed in 1848 to be men's and women's common humanity. 'Woman and man are two in variety and one in equality. Their physical frames are as various as are the stems of the poplar and of the oak, but yet should the sun of equal right be alike shining upon them.' In 1889 Helene Lange took up that image. Instead of the 'angelically clouded ideal of a woman', and of 'oak and ivy', the ideal should be 'the image of sister trees, which together gravitate towards the light'.[53] The women's movement used both old and new forms of the division of labour as an argument for the right and duty of women to overstep domestic boundaries. 'Maternal mission' or 'female cultural influence' also implied criticism of the unbound Prometheus of an increasingly competitive economic and social order. Efforts by the French and also by the international women's movement for *egalité dans la différence* meant equality in liberty. Whether the female sex was faced with limits, and whether these were in fact different from those of men, would remain to be seen until not men but women decided and when women enjoyed full freedom to explore the matter independently. 'Woman' did not exist in the singular but the plural: 'We do not talk about Woman with a capital W. That we leave to our enemies', wrote Millicent Fawcett in Stanton's volume of 1884. Not only the maternal mission but also Margaret Fuller's claim in *Woman in the Nineteenth Century* (1845), 'Let them be sea-captains, if you will', was part of the liberty which feminists strove for. And Fuller's claim spread beyond national borders. In 1874 Hedwig Dohm made reference to it, and Helene Lange cited it at the turn of the century, when women's suffrage had finally made it to the European agenda.

4

From the Social to the Political

The entire women's movement meant suffrage movement to me.
                                        Helene Lange, 1921[1]

The American Theodore Stanton opened his anthology on European women's movements by pointing to suffrage as the *summum bonum* of the age. Yet the articles, covering about twenty countries, hardly did justice to the dictum, since the only country in Europe that had a genuine suffrage movement at that time was Britain. Still rather modest in number, the suffragists were incredibly active, having just taken on the challenge of pushing through women's suffrage in the upcoming Third Reform Act (1884). But most feminists in Britain, and even more so those on the continent, had other priorities in the 1880s; at most they agreed with Theodore Stanton in viewing the British suffragists as a shining example and suffrage as the distant capstone of feminist endeavours. Within hardly a generation, however, the relationship would be reversed. In 1896 Helene Lange had published *Frauenwahlrecht*, one of the first German treatises on women's suffrage, and the most comprehensive, in the international journal *Cosmopolis*. At the 1904 Berlin conference of the International Council of Women she declared that suffrage was not the ultimate goal but the cornerstone and means through which women would gain ground and 'the steady expansion of the scope of their civic duties and rights', and by which to restructure 'gender relations within the social order'. In the course of that generation, suffragism grew into a transnational movement. Additional thrust came in 1893, when New Zealand became the first country to grant political participation to women, albeit only through ('active') voting rights and not full suffrage that included the ('passive') right to stand for election, which was not granted until 1919.

The women's temperance movement in New Zealand had been the major driving force and Frances Willard, suffragist and leader of the women's temperance movement in the United States, commented on this victory by declaring, 'What fine men you must have in New Zealand!'[2] For it was in fact only men who decided on women's suffrage. Consequently, in taking the step from the social to the political, the women's movement had to go beyond earlier and enduring forms of self-help and address not only the female but especially the male public sphere.

National and Transnational Movements

> Authority is male; this sentence is actually self-evident.
> Heinrich von Treitschke, 1897[3]

Suffrage first became the *summum bonum*, or 'la grande affaire du XIXe siècle' (Pierre Rosanvallon), for the male sex. The European path from 'kings to people' (Reinhard Bendix) or to 'male democracy' (Stein Rokkan) went via a parliamentary, constitutional order that gave legitimacy to suffrage by limiting it to certain groups of men. Usually the franchise was granted by virtue of property or taxes, sometimes – as in Britain – on the grounds of an independent household, and more seldom – as in Italy or Portugal – of basic or higher education. The nineteenth century was characterized by the struggle to extend the franchise, which was carried to some extent by the liberals, though mainly by the labour movement. In Britain the route began essentially with the Great Reform Act of 1832; in France with the Great Revolution and again with the July revolution of 1830; in Belgium when the country revolted and declared its independence in 1831; in Norway with the constitution of 1814; in Switzerland with the constitution of 1815; in Germany with the early constitutionalism in most federal states (the first being the Baden constitution of 1818); in Portugal in 1822, Denmark around 1834, the Netherlands in 1848 and in Sweden in 1866. The length of the journey that eventually led to political participation for women – either some or all of them – varied from country to country. In twenty-one European countries women's suffrage was introduced in the early twentieth century, mostly after World War I: from the first-comers Finland (1906) and Norway (1907) to seventeen others between 1915 and 1922 (1920 in the United States), to Spain and Portugal in 1931. France, Italy, Greece and Switzerland were the late-comers (1944, 1945, 1952, 1971, respectively), though all four are usually considered cradles of ancient or modern democracy. Despite such a large chronological divergence the developments of suffragism in the various countries resembled each other, not only with respect to the point in time the aim was achieved in most countries but in three other aspects as well.

First, women everywhere began demanding the franchise at a time when they saw some chance of success, and only at such times; namely, when democratization for men was on the political agenda. Hence, national differences in historical timing were based not so much on differences in the history of the women's movements as on those in the history of men's movements and constitutional developments, as well as the political culture in the respective countries. In Britain the first modern appeal for women's suffrage was the *Appeal of One Half the Human Race, Women, Against the Pretensions of the Other Half, Men,* by Anna Wheeler and William Thompson (1825). This treatise stood in the context of the history leading up to the Reform Act of 1832. When the bill was introduced in the House of Commons, Mary Smith, a loner about whom virtually nothing is known, petitioned for women's suffrage on the grounds of the same property qualifications as for men (since married women could not own property this applied only to unmarried women). A member of parliament took on the matter, and it was the third time that a European parliament had even briefly discussed national suffrage for women. Norway was first, where the Storting had discussed the issue in 1818, and in Portugal suffrage for mothers with six or more children had been proposed in the Cortes in 1820. (In other countries national women's suffrage was not brought up in parliament until much later: 1851 in France; 1867 in Italy; 1877 in Spain; 1884 in Sweden; and 1887 in the Netherlands.) As would continue to be the case for a long time, Mary Smith's courageous proposal served merely as a source of amusement. Hardly any male and very few female Chartists spoke out in favour of women's suffrage; like the English reform movements since 1770, they demanded 'universal' suffrage for 'every man'. Anne Knight and the Female Reform Association of Sheffield protested in 1851 against 'calling that universal which is only half of it', and the Association demanded women's suffrage in a petition to the House of Lords and called for 'all the political, social and moral rights of man'.[4] Prior to the Second Reform Act (1867), which would turn out to be significant not only for Britain but for all of Europe, the recently founded Women's Suffrage Committee submitted a petition in 1865 that 1,500 women had signed within only two weeks. The committee activists, especially Barbara Leigh Smith-Bodichon, Emily Davies and Jessie Boucherett, had already been active for years in projects offering care to the poor and promoting education and employment for women. The petition was introduced in the House of Commons by John Stuart Mill – who had spoken in favour of women's suffrage in his 1865 election campaign – and Henry Fawcett. Mill demanded that unmarried women be granted active (but not yet passive) voting rights under the same conditions as men. Though his motion to replace the word *man* with *person* did not pass, it did receive seventy-three 'ayes'. From this point on suffragism became consolidated, albeit as a minority within the broader women's movement. Millicent Garrett Fawcett soon took over its leadership. Some suffragists, such as Emily Davies, later preferred to dedicate their activism to promoting female education.

In the United States national women's suffrage was demanded publicly for the first time in the summer of 1848. Although the issue was highly disputed at the legendary Seneca Falls Convention, in the end it was included in the Declaration of Sentiments. (This Declaration was modelled after the Declaration of Independence, much like Olympe de Gouges's declaration was modelled after the Declaration of the Rights of Man and Citizen.) The suffrage initiative developed in part out of the abolitionist movement, in the context of which women – against considerable resistance – claimed the right to speak in public; it also evolved from a movement for married women's property rights, which enjoyed some success at this time, in contrast to the situation in Europe. The first suffragist organization and campaign were launched in 1867–8, when suffrage for black men was on the political agenda and women could hope – albeit to no avail – that the 'negro's hour' would also be the 'woman's hour'. In France, Germany and Austria some voices for suffrage were heard before and during the 1848 revolutions. They rang most clear in France; mostly surrounding the journal *La Voix des femmes*, some well-known and some anonymous women – Jeanne Deroin, Dickens translator Eugénie Niboyet and 'artists, workers, writers and teachers' – took up *suffrage universel* (the expression had become common in the 1830s), the great issue of the February revolution and its antecedent period, and demanded full civil, political and social rights. Compared with other countries, this early women's movement in France can be viewed as the most progressive from a political perspective. During the struggle for the Third Republic and the restoration of manhood suffrage, Hubertine Auclert created the Droits des femmes suffrage committee in 1876, and later one called Suffrage des femmes. Through her work and her journal, *La Citoyenne*, she became the most radical, untiring and best-known French suffragist from the 1880s up until World War I. Around the turn of the century, when a majority of feminists began joining her views on suffrage, she was willing to demand, as a first step, suffrage only for unmarried and widowed women, in view of the legal subordination of married women.

In 1840s Germany it was Louise Otto especially who demanded active suffrage for women, under the slogan of her newspaper, *Frauen-Zeitung* (which was as short-lived as its French counterpart due to the repression that began a short time later): 'I recruit women citizens for the realm of freedom' (*Dem Reich der Freiheit werb ich Bürgerinnen*). The issue of manhood suffrage was suddenly raised in March during the German revolution, with hardly any prior debates (as in France or Britain) that women could have joined. Leading up to Bismarck's 'revolution from above', that is, manhood suffrage – first in the North German Confederation (1867) and then in the Reichstag (1871) – there were no public debates on the issue which women could have joined. Thus it was all the more remarkable when Fanny Lewald asserted in 1870 that women's suffrage was reasonable and necessary, but, realistically speaking, that the time was not yet ripe in Germany. After the election of the first national parliament, and making reference to it, Hedwig Dohm, also of Jewish descent, published her bold polemic *Der Jesuitismus im Hausstande* (1873) and *Der Frauen Natur und Recht* (1876, Women's Nature and Women's Rights); it also appeared in Italian (1878) and English (1896). Suffrage seemed to her merely a 'matter of time' – she thought it would take about fifty years – and she called upon women to organize. In contrast to the lone fighter Auclert, Dohm did not attempt to organize and turned, like Emily Davies, to the problem of higher education for women. Moreover, in Germany and some other countries in continental Europe, throughout most of the nineteenth century suffrage had (in the words of one feminist) 'such limited practical value' – the government was not held accountable to the parliament until much later than in the United States and Britain – that most women did not take up the cause until this situation gradually started to change.[5] In Spain some women first demanded political rights in 1854 at the beginning of the *bienio progresista*. Starting in 1861 with the petition of a Lombardian group of *cittadine italiane*, women's claims in united Italy precisely followed the suffrage debates and reforms of the liberal period that pertained to men. Anna Maria Mozzoni demanded at least active, if not also passive, suffrage in 1864, three years after the first Italian parliament had been elected. She continued to be active for this cause, especially with her important petition of 1874, and again after the left took power in 1876, together with other women and philogynist Salvatore Morelli. In Switzerland political demands by and for women were first voiced in the 1860s, during the debates for constitutional reform in German-speaking cantons. They were then firmly articulated in the 1880s by the rebellious aristocrat Meta von Salis and the liberal Vaud philosopher Charles Secrétan. In Norway Gina Krog was the first to make a public issue of women's suffrage, in 1884, in parallel to the male-related liberalization efforts of the 1880s. In Sweden the early demand of 1899 was part of a broad-based movement that then strove in the 1890s to reform male suffrage. In Finland such claims were also voiced around the turn of the century, and in Russia they were raised within the context of the 1905 revolution. Portuguese women petitioned for their enfranchisement directly before and after the republic was declared in 1910.

Hence, women closely followed and carefully observed the secular debates on modern democracy, but they were in a far worse position than reform-seeking men. The reason lay in a second aspect of international common ground, namely, an explicit masculinization of political participation in the nineteenth and early twentieth centuries. Although women had first and foremost been excluded from politics on the basis of long-standing tradition, now their exclusion was expressed explicitly – often as a result of debate – in proportion to how loudly their demands were perceived and heard. Thompson's and Wheeler's appeal of 1825 had targeted the dictum of the influential liberal, utilitarian reformer James Mill, which had been valid throughout the *ancien régime* in Europe, remained valid, and would soon be attacked by his son: 'All those individuals whose interests are indisputably included in those of other individuals' do not require the franchise; among them were women, 'the interest of almost all of whom is involved either in that of their fathers, or in that of their husbands'. It was the concept of vicarious or virtual representation against which the American colonists, who lacked representation in the British parliament, had once rebelled. And in fact in the nineteenth century, male suffrage – whether limited or full – was not about individual citizenship; it was about a citizenship, the principal bearer of which was the male head of the family, just as Portalis had once pronounced. Marriage and family were no less important for the concept of the citizen-man – not to mention his social status – than they were for women's social status (though not her citizenship).

During the constitutional monarchy in France, the assets required for the franchise (initially 300 and later 200 francs) were measured not only on the basis of the male income but that of the entire family (this was later also the practice in Greece); when manhood suffrage was introduced in 1848, the head of the family, including unmarried men as potential family heads, was regarded as a political individual.[6] In Britain, all that Mary Smith's 1832 petition accomplished was that women were now also explicitly excluded from suffrage. The Great Reform Act of 1832 applied only to 'male persons'; the radical reform movements that had started in the 1770s had in any case used the same wording. Masculinity as a prerequisite for enfranchisement was also introduced in the British Municipal Corporations Act of 1835. The central concept in the Reform Acts of 1832, 1867 and 1884 was that of the householder, the male head of the family, who represented not only the women in his family but, in contrast to the situation in France, unmarried sons as well if they lived in his household. (The Prussian Municipal Act of 1853 also included the phrase 'every one who has his own household'.) Demands for 'manhood suffrage' in Britain since mid-century stood either side by side with this concept or opposed it, generalizing the masculinity of the political individual. English was thus the only European language that precisely articulated what was referred to elsewhere as 'universal' (in the Italian parliament in 1881 women's suffrage was called *suffragio univer-salissimo*, in contrast to *suffragio universale*, but this profound irony did not catch on). John Stuart Mill complained of the terms in 1859, finding 'the name of universal suffrage ... misapplied' and manhood suffrage 'silly and insulting' to women. When in 1917 the House of Commons discussed the franchise for all men over the age of twenty, the Speaker emphasized that 'the right that a man has for a vote is that he is a man'.[7]

In 1868 in the United States, the male-specific sense of the 'negro's hour' was underscored when the fourteenth amendment inserted specific reference to the 'male citizen' as eligible to vote into the previously gen-der-neutral wording of the constitution. A similar amendment was made in 1887 to the constitution of the Netherlands. In 1865 the Italian local and provincial election act disenfranchised female tax-payers, who had voted in Tuscany and Lombardy-Veneto under the Hapsburg monarchy. In Austria, too, tax-paying women were stripped in the 1880s of the active provincial voting rights they had enjoyed since 1861. When in Prussia the older social definition of communal citizenship (which re-quired payment of a certain sum) was replaced by the modern political concept, women were excluded. Especially in the German-speaking realm, there emerged the political theory of the state as being of 'male gender', of 'purely male essence' (Wilhelm Heinrich Riehl); historians and politi-cal theorists particularly excelled in such theories. According to the Swiss Johann Caspar Bluntschli (father of the Zurich civil code), the state was 'without a doubt essentially male', and Swiss women were also confronted with the widespread adage 'to the man, the state; to the woman, the family'. Theodor Mommsen's statement, that 'political action is man's duty', was harshly criticized by German women, as was Otto Gierke's vision of 'the historically proven ideal of the male state'. The men of the Frankfurt Parliament still rejected explicitly naming masculinity as a con-dition for suffrage in 1849, since it was 'taken as self-evident', thus op-posing the opinion that the wording had to be more precise in view of 'efforts of recent times for the political emancipation of women'.[8] But when one-quarter of the German states abolished the suffrage limita-tions after 1900, the older, gender-neutral wording was in fact replaced by the requirement of belonging to the 'male gender'. This form of mod-ernization also took place in Austria (1907) and Italy (1912), when man-hood suffrage was instituted, and in 1913 in Portugal. In the 1911 elections to the Portuguese constituent assembly, the physician, suffragist and widowed mother Carolina Beatriz Angelo managed to vote and have it legally recognized by referring to her status as head of a family. After this, however, only (literate) men were permitted to vote.

Thus there was by no means gradual, linear progress in the acceptance of female citizenship. Instead, the controversy between advocates and adversaries intensified. At the same time, however, some countries did indeed report of progress at the level of local and regional suffrage. The social commitment of British women was one reason for their being granted local voting rights in 1869, which were implemented by means of a linguistic rule: 'Whenever words occur which import the masculine gender the same shall be held to include females.' This applied only to active suffrage, not passive, and only to tax-paying women and – due to the institution of coverture – only unmarried women; it was, however, extended to married women in 1894, thus finally eliminating the problem of coverture at this level once and for all. Step by step, all women became eligible for all local offices by 1907, including school boards and Boards of Guardians – a concession that would not be granted German and Italian women, despite all their efforts, until far into the twentieth century. This marked a significant difference between the British women's movement and some of its counterparts on the continent. Women were granted local or other specific, non-political voting rights in Sweden, Russia and Finland (1862, 1864, 1873, respectively), Italy (1890–1911), France (1898–1908), Norway, Denmark, Iceland and Bulgaria (1901, 1908, 1909, 1937, respectively). In the United States, women had received similar functional rights at school and local levels by 1910 in twenty-five states.

On the other hand, the number of men as well as women who organized against suffragism and claimed to speak for the silent majority of women started to grow in the late nineteenth century. From eastern Europe to the western United States, a number of variants of the Polish Pater Kaplanski's claim around 1900 could be heard: 'Under the guise of equal rights women are seeking supremacy over men [almost two thousand years before, Livy had written the same in the 34th book of his *History of Rome*]. If that happens our nations will be faced with a disaster greater than the partition, for if this unhealthy principle spreads among our women, if they seek to rule under the guise of equal rights, their antipathy towards men will increase, and men will lose the respect and adoration they have towards women out of fear of having emancipated wives. Fear will stop them from marrying, childlessness and licentiousness will prevail and male depravation will result in the decline of families, the debasement of society, and loss of the nation. For those reasons the emancipation of women is the mortal enemy of every nation.'[9] The male-dominated German League to Combat Women's Emancipation

(Deutscher Bund zur Bekämpfung der Frauenemanzipation, 1912) modelled itself after the female-dominated National Association Opposed to Woman Suffrage in the United States (1911). Both combined conservative gender ideology with pessimistic spectres of the decline of nation and state and with racist – in Germany and Austria also anti-Semitic – ideologies (Karl Lueger appealed to the Christian women of Austria 'to forgo the suffrage' as long as 'for every Christian woman there are ten Jewesses').[10] In Britain one hundred influential men and women had already signed an anti-suffragist appeal in 1889 – including the social reformer Beatrice Potter (married name: Webb), who, however, soon dissociated herself from it. Yet the main thrust of this appeal was not to restrict women to domesticity and motherhood but to strictly separate the local, social level, where public involvement by women was encouraged, and the national, political level, which was to be retained for men, since statehood was assumed to be based on violence. On that point they agreed with the German historian Heinrich von Treitschke, who argued that 'Government means ordering armed men' and 'armed men do not let themselves be ordered around by a woman.'[11] In Italy there was no organized anti-suffragist movement; in Switzerland there seemed to be more women among the anti-suffragists than elsewhere. Whether organized or not, opponents helped give great symbolic value to national suffrage, define the political sphere and draw a distinct line between the social and the political, a line that feminists were striving to cross.

Yet around this time the symbolic value of suffrage also increased among feminists. This marks the third aspect of the transnational community of suffragism: although the franchise was always viewed within the logic of a national context and symbolized primarily affiliation to the nation, as had already been true during the French Revolution, the national beginnings of suffragism developed into a transnational movement, similar to the path that led to male democracy. The first American women's rights convention (in Worcester, Massachusetts in 1850) inspired John Stuart and Harriet Taylor Mill to publish their first public appeal, in 1851, in the *Westminster Review*. (Sigmund Freud later translated it into German 'out of boredom' during his military service.) As of 1867 there was hardly a women's suffrage initiative in Europe that was not inspired by John Stuart Mill's 1867 speech in the House of Commons, not least because his international fame gave his words greater weight than those spoken by women. Of course anti-suffragists, too, usually made reference to him. In the French debate of the 1860s on the restoration of manhood suffrage Mill's position was often reviewed, such as in the *Revue des Deux Mondes*, and, as regards women, rejected. In Germany, where the General German Women's Association (Allgemeine Deutsche Frauenverein) had initially tabled the question of political rights for more favourable

times, Franz von Holtzendorff, liberal head of the Lette-Verein for vocational training, expressed himself very clearly in late 1867 and 1868
('Women have a right to demand it'), but he found little support among
his co-liberals. He pointed to British events and was encouraged by Jessie
Boucherett, co-founder of the English Women's Suffrage Committee and
the Society for Promoting the Employment of Women, which served as a
model for the Lette-Verein. Starting in 1883 Elizabeth Cady Stanton,
together with other Americans and some British women, pushed for an
international suffrage association. This idea was met with scepticism by
many, but – through the conferences of 1888, 1889 and 1902 – it was
finally founded in Berlin in 1904. From the 1890s suffragism was no
longer driven only by the constitutional, political developments in the
respective countries but also by transnational communication among the
suffragists themselves. The years 1895 to 1914 were the zenith of the
broader women's movement, and suffragist debates and campaigns started
or became revived after a period in the doldrums, after short-lived earlier
beginnings or fruitless conflicts.

In the United States, the founding of the National American Woman
Suffrage Association (NAWSA) in 1890 brought an end to the competition and mutual obstruction of two national organizations, but the campaign at the state level usually led initially to defeat. Not until after the
turn of the century was the subject successfully introduced into the public arena, this time at the national level. NAWSA developed into an efficient, albeit hierarchical, lobby. The General Federation of Women's Clubs
did not finally include suffrage in their platform until 1914 (at this time,
however, 1.8 million women had already received active and passive voting rights for the federal government, since in the United States, in contrast to German and Swiss federalism, the states decided on national
suffrage). In Britain the founding of the National Union of Women's
Suffrage Societies (1897) and later the Women's Social and Political Union (1903) symbolized a new start, after futile attempts and the defeat of
1884 (from 1907, supporters of the Social and Political Union were called
'suffragettes', which had initially been a derogatory diminutive for 'suffragists'). On the European continent, there was heated debate whether
suffrage would be better promoted by the general women's associations
or by newly formed single-issue societies. In the course of the next two
decades, most feminist umbrella organizations that had emerged since
1893 took up the suffrage issue in their platforms. The Federation of
German Women's Associations (Bund Deutscher Frauenvereine), founded
in 1894, did so in 1902; Federation president Marie Stritt had announced
at the conference of the International Council of Women in 1899 in London that the Federation had 'unanimously resolved to take its stand for
the Suffrage' in 1898. Whereas the General Austrian Women's Associa-

tion (Allgemeiner Österreichischer Frauenverband) had promoted suffrage since its inception in 1893, the considerably older General German Women's Association did not officially take up the suffrage issue until 1905. Its president, Helene Lange, was the driving force for suffragism; her treatise *Frauenwahlrecht* had been reprinted numerous times even before the turn of the century. At the next conference of the International Council of Women (in 1904 in Berlin), Lange was one of those responsible for the inclusion of suffrage in the Council's platform. At the same time, the German 'radicals' who had appeared around 1894 took up the issue after initially giving priority to efforts for the reform of marital law. The first two appeals for women's suffrage by German 'radicals' appeared in their journal *Die Frauenbewegung* (The Women's Movement) in 1895 and 1896, and Anita Augspurg followed in 1897. In 1902 she founded the first German organization devoted specifically to suffrage. Single-issue organizations for suffragist activism started appearing all over between 1895 and 1918 and joined the International Women's Suffrage Alliance, which was formed in 1904 in Berlin. At first there were six member organizations, four of which were European. By 1913 the number had grown to twenty-six, and in 1929 there were fifty-one, including South Africa, China, Egypt, India, Palestine and Syria. All of them were not 'merely' organizations. Even if bureaucracy and hierarchy did play a part, their main impact was twofold: first, the practical exercise of democracy and representative structures; and second, networks of friendships were formed, often beyond national and continental borders, which promoted mutual support and exchanges, including those with respect to their political language.

Equal because Different: The Political Discourse of Suffragism

> With regard to the differences between men and women, those who advocate the enfranchisement of women have no wish to disregard them or make little of them. On the contrary, we base our claim to representation to a large extent on them.
>
> Millicent Garrett Fawcett, around 1890[12]

The women's suffrage movement was not merely a later supplement to other democratization movements; instead, it must be viewed within the context of the broader women's movement, which fought for political equality as well as female autonomy. Their efforts to democratize the 'male state' were based on their own concepts, which brought out the situation and interests of the female sex. On top of the classical themes of liberty, equality and – real or alleged – individual citizenship came a particular female focus, one which assumed the common interests of women on the basis of their shared discrimination, domestic and other responsibilities and their cultural qualities.

The political discourse of suffragism developed over the course of several generations from the conflict between women and men, between (male and female) suffragists and (male and female) anti-suffragists, in transnational communication and in words and images. An expressive, utopian or satirical imagery emerged, especially in the flyers, posters, magazines and pamphlets of British and American groups. There was also renewed discussion on what women or the sexes were or should be; it escalated as the subject moved to politics and debate on current political theories, of which there were three main ones: the rights, duties and equality of 'man' as citizen in the tradition of the Enlightenment and French Revolution; the doctrine of the male state and male citizenship; and the theory of parliamentary representation, with its class-specific connotations as it had been developed especially in Britain. Despite historical experience that precisely the universalistic vision of the rights of man and citizen had not offered women a chance and had in any case suffered a bitter defeat, feminists of all currents – whether radical or moderate – continued to refer to it, for example, the moderate General German Women's League in its journal *Neue Bahnen*. They often countered the 'male state' by indicating their own social practice. Henriette Goldschmidt's dictum of 1873 became a common saying: 'We need not only fathers of the city, but mothers too.' This echoed Anna Jameson's words of 1859: 'The *maternal* as well as the *paternal* element should be made available, on the principle . . . that the more you can carry out the family law, the "communion of labour" into all social institutions, the more harmonious and the more perfect they will be.' In 1896, Helene Lange contrasted the 'proven ideal of the male state' with its reality: 'Technically and intellectually at a peak, but at the end of the century the peoples of the world face each other armed to the teeth. For the *ultima ratio* of the male state today is still physical violence, war.' Using almost the same words, Millicent Fawcett had described the situation a short time before as a consequence of the exclusion of women and of the 'domestic interests of the nations': 'We have before us the picture of the whole of Europe armed to the teeth, and the great neighbouring nations ready to spring like wild beasts at each other's throats, all for the sake of fancied political advantage.'[13]

However, the most important and concrete component of suffragist discourse was the language of parliamentary representation. It had appeared during the French Revolution and shaped English liberalism and utilitarianism, which was influential throughout Europe. That language was used both to exclude women and to include workers and blacks.

John Stuart Mill contradicted his late father James using this vocabulary in May 1867 when he addressed the House of Commons: 'The interests of all women are safe in the hands of their fathers, husbands, and brothers, who have the same interest with them, and not only know, far better than they do, what is good for them, but care much more for them than they care for themselves. Sir, this is exactly what is said of all unrepresented classes. . . . Are not the interests of the employers and that of the employed, when properly understood, the same? . . . [But] I should like to have a return laid before this House of the number of women who are annually beaten to death, kicked to death, or trampled to death by their male protectors. . . . Sir, before it is affirmed that women do not suffer in their interests, as women, by the denial of a vote, it should be considered whether women have no grievances.'[14]

Criticism of vicarious representation, along with the very language of representation, characterized the suffragist discourse and sometimes eclipsed the concepts of 'nature' and 'universality'. Jeanne Deroin had at first affirmed *liberté, égalité, fraternité* in a flyer in 1849 before adopting the language of representation, declaring that 'a legislative assembly composed only of men is just as unable to pass laws intended to regulate a society of both men and women as an assembly of privileged persons would be unable to discuss the interests of workers'. In 1871 Millicent Fawcett claimed that the strongest objection to women's political participation was the assumption that 'women are sufficiently represented already by men, and their interests have always been jealously protected by the legislature'. She drew attention to the important role that the parallel argument had played in 1867 for those opposing voting rights for male workers. Hedwig Dohm expressed this idea in a similar way in 1876: 'Men, they say, represent women. When did women give men the right to represent them? . . . With just as much right the slave-holder [can] declare that he represents his slaves. It is an old argument that the workman can be represented by his employer, but it has not convinced the workman, and he has refused such representation with the greatest energy. And women are expected to accept it? Never!'

Anna Maria Mozzoni justified her suffrage petition in 1874 by arguing that men were by no means 'the natural representatives of women's interests'; her petition was still submitted in 1907 with 10,000 signatures. Hubertine Auclert ran for office (extra-legally) in the 1885 French parliamentary elections on the platform that only women could represent their interests; then the 'Minotaur State' would be replaced by a 'motherly state' guaranteeing peace and welfare. Helene Lange considered male representation of women – and thus the male claim to represent the common good – to be a fiction. In 1896 she maintained that 'Just as one social class cannot speak for another, one sex cannot speak for the other', and 'such vicarious representation between the sexes' is even more unthinkable 'than between different social classes and even races'. For 'only woman completely understands all the needs and interests of her sex and . . . only women's suffrage will make the so-called universal suffrage more than empty talk'. Lange referred to French and English suffragists and quoted the American Thomas Wentworth Higginson (who had participated at the 1851 women's rights convention): 'All theories of chivalry and generosity and vicarious representation fall before the fact that women have been grossly wronged by men.' In 1895 the long-standing democrat Louise Otto used the argument in her last treatise before her death, in which she again, as in 1848, appealed publicly for women's suffrage. In 1911 Catherine Marshall defended suffrage against a British opponent: 'You say that "speaking generally, there is no woman who has no man to represent her". . . . But . . . with the best will in the world men cannot have the same knowledge and experience of women's needs that women have, for the simple reason, so often used as an anti-suffrage argument, that "Men are men, and women are women."'[15]

At this time Catherine Marshall was the leading figure on the path to a coalition of suffragists and labour. Her argument made reference to the discourse on 'peculiar qualities' and 'separate spheres' in the sense of female inferiority. Suffragists no longer merely rejected this by stressing the value and dignity of the female sex; they translated the discrimination in custom and rights into the language of different interests between the sexes and thus between 'common good' and 'female good'. This difference became the discursive grounds for claiming equality and political participation, just as in Higginson's statement, which was often cited explicitly or implicitly, that 'the more you emphasize the fact of sex, the more you strengthen our argument'. In Hedwig Dohm's words in 1876, 'I believe in the difference between male and female minds'. And, she continued, 'the more the difference of the sexes is highlighted, the more clearly we see the necessity of a representation of women', since women have 'other interests' than men do, 'other mental, spiritual and bodily needs'. Helene Lange argued in 1896 that precisely because of their peculiar abilities and interests, as they found expression in the practice of social reform, women could supplement and change male politics. The metaphor she used was taken from a British suffragist journal, 'The women's movement is organized mother-love'. Millicent Fawcett highlighted sexual difference for the sake of political representation – more militant suffragettes did so as well, and even more strongly – using the same metaphor: 'If men and women were exactly alike, the representation of men would represent us; but not being alike, that wherein we differ is unrepresented under the present system. The motherhood of women, either actual or potential, is one of those great facts of life which we must never lose sight of. To women as mothers is given the charge of the home and the care of children. Women are, therefore, by nature as well as by occupation and training, more accustomed than men to concentrate their minds on the home and domestic side of things. But this difference between men and women, instead of being a reason against their enfranchisement, seems to me the strongest possible reason in favour of it; we want the home and the domestic side of things to count for more in politics and in the administration of public affairs than they do at present.' On the eve of the first Italian elections on the basis of manhood suffrage in 1913, Emilia Mariani wrote: 'Women, you are victims of unjust and biased laws, because they have been made only by men and in their interests alone. When you are told it suffices that men make the laws also for women, then you must answer, *That is not true.* Answer that the male soul is far too different from that of the female and that the interests of men and women are different and often contrary.'[16]

Just as the notion of gender difference had become a vehicle for the expansion of the female 'sphere' by way of social and moral reforms, it also became a vehicle by which to demand participation in politics. Far from accepting traditional gender roles, this language of difference took up the language of representation of interests that had hitherto been neglected; just as in the case of workers, this was not a matter of ontology but of historically based interests. It was all the more clear considering that the language of difference was combined with the language of equality. Not only in Europe but also in the United States, New Zealand, Australia and Canada, it was commonplace around the turn of the century to speak in terms of bringing the 'motherly influence' into politics and of becoming the 'nation's housekeepers'; most suffragists claimed equal human status at the same time as eliciting women's particular virtues.[17] This applied just as much for radicals and militants as for moderate suffragists. The various wings differed more in their methods and style than in their principles. Reference to femininity overlapped with statements such as 'equal brain, equal soul, equal rights' – according to the moderate German journal *Neue Bahnen* – or 'same spiritual power' and same 'reason' (Helene Lange). Precisely within the suffragist context many feminists, including Dohm and Lange, linked the notion of gender difference with sharp attacks on traditional sex roles. Both Dohm's and Lange's focus on difference culminated in an appeal for equality, and Lange quoted from the constitution of Wyoming, which introduced women's suffrage in 1869 when it was still a territory: 'Since equality in the enjoyment of natural and civil rights is only made sure through political equality, the laws of this state affecting the political rights and privileges of its citizens shall be without distinction of race, color, sex.' What nowadays might seem contradictory to some was perfectly consistent for the protagonists. On the one hand, it was a product of the diversity of available political languages and the contradictions of the gender order; on the other hand, it was derived from the insight that equality and difference are compatible, while equality and subordination are not.

Again, the discourse was shaped by historical context and target group. This also applied to Clara Zetkin when she sought with her internationally circulated manifesto of 1907 to give legitimacy to suffrage while at the same time denying the legitimacy of the 'ladies of the bourgeoisie' with their 'bourgeois women's rightism' (that became the doctrine of the Third International in 1920), with the argument – intended to be denunciatory – that the middle-class women claimed 'even today, women's suffrage as a natural right', much like the 'bourgeoisie' in the eighteenth century. Zetkin preferred to point instead to that which 'woman as wife and mother achieves for society at large' and to the 'recognition of her highly significant activities as mother'.[18] The fact that on this point she agreed with the 'ladies' (albeit not in her 'struggle against the bourgeois democracy') underscores another important element of the discourse; namely, legitimizing the franchise on the grounds of actual or potential motherhood always aimed to extend political rights – beyond those of a limited franchise, including the much-debated exclusion of married women – to all women, whether married or not, and whether propertied or poor. This was a challenge to the age-old argument according to which women were incapable of making political judgements and taking political action because of their duties as mothers. Condorcet, de Gouges, Wollstonecraft and Hippel had challenged that argument; but in 1917 it was, together with the danger of a 'leap in the dark', still being raised in the German parliament against women's suffrage.

Feminist discourse on representation was probably strengthened by the fact that the labour movement in many European countries had been fighting for proportional representation since the end of the nineteenth century. Rights viewed as individualistic or natural had long since receded from the spotlight; instead, the idea took hold that the interests of social groups should be represented in accordance with their proportion of the population. Yet discussion on women's suffrage was not limited to the language of legal equality and theories of representational difference. Other arguments were hardly less important in getting sceptical women and male decision-makers ultimately to accept votes for women – against the drumbeat of warnings against 'women's regiments', neglected husbands and babies, 'feminization' of the men and 'masculinization' of the women. Suffragists pointed to the utility of women's vote, to its expediency in contrast to abstract rights that John Stuart Mill had presented as his major argument in 1867 before the House of Commons, in the sense of a happy coincidence between female good and common good. As

Condorcet as well as Hedwig Dohm and the dedicated conservative suffragist Frances Power Cobbe had done, suffragists discussed the contradiction that independent and educated women were not allowed to vote while dependent and uneducated men were. In some places this argument took on racist or nativist undertones. But suffragists from all camps especially used the passionate or pragmatic language of history. They showed that in Europe's *ancien régime* some women were allowed to vote, albeit through male proxies, and that women had been allowed to vote in New Jersey from 1776 to 1807 (German feminists also liked to point to this historical fact). They also evoked the historical change, the rise in women's industrial work, the international forerunners – Wyoming, the Isle of Man, where women were granted suffrage in 1881, New Zealand, Australia – the battle cry 'no taxation without representation' and the expanding presence in many places of women voting and getting elected to local administrations, school boards, poor relief and labour and trade boards.

The language of nation, nation-state and nationalism, which had long been considered men's business, was of great significance. This language was used all over in the service of male suffrage, whether in the centuries-old tradition of the citizen-soldier or in its modern variants of the French National Guard or Germany's compulsory military service. The franchise meant more than having a voice in decision-making; first and foremost, it symbolized affiliation to a nation. Olympe de Gouges had justified female citizenship by asserting that *la nation* was not male but that it united men and women. The British suffragists stressed in their 1865 petition that women were 'no less a constituent part of the nation' than men were. Louise Otto, too, used the language of German national unification (though she opposed the Prussian solution). Anna Maria Mozzoni demanded suffrage as an element of a *risorgimento delle donne* and the path to the freedom of the nation. Many women saw themselves as pillars of the nation and the nation as a great family in which men and women cooperated. When the first European country granted the vote to women – Finland in 1906 – it was done in the enthusiasm for the national liberation from the Russian yoke, to which women had contributed just as men had. This was the reason why Finland became a forerunner and why women there were granted full suffrage at the same time as men. The situation was similar in Norway, where women wanted and were expected to show that they deserved suffrage by supporting the break from Sweden. To this end they organized a broad-based petition campaign in 1905. When they were granted the vote, with a property qualification, in 1907 (as the first sovereign state in Europe, which then lifted the special women's qualification in 1913), it was justified on the basis of their efforts for the sake of the nation. On the other side of the border, Swedish women declared their responsibility as 'one half of the nation' in the crisis of 1905, but they were not granted suffrage until 1919. The British women's movement was divided with respect to Irish Home Rule (Fawcett took the side of the Unionists). Irish suffragists supported national independence but when the Home Rule party did not come out for the women's vote they were not agreed on whether to place their primary loyalty with their gender or their nation. They countered the male definitions of Irish tradition with an ancient national tradition of Irish women's rights and obtained the vote in 1922. The old question whether or not women were human assumed a new variation in a national context: did the French, the Swiss and the Germans, as usually mentioned in their respective statutes, also include women? In many countries suffragists tried to vote, pointing to apparently gender-neutral constitutions or (suffrage) laws, but all of these attempts failed, either at the polls or when court rulings were later handed down.

It was precisely in Europe that nationalism was not just a national phenomenon but an international one. Women's nationalism, much like nationalism in general, oscillated between participation – national loyalty and citizenship appeared inseparable – and exclusion, or even aggression. World War I, the first 'total' war of unprecedented magnitude, brought both varieties of nationalism to a peak, in the women's movements of the warring countries as well. The war interrupted the suffrage movement at its zenith, when the goal seemed so near. Under the wartime 'truce in class struggle' (*Burgfrieden*) in Germany and *Union sacrée* in France, most suffragists, national associations and moderate, radical and socialist women turned to social welfare, especially for women employed in war-work. The militant British suffragettes supported male honour, pasted recruiting posters that read 'Women of Britain say "Go!"' and identified themselves as patriots in the struggle against 'Huns' and 'Bolsheviks' in their newspaper, whose name was changed from *Suffragette* to *Britannia*. Jane Misme made an appeal in 1914 in *La Française* that 'as long as the war lasts, the enemy's women will also be the enemy'. And Gertrud Bäumer argued in 1915 that 'it is obvious for us that during a national struggle for existence, we women belong to our people and *only* to them.'[19]

In 1916–17 women in many places took up the suffrage issue once again. They had already been successful in Denmark in 1915. The postwar successes were accompanied by a chorus of voices that now – just as in the case of male 'votes for heroes' in Britain and the merits of the Prussian soldiers – justified the franchise with women's contribution to the war. It was, however, a predominantly male chorus. The Federation of German Women's Associations demanded full suffrage in 1917 but publicly refused to accept it as compensation for the female war effort.

When women's suffrage was rejected by the Senate in France in 1922, the explanation was that French women did not want to be paid for their war effort with filthy lucre. The vote as women's 'war profits' was the – retrospective – justification used by those who needed a new argument to compensate their former opposition to a 'women's regiment'. It was not the war that ushered in women's suffrage but a transnational development, the groundwork for which had been laid by the transnationalism of the suffrage movement starting at the end of the nineteenth century. But why did women's suffrage come at all, after a century of intense resistance and after the often dramatic invocation of the 'male state'; and why did it come throughout almost all of Europe at approximately the same time as the United States, where suffragism was so much stronger (not in comparison with Britain, but definitely with respect to continental Europe) and where a democratic culture had become much more firmly anchored? Why did some European countries follow such an incredibly long time later, not until after World War II?

First-comers and Late-comers: European Paths to Women's Suffrage

One man, one vote, one value, one gun.

Women were admitted to political participation earliest in countries where there was no, or at most minimal, class tension – among whites, at least – and where suffragism was supported by strong female temperance movements. This was true for New Zealand, where women obtained the vote only four years after men received full suffrage, and for Wyoming and other western states in the United States. On the other hand, the American alcohol lobby (especially the beer industry, dominated by German immigrants) was among the strongest opponents of women's suffrage around the turn of the century, since they feared that women would support prohibition (which then came in 1919 with the Eighteenth Amendment to the US constitution). Other opponents were the party machineries and especially the southern states, which saw women's suffrage as a threat to the racist Jim Crow laws. For free – that is, white – men, the franchise limitations of the early republic had already been lifted in the 1820s and 1830s, long before women publicly raised the issue of their own suffrage; there had been virtually no social movements or struggles in connection with elimination of the voting qualifications for men. There was, of course, the Civil War and the initially successful struggle to enfranchise black men (the effect of which was subverted soon afterwards until the mid-twentieth century). On the one hand, however, the thrust of the 'race question' was very different from that of the European 'class question'. On the other hand, in Europe the men of the most significant ethnic and religious minority, the Jews, had enjoyed equal political rights almost everywhere, except Russia, since the 1860s. In the United States women had to gain suffrage against the background of the full enfranchisement of white and, to some extent, black men. Thus it could be assumed – and was – that women's struggle would be easier in the United States than in Europe since only one more step had to be taken. But the American path to national women's suffrage would take almost a century.

The historical constellation was different in Europe. Here, the path to women's suffrage ran parallel to and almost simultaneously with that of the fiercely contested abolition of voting qualifications for men. 'One man, one voice' was their slogan; 'one value' was later added, as was often 'one gun' (the right to bear arms was guaranteed in the Second Amendment in the US Bill of Rights of 1791 and was a significant issue in Europe, too). Manhood suffrage was introduced at the national level, and sometimes in stages, between 1848/51 (France and Switzerland) and the time around World War I in Italy, Portugal, Iceland, Denmark, the Netherlands, Sweden, Britain and Ireland. In between came Germany (1867/71), Greece (1877), Norway (1898) and Austria (1907). Suffragism, the struggle to enfranchise the 'second sex' – sometimes women were referred to as the 'fifth estate' – was thus at the interface between the women's movement at large and the efforts of the fourth estate, as the lower classes were often called. Although women in both the United States and Europe were excluded in the same categorical way by virtue of their sex, this issue was more manifest in the United States than in Europe, where it was long overshadowed by the fact that most men were also excluded. Yet the class barrier was clearly less fundamental than the sex barrier (and the race barrier), since poor men could become tax-payers, and the uneducated could receive an education. Hence the period spanning the institution of full suffrage for men and that for women varied considerably from country to country. In Austria and Britain it took ten years; in Italy, almost thirty; in Germany, fifty; Spain and Denmark, over sixty. The time periods seem short – with the exception of Greece (seventy-five years), France (one hundred) and Switzerland (one hundred and twenty) – as compared with the United States, but very long in comparison with Finland, the Netherlands and Ireland, where womanhood suffrage was introduced together with manhood suffrage. (This was later also the rule in many developing countries that had a national liberation movement.)

The major reason why women's suffrage took so long, why the respective length of time was so different and, finally, why it came at all was its particular relationship to the various national paths to manhood suffrage. A decisive factor was the relationship of suffragism to liberalism, on the one hand, which at least in theory stood for progress, and to the labour movement, on the other hand, though the more radical it was, the more it considered political rights to be merely 'formal' anyway, speaking out instead for the social emancipation of the lower classes. Liberalism, with which suffragists had sympathized since the 1860s, continued to hold to more or less drastic property qualifications for the franchise. This was by no means due only to conservative motives, but was also part of the controversial tension between the 'sovereignty of the people' and a 'government of reason'; in Britain it was referred to as popular versus good government; in France, as *le nombre et la raison*; and it had been a major subject of constitutional political thought throughout Europe since the French Revolution. John Stuart Mill was highly committed in his campaign against the sex barrier, but he called for a graduated suffrage – independent of sex – that was graded according to level of education. Mill, like most liberals, saw the road to prospective full democracy as a gradual one, the steps depending on the spread and level of education and independence. The liberals felt confirmed in their fears when the new manhood suffrage in France led not to democracy in 1851 but to a plebiscite dictatorship and the reign of Emperor Napoleon III (in Portugal, as well, a dictator came to power in 1917 as a result of manhood suffrage). In Britain conservatives, too, were sometimes able to benefit after 1867 from the expanded franchise as introduced by Benjamin Disraeli; in Germany Bismarck's introduction of manhood suffrage for the Reichstag, the national parliament, initially strengthened the conservatives. (This had already been the case regarding the elections to the Frankfurt Parliament in 1848. The broader the suffrage in the individual German states, the more conservative the elect.) Extensions of the franchise for men by no means originated merely in pressure 'from below' but often in the efforts by leaders in parliament and government to mobilize new voters for their own party. Whereas male reason was conjured up to oppose women's suffrage, this image of man was revised (and not entirely without reason) in the debate on manhood suffrage and the franchise of the 'rabble'. Experience had taught leaders to measure the suffrage extensions not solely by the legitimacy of rights and duties but first and foremost according to *cui bono*: which party would benefit? In a similar way, women's suffrage was discussed under a phrase that Lord Palmerston had coined in 1859 with respect to suffrage for male workers: 'a leap in the dark'. Starting in the late nineteenth century, this topos became popular in reference to women in virtually all European parliaments (in Germany *Sprung ins Dunkle*, in France *le saut dans l'inconnu* and in Italy *il salto nel buio*).

The configuration of liberalism, labour movement and women's movement changed around the turn of the century. Many believed that the elimination of the class barrier, as well as the sex barrier, was a matter no longer of principle but of time and timing. To avoid the worst, all conceivable forms of specifically female suffrage qualifications were discussed. Particularly in Britain there was continued wrestling whether – if at all – only the simple sex barrier should fall or also the double barrier that faced married women. Or, as in Italy, whether or not prostitutes should be excluded and if the *voto amministrativo* alone or also the *voto politico* would be acceptable. Filippo Turati, the leading Italian socialist, complained in 1910 about 'the very underdeveloped political and class consciousness of the female proletarian masses'. Italian and other socialists viewed the call for women's suffrage as 'bourgeois' and as a dangerous obstacle on the road to full worker suffrage.[20] Thus, the conflict discussed throughout Europe was the following: If democratic participation was just a question of time, but the simultaneous elimination of the class barrier and the sex barrier appeared to be too great a 'leap in the dark', who should be admitted first? The labour movement and especially the socialists feared that admitting women to a franchise with property qualifications would benefit the liberals or conservatives. Socialists and liberals (especially in France, Belgium and Italy) feared that it would strengthen the clerical parties. The conservatives feared the opposite, namely, female support for the left and the liberals and the danger that a female suffrage with qualifications would be the first step to full emancipation of women. The suffragists had good reason to assume that the labour movement was interested only in its own manhood suffrage and that the socialists sought not a parliamentarian democracy but to overthrow 'bourgeois society'. Thus there were numerous variants that gave priority either to class or to sex. In the end, class won out. Virtually nowhere in Europe were women admitted to national suffrage before all class barriers had fallen for men, and nowhere were they admitted to an existing system of qualifications for men. In fact, the internationally widespread women's demand, 'suffrage as it is or may be' (it had also been supported by John Stuart Mill and Anna Maria Mozzoni), did not stand a chance, although – or precisely because – it was criticized by the left as conservative, whereas the conservatives rejected it as well. Hence women were consistently associated more with a sex than with a class. Only in Portugal were they granted suffrage before the male-specific class barrier was abolished, but this was only on the grounds of a women-specific qualification: in 1931, when literacy became the prerequisite for male suffrage, higher education became required for women voters. And only in Norway, long after the class barrier was eliminated, were women admitted on the grounds of a (short-lived) women-specific property qualification. In Iceland and Britain (after the class barrier was removed) there was temporarily a higher minimum voting age for women than for men. In Belgium, women's family status became crucial in 1920 (mothers and widows of fallen soldiers were allowed to vote), and in Austria and Belgium prostitutes were initially excluded from the suffrage.

Democratization, regardless of whether or not it seemed desirable, was understood as the extension of the franchise to men ('downward') but not to women. Hence, the priority that was given to class over gender was an important reason why the path to female citizenship was such a long one. John Stuart Mill had already sensed that in 1870 when he stated that 'To combine the two questions would practically suspend the fight for women's equality, since universal suffrage is sure to be discussed almost solely as a working men's question: and when at last victory comes, there is sure to be a compromise, by which the working men would be enfranchised without the women, and the contest for women's rights would have to be begun again from the beginning, with the working men inside the barrier instead of outside, and therefore with their selfish interests against our cause instead of with it.'[21] It was nevertheless a question not only of priority but of a specifically European interaction between the elimination of the class barrier and the sex barrier. In its wake womanhood suffrage usually followed more closely after manhood suffrage in Europe than it did in the United States. A comparison of developments in Britain with those in Germany can serve to illustrate this situation.

In early twentieth-century Britain increasing numbers of men, especially liberals, supported both moderate and more militant suffragism, actively and often with great personal dedication. The number might have amounted to several thousand (this form of liberalism was absent in Germany, where far fewer men spoke out for women's suffrage than was the case elsewhere). The rank and file within the Liberal Party generally supported the suffragists, while the leadership opposed suffrage. The situation was reversed among the conservatives, while there were hardly any men in the Labour Party around the turn of the century who considered the removal of the sex barrier to be more urgent than – or at least just as urgent as – the removal of the class barrier; James Keir Hardie, an eloquent socialist radical democrat, was an exception to the rule. Instead, Labour supported adult suffrage. Irrespective of the gender-neutral word and to the dismay of the suffragists, this essentially meant nothing more than the familiar manhood suffrage, and the conflict between adult suffrage and women's suffrage remained undiminished for years. The small Social Democratic Party was not at all in favour of women's suffrage and, considering it was revolutionary, did not think much of suffrage at all. All political parties sometimes took advantage of the active support of women (usually wives of party members) in election campaigns. The situation of the British suffragists was no less complex.

The overwhelming majority of female as well as male suffragists (after 1897 they were represented by the National Union of Women's Suffrage Societies) demanded, from 1866 until after the turn of the century, 'equal suffrage' for women, that is, the franchise 'as it is or may be granted to men', admission of women to the current suffrage with prospects of extending it for both sexes in the future. This demand was expressed in political agitation as well as in the roughly thirty women's suffrage bills, which often received an impressive number of 'ayes' in the House of Commons; by 1907 such bills had received a majority five times but were then blocked on points of order. The minority wing that emerged in 1903, also called militants – and consequently, the majority suffragists called themselves constitutionalists – had initially cooperated with Labour but broke with them in 1907, disappointed because Labour still acted with great reluctance with regard to women's issues. Now the suffragettes also propagated the old formula of non-partisanship and equal suffrage; moreover they were committed to civil disobedience and, after 1912, provocative violence. Theirs was not revolutionary but symbolic violence, which served to shake up the public in those years of fierce conflict, though at the same time it estranged the women and men of the Labour Party from the suffragettes even further. Meanwhile, Labour's leadership finally started to realize that agitation for women's suffrage could also benefit the struggle for adult suffrage through the popular support by working-class women, who had already started a suffrage movement in the 1890s that had found little support among the male comrades. The turning point came between 1910 and 1912, when the Conciliation Bill was introduced to mitigate the confrontation between adult suffrage and women's suffrage. The bill was torpedoed by the Liberal Asquith government. Labour finally declared its clear support for women's suffrage in 1912; and suffragists of all social classes decided it was more promising to cooperate with Labour than with the Liberals, who had continually disappointed their hopes since their landslide election victory in 1906. The new alliance was negotiated starting in 1912 with highly complex arrangements that bring to mind modern-day coalition agreements (for the women, negotiations were handled not by the suffragettes but by the constitutionalists). It even came about that Labour rejected the government's offer to institute manhood suffrage if it did not also consider the women's cause. The cooperation with Labour led to a compromise, and the price that British women would have to pay was that men received full active and passive suffrage in 1918 provided they were at least twenty-one years old, while special suffrage requirements were introduced for women. They had to be over thirty years of age to receive active voting rights (and twenty-one for passive); they had to be either married to a man eligible to vote, or head of a household or a university graduate. Former women workers in the war industry remained largely excluded because they were too young; that is, they were certainly not rewarded for their contribution with the franchise. Not until 1928 was the minimum voting age for women adjusted to that for men.

Germany took a dramatically different path to democratic suffrage than Britain did. For men as well as women, the British route was gradual, while the German one was revolutionary. It was revolutionary in the sense of Bismarck's 'revolution from above', which brought manhood suffrage for the national elections, and also in the sense of the 1918 revolution, which introduced manhood suffrage for all state parliaments that had not already instituted it and, in addition, women's suffrage for all parliaments. Nevertheless, there are still structural similarities with respect to the interaction of male and female suffrage. Similar to the case of Labour in Britain, it corresponded to the party interests of the Social Democrats (SPD) and especially to the fact that they were strong in the national parliament, the Reichstag, precisely because of manhood suffrage, which did not exist in Britain. The SPD had put women's suffrage on their platform in 1891, but the resolution had come from the party leaders and triggered obvious reservations from the rank and file. August Bebel gave a moving address to the Reichstag in 1895 in support of women, but it would take over a decade until the Social Democrats took any concrete actions, except for Clara Zetkin's articles in her journal *Die Gleichheit*, in which she often recommended women's suffrage as a 'weapon' or 'bullet' against 'bourgeois society'. Germany was one of the few European countries in which no one – not even the Social Democrats – had ever made a parliamentary motion to allow women to vote in the national elections (admittedly, nowhere in Europe were so many motions made as in Britain). The Social Democrats only actively supported women's suffrage where they could use it to promote their interest in expanding male suffrage and where they could certainly use the female support, that is, at the level of the 26 single states. SPD critics continued to draw attention to this deficit in logic, after Bebel's speech in 1895, for instance, or in the 1913 Reichstag session: 'If women's suffrage is truly so deeply grounded in all directions, as he has tried to illustrate, then the motion . . . is far too narrow; then you must demand women's suffrage first and foremost for the national elections before you demand it for the elections in the individual states.'[22] A position such as Keir Hardie's, to admit women to the limited suffrage of the states, did not exist among German Social Democrats, except for the isolated voice of Wally Zepler, which was quickly silenced. From 1900 on, one in four states, especially in the liberal south and south-west, but also in the northern state of Oldenburg, successively introduced manhood suffrage. On those occasions some Social Democrats, in Bavaria for example, also demanded women's suffrage, but in contrast to the situation in Britain no one in Germany recommended that a bill be rejected because it did not consider women. Starting in 1902 Clara Zetkin spoke out expressly against such a possibility, since the class interest of the proletariat must 'take precedence over woman's special interest'. She harshly criticized Norway's first step towards women's suffrage in 1907 and naturally considered the Norwegian suffrage requirements to be 'reactionary'. As leader of the socialist women's international (1907), Zetkin declared that wherever male suffrage was an issue, there – and only there – should the Social Democrats also fight for women's suffrage. Concrete activities on the part of the SPD, including their women's organization, did not start in Germany until quite a while after 1903, since that was the year the SPD campaigned for the Prussian state elections for the first time and so placed the reform of male suffrage in Prussia on their agenda. In Prussia all men were eligible to vote, but their votes had different values according to the amount of tax they paid (in Britain at this time two-thirds of all men were eligible to vote, including half the working class). In 1911 the SPD, including their women's organization, called upon workers in Berlin to participate in the first demonstration for women's suffrage, in connection with the ongoing election campaign.

At the same time demonstrations also took place elsewhere which included the participation of middle-class women. The class barrier or the suffrage requirements played the same role for German suffragists as for British. Until the turn of the century, they had advocated a gradual process that would start with local suffrage, as in Britain. But then national suffrage moved to the foreground. Like the British, most German suffragists insisted upon non-partisanship with an implicit preference for the Liberals, who disappointed them just as the British Liberals had disappointed their British sisters. When the ban on women's political associations and assemblies that existed in Prussia and eight other states was lifted in 1908 by Reich legislation, feminists could finally become party members; leading feminists joined the German Democratic Party. Many German suffragists adopted the British slogan, 'suffrage as it is or may be granted to men', and debated as controversially as the British women. German single-issue suffrage organizations were divided along party lines with respect to voting qualifications, whereas the feminist majority preferred a non-partisan 'wait and see' attitude to the division. The British slogan assumed a much more progressive meaning in Germany than it had in Britain. Where men had already been granted full suffrage – for the national Reichstag elections and one-fourth of the states – it meant a firm commitment to full democratic suffrage. The year 1917 appeared to represent a real chance, a time when women in the other warring nations were also taking up the suffrage issue again. Emperor Wilhelm II promised manhood suffrage for Prussians in his 'Easter address' (as a reward for the war effort), but he made no mention of women. In addition to many other Liberals and of course the SPD, Max Weber, who had previously expressed support for feminist positions, spoke out in 1917 for suffrage reform in recognition of male contributions to the war effort. But he too made no reference to women. Moderate, radical and social democratic suffragists protested firmly against the words of the emperor. That same year they formed a coalition, promoted by the fact that the three factions had already worked together during the war in the National Women's Service (Nationaler Frauendienst) and the Social Democrats were no longer dominated by Clara Zetkin with her insistence on 'clean separation'. Women's suffrage was instituted in late 1918 by the provisional revolutionary government, that is, the Social Democrats. And their present interests were no less important than their platform of 1891. They needed the support of the masses more desperately than ever and they got it. In 1919 female voters clearly chose the democratic Weimar coalition of the SPD, the Democratic Party and the Catholic Party.

The old platform and new interest of the Social Democrats were certainly more important for the introduction of women's suffrage than the two major manifestos of the German suffragist coalition of 1917 and the suffrage associations before 1914, which were divided on the issue of suffrage qualifications. To some extent German women were handed suffrage in 1918 just as the German workers had been handed it in 1867 and 1871. Yet the fact that there was no notable opposition after the war and the turnout rate of women at the polls in 1919 was 89 per cent was a result of the German and transnational efforts by women since the 1890s. Moreover, in contrast to Britain and most western countries, women's suffrage was not resolved in Germany by a male parliament – in such a case strong opposition would have emerged – but by the constituent assembly in 1919. Thirty-seven women were members of this assembly (in the individual state parliaments there were 117 women). The price that German women paid for their enfranchisement was a revolution that would not have occurred without the war, and they now shared the responsibility for the difficult task of building up a democratic Germany. Might the road to democracy have been travelled without violence if women had been made 'active voters' decades earlier, when the transnational women's movement had reached its zenith and confronted the 'male state, armed to the teeth' with its vision of peace? Hippel had speculated along those very lines with reference to the French Revolution, as had French feminists at the start of World War I. The fact that female citizenship was recognized at all in 1918 must essentially be attributed in both Germany and Britain to the conflict-ridden interaction between efforts to eliminate the class barrier and those to eliminate the

sex barrier. On the side of the labour movement, their own political interest played a crucial role. Already in 1896, the realist Helene Lange had
predicted this situation. If women were enfranchised, it would hardly be
due to 'a sudden attack of justice frenzy in our parliaments'; instead, 'The
men will not give women the suffrage until it serves their own interest.'[23]

In France (1944) and Italy (1945), too, women's suffrage was first
instituted by provisional governments. In 1919 in Italy the *autorizzazione
maritale* was abolished, and civil and political rights for women appeared
on the horizon when that same year the Chamber, with the support of
the Catholics and socialists, approved both 'administrative' and political
suffrage, though they were divided on the issue of voting rights for prostitutes. The resolution did not become law, however, since the Senate's
legislative period had been ended early (perhaps the Senate would have
rejected it anyway). The fascists planned both forms of suffrage directly
after the war, and Mussolini promised at least administrative suffrage in
1923. But shortly after the law was finally passed in 1925, for women
with schooling as well as mothers and widows of fallen soldiers, local
elections were abolished and Italy became a one-party dictatorship.

In France and Switzerland, on the other hand, it was not a dictatorship
that blocked women's suffrage or made it irrelevant, but the republic.
This can again be explained by the specifically European interaction between class and gender and the priority given to class. Many French and
Swiss women had firmly reckoned on admission to political representation after World War I, especially in view of the international tide of
franchise extensions. And they had good reason to do so. The movements in both countries did not differ significantly from those in the rest
of continental Europe. If anything, the French movement was stronger
than elsewhere (as indicated, for example, by the large *manifestation
Condorcet* in July 1914 in Paris), and the arguments were the same as
those in the transnational suffragist and anti-suffragist discourse. Wom-
en's suffrage first appeared on the agenda of the Swiss national legislature in 1919. The National Council approved it and passed the matter on
to the Council of States (*Bundesrat*), where it was referred back to the
cantons. The cantons decided to require referendums, that is, a vote by
all men. The motions or petitions of the women, it was argued, did not
represent the people's will. Referendums, however, represented the greatest
hurdle, as women in many states of the United States had already experienced starting in 1867. The sovereign of five Swiss cantons also rejected
women's suffrage in 1920. The 'people' had shown, it was declared, 'that
they stand firm and steadfast to their democratic state'. After the referendums, there were reports that 'Hein, c'est encore nous les patrons!' ('Hey,
we are still the bosses!') and many 'red patriarchs' also wanted to remain 'the lone chef in the political kitchen'.[24] In France a majority of the

Chamber voted for women's suffrage in 1919, but after a three-year delay the Senate decided not to put it to a vote in 1922, after two weeks of debate, and so the bill was rejected. The Senate resolution had received most of its votes from the republicans, the *radicaux* and the *socialistes radicaux* (the Chamber's earlier 'aye' only came about because many representatives had reckoned on the later rejection by the Senate). The radical senator Alexandre Bérard, an anti-suffragist, played a decisive role with his notorious report to the Senate in 1919, in which he made use of the classical counter-arguments and added a few new ones as well: 'A leap in the dark' might produce clerical rule or the election of a 'new Bonaparte' as *suffrage universel* had in 1848, and might thereby lead to a 'new Battle of Sedan' (this was the site of the French defeat in 1870 in the Franco-Prussian War). Obviously devoid of all logic, he continued that it would also bring with it the danger that women would vote for a Bolshevik revolution. Indeed, they did not expect anything for their war efforts since 'they did so for love of the *patrie*, not in the expectation of a reward.'[25]

Catholicism was not responsible for the Sedan of French women's suffrage, nor for that of its Swiss counterpart. Catholic countries such as Austria and Poland (1918), Ireland (1922) and Spain (1931) granted women political citizenship; Belgium granted at least mothers and widows of fallen soldiers the so-called *suffrage des morts* (1920), and Portugal did so for educated women. The Catholic women's movements in France and Belgium had supported women's suffrage and in 1919 even the pope had been 'converted'. The cause of the defeat was not Catholicism but two other reasons. First, it was feared that women would vote in favour of the conservatives or even the clerics. This fear was widespread internationally and by no means referred only to Catholicism but had more profound significance among the French Democratic Left. There was a long-standing national myth (given urgent expression by Jules Michelet in 1845) that women had betrayed the revolution by resisting the 'cult of reason' and cooperating with the clergy. This myth was rekindled in the fierce conflict between the republic and the Church that shaped French domestic policy at the time of the great suffrage debates. The fact that the pope and the Catholic women's movement supported women's rights merely served to reinforce the anti-feminism of the leftist republicans. Thus it was not Catholicism but republican anti-clericalism that blocked women's suffrage.

The second reason applies to both France and Switzerland. Both countries lacked one factor that promoted women's suffrage elsewhere in Europe, no matter how ambivalent it had been; that is, the struggle to abolish the class barrier. In both countries all men had long since become eligible to vote. Thus it was not a heyday for group theories of parliamentary representation, nor did male citizens need the support of women to obtain the franchise for themselves. Furthermore, efforts to create alliances among liberalism, the labour movement and suffragists were consequently less intensive and less effective. Finally, the suffragists were also republicans, and French women also shared fears for the good of the republic. 'Long live the republic, in spite of everything!' shouted the radical suffragist Maria Vérone from the overflowing gallery of the Senate after women's suffrage had been defeated. Women's suffrage was also absent from the platform of the campaign coalition that brought Socialist Léon Blum to power in 1936 – 'this ostracism has continued for one hundred and fifty years', exclaimed enraged feminists in 1939 on the occasion of the 150–year anniversary of the French Revolution, and the Resistance, too, omitted it from their programme.[26] It was finally de Gaulle who in 1942 announced women's suffrage, and in 1944 he included it on the platform of his provisional government in Algiers. In the cantons of Switzerland, men voted sixty-three times by 1971; women's suffrage passed for the first time in 1959 and 1960 in the three French cantons, but it was defeated in a national referendum in 1959. Still in 1971, the 'assembly of citizens fit for military service' was asserted to be the 'most direct democracy', but that year women's suffrage passed at the national level owing to changed political circumstances (including the European and United Nations' Human Rights Declarations, the new women's liberation movement, though it considered suffrage to be of secondary importance, and above all the indefatigable efforts of the traditional suffragists). Even after 1971, some cantons still denied women the cantonal suffrage. France and Switzerland were late-comers, not *although* they were the oldest male democracies in Europe but *because* they were. And the first would be the last.

Citizenship and Mothers' Rights

The work of motherhood is a veritable social labour.
                                                                Bertha Novich, 1907[27]

As Thomas Marshall showed in 1949 for the British case, for the men of Europe gradual access to political participation was based on the civil rights they had already achieved. Usually social rights followed some time later, providing protection against work disability (due to sickness, invalidism, age and later unemployment). The improvement and systematization of these rights in the twentieth century led to the modern social or welfare state. Women, on the other hand, had to fight simultaneously for civil, political and social citizenship, and in the two decades prior to World War I they took up the issue of social security. Suffrage itself was for the suffragists not merely the epitome of their formal equality, not simply a symbol that they belonged to the community of a municipality, church or nation. Above all, it was a means of achieving social reforms they hoped to set in motion. Women everywhere did not merely seek access to the political sphere that men had long since defined; instead, they sought to redefine it. Social reform and social rights were integral elements of the women's movement at large. As suffragism coincided with the path to manhood suffrage, social reforms as envisioned by and for women overlapped with the beginnings and the consolidation of the welfare state. For men the issue was the relationship among employment, disability and leisure time; for women it was the relationship between employment and family work. This led again to a genuine gender dispute, which up to World War I can be divided into three different strands: the meaning of gender-neutral social security for women, legislation to limit women's wage-work – female factory legislation in the strict sense – and legislation ensuring the social security of mothers, wage-earners as well as non-wage-earners. Since the turn of the twentieth century, the third strand has been referred to in France as *protection des mères* and in Germany as *Mutterschutz*.

The first of the three strands can be illustrated using some national parallels and differences in old-age pensions. In Britain and Germany there was much criticism leading to the recognition of poverty as a problem desperately in need of a solution. In both countries a disproportionately high percentage of those living in poverty were female. Germany tackled the problem in the 1880s with legislation (dealing with risk of sickness and, for factory workers over the age of seventy, with age and invalidism) setting up an insurance model. It based social citizenship – the obligation to pay premiums and the right to receive benefits – on employment and wage level. Men were thus advantaged over women: men earned more, only 18 per cent of factory workers were women, only 13 per cent of all employed women worked in factories and women were employed with less regularity than were men. Britain responded differently (and with a highly publicized dissociation from the German insurance model) with the Old-Age Pensions Act of 1908, a non-contributory, state-financed scheme. All former wage-earners over seventy years of age who had been at the lower end of the wage scale (having earned less then 21 pounds annually) received five shillings per week. Accordingly, of the half million individuals who received their pensions for the first time in 1909, more than half were women. They received little, as is the case with all non-contributory schemes, but more than German women received. The difference between the German and the British models was not coincidental; it was political. In view of the threat to the state that, in the eyes of the Bismarck government, social democracy posed, social security was primarily conceived not as a means of combating poverty but as a supporting measure to combat social democracy by integrating rebellious – male – workers socially. In contrast, the social security system in Britain aimed to offset the drastic consequences of the New Poor Law of 1834. By 1900 pauperism, especially that of women, had become a focus of public indignation. Female poverty was also expressly considered in the British health insurance scheme of 1911. Women paid a contribution of three pence per week; men paid four, though everyone received nine pence if ill (in Germany, both contributions and benefits were graded according to wage level). But irrespective of the differences between the British and German models, a 'two-channel system' ensued in both countries, as well as in many others. Men profited more from the new social policies and women continued to be dependent on poor relief more than men did. Uninsured widows did not receive any benefits in Germany until 1911 (initially only if they were unable to work); in Britain not until 1925. In both countries World War I and, consequently, the massive number of women who were widowed played an important role in improving the situation of widows, especially younger ones. The war left roughly 600,000 widows each in France and Germany, and 200,000 in Britain. Unemployment insurance in most countries usually paid family supplements to men, whereas women were often excluded from unemployment benefits because family responsibilities appeared to prevent them from being available to the labour market. Here and in other areas social security for non-wage-earning women was not considered, and if it was, then it was with an eye towards their dependence on a 'breadwinner'.

The second strand of the emerging welfare state, factory legislation, was handled very differently in the respective countries. With respect to women, it was epitomized by the ban on night work (introduced in Switzerland in 1877, in Britain and Germany in 1878, in France in 1892, in Sweden in 1909, in Greece in 1911, in Spain in 1912, in Russia in 1905, in the Soviet Union in 1918, in Portugal in 1927). This legislation also included a ban on women performing extremely hard labour or work hazardous to health, which was introduced in Britain through the Mines Regulation Act of 1842 and intensified in successive acts; the state-regulated limit on the length of the workday for women (in Britain in 1844 to twelve hours and then reduced in 1847 to ten; in France in 1892 to eleven hours; in Italy in 1902 to twelve; and similar limitations in twenty states of the United States between 1909 and 1917); a longer lunch break for women who had to run a household (in Switzerland in 1877, in Germany in 1891 and soon afterwards in the Netherlands); and in some countries state-fixed minimum wages (in Britain around the turn of the century in the struggle against the sweating system, in some states of the United States, and in 1895 in Australia). This was a transnational development, promoted since 1890 through several international conferences. The International Labour Organization in Geneva, founded in 1919, developed out of these conferences. Government representatives and labour organizations participated and the conferences were also supported by the Socialist International. The transnationality resulted especially from the need to block competitive advantages that would result from the unrestricted cheap labour of women in individual countries. Though women could not vote for the legislation, some were permitted to speak at these conferences and many spoke at the almost twenty international women's meetings that took place on this subject between 1878 and 1914.

Female factory legislation was extremely controversial. The conflict was about the vision of women and gender relations; the fronts often cut across the usual political and social camps. Industrialists were at first against giving women 'privileged' status, since it would raise labour costs and the factories would not be utilized fully at night. Supporters cited the 'weakness' of women, pointing to (disputed) surveys and physicians' opinions. Mostly women's double burden – quite the opposite of 'weakness' – was brought up and the argument that women were primarily responsible for the welfare of their families. Soon it was extended to include not only the welfare of their family but that of the nation, the 'race', the state and its position as a world power. In Britain workers were accused of forcing their wives to work in factories in order to supplement the family income. The labour movements were initially strictly opposed to state intervention, but soon they started assuming that alleviation of hardship for women would also bring the same for men. In only a few countries did the restrictions apply to both sexes, but even then – in Switzerland, for example – they were often enforced more for women than for men. In fact, however, restriction of the male workday – through not state intervention but wrangling between capital and labour – usually preceded the restriction for women. The labour movement (and Social Catholicism) was in favour of female-specific restrictions in the hope of barring all or at least married women from the labour market. It coupled its hopes with a demand for a family wage for (both married and unmarried) men, and sometimes with demands for 'equal pay for equal work', in order to secure men's jobs from the intrusion of poorly paid women. Nevertheless, women's wage work remained absolutely essential. Nowhere was there a law excluding women from factory work (much less domestic industry), not even one applying only to married women. In view of the considerable share of women among all wage-earners, such a ban would have been neither realistic nor desirable in the eyes of legislators and lobbyists. (The situation was different in better-paid professions, especially among female civil servants, who in many countries had to give up their jobs when they got married.)

Women themselves, internationally and whether from the middle or working class, whether in women's organizations, trade unions or political parties, were at first just as divided as the men. Opponents criticized either alternately or simultaneously the fact that female factory legislation gave women privileged status or that it classified them as inferior. Conversely, supporters saw it as a means of challenging the inferior status of women. Feminist opponents and supporters disagreed as to whether they viewed women's industrial labour as independence and liberation or as bitter necessity and exploitation. Opponents used arguments of classical economic liberalism to make their case against state intervention and for freedom of contract and competition: 'If man and wife like overwork, let them'; 'hard work really hurts nobody'. Emmy Paterson, the most significant British spokeswoman, said she 'would rather women suffer the evils of overwork so that they should in this way come more fully to an understanding of the unsatisfactory state of their position and the need to form trade unions for themselves.'[28] Supporters, on the other hand, including the national and international organizations of Jewish women, demanded state intervention since they felt the interests of working women got lost amidst the profit interests of the capitalists and the egoism of the unions. They did not merely want the same opportunities on the free market but, like the male unions, they wanted equality as a result of restricting an absolute free market. In modern terminology, they wanted not only equal opportunity but equal results, affirmative action or 'positive discrimination'. But in contrast to many male supporters, feminists never demanded a general ban on employment for women or wives. Women who opposed legislation largely had their eyes on well-paid positions (such as women in the printing works), but they cautioned that protective legislation would end up excluding all women from wage-earning and they brought major differences among women to bear: married and unmarried, with and without children, young and old, strong and weak. Women who supported it made more reference to the miserable working conditions, pointing to the double burden and health risks. With respect to night work and measures to separate the sexes during work, they attacked sexual harassment at the workplace under the category of 'morality', much like the female temperance movements and the feminist attack against the sexual double standard.

British working-class women were also divided. There were 5,000 signatures collected opposing the Factory Act of 1874, 95,000 in favour of it. In 1887 female miners protested before the House of Commons against the exclusion laws and a short time later 66,000 washerwomen demanded the statutory eight-hour day for themselves. In a number of countries the protest came from highly qualified women employed at printing works who lost valuable income when night work was prohibited. Social Demo-

crats in Sweden and Denmark protested against the women-specific enforcement of gender-neutral legislation. In 1889 Clara Zetkin rejected
the protective legislation with the argument that 'we do not recognize
any special woman question – we do not recognize any special women
workers' question!' Then she accepted it as of 1891: first, 'in the enduring class interest of the proletariat', for which the woman worker shall
'bear healthy children' and 'see that tomorrow there is a proletariat able
to fight'. Second, because at that time she was consolidating her powerful position within the Social Democratic Party and they had spoken out
in favour of protective legislation. Third, because she wished to relieve
the condition of working-class mothers, which she considered to be 'social murder'.[29] Middle-class German feminists also decided in 1900 to
advocate the legislation, despite their differences with the socialist women.
They did so because they were committed to the improvement of lower-
class women's lot, but also under the influence of the now-powerful social democracy. Even earlier the British Women's Trade Union League
had spoken out for protective legislation, followed soon afterwards by
most British as well as American feminists. Feminists remained solidly
opposed in Denmark, Sweden and the Netherlands, where the proportion of women working in factories was low or where factory work was
of minor significance. When the International Labour Organization recommended the ban on night work for women in 1919, it was supported
by a strong international women's lobby.

There was considerable symbolic, albeit minimal practical, value to
the heated dispute on the question of what and how women were and the
role of the state. It cannot be confirmed and is rather improbable that the
laws actually served to reduce the extent of women's employment (except for those working in mines and printing works). At first the laws
applied only to women working in factories and mines, which comprised
a small minority of female wage-earners; they were extended to other
categories only gradually. In times of economic bottlenecks, such as World
War I and during the period of Russian War Communism (1917–21),
the laws were rescinded or circumvented. Nurses were never banned from
working at night. The number of regulations were probably surpassed
by the number of exceptions. Many factories avoided the rules illegally;
if this was discovered by trade inspectors, the penalty was mild. In 1921
in Spain, illegal night work was identified in more than one-third of the
factories. Women workers themselves found a number of ways to cir-
cumvent the rules when they functioned counter to their interests. If they
were caught, they were not punished, since the bans were directed against
the employers. A majority of feminists did not condemn pro-tective legislation as discriminatory until the emergence of second-wave feminism
in the 1970s, at the same time and to the same extent as the working

conditions of lower-class women had very much improved and quotas and other forms of positive discrimination were demanded for women in the higher professions. When in 1991, almost a century after the great debates on female labour legislation, the European Court of Justice ruled against the ban on night work because it seemed to conflict with the 1976 anti-discrimination rule of the European Community (German law complied with the ruling immediately), objections came from France. It claimed that women had always been able to work at night, despite the ban, and that night shifts made them especially vulnerable to sexual harassment or even violence and could not be reconciled with women's family duties. The logical counterpart to the 1991 decision came in 1997: the Court of Justice rejected discrimination of men in such – higher – professions where preferential treatment for women with equal qualifications had been hard won by feminism.

In contrast to the emblematic ban on night work and other regulations of exclusion, the third strand of early state welfare in Europe (initially in the United States as well) would have a greater future: maternity protection. Many of the European feminists who had spoken out in favour of restrictions on competition for women workers had done so because the restrictions were placed on the agenda together with maternity protection, even though the two were anchored in different legal categories. Virtually all feminists who opposed limits on the length of the workday and minimum wages, which were often given legitimacy in the name of motherhood, spoke at the same time in favour of state intervention that aimed truly to improve the situation of mothers. It was largely to the credit of the women's movements that maternity protection also became a transnational movement around 1900. The American Katherine Anthony referred to it in 1915 as a 'dollars for women movement', in addition to the 'votes for women movement'.[30] At issue were not merely restrictions without financial compensation but also benefits for pregnant women workers and those in childbed; security against the female poverty risk of motherhood (parallel to the security against male life risks); and the option for mothers to combine wage-earning and family work. Above and beyond that, maternity protection was soon not only discussed with respect to needy and working mothers, but the discussion was extended to deal with the social role of maternity in general and thus the legitimacy of the male family wage, the income gap between male and female wage-earners and an income transfer from men to women guaranteed by the welfare state.

Many feminists claimed that the activities of mothers and housewives did not belong to the domain of nature, but was labour, albeit of a special kind. The German radical Käthe Schirmacher declared in 1904 that housework was 'real', 'productive work' that 'produces, preserves and distributes value'. There is 'no more productive work than that of the mother', she argued, who 'creates the value of values, the thinking and acting value called a human being'. She continued that domestic women's work was 'the *conditio sine qua non*' of male employment and it was a fallacy that the man worked for two, when 'in fact he is merely pocketing for two'. The 'sex bonus' to the male breadwinner wages – Schirmacher borrowed the expression from Max Weber – should really go to the wives. She protested against the 'exploitation of housewife and mother'; rather than exploiting her again outside the home for the sake of a doubtful emancipation, domestic work should be recognized socially, politically and economically. Whereas some feminists rejected her argument as too 'individualistic', Schirmacher met with approval from housewives.

Schirmacher had taken her ideas largely from France, where they had appeared earliest. At the International Congress for Women's Rights in 1878 in Paris, demands were expressed for municipalities to support poverty-stricken women for eighteen months after they gave birth. In 1892 the first French women's conference that called itself 'feminist' (General Congress of Feminist Societies) reiterated the urgent need for a *protection sociale à toutes les mères*. The indefatigable suffragist Hubertine Auclert, the first woman to call herself 'feminist', wished that the future 'motherly state' would secure assistance to children. In 1899 she demanded a maternity allowance financed by a paternal tax levied on men and, finally, a payment to mothers 'for indispensable service to the state'. At the International Feminist Congress of 1896 in Paris, the socialist feminist Léonie Rouzade took up an expression that had emerged a short time earlier, which from this point on granted legitimacy to such demands: motherhood was a 'social function', not a natural, private or individual one; it was 'the principal social function', 'the source of the race' and therefore it 'deserves to be subsidized by the state'. At the International Conference on the Conditions and the Rights of Women (1900 in Paris), Marie Pognon demanded a government fund to support children that would be accessible to all women, whether married or not, to make them independent of the fathers of their children, rendering the problem of paternity suits irrelevant. The conference recommended the establishment of a *caisse publique de la maternité* and the right of employed women to receive paid maternity leave. The Conseil National des Femmes Françaises, founded in 1901, and the national suffragist organization (1909) also adopted the concept of motherhood as a social task. Marguerite Durand, editor of the feminist daily *La Fronde*, called for a maternity insurance as well as equal pay for equal work outside of the home. The more radical Nelly Roussel claimed women's right to decide for themselves whether or not to have children, as well as a *salaire de la maternité*, a 'fair wage for the noble work of motherhood', which would allow mothers to dedicate themselves entirely to their children. In the anthology *Mutterschaft* (published in 1912 by Adele Schreiber), which presented the European efforts and the 'social, public function' of mothers, Roussel defined for German-speaking readers the 'ideal of the women's movement' as the 'recognition and material valuation of motherhood as a social contribution that is valuable to the state'. As a pacifist, she proposed the 'budget of life' to oppose the military 'budget of death'. The German Marie Stritt wrote of 'the mother as citizen', whose rights – in contrast to those stated in the civil code – should no longer be placed behind those of single women.[31] To these feminists, equality did not mean sameness but independence (from employer and husband) and equal liberties. With the slogan that motherhood was a social and political function, they fundamentally questioned the separation of the private and the public, female poverty and the distribution of paid and unpaid work between the sexes.

French women had an additional motive for insisting on the rights and duties of mothers. In France pro-natalist opinions were voiced early on demanding a rise in the birth rate, which had dropped in France earlier than elsewhere (around 1900 the birth rate in France was 21 per thousand, in Sweden, Britain, Wales and Norway it was between 27 and 29, in Italy, Spain and Germany it was between 33 and 36, with a downward trend everywhere). *Dénatalité* and *dépopulation* were considered public and political problems, especially since the French defeat in 1870 in the war against the more populous Germany. The subject was charged – in France and later in most of Europe – with the issue of national grandeur, European hegemony and imperialist aspirations. French pro-natalism was propagated by men who had united in 1896 in the influential National Alliance to Increase the French Population and differed dramatically from the maternalism of the women's movement. The Alliance saw the reason for the decline in the birth rate not as a crisis of femininity but one of virility, which was why it focused on protecting paternity and demanded father-oriented reforms. Men were called upon to father more offspring ('let us prepare our children to become fathers!') and financial incentives were demanded for fathers, especially deductions for wives and children in income and inheritance taxes. Since that time tax exemptions became the most important proposal of pro-natalist propaganda, which pursued the revaluation of fatherhood. Conversely, the Alliance proposed a medal for mothers. The proposal prompted Maria Martin and Hubertine Auclert in 1903 to insist on state maternity allowances with greater vehemence than they had previously, now spiced with sarcastic criticism. But aside from the basic difference between maternalism and paternalism, the French women's movement was not afraid of pro-natalism; on the contrary, it sought to exploit it for its own purposes. As Maria Martin declared at a women's conference: 'If you want children, learn to honor mothers.'[32]

Radical, moderate and socialist women proclaimed this utopia, or more realistic variants, and formulated practical suggestions. The Norwegian Katti Anker Møller, who advocated the 'emancipation of motherhood' and a state-financed wage for mothers until their children started school, and Eleanor Rathbone of Britain developed comprehensive theories of a society in which independence and social security were based not only on employment but on work in the family as well. Italian feminists struggled for a *cassa di maternità*, a maternity insurance for women workers. Paolina Schiff made the first such proposal on behalf of the Milan-based League for the Defence of the Interests of Women in 1894, and soon the Unione femminile nazionale took up the subject. In Germany the Bismarckian health insurance model was used as a basis for demands. The Industrial Act of 1878 had banned work on Sundays for factory workers and introduced a mandatory maternity leave of three weeks after parturition. Starting in 1883 self-insured working women received a modest albeit highly insufficient maternity benefit from the newly established health insurance scheme. (A similar law followed in Austria in 1888; in Switzerland mandatory leave was established, but without financial compensation.) From 1897 this was then the point of departure for the German women's movement, which demanded an extension of the leave to include the late phase of pregnancy, full compensation of wages and an independent maternity insurance in which maternity was not defined as a sickness and which would add maternity to employment as a source of entitlement. Mothers were to be recognized as subjects of social and political citizenship. Around 1897 suffragists Lily Braun and Anita Augspurg started calling for payment of mothers in the first year after confinement. (Braun advocated payment for women workers only; Augspurg for all mothers. From this perspective Augspurg founded an international league in 1897 that opposed the *recherche de la paternité*, for which most French feminists were struggling at the time.) Some members of the radical League for Maternity Protection demanded such compensation in 1905. Alice Salomon, who stressed mothers' need for protection more than their work for children, and Henriette Fürth instantiated the suggestions for employed pregnant women and mothers. The Jewish Women's League (Jüdische Frauenbund) advocated recognizing the value of mothers' work, as did the General German Women's Association in its 1905 programme. However, Helene Lange felt it was too early to measure its value in precise figures because such an approach was 'not yet a part of the general moral consciousness'. Since in Germany the insurance model had become indisputably well established and health insurance for women workers covered the postpartum period, further-reaching demands that took all mothers into consideration would have no future among German feminists. The major obstacles were the contributions of the insured and the costs to be borne by the state – who should pay for an independent maternity insurance?

In 1896 amidst the public discussion in Britain on the miserable conditions facing women, and especially mothers of small children, Alys Russell (wife of Bertrand) demanded 'payment of motherhood'. She criticized August Bebel for viewing women only as factory workers and not as mothers, and for expecting their emancipation only from collectivization and not 'in an individualistic state of society'. An impressive and organized mothers' movement emerged at this time. The women of the Labour Party were among the first who discussed a 'motherhood endowment' (the term was coined around 1904), which should enable women to tend to their young children without having to work for wages and without being dependent on the husband, especially if he did not bring home a family wage. The Women's Cooperative Guild, which mobilized primarily working-class women, was especially active in this area ('Because a man sells his labour while the mother applies hers directly in the home, why should he claim to be the breadwinner?'), as were the Women's Industrial Council and the women's group of the social reform-oriented Fabian Society. Mabel Atkinson, a Fabian, argued that working-class women, who had to be wage-earners for subsistence reasons, were not demanding 'the right to work but rather the protection against the unending burden of toil'. She saw the 'State endowment' as 'coming to be realized more and more clearly as the ultimate ideal of the feminist movement', since 'no act of citizenship is more fundamental' than childbearing and child-rearing. The endowment should be paid for the period in which women devoted their time to mothering. In Britain as elsewhere women declared that they did not need to become citizens first, but by virtue of their diverse contributions to society, including that of motherhood, they already were de facto citizens. Suffrage would serve to acknowledge that fact. In the United States radical feminist Crystal Eastman, who was also an active supporter of birth control, advocated the recognition of child-rearing 'as work, requiring a definite economic reward and not merely entitling the performer to be dependent on some man'.[33] Similar claims were raised by three other groups: social reformers of the Progressive era such as Jane Addams and Sophonisba Breckinridge; feminists who founded and directed the Children's Bureau in the US Department of Labor (1912), especially Lillian Wald, Florence Kelley, Julia Lathrop and Grace Abbott; and the mothers' movement launched in the 1890s, which was organized as the National Congress of Mothers. The last-named was largely responsible for the emergence of a broad-based movement that demanded 'mothers' pensions' for widowed and other very poor mothers. Claims for a maternity endowment to be granted to all, or even only to employed mothers, were rarely raised in the United States. Nevertheless, mothers' pensions were justified (or attacked) on the grounds that they were not alms but payment for work. Many (advocates and opponents alike) saw the mothers' pensions as a first step to a universal maternity endowment and many mothers saw them as their right.

Although the dignity, 'social function' and value of motherhood were declared loudly and frequently in women's movements throughout Europe – and beyond – there was disagreement whether, and if so how, these values should be expressed through state support. Praise of motherhood and complaints about the actual circumstances ('It is in maternity ... where the deepest roots of either slavery or liberty of the female sex lie', or 'Why should the greatest achievement of woman be at the same time the foundation of her servitude?') could be used either to recommend a mother's endowment (Helene Stöcker) or to reject it (Madeleine Vernet). A common objection – which Schirmacher was confronted with – was that the demand was too 'individualistic' and egotistical. Katherine Glasier of the British Independent Labour Party condemned it in 1909 as the 'sheerly individualist "revolt" stage of our women's battle for freedom', and Ramsay MacDonald of the Labour Party called it 'an insane burst of individualism'. Others viewed payments to mothers as inappropriate distrust of the husbands and their use of the family wage. According to the British social worker Anna Martin and the German Marianne Weber (Weber's position was adopted by the German women's movement), maternity endowments and 'wages for housework' would serve to relieve husbands of their responsibility for wife and children, thereby undermining male work ethics. Instead, they preferred a wife's right to a share of her husband's wages, as household and spending money. In 1912 Millicent Fawcett called for the recognition of the 'economic value of [the wife's] work in her household', payable in the form of 'a definite sum as wages' or at least 'a proportion of her husband's wages'.[34] Some were concerned that state benefits, especially for unmarried women, would encourage immorality and sexual promiscuity. Others, such as Weber in Germany, Glasier in Britain and Vernet in France, thought state resources were insufficient and that the shift from a 'labour of love' to a monetary value was 'unnatural', 'immoral' and 'monstrous'. Finally, there were some who thought marriage law reform was more important than state benefits, viewing the economic side of female independence exclusively in women's wage-earning potential, which had somehow to be combined with domestic work. Virtually no feminists feared that providing benefits for mothers would bind them against their will to hearth and husband. It was acknowledged that poverty and dependence did not come from access to their own means but from the lack of such access, and at any rate childcare was generally viewed as women's work, albeit not necessarily for all women.

Social Policies for and against Women

[T]he information might prove useful to the people of one of the few great countries which as yet have no system of State or national assistance in maternity – the United States.

Julia Lathrop, US Children's Bureau, 1917[35]

Female labour legislation divided feminists in some countries; in others they were clearly either for or against. On the issue of maternity protection for women workers, however, they were all agreed. There had to be maternity leave after (and soon also directly before) confinement, and loss of wages had to be fully compensated. When heated debate was ignited on this issue in 1891–2 in the French Chamber of Deputies, some deputies drew attention to forerunners Switzerland, Germany, Austria, Belgium and the Netherlands, to the backwardness of Russia and especially to the International Conference for Protective Labour Legislation in 1890 in Berlin, which recommended maternity leave for women workers for four weeks after parturition. Prenatal leave had not been envisioned, nor was wage compensation. Nonetheless, it had long been known that women workers could only take advantage of the leave if they were compensated for their lost wages. The women's movement especially, although not exclusively, drew attention to this fact. Workers often concealed their pregnancy or worked illegally, and this usually met with the tacit acceptance of their employers. Of the countries that had already instituted maternity leave (Switzerland with eight weeks, Germany with three, Austria and the Netherlands with four), only Switzerland had a prenatal maternity leave of two weeks prior to the due date. Until 1882 in Switzerland, half of all industrial workers were women; in the textile industry it was even 64 per cent. Following the 1890 conference, Britain, Portugal (1891) and Sweden (1900) introduced a four-week maternity leave, followed by Norway with six weeks (1892), Denmark (1901), Italy (1902), Greece and Russia (1912). Initially, only Germany and Austria offered maternity benefits (since 1883 and 1887, respectively), amounting to roughly half of the already modest wages. France as well as Italy, Denmark and Russia followed a long time later.

The debate in the French Chamber was lively and fundamental. Was there really a need for a four-week maternity leave to recover after giving birth and to tend to the child? A deputy of the Radical Left thought not, considering the leave to be an attack on individual liberty and an attempt to treat women as inferior. A physician and liberal republican asserted that 80 per cent of women in childbed could return to work three days after the birth without any difficulties. He summarized the common, though in view of the *Code Napoléon* very dubious, opinion that legislators should not invade the private sphere, that 'one should not regulate domestic life through laws'.[36] The only principle that found widespread support was that all legislation should also apply to agricultural workers; this was a major category of female employment in France. No maternity leave legislation was passed (only the ban on night work went through), but the debate was nevertheless pioneering, since it raised the issue of financial compensation and the value of motherhood. A deputy who was at this point a lone voice called enthusiastically for compensation of one franc for new mothers on leave who had earned two francs per day; though that was a considerable investment, he argued, 'the children' whose health was insured in this way would one day be able to defend France's borders. The most zealous defender of maternity leave vehemently rejected a benefit. A year later – only a few months after the first 'feminist' conference in 1892, where 'social protection for all mothers' was demanded – Paul Lafargue and other deputies of the French Labour Party demanded a *caisse de maternité* to be financed by the state, the municipalities and the employers. They justified it by asserting that *toute citoyenne*, whether married or not, who brought a child into the world performed 'a sacred task and satisfies a social function'.

The heated debate ended without a law. But in 1893 (and soon afterwards in Denmark), it was made possible within the medical poor relief services for needy new mothers to be given the opportunity to receive medical services at the expense of the municipality or the district. This law emphasized that 'women in childbed shall be considered as being ill'. The terms of an international debate and development were thus laid down, and were also adopted by the German Reichstag when the health insurance act was amended in 1891–2 (in 1891 maternity leave was extended to four weeks): Was giving birth an illness? Feminists generally rejected such reasoning. Was it the responsibility of health insurance to cover maternity costs, even if no premiums had been paid? German Catholic Party representatives were opposed and referred instead to the Catholic charity organization. Should distinctions be made between healthy and 'truly sick' pregnant women? Should the state also provide financial benefits for unwed mothers and thereby promote immorality? Catholic and other representatives of both countries found that to be cause for concern. Should only wage-earning mothers, only needy ones, only unwed ones or all mothers receive benefits? Only feminists supported the last-named option. For how many weeks before or after the birth should benefits be paid, and how high should payments be or what kind of services should be granted? A small number of weeks and a small amount of money became a bone of contention among legislators. But the Reichstag representatives did not even discuss the matter that confounded their French counterparts around the same time: 'motherhood as a social function'. Because of the predominance of the insurance model in Germany, from the very beginning maternity benefits applied to wage-earning mothers only. In 1904 there were already 2.7 million women with health and thus maternity insurance in Germany (52 per cent of employed women). The health insurance offices paid a total of roughly twelve marks per woman who had recently given birth.

Amendments to the German industrial and health insurance laws in 1903, 1908 and 1911 were followed closely by lively debate within the women's movement. The reforms extended maternity leave to eight weeks, raised maternity benefits and included compulsory health insurance for domestic servants. In France the reforms in state welfare began with the Engerand Act of 1909, which guaranteed job security to women who took maternity leave of up to eight weeks before and after giving birth. But this leave was neither mandatory nor was any financial assistance available for this time (though public school teachers became entitled to full wage compensation as of 1910). It took another four years of pressure and close cooperation between feminists and the few deputies who supported their cause before major changes were enacted. The Strauss Act of 1913 and another financial law required employers to grant maternity leave and awarded allowances to certain categories of women workers; these payments were financed by the municipalities, *départements* and the government. In the same year, allowances were introduced for needy families with four or more children; also, special benefits became available for civil servants. In both cases – in contrast to the Strauss Act – payments were made to the fathers, so feminists unsurprisingly railed against them. Together, these three laws paved the way for the French welfare state. The Social Insurance Act of 1928, which was modelled in part after its German counterpart, integrated the laws of 1913 into a health insurance scheme (once again feminists opposed the equation of pregnancy and birth with sickness). This law applied to insured, that is, employed women and the wives of insured men. It guaranteed medical care at no charge during the postpartum period, and also extended the length of maternity leave and raised maternity benefits.

In Italy it was largely the lobbying by women's organizations that led in 1910 to the establishment of the national *cassa di maternità*, a fund to finance maternity leave. It was based on an insurance model; the mandatory premiums were to be paid by the female workers themselves but not the male ones – this was unique compared to other countries and was not supported by the women's movement. The fund was supplemented by employers, donations and state subsidies. But benefits were too low and premium payments too high for most women, so they often resorted to working illegally; consequently, the *cassa* was initially a fiasco. In the United States – up to today, in contrast to Europe – there has never been a law guaranteeing maternity leave with wage compensation. From 1911 to 1939, however, thirty-nine states introduced mothers' pensions. They were usually intended for needy, widowed women; in some states unwed mothers or those abandoned by their husbands were also eligible. Mothers' pensions were part of poor relief. In Europe, on the other hand, maternity benefits were integrated within the health insurance systems (except for Italy and France, which did not yet have one) and were therefore reserved for employed women. In Sweden, despite much protest, especially after women entered the parliament, it took more than three decades after the introduction of a four-week maternity leave (1900) until financial compensation was granted. Efforts were blocked with the argument that assistance could only be paid by a health insurance system; this was finally established in 1931. In Norway (1909), the Netherlands (1913) and Denmark (1915) maternity benefits were also coupled with the new health insurance system. State assistance for unwed mothers was instituted in 1915 in Norway against fierce protest by the conservatives; the women were expected to have jobs in addition to caring for their children, however, and the payments were small and discriminatory. More important was the innovation that non-insured wives of insured workers were also entitled to maternity benefits (1915). This was not introduced in Germany until 1924, led by the Social Democrat women, with the united strength of the women in the parliament of the new republic. By the time it was instituted in France (1928) and in Sweden (1931), it had become almost self-evident. The issue had caused a stir in Britain more than a decade earlier, when the National Insurance Act was enacted in 1911. The Women's Cooperative Guild succeeded in inserting a maternity benefit into the bill, not only for self-insured women but also for non-employed dependants of insured wage-earning husbands. According to the law, the maternity benefit was to be paid to the husband. The Guild once again waged a battle and won. As of 1913 the mothers were entitled to pick up the 30 shillings themselves at the post office. From this point on, the issue of whether wives had an independent right to benefits that were paid to them as 'dependants' took its place on European social policy agendas.

Julia Lathrop, head of the Children's Bureau of the US Department of Labor prepared an impressive international survey in 1917 of state-sponsored or subsidized maternity benefit schemes, criticizing the fact that such a system was lacking in the United States. The Australian law of 1912 was unique in granting maternity allowances to its 'citizens' regardless of marital and occupational status. In this respect it was more advanced than the European insurance model. However, the insurance model that applied to employed women and other women as 'dependants' of an insured male had the advantage that it was independent of citizenship and thus also applied to foreign workers. Largely as a result of women's lobbying, the International Labour Organization recommended, in the Washington Convention of 1919, legislation granting a maternity leave of six weeks before and after parturition, full wage compensation and free medical services. Germany's Maternity Protection Act of 1927 was, along with the Unemployment Insurance Act of 1927, the most important welfare law of the Weimar Republic. Germany thus became the first major industrialized country to implement the Washington Convention, combining it with job security during the maternity leave. Again, it was female representatives – social, liberal and moderate – who carried the parliamentary work and lobby. In 1942 the law was modified in two ways characteristic of Nazism. First, it excluded 'racially inferior' women, especially forced labourers and Jewish women, from maternity protection. Second, it provided for the increased establishment of childcare facilities in order to promote women in wage-earning positions necessary for the war effort. In 1945 the law was annulled by the Allied forces. In West Germany, a new act to protect employed women during maternity was passed in 1952 which had no exclusionary stipulations; a corresponding law was passed in East Germany in 1953.

The European development of maternity protection – extension of maternity leave and, as slow as it was, benefits approaching full wage compensation – laid the groundwork for women to be able to combine wage-earning work with family and housework. The forces and arguments that advanced the cause of state recognition of motherhood over the course of two generations, at least with reference to wage-earning, were numerous and varied. The motives, arguments and lobby of the women's movement were only one factor among many, and the notion of 'motherhood as a social function', with all its implications, was irrelevant for the legislators. In all major industrialized countries the 'people', 'nation', 'species', 'race' or 'human race' had to be summoned to convince legislators, industry and the public sphere that time and money for mothers were not only in the mothers' interests but were also for the 'common good'. Alongside humanitarian motives, the battle against poverty and the attempt to integrate the labour movement there was increasing paranoia that women were afraid to give birth, about abortion, infanticide and the decline in birth rates. The issue of maternity protection joined forces with the struggle against the mortality of infants, children and mothers. It also stood in the context of pro-natalist rhetoric and politics that promoted maternal welfare as a means of encouraging women who could not afford children due to poverty and overwork nevertheless to become mothers. This rhetoric and politics developed against the background of the continuing decline in the birth rate, the low point of which was reached in Britain, Germany, Norway and Sweden around 1933, and somewhat later in France. That rhetoric and politics remained influential well into the 1930s, to varying degrees in the respective countries. Yet the most significant factor was the general trend towards the European welfare state. Once a novelty, it became commonplace for the state to intervene in the 'freedom' of the market to solve social problems. Which social problems were considered worthy of being solved was dependent on the public awareness they were able to cause, which was fed by highly varying motives. Irrespective of the motives that had led to the introduction of maternity benefits, and parallel to the general rise in both male and female wages (though the gap between the two remained almost constant), maternity protection raised the price of women's labour considerably. Only an expanding economy could afford it. In the 1930s Russian women were granted paid maternity leave, leave to care for sick children and an early retirement age. In the 1990s, in view of the new demands for efficient production and of rampant poverty, many women were laid off because their labour appeared too expensive as compared with that of men.

5

Between Extremes

In spite of everything there have been revolutions for the better in this century . . . , the rise of the fourth estate, and the emergence of women after centuries of oppression.

Rita Levi Montalcini[1]

The twentieth century was, for the women of Europe as well as for the men, a century of extremes poised between the Roaring Twenties and the murderous forties, between democracy and dictatorship, peace and war, welfare state and genocide, between liberty, murdering and being murdered. The path leading from 'kings to people' was obstructed in parts of Europe by dictators who found a broad following. Important trends in women's history, especially the question of civil, political and social rights, were interrupted by events not rooted in gender relations, yet which nevertheless were crucial for women's history. Two world wars, the catastrophic force of which was unleashed primarily in Europe, and the Holocaust threw dark shadows not only over the time in which they raged but over the entire twentieth century. Both sexes have been affected by the questions of contempt for human life, of guilt and responsibility, consensus and collaboration, of complicity and resistance. The wars left sixty million dead in their wake, mostly soldiers (as a result of which the century saw a feminization of widowhood) but also women and men from the civilian populations of all belligerent countries, and there were millions of refugees. In both wars millions of women and men became victims of forced labour, especially for Germany, and many did not survive. There were millions of victims of the Holocaust, including six million Jews from throughout Europe, as well as Romany (Gypsies) and segments of the Slavic peoples. The history of women had always been very diverse, individually and with respect to their affiliation to 'imagined communities' such as class, religion or nation. In the twentieth century, however, this diversity was as extreme as that of life and death, 'worth' and 'inferiority', depending on affiliation to the 'community' of a particular 'race', on ethnicity, on descent and descendants.

Female Citizens and the New Woman

When we got to the university, it was absolute bliss. We were ambitious and wanted to do great things and were incredibly proud. And what has happened hardly fifteen years later? The flapper has come.

Gabriele Tergit, 1927[2]

Twenty-seven million men were drafted during World War I in Great Britain, France and Germany; in Russia there were over ten million soldiers. In France, 60 per cent of the working male population went off to the military, making female wage-earning all the more important. Female employment rose most dramatically in Great Britain, where it had been relatively low; the increase was less drastic in France and Germany, where there had been a higher female employment rate (especially if agriculture is taken into account, which was significant in times of both war and peace). All over, many women who had been working in the largely women's fields of domestic service and agriculture entered industrial professions for the first time, mostly in the armaments industry (especially chemical, electrical and heavy industries); hence in France they were called *munitionettes*. Skilled specialists were replaced systematically by untrained and semi-skilled women in Britain. In the many parts of Germany where domestic industry was widespread, it was redirected into war production. Sometimes the women were attracted by the high factory wages (though these differed greatly depending on branch and level of training), sometimes they were pushed by dire need or by recruitment measures or campaigns, which the women's movements also supported. Many women worked for the sake of their independence, but a far greater proportion took up employment in order to support their families, as had been the case earlier. More significant, however, were the diversification of women's labour, especially for public opinion, which saw it as the collapse of the traditional gender order, and the obvious albeit relative social rise of a female minority. In France women became bank employees. Throughout Europe women took over as ticket sellers and conductors for the transit systems. The number of nurses rose enormously and many saw their work as equivalent in worth to male military service – Hertha Nathorff, for example, who later became a doctor and was then forced to leave Germany since she was Jewish. Many worked not on the home front but the military front. 'You are free of the confinement at home and can get involved in a great task', wrote one nurse. They were shocked at the atrocious suffering and worked incredibly hard day and night, often using family metaphors to refer to their relationships to the soldiers. German nurses named a military hospital for eighteen-year-olds the 'nursery' and to one of them 'the best wage for my work was being called "our sister" by the troops and officers'. In France the image of nurses oscillated between that of nun, angel and mother of the *petit poilu*, as the combatants were called – *la vraie, la sublime* or *la Dame blanche*. Some of the nurses received a military medal or were buried alongside soldiers. The International Red Cross awarded Florence Nightingale Certificates, decorated with a symbol of the Pietà, for 'The Greatest Mother of the World'.[3] Men as well as women suffered in Belgium and northern France under German terror, looting, forced labour, mass deportations. Edith Cavell, a British nurse who ran a nursing station in Brussels, was executed by the Germans for her resistance.

After World War I nurses and *munitionettes* were laid off in all countries involved in the war, as were other women in areas that had been important for the war effort and other fields in which they had to step down to make room for discharged soldiers. Women's movements protested against the dismissals but there was no mass protest by women at large. They knew all too well that the new opportunities had been war-related and most of them were all too happy to be reunited with the men of their families, if that was the case at all. The end of the war brought a veritable surge back to the private sphere. But the clock could not be turned back on the expansion of women's wage-work. Soon the official employment rate of women had reached 54 per cent in France (1921), 35 per cent in Britain (1921) and 48 per cent in Germany (1925). The proportion of married women is even more revealing. Whereas in interwar Britain only 10 per cent of all married women were employed, the figure for Germany was between 29 (1925) and 34 (1939); for Italy between 12 per cent (1931) and 21 per cent (1936); and in France the figure was even higher. But the distribution of women working in various sectors and branches changed very abruptly as compared with the pre-war period.

Building on the two earlier international women's associations and the Women's International League for Peace and Freedom, which was founded in 1919 from the smaller women's peace movement that had been developing since 1915, a wide-ranging international feminist network emerged after the war. Because financial resources were necessary for such a global mobilization, the network included not only an intellectual and political 'feminine elite of the world' (as a member of the German League of Jewish Women put it in 1926) but also an elite with independent means.[4]

These women were also active in the International Labour Organization, the League of Nations and later the United Nations. Peace, disarmament and gender equality were their major goals. Most of the German women's movement did not initially join the new internationalism because they viewed the Versailles Treaty as unjust, but in 1922 they resumed their cooperative efforts. At the 1926 convention of the International Alliance for Women's Suffrage at the Parisian Sorbonne, the black, white and red flag was erroneously raised for the German delegation. When the error was discovered and the flag was replaced by the black, red and gold one, Gertrud Bäumer defended the new flag against the German nationalist women who were present. (Bäumer was vice-president of the German Democratic Party and the Federation of German Women's Associations, Reichstag representative, civil servant in the Ministry of the Interior, German delegate to the League of Nations and advocate of a cautious course between nationalism and internationalism.) The threat of fascism, Nazism and Communism, and later the politics of appeasement *vis-à-vis* Hitler, led in the 1930s to heated conflict over the legitimacy of war. The three international women's associations protested against the spreading anti-Semitism, and after the Federation of German Women's Associations disbanded in May 1933 to avoid being Nazified the International Council of Women refused to allow any German – that is, Nazi – representatives in their ranks.

Women had meanwhile entered the national parliaments, at a time when Europe, bled dry and torn by revolution, fear of revolution and reaction, was waiting for reconstruction and a stable democracy. The last anti-suffragists, largely those who had supported the war most enthusiastically, had conjured up the 'danger' that women now made up a majority in view of the male war casualties. But women's suffrage was not seriously attacked any more, except in the upcoming dictatorships, which, however, rescinded the suffrage for men as well or perverted its meaning. Women's entrance into the parliaments was not especially triumphant in quantitative terms. The German Reichstag had the highest share of women; initially 10 per cent, 7 per cent in 1930, and in November 1933 women were once again prohibited from standing for election. In Finland women made up 9 per cent and in the Netherlands, 7. In 'The Mother of all Parliaments' only one of seventeen female candidates was elected in 1918, but she never took office since she was not only Irish but a member of Sinn Féin. In 1919 Lady Astor moved up and thirty-six women became members of parliament (MPs) in the interwar period. A peak was reached in 1931, with fifteen (2.5 per cent of all MPs). They were all elected via the traditional parties, except for suffragist and social reformer Eleanor Rathbone, who took a university seat as an independent in 1929 and retained it until her death in 1946. Soon after she was elected Rathbone spoke out clearly against Nazism and anti-Semitism. She had succeeded Millicent Fawcett as president of the National Union in 1919, which later changed its name, as did many other suffrage organizations once their goal had been achieved, to the National Union of Societies for Equal Citizenship (the General German Women's Association became the German League of Female Citizens [Deutsche Staatsbürgerinnenverband]). Irrespective of the voting system – majority vote in Britain; elsewhere the Labour parties usually managed to push through the proportional vote – women were usually placed by their parties in the most hopeless positions. The proportional vote, which had been conceived so that the parliament could accurately reflect the social composition of the population, now reflected only the relative strength of the parties. Whereas suffrage was democratized, the parties were not, and so women remained largely excluded from 'passive' suffrage.

There were other problems, too. Many demands on representatives, including fundraising and looking after the constituency, were taken care of by a presentable and cooperative wife – no wonder, then, that a female British MP sighed, 'What I need is a wife'.[5] Party decisions were made not only during commission meetings but also in men's clubs and at bars; Helene Lange often joked about male 'smoke' and 'fug'. It is unclear whether or not newly admitted female voters tended to vote for women; more likely they voted for 'their' parties. The goal of suffragism had been to represent the female good and thus also the common good. But now, for lack of a common goal, the women's movement fell apart, or else it expanded into numerous separate interest groups. By no means did all the women in the parliaments share the former goal, and both the female good and the common good remained highly controversial. In some countries there were plans for a women's party or a party with exclusively women on its parliamentary candidate list. But the example set by the US National Women's Party, which never caught on, could hardly serve for encouragement, and a British initiative of 1920 failed as well. Should feminists or women in general vote only for women, or even only for feminists? What platform could a majority of women, or even just feminists, agree upon?

The main reason, however, why few women were elected was that they were still not fully accepted as 'representatives of the people', that is, as representatives also of men. Such acceptance would have required – as many women had been emphasizing since the French Revolution – not only a political revolution in a narrow sense, but a cultural revolution. It would take half a century before the true implementation of passive suffrage – that is, not merely the eligibility to run for election but actually getting elected – was to take its place on the political agenda. Only through the pressure of the second-wave women's movement, public opinion and quotas for women (contrasting as well as parallel to traditional male quotas) was it possible to even embark on the path 'from votes to seats'. But the old suffragist claim that only women could represent women had now all but disappeared.

And yet female representatives played an important role in their respective national parliaments during the 1920s. They rarely got a foot in the door to 'male' domains such as foreign policy. Gertrud Bäumer was the first woman in Germany to hold a speech on foreign policy (in 1928 to the International Court of Justice in The Hague). To some extent female parliamentarians were kept out of such areas; to some extent, they set their own priorities elsewhere. Above all they dedicated themselves to issues they had long dealt with, social policy and the aspects of it that concerned women. Criticism that female representatives concentrated their energies on such 'women's issues' (though these had been entirely 'men's issues' until a short time earlier) was voiced as early as the 1920s. Gertrud Bäumer responded that, after all, laws were now being passed that were influenced by women. Although the traditional politics of 'reason of state' still prevailed, women in the parliament were succeeding in changing politics. Besides, she continued, it was an 'irony' of the new situation that even women were now judging the legislative areas 'by the old standards, according to which public welfare seems less important than state policy'.[6]

In cultural terms, the Roaring Twenties were less influenced by the new female citizens than by the New Woman: The *garçonne* in France, the flapper or nymph in Britain, the *maschietta* in Italy, and women with bobbed hairdos, the *Bubikopf*, in Germany. The New Woman was not all that new; she had already entered the stage around the turn of the century and came in many varieties. In France of the Belle Époque, where music halls, vaudeville theatre and serialized novels had their heyday, a new role for women was in the limelight of public interest. Imagery of the *années 1900* was marked by the *femme nouvelle* and the *femme fatale*, by androgynous hermaphrodites and women portrayed as profligate and excessively feminine. Actual women, too, had a growing influence on the culture of the generation. There was an abrupt rise in female authors, including Rachilde, acclaimed literary critic and author of scandalous best-sellers, and Colette, whose *Claudine* novels were her first literary success. The New Woman of the turn of the century, as she was portrayed in the media, was especially the professional or the student, unmarried academics, dancers and actresses, bicycle riders and athletes. Their life plans and their public presence illuminated the new options open to them. In many places the appearance of the *femme nouvelle* went hand in hand with a wave of misogyny and a politically consequential crisis in men's self-esteem. Especially in *fin de siècle* France, a feeling of cultural decadence prevailed that left its mark on the style of the epoch, and broad political circles responded with a strongly nationalistic form of anti-feminism.

In the *années folles* the New Woman was again discussed throughout Europe. She appeared to take over the streets, cafés and dance halls of the metropolis with her boyish silhouette, bobbed haircut and knee-length dresses. This was the image of a generation of women that became a symbol of the 1920s. Behind the symbol, which dominated magazines, light fiction and the movies, were the actual lives of young women whose lifestyle differed from that of their middle- or working-class mothers and grandmothers. Reluctant with respect to marriage and family life, these office workers, university students and journalists developed new values regarding sexual conduct, partnership, and private and work lives. Sex was no longer taboo; it was public. *Ideal Marriage* by Theodoor Hendrik van de Velde of the Netherlands appeared in Dutch (1926), went into thirty-five editions in German by 1929 and was also translated into English, Italian, Spanish, French and Swedish. It explained in detail the 'physiology and technique' of sexual desire and love games between a man and a woman. Everywhere, the number of female office workers rose; it tripled in Germany (the number of male office workers doubled). In the Netherlands in 1931 the female journalist Matty Vigelius wrote: 'In the morning quite a little army of cheery, sporty girls hastens to the city centre either by bike or by tram. With their happy, laughing faces, cheerful, naughty bonnets and hats, and sparkling eyes, they form a most agreeable decoration to the awakening town. . . . The girl has started her daily work, the work which will give her satisfaction and hence happiness in life. For woman has conquered the office.'[7] She conquered more than that. In early January 1933 Erika Mann opened her cabaret *Die Pfeffermühle* (which Thomas Mann called the 'swan song of the German Republic'). Forced to leave by the Nazis, she took it on tour throughout Europe and tried to start it up again in 1937 while in exile in the United States. Stage actress Marlene Dietrich – whose image combined the *garçonne* and the vamp – became the symbol of a woman's dream career, working her way up from modest living conditions to become the idol of female office workers. After her film *The Blue Angel* (1930), Dietrich went to the United States where, in view of Nazism, she became a dedicated exile. Many French artists and bohemians from the provinces found a second home in the metropolis on the Seine; in addition to Gertrude Stein and Djuna Barnes, black entertainers such as Josephine Baker charmed audiences.

The new, functional fashions and the new roles did not find much approval among many of the older generation. Colette, once a New Woman herself, commented ironically on the Parisian spring collection of 1925: 'Short, flat, geometrical, square; women's fashions follow the pattern of a parallelogram.' Victor Margueritte's successful novel *La Garçonne* (1922) provoked harsh reactions. The author was soon expelled from the Legion of Honour and the book was censored in Germany. The nationalist Drieu de la Rochelle vehemently attacked the new 'civilization without sexes'. The women's movement complained about the supposed decline in morals of the new generation and the fact that the young women no longer spoke out in favour of the old feminist goals. On the other hand, another variant of the New Woman started spouting polemics in Germany: the young ethnically conscious or even racist women who would soon join the Nazis, opposing 'the ever-senile and liberalistic women's movement'. Aside from myths and complaints, there were also pragmatic observations. Economists and advertising strategists recognized the major role played by women as consumers of clothing and cosmetics, movies and mass culture. 'What would happen if women suddenly got the idea to start knitting socks and weaving clothing again?' asked someone at the time; he answered the question himself: 'Entire industries would go bankrupt; unforeseen misery would come to pass.'[8]

Maternity and Paternity in the Welfare State

The first of my books in which [Harriet Taylor's] share was conspicuous was the *Principles of Political Economy.* . . . [H]er influence . . . consisted chiefly in making the proper distinction between the laws of the Production of Wealth, which are real laws of nature, dependent on the property of objects, and the modes of its Distribution, which . . . depend on human will.

John Stuart Mill, 1873[9]

World War I brought yet another innovation. All warring countries except for the United States had introduced separation allowances, called family support in Germany; these were state benefits paid directly to wives, widows or other female family members of absent soldiers, for themselves and for the care of their children. The level of the separation allowances was sometimes dependent on the number of children (the more children, the higher the benefits); elsewhere it depended on the wages earned by the woman (the higher the income, the lower the benefits). Often, the allowance was paid not only to married women but also to women who lived with a soldier in a common law rather than civil marriage. The separation allowance, which was increased in the course of the war but remained nonetheless modest, was based on the assumption that the women were dependent on the income of the male head of the family. It was paid in the interest of the fighting soldier as well as for the welfare on the home front. But many recipients considered themselves by no means to be 'dependants' and they viewed the benefits as payment for their domestic and family duties. In 1917 in Germany 'they saw it as their right to *demand* that the state support them; they did not need to *beg* for it'. Women who performed both child-rearing and housework as well as wage-work protested against the fact that their separation allowance was lowered because of their income. They argued with the authorities and even submitted petitions and organized demonstrations. 'If we torment ourselves more than the others do, then we want to get something for it.' In 1915 in Germany the eight-week maternity allowance – originally intended only for women workers who paid for health insurance – was extended to include women who were insured neither on their own nor through their soldier-husbands. Moreover, similar to the practice already established in France, they now received a nursing allowance. Julia Lathrop and her staff in the US Children's Bureau saw separation allowances, based on the 'most advanced and liberal ideas', as a model for future policies in the United States.[10]

Women did indeed continue to use their voices as citizens to improve the situation of mothers across class lines. These policies even came to the fore after suffrage was no longer a uniting goal, and they were the most significant contributions by and for women in the beginnings and consolidation of the European welfare states. Compared to the pre-war period, however, utopian expectations gave way to more pragmatic approaches. The pathos with which the exploitation of mothers had once been denounced disappeared along with the straightforward glorification of motherhood. The Sheppard-Towner Maternity and Infancy Act of 1921 in the United States, the first welfare law at federal level, was the goal and earliest political success of the new female citizens. It provided for federal subsidies for preventive health services for mothers and children, which were administered by the Children's Bureau. Opponents accused it of introducing Communism and collectivization; when opposition gained the upper hand, the law was repealed in 1928. Maternity was again perceived as a purely individual or familial responsibility, not a social one. But owing to the Children's Bureau's unwavering efforts, federal funding was reinstated in the midst of the Great Depression within the scope of the 1935 Social Security Act, as 'aid to dependent children' and as part of poor relief. After World War II this modest support was paid primarily to unmarried black 'welfare mothers'. Thus in the United States 'welfare' took on the stigma of poverty.

Developments in the United States differed greatly from those of the European welfare state, despite similar hopes of women internationally. In Europe women's involvement and children's needs, often those of their mothers and parents as well, were significant, albeit to different extents and in different phases. In the Weimar Republic, where equal rights of men and women as well as maternity protection were anchored in the German constitution, female members of parliament from all parties (except the Nazi Party, which had none) cooperated and were fairly successful in preserving and raising maternity and nursing benefits for insured women and dependants of insured men. Their efforts culminated in the passage of the 1927 Maternity Protection Act. But despite lasting rhetoric on motherhood, German feminists and politicians no longer advocated a universal motherhood endowment regardless of occupational status. The situation was different in France, the European country where pro-natalism was most pronounced among politicians and organized population experts as well as in the popular culture and the influential social Catholicism. The call to raise the birth rate and provide care for children continued undiminished in the interwar period, as a baby boom of the early 1920s proved short-lived and the birth rate continued to decline, reaching a European low of 13 per thousand in 1938. In 1920 the *fête des mères* was created (as of 1912 there was already a Mother's Day in the United States and, a short time later, in Canada, Britain and Germany). In addition, medals were awarded to mothers with five or more children, an innovation that would remain uniquely French for another twenty years. Anti-natalist propaganda was prohibited in 1920, which was a great blow for neo-Malthusian associations aiming to combat poverty by lowering the birth rate among the poor. A 1923 law lowered penalties for abortion, at the same time providing for the stricter enforcement of the prohibition. However, pro-natalists were more successful convincing parents that France urgently needed pro-natalist legislation than in convincing them to have more children.

French women's associations too supported the family-oriented and pro-natalist consensus, continuing the debate on maternity as a 'social' or a 'family function' in the 1930s. Supporters of the (private) 'family function' rejected universal maternity allowances, while supporters of the (public) 'social function' favoured them. Jewish feminist Cécile Brunschvicg, who would later become an under-secretary in Léon Blum's government, spoke out in 1931 for a compromise that limited the 'social function' to mothers without a breadwinner. But the Women's Civic and Social Union (Union Féminine Civique et Sociale), which was inspired by social Catholicism, continued to insist on the 'social function' of maternity, in contrast to the largely Protestant leadership of the secular women's movement. The Union Féminine agreed with the male family wage, which was advocated by the labour movement and the pope in his encyclical *Quadragesimo Anno* of 1930, but the Union went further, demanding also a maternity allowance for non-employed mothers (*allocation de la mère au foyer*), arguing for the mother's right to dedicate herself entirely to her small children. The French suffragist association (Union Française pour le Suffrage des Femmes) also supported this goal.

Furthermore, French women advocated universal and state-financed family allowances. These grew out of a series of precursors: the 1913 laws on benefits for needy families and for civil servants, and the business-sponsored child allowances (*allocations familiales*), which were widespread in the 1920s but remained limited to individual regions and branches of industry (similar business-sponsored allowances already existed in Belgium, Austria and Germany). The earlier *allocations* had been introduced because some employers supported the family ideal of social Catholicism; in other cases, they wanted to win over workers or keep wages down by distinguishing between workers with children and those without. The *allocations* were financed through equalization funds (*caisses de compensation*), into which several employers paid a contribution. Although the labour unions rejected them, many workers and their families benefited from such allowances. Given the high rate of French women's participation in the labour force, the allowances were often paid directly to the mothers. The Family Allowance Act of 1932 – the first of its kind – obliged all employers to join and contribute to these equalization funds. Although the law was implemented very slowly (it was difficult to apply in agriculture), it transformed an industrial wage policy into a national family policy inspired by the idea of family-based distributive justice, transferring income from people without children to those with children. The law was extended in 1938 and systematized in the *Code de la famille* of 1939. The amount of the benefits varied according to average wage levels of the respective region. The allowance consisted of a one-time bonus for the first child (if born within the first two years of marriage), and an allowance of 10 per cent of the wage for the second child and 20 per cent for each additional child. On top of that there was an *allocation de la mère au foyer* of another 10 per cent for non-employed mothers (this also applied to families in which the mother, not the father, was employed). The Vichy regime no longer paid maternal allowances separate from wage-dependent family benefits but combined them in a payment to the (main) breadwinner, usually the father. This combined allowance was called the *salaire unique* (much to the dismay of the Catholic women's association, who wanted women's share to be separate and visible); it was intended, as in similar practices in all authoritarian and dictatorial regimes of the period, primarily to improve not the situation of mothers but the 'living conditions of family fathers in the labour force'.[11] At the same time child allowances were increased, also by the Fourth Republic, which integrated them into a comprehensive social security system in 1945. In addition to the *prestation familiale* there was now an *allocation de maternité* and an *allocation prénatale*; all of them required at least one parent to be employed in order to avoid having recipients live 'idly' from the benefits. All those gainfully employed were now entitled to these benefits, including foreigners. None of these laws referred to 'motherhood as a social function'; even so, a higher proportion of the national income was redistributed in France than elsewhere, primarily from non-parents to parents but also from men to women. In spite – or because – of this, the level of women in the labour force was maintained at a higher level in France than in the rest of western Europe.

In Britain, Eleanor Rathbone's efforts as the administrator of wartime separation allowances inspired her to dedicate her life to the struggle for a universal maternity endowment. Her extensive work *The Disinherited Family* (1924) was the most significant economic analysis to date of the need for state benefits to mothers and their children. Rathbone calculated the social costs of the procedure by which the earned income distribution was left strictly up to wage negotiations at the production site. Wages did not take family needs into consideration and were paid disproportionately to adult men, irrespective of the number of children or the needs of the women who tended to them. The resulting poverty of families with small children – as compared with childless workers – could not be prevented by increasing wages. The wage system itself produced a drastic gap in living standards within one and the same social class. This is why she advocated considering the costs of children a social responsibility and guaranteeing the mothers an income, as an alternative to a social order based entirely on the wages of the male breadwinner. Rathbone also took a definite stand against the rising tide of eugenicists, especially their argument that allowances for lower-class mothers who had too many children anyway would encourage them (and their husbands) to procreate even more. Rathbone countered with the claim that a higher standard of living would in fact induce them to practise birth control of their own accord.

Rathbone faced considerable criticism. Economists viewed childcare as the individual duty of the parents; conservatives sought to limit public expenditures; labour unions saw their struggle for a male family wage in jeopardy. Some feminists did not want women to be treated differently from men, believing that mothers should receive benefits, if at all, only for the needs of their children and not as payment for their services; they thought women should instead seek their independence on the labour market. Rathbone accepted some of the criticism and soon no longer spoke of *motherhood endowments* but of *child* or *family allowances*, though they were still to be paid to the mothers. But Rathbone also enjoyed a lot of support: from the lower-class women of the

Women's Cooperative Guild, from William Beveridge, the future father figure of the British welfare state, and from Virginia Woolf, who not only spoke out against anti-Semitism and racism and demanded 'a room of one's own' for women but, in *Three Guineas* (1938), also called for wages for motherhood. The earlier pathos was once again given a voice. Civil servants of all kinds were well paid with tax revenue, 'but wives and mothers and daughters who work all day and every day, without whose work the State would collapse and fall to pieces, without whose work your sons, sir, would cease to exist, are paid nothing whatever. Can it be possible?'

British women's organizations, including the National Union and the women of the Labour Party, had been integrating the demand for child allowances into their programmes since the 1920s, sometimes alongside the demand for free access to birth control. In 1945, after decades-long debate, a bill for universal, state-funded child allowances independent of marital and occupational status was introduced in the House of Commons, providing for five shillings per week (instead of the eight shillings recommended by the well-known 1942 Beveridge Report). It differed from women's proposals, which included the first child, instead providing for payments starting with the second child to be paid not to the mother but to the 'head of the household'. Rathbone and many other women spoke out against the bill, both within parliament and outside, on the grounds that it 'will not raise the status of motherhood but will actually lower it' by treating the wife 'as a mere appendage' of her husband. Women's protests succeeded in making the allowances payable to the mother, to be picked up at the post office. Measured against the earlier feminist visions of redistributing earned income from men to women, the Family Allowance Act, the first law of the modern British welfare state, must be viewed as a defeat. But it was also a victory in its recognition of mothers' right to some payment outside the wage structure, and it granted legitimacy to transfer payments not only for those unable to work, but for people whose labour was considered 'priceless'. Unlike the situation in France, the payments were very small, not least due to the opposition of the labour unions. The low level of the benefits, together with the privileged status of married men (and unmarried women) in relation to married women in other areas of social security (especially unemployment insurance, which provided bonuses to men with wife and children, and excluded even insured women if they had a 'breadwinner'), strengthened the figure of the male breadwinner. In 1960 family allowances made up 35 per cent of all social security benefits in France and only 12 per cent in Great Britain.[12]

In Norway, too, praise for motherhood and demands for its social recognition had receded into the background in the 1930s. Child allowances (*barnetrygd*) were instead on the agenda; their focus was not on the mothers but on children and families. Should child welfare be supported through wage supplements or state allowances, service benefits or benefits in kind? In contrast to Britain, in Norway the labour movement advocated allowances but rejected wage supplements and supported financing the allowances through taxes. Socialist and non-socialist feminists continued to demand that payments be made exclusively to mothers. When universal child allowances finally became law in 1946, they were made payable to mothers but were far too small to be regarded as 'mothers' wages'. Needy mothers were left to municipal poor relief until 1964, when widows and single mothers became entitled to payments. In Sweden state maternity relief was granted in 1937, and over 90 per cent of all mothers were entitled to it. Additional benefits were awarded to needy mothers. These reforms were mainly due to previous proposals and pressure by the women's movement, but also to a new social democratic family policy combining pro-natalism with social reforms, based largely on proposals by Alva and Gunnar Myrdal. Universal child allowances were introduced in 1947; as in other democratic countries, they were made payable to the mothers.

Women's demands were silenced in the rising dictatorships and the official praise of motherhood degenerated to empty rhetoric. In Franco's Spain and fascist Italy an extremely aggressive pro-natalist rhetoric prevailed, supported by male-dominated Catholicism, in spite of which the birth rate continued to drop (to 23 per thousand in Spain in 1943; and to 23 per thousand in Italy in 1935, with much higher figures in the south than in the north, and the highest in rural areas and the lowest in the urban service sector). From the very beginning of fascism, *virilità* was at its centre. Five years after Mussolini took power, he initiated a *battaglia demografica* in the daily press. A rising birth rate was now seen as an expression of *virilità nazionale* and, in the 1930s, a foundation of the empire. Mussolini's policies corresponded to his proclamation in 1927 (in reference to Georg Wilhelm Friedrich Hegel) that 'He who is not a father is not a man'.[13] Taxes for unmarried men (1927) and tax deductions for wife and children on the income of the heads of families (1933) were introduced. Starting in 1936, state-funded allowances for the wife and each dependent child (*assegni familiari*) were granted to wage-earning fathers; even birth premiums became available for fathers in 1939, replacing the former, feminist-inspired *cassa di maternità*. All pro-natalist measures focused on paternity and virility. In Spain, where the women's movement had once stressed the upgrading of motherhood rather than political rights, new measures gave greater value to paternity, reinforcing the figure of the *jefe de familia*. State family allowances (*subsidio familiar*) were introduced in 1938 and family bonuses (*plus de cargas familiares*) for a wider population in 1945. Both were payable to the fathers, as was also true for the family allowances introduced in Portugal in 1942.

   National Socialism, too, pursued a cult of fatherhood and masculinity. This initially brought criticism from some women, who claimed that, contrary to their hopes, this was 'male domination' and that nothing but lip service was paid to the 'cult of motherhood'. As late as 1934 some women still demanded a 'mother's wage' independent of the income of the husband. But the equalization of family burdens, politicians were agreed, should equalize the burden between childless men and fathers, 'so that a man, simply for having satisfied his duties to his nation, would no longer be in a worse situation financially or non-materially than the so-called clever bachelor in the competition'. Accordingly, marriage loans were initiated in 1933 in Germany (followed soon afterwards by Italy, Sweden and Spain) which were paid to the husband, as were the monthly child allowances of 10 Reichsmarks from 1936. Allowances were initially paid starting with the fifth child; as of 1939 payments were made starting with the third child. Unmarried mothers received them only if the father of the child was known to the authorities and was considered irreproachable. The tax reform acts of 1934 and 1939, which were much more far-reaching in the equalization of family burdens, were geared towards 'the right of the father of a family': income tax for people without children (unmarried men and women as well as couples) was raised and in turn a tax rebate for wife and children was granted the head of a family. The support was based on the husband's earned income level. The head of the Nazi Public Welfare Office, with its 'Mother and Child' department that provided support for the needy, expressed the inverse ideal that: 'There is no more beautiful image of selfless service than that of the mother and her children. Again and again she gives of herself, showing her child love and more love without ever giving a thought to whether she might ever get anything in return. . . . The moment she would attempt to offset her services, she would cease to be a good mother.' Accordingly, starting in 1939 – based on the French model of 1920, and also introduced in the Soviet Union in 1944 – mothers received a medal, unconnected with any financial award, for having four or more children. Robert Ley, head of the German Labour Front, the Nazi surrogate trade union, did suggest in 1942 that mothers receive not only a medal but a pension, and that the same benefits as for employed mothers be granted also to those who were not wage-earners (especially the needy mothers among them). His reasoning was that these mothers created 'worth that goes into the thousands of millions' and thus had earned 'economic recognition'. But Hitler rejected it on the grounds that the 'most difficult tasks imaginable' of the near future were far too expensive.[14] These tasks

– race policy – were at the core of Nazi family policy from the outset. Thus husbands and fathers who were considered eugenically or ethnically 'inferior' – first and foremost the Jews – were excluded from all forms of family burden equalization. After reaching a low of 15 per thousand in 1933, the birth rate rose to the 1928 level by 1939 and then declined again until 1942 to the 1933 level.

The paths taken by modern welfare states towards a redistribution of family income resembled each other to some extent in the interwar and early post-war periods, and were in part different. Nowhere was the feminist utopia achieved in which motherhood was recognized as a 'social function'. But unlike the situation in the United States, in Europe (and also in Canada, New Zealand and Australia) considerable transfer payments were approved. In all of these cases, albeit to differing degrees, pro-natalist motives came together with those for social reform. But even within Europe there were obvious differences. In the democratic countries sometimes a minuscule share of the national income was reserved for such payments, and sometimes a larger one. The discrepancy between the British path, which always focused on the male breadwinner, and the French one, which put both parents at the centre, has been explained precisely by the fact that British women, unlike French women, were so incredibly vocal in expressing their demands and so eloquent in opposing the male family wage. But what the French women gained financially they lost – unlike the British women – on the legal front. In 1938 France granted wives the right to conclude contracts (1935 in Great Britain), but the same law – following heated debate – also declared that 'the husband is the head of the family' and he could veto his wife's decisions. Far more extreme was the divergence between the European democracies and the dictatorships. In the democracies the transfer was not only from people without children to parents but also from men to women. In the dictatorships it was only between the childless and fathers. The Nazi dictatorship was unique in that its family allowances were never universal. 'Inferior' parents and their children were regarded as undesirable. In view of its racist policies, therefore, Nazi Germany cannot be considered a welfare state.

Paths Leading to Dictatorship: The Political and the Private

Can woman under fascism and on behalf of fascism think and act for specific ends with ideas and abilities of her own? We firmly believe so!
Giornale della donna, 1928[15]

The European crisis of liberalism and the newly emerged republics led after World War I to a series of dictatorships whose power, violence and terror would shape the twentieth century. More so than for any other period, it is virtually impossible here to write the history of women without including that of the men. In Russia, where liberal traditions were weak, Tsarist rule ended with the February Revolution of 1917. That authoritarian style of rule would reappear in Bolshevism, which put an end to the young republic in the October putsch. The rise of the former socialist Mussolini and his *fasci* starting in 1922 led to a one-party dictatorship that became firmly established in 1926. The Portuguese republic declared in 1910 was replaced after sixteen years by a military dictatorship and in 1933 by Salazar's authoritarian *Estado Novo*, which took up the cause of *Deus, pátria, família*. After generations of change in Spain from constitutionalism to Bourbon restoration and then military dictatorship, the Second Republic of 1931 gave way within eight years to Franco's autocratic *Nuevo Estado*. Greece followed with Metaxas's dictatorship from 1936 to 1941. In Germany the Nazis took power in 1933 and annihilated any opposition. France's defeat in 1940 led to the 'national revolution' of the *Nouvel État* of Vichy, with its slogan *travail, famille, patrie*. In some cases the transitions were accompanied by civil war. There were almost half a million casualties in Spain, roughly ten million in Soviet Russia (two million died in the Hunger Winter of 1920–1 alone), including many women. The movements and parties on which the dictatorships were based were a male domain from the outset and wholly condemned the feminism of the preceding generation. In the Soviet Union, the liberal, autonomous women's movement was brought to an end in 1917. One of the leading spokeswomen of the time was the self-proclaimed anti-feminist Alexandra Kollontai, who regarded feminists as 'our enemy'. Following socialist tradition 'feminism' became a denunciatory word, equivalent to 'bourgeois'. Russian suffragists, who had won the struggle for women's suffrage on 20 July 1917, were considered just as bourgeois as parliamentary democracy; only here does suffrage make sense as a mode of political participation. But now, it was claimed, something more important was at stake, namely, the men and women of the proletariat. In Italy Mussolini declared that 'Woman must obey. My idea of her role in the State is in opposition to all feminism.'[16] The Nazis in Germany proclaimed 'emancipation from women's emancipation', condemning the women's movement as having been inspired and dominated by Jews. Especially in Germany, Italy and the Soviet Union, the radical changes were accompanied by imagery of the 'new man'. In fascism it was marked by an extreme, at times even obscene, cult of masculinity that was fed by futurism; in Nazism this imagery was marked by the 'Nordic', 'Aryan' or 'hereditarily sound German'; in the Soviet Union, by industrial technology and the male proletarian cult.

Regardless of their shared anti-feminist tendencies, the dictatorships varied in a number of ways in their attitude to the female sex and the women's movement, depending on their historical points of departure, their goals, the social situation and reactions by women. Contradictions, either from the start or over time, were inevitable: in the Soviet Union in the period up to 1989; in Spain until Franco's death in 1975; in Portugal up to the Carnation Revolution in 1974; in southern Italy until 1943 – in northern Italy until the end of the fascist republic in 1945; and in Germany until 1945, the year of defeat for many, but for most, including those in the conquered territories of Europe, the year of liberation. The relationship between tradition and innovation led to shifting and ambivalent gender policies that were subordinate to the primacy of 'nation', 'people', 'race' or 'class'. Common to all the dictatorships was a special relationship between the political and the private, between the public realm and individual existence. This can be seen in the role of women during the rise of these dictatorships; in the relationship of the women to the former (and, in the democracies, lasting) autonomous women's movements; and in the paradox of mobilizing masses of women in authoritarian and totalitarian regimes where, on the one hand, women were to be relegated to the private sphere and, on the other hand, where the separation of the private and the political, of centralist state and civilian society, was dissolved.

The February Revolution in Russia was triggered by hungry women workers and housewives whose hardship caused by the war stirred them to revolt against low wages and high prices (in 1917 women made up half of the factory workforce). A month later in Petrograd, alongside the organized women's movement, they demanded equality, protective labour legislation for women and children – especially a ban on night work – the eight-hour workday, land for the peasants and a democratic republic. When happy feminists informed the women on the streets after 20 July that they were now citizens, they were at first confronted with a lack of comprehension. But when a soldier asked, 'Does that mean I can't hit my wife?', they started to understand. 'None of that. You just try it. Nothing doing. Let ourselves be beaten anymore? Not on your life. Nobody has the right now.'[17] Male violence in the family was widespread and alcohol consumption – within the working class a symbol of masculinity – played a significant role in family violence. When the male family wage was divided between alcohol and the family needs, wives often tried to favour the latter. But the simple understanding that the new citizens had of the relationship between the political and the private, between suffrage and sexual violence, would be taxed to the limit in the period leading to Stalin's dictatorship.

In December 1917 a decree had already taken up an old feminist slogan, 'The bearing of children is a social function'. Occasionally it was supplemented by the slogan that motherhood was 'the duty of women as citizens'.[18] The People's Commissariat for Social Welfare, initially under Kollontai's direction, aimed to expand protective measures for mothers and infants. These were later placed under the Ministry of Health. The meaning of the 'social function' slogan was much more one-sided than it had been in the women's movements. Whereas the women's movements always stressed that a choice between wage-earning and motherhood should be possible, the revolutionary context considered only a combination of the two. Mothers were to be integrated into production outside the home, which is why, especially for the five-year plan (1929–32), they were to be freed of child-rearing and of work for the family. Consequently, maternity leave of eight weeks before and after giving birth was introduced in 1918 for women workers (this, too, had been an old demand of both Russian and western feminists). It included full wage compensation and, when the women returned to their job, it provided for six-hour days with nursing breaks. In view of the post-war unemployment level and the general hardship and chaos of the civil war, however, few women were able to take advantage of this benefit. Socializing child-rearing was supposed to serve 'Communist education' (this was the title of the first Communist International Women's Day in 1926), the aims of which were very distinct from women's movement's ideas on education. In Russia, as elsewhere, the women's movement had oriented its philosophy on the ideal of the autonomous personality, as conceived by Friedrich Fröbel, and later by the Italian Maria Montessori.

Prominent revolutionaries (albeit not the male rank and file) agreed that women should be liberated from 'domestic slavery' and that housework, as Lenin put it, was 'unproductive, petty, nerve-racking, stultifying and crushing drudgery'. This pertained, in their view, only to individual housework but not to the collectivized tasks to be performed by women working as professional cooks and cleaners. Lenin's aversion to individual kitchens, pots and pans bordered on an obsession, and Kollontai saw the need to separate marriage and kitchen as just as pressing as the need to separate Church and state. But the children's houses, kitchens and dining halls, and their female staff, were miserably equipped, a situation that would continue into the future. Gangs of neglected and homeless children (*besprizorniki*) that roamed the countryside in the 1920s left a greater mark than the kindergartens. These children earned their subsistence through begging, theft, murder and prostitution. There were seven million of them in 1921, including thousands of former foundlings. An attempt was made in 1926 to solve the problem in a private way by permitting adoption again after it had been abolished in 1918 because of the inheritance issues it raised. But it was precisely among the workers that collective housework proved impossible to implement; for the peasant population (roughly three-quarters of Soviet women) it was also irrelevant, especially when mandatory collectivization was initiated in 1928, bringing mass deportation and persecution of peasants (kulaks) and, consequently, a period of famine from 1930 to 1932. On top of the six million deaths that resulted there were a further 2.5 million victims of political persecution. Starting in 1934, wives and sisters of 'enemies of the people' were threatened with arrest and deportation for being related to 'enemies of the people', and their children were put in orphanages.

The interplay of civil war, War Communism and the New Economic Policy (1921–4), of low wages, unemployment and housing shortages, of the cult of the proletariat and forced collectivization was allied with a truly bold moral and sexual policy in the Soviet variant of the Roaring Twenties. Its main principle was that 'all relations between the sexes are a matter of private concern'. This corresponded to the old socialist assumption that 'bourgeois' marriage was a product of private property and capitalism. Yet it was clear from the very beginning that the private sphere was not just private, and it became even more clear in the year-long, nationwide, virtually democratic debate that took place in 1926 about the new family code. Abortion had been permitted as of 1918 and the measure was considered a 'widely organized rationalization of the reproductive urge' and 'the first model of planned and implemented population policy'. It was also presented as 'the first legal recognition of woman's right, demanded by the feminist movement, to possess her own body' (although feminists had viewed abortion as a last resort and unrestricted abortions as a license for irresponsible men) and as 'one of the great achievements of Soviet Russia's constructive will'.[19] Free 'abortaria' were opened in Moscow for poor women. According to a 1927 survey, only 6 per cent of the clients truly did not want the child and the rest sought the services of the clinic because they were desperately poor. In 1928 there were 50 per cent more abortions than births nationwide; in Moscow there were three times as many. More and more children were abandoned, and orphanages turned into hospices for the dying.

Divorce was introduced in 1917 after having been virtually impossible under the Tsar. It was free of charge and mutual consent was sufficient grounds, though divorce was even possible on the request of only one party; after the marriage reform of 1926 it could be obtained by written request ('postcard divorce'). In 1927 in Moscow there was one divorce for every two marriages. Non-married cohabitation (so-called de facto marriage) was recognized as of 1918 and legitimated by law in 1926 in order to create stability and facilitate enforcement of paternal duties. But paternal alimony to the woman, when she and the children were abandoned by her partner, existed on paper only. In reality paternity was difficult to prove (it was a popular literary theme), and it was equally difficult to collect the support payments. Fathers disappeared or were too poor or had too many children. The de facto marriage was exploited especially by men – usually workers – at the expense of the women. Abandoned, impoverished de facto mothers populated the cities; in some places 70 per cent of divorces in cases of de facto marriages were initiated unilaterally by the men. Young husbands complained, 'If a child comes, that's the end of freedom'. In the cities it was not unusual for marriages to last a day, a week or a month. The age at which young people first engaged in sexual activity dropped dramatically and the result, as a foreign journalist put it, was 'equality, liberty, maternity'. There was widespread debate on short-term and noncommittal sexual relations and the relationship between sexuality ('proletarian' physiology) and Eros ('bourgeois' psychology). A prostitute complained of falling prices and presumed it was due to 'free marriages'. The subject of de-eroticization influenced images of the New Woman. Once it was the member of the Red Army who was 'willing to sacrifice herself sexually' to her comrades; later it was the stern, progressive worker with a red scarf around her neck – in contrast to the backward peasant with a white kerchief on her head – the militant comrade of a Komsomol or the flirtatious stenotypist who would do anything for some French perfume and looked like the western flapper. There were proposals to have special houses for sexual intercourse and a (presumably ironic) play considered a 'Five Years' Plan of having children': 'Give us a bedroom factory! Twenty thousand sexual acts per day!' Virtually every facet of the 'sexual revolution' was played out, whether in theory or in practice. What was missing among all these images, proposals and reforms, however, were measures against the sexual violence that those women had referred to in June 1917 when they became citizens.

Against this background of libertarian reforms along with uprooting and upheavals, it was not surprising that critical voices became louder in the late 1920s. All observers were agreed that the child gangs were connected to the instability of marriage. It was especially women who complained about the innovations; a leading Bolshevik woman protested against the fact that every student or Komsomolka who was not willing to give herself to a man was said to be 'petty bourgeois', and a young woman said that she would rather work sixteen hours a day than return to the co-ed dormitory of the Komsomol. Male and female peasants (as long as peasants existed) expressed their doubts about the individualistic right to divorce, since it interfered dramatically with collective property and inheritance customs. Many women, workers and peasants alike, spoke out against the absolute freedom of divorce: 'It is inexcusable when a man lives with a woman for twenty-five years, has five children with her and then decides he doesn't like her anymore.' In Kollontai's last campaign in 1926 she demanded an annual tax of two roubles to finance children's homes and support unemployed and unwed mothers. Other women responded with their own view of the relationship between the private and the political: 'If such a tax were introduced, the men would lose all shame and universal license would be the result'; or 'The mother should pay too. It may serve as a lesson to her!' and 'What has it to do with all men, when only one man is concerned in the begetting of a child? ... If you are the father, you must pay!'[20] More important than having their own sexual freedom, these women wanted to limit the sexual freedom of men – quite comparable to the old feminist struggle against the double standard.

Among politicians and many other men, these gender issues were discussed 'politically'; that is, using the vocabulary of 'bourgeois' or 'petty bourgeois' versus 'proletarian', and 'revolutionary' versus 'counter-revolutionary'. Critical women's voices in particular were considered backward or conservative. Lenin viewed sexual promiscuity as bourgeois, whereas Bukharin considered any possible party intervention into family matters to be petty bourgeois. Kollontai's visions were condemned as bourgeois 'George Sandism'. Wilhelm Reich visited the Soviet Union in 1929 and was inspired by revolutionary sexuality; he too condemned the criticism as bourgeois (his ideas would subsequently gain influence in the west in the 1960s). The confusion of these social (class) categories, which had long since become political ones, reveals, on the one hand, the insecurity and ignorance in dealing with gender relations and, on the other hand, the confusion over what sexual gender relations were historically, in theory and practice, within the bourgeoisie. This debate compressed into a few years what had taken over a century in western Europe and was not yet concluded there. Marxist scholar David Ryazanov defined the problem in 1927 in terms of the relation between the public and the private: 'We should teach our young Komsomols that marriage is not a personal act, but an act of deep social significance, demanding interference and regulation by Society.'[21]

Stalin put an end to the debate. Without further ado he took the side of women and within ten years had turned the tide. Now whatever served to rehabilitate the family was considered proletarian and revolutionary. The state-supported duties of women were no longer limited to production (in 1940 women made up 43 per cent of the industrial workforce and soon 70 per cent of agricultural workers); now it included motherhood, too. For Stalin, this was 'certainly not a private affair but one of great social importance.'[22] The new family code of 1936 prohibited abortion except on medical grounds. Nevertheless, for a long time it remained the only family planning option and the birth rate continued to decline (to 31 per thousand in 1940). De facto marriage was still legal, but divorce now cost 50 roubles the first time and 300 roubles the third time (in 1944 the fees were increased), and not just one but both parties had to appear in court. Alimony payments were increased. Mothers, whether employed or not, were granted a child allowance. Childcare for school-age and pre-school children was expanded. In 1944 payments to mothers were increased, mothers who had a large number of children received a medal, and special taxes were levied on unmarried people and on child-less couples. De facto marriages were stripped of all financial rights, but the child bonuses for loyal male functionaries, payable in cash ('enve-lopes') or in kind, were in any case more significant from a financial perspective.

Two other factors were more important for women's lives. First, women continued to suffer under the double burden of working both in and outside the home (including the army). Second, life had long since been overshadowed by death, mass arrests – seven million in the years 1937 and 1938 – and spectacular show trials. Three million people were shot or perished in camps, one in seven of them women. Twenty million So-viet citizens died in World War II, including nine million civilian men and women. More than one million women and almost as many male civilians were brought to Germany to perform forced labour, often un-der murderous conditions. After the war almost 30 per cent of all house-holds were headed by single women, and women made up half of the workforce. Factory legislation for women and maternity protection had been largely eliminated during the war, but they were reinforced in 1956 during the period of political thaw. Russian women bore a dispropor-tionate share of the burden of an industrial development that took a century elsewhere and here had been pressed into two decades, accompa-nied by war, civil war and changes in political direction. Despite their being overburdened, Soviet women appeared to be 'a pillar of the re-gime' – sober, enduring, conscientious, disciplined, and willing to make a sacrifice both in and outside the family.[23]

The European dictatorships mobilized women in masses in order to integrate them into their respective policies. In 1917 Lenin said that it was 'impossible to win the masses for politics unless we include the woman. . . . Without the women there can be no true mass movement'.[24] The mass mobilization was an innovation, not only in comparison with the traditional lack of interest that male politicians showed women but also with respect to the kind and size of organizations that women had previously founded on their own. Women who had traditionally belonged, or were supposed to belong, to the private sphere moved into the spot-light of an organized public sphere. Also of interest is the relationship between the new organizations and the earlier women's movement. No-where were women recruited within the framework of the respective State

Party; their proportion in the Party was relatively low everywhere (in Soviet Russia it rose from 8 per cent in 1924 to double that figure in the 1930s and 1940s; in Germany it was 6 per cent in 1934; in Salazar's National Union a constant 4 per cent was maintained). Furthermore, there were virtually no women in higher Party or government ranks. Instead, they were mobilized in special organizations and campaigns instituted from above and affiliated with the Party which aimed either to answer to women's needs or to combat their 'backwardness'. This was the main task of the *Zhenotdel* (the women's departments of the Central Committee and at all other levels of the Party hierarchy), founded in Soviet Russia in 1919.

First, the Bolshevik women in the *Zhenotdel* were involved in winning over female masses for the revolution and Soviet power, for production and collectivization. However, as Kollontai reported in 1921, most women were afraid of losing their children and having their family dissolved and the Church destroyed. The agitprop courses and trips organized by the *Zhenotdel*, which also taught reading, writing and dealing with authorities and Party, had reached almost ten million women by 1930 and won over those who had been elected as delegates. The proportion of literate women rose from 37 (1926) to 72 (1937) per cent. Second, the *Zhenotdel* had to deal with woman-related problems in order to achieve its goal and revolutionize the consciousness of the women workers. This included the same social issues that the women's movement had once rallied around (aid for mothers and children, especially the poor and orphans, health care and food distribution, school and educational issues and finding jobs, especially for prostitutes). It was not by chance that Kollontai had to confront the charge that her aims were 'feminist'. Third, the official subordination of women's interests meshed with the thrust of the separate women's associations when they threatened to become too autonomous. As of 1923 the *Zhenotdel* departments were accused of a 'feminist' deviation and gradually dissolved by 1930, when the 'woman question' was officially declared to have been resolved. It did not help their cause that they chose '100 per cent collectivization' as the slogan for the 1930 International Women's Day. Thereafter women's politics were undertaken exclusively by men. However, women retained certain spheres of action at local levels, albeit within the strict framework of Party directives.

In Italy too the transition took a decade. Unlike the situation in the Soviet Union, however, in Italy it led not to the elimination of separate women's organizations but to their being reinforced by the fascists. Until 1925, when Mussolini still declared his support for women's suffrage, and even several years later, many Italian feminists, including many Jews, thought they would be able to achieve at least some of their goals under the new regime, especially the improvement of women's status through social involvement. The *fasci femminili* – mostly young, pugnacious women, like the early Communists and Hitler supporters – were a small minority in the 1920s. They occasionally even raised their voices against fascist anti-feminism. The Marchesa Maria Spinelli Monticelli protested in 1926 against the elimination of local elections by disbanding her *fascio femminile* in Milan; consequently, she was expelled from the Party. Socialist and suffragist Teresa Labriola, at the time the best-known Italian female intellectual, gradually shifted to fascism, trying to reconcile it with a *femminismo italico*. Her idea was that 'women *must also acquire male qualities* which consist in the consciousness of belonging to a race and a nation'. In 1927 she argued that 'Participation in social life does not belong only to a democracy; it can also be advocated by those who are fighting against parliamentarianism, . . . and it by no means contradicts the doctrine and practice of fascism'.[25] The National Agency for Maternity and Infancy (ONMI) was founded in 1925 and financed through donations and state subsidies. In it, though almost totally excluded from leadership positions, women worked in health education and to support poor and unwed mothers, even in the remote rural regions. Olga Modigliani, a feminist from an old-established Jewish family, had been active for a long time caring for single mothers. Before ONMI was founded Modigliani had advised the responsible commission in Mussolini's first cabinet, and in 1934 the Paris conference of the International Council of Women admired the fascist welfare services for mothers and children. Philanthropist Daisy di Robilant of Piedmont was the vice-president of the Roman section of ONMI and was elected in 1931 to head the National Council of Women, founded in 1903. Women were hardly represented on the Superior Council of Corporations (1929), which brought protest from some fascist women. However, the president of the Midwives Corporation was appointed. Giuseppe Bottai, then under-secretary of the Ministry of Corporations, also appointed Adele Pertici Pontecorvo to be the first (of three) women counsellors in 1931; that would have been impossible in Nazi Germany, where there were virtually no opportunities open to female jurists. Pertici Pontecorvo was an expert in labour law, an advocate of women's rights and had been Italy's first female notary public. During the fascist period she brought a number of sex discrimination cases before the highest court.

Only late and gradually did fascism mobilize one-quarter of the adult female population: just prior to the Italo-Ethiopian War and then once the war started in October 1935. It did so in reaction to the economic sanctions of the League of Nations and the subsequent policy of autarky (now the ageing futurist Marinetti declared spaghetti to be 'anti-virile' since wheat was an import good and the women had better things to do than to work in the kitchen). First the *fasci femminili* were turned into a mass organization with recruiting drives from the early 1930s; the former women's movement newspaper, *Giornale della donna*, became its official organ and Teresa Labriola was one of its contributors. By the late 1930s there were about 750,000 members of the women's *fasci*. The association of rural housewives followed (there were 1.5 million *massaie rurali*), and the women's factory and homeworker association (half a million), which charged lower membership fees than the Party and was thus more attractive. Only from the mid-1930s were the remnants of the former women's movement eliminated (some of its activists, such as Ersilia Majno Bronzini, had died earlier). The internationally oriented Federation of University Women (with many Jewish members) was superseded by a fascist association in 1935 and, according to the authorities, had to 'dissolve itself spontaneously'.[26] The racial laws were enacted against the Jews on 17 November 1938, and later that same year the National Women's Council and the time-honoured Unione femminile were banned on the grounds that they had a large number of Jewish members. At just the same time in Germany, in the aftermath of the November Pogrom, the Nazis dissolved the League of Jewish Women. In both countries this was, in retrospect, the beginning of the end, but the murder of the Jews in Italy was essentially the work of the Nazis, not the fascists.

There was no transition period in Germany as there was in Italy. Between Hitler's becoming chancellor of the Reich on 30 January 1933 and the (last free) Reichstag elections on 5 March, the Federation of German Women's Associations protested against the threat the Nazis posed to women's citizenship, their access to public office and their career options. Gertrud Bäumer, who had considerable international experience, was vice-president of the Federation; like the Italian feminists, she remained hopeful. With an eye towards Italy, she wrote in March 1933 (the Nazis had just won 44 per cent of the seats in the Reichstag) that especially now there was a need for 'women to get involved', no matter 'if it is a parliamentarian, democrat or fascist state' that was to come. She dissociated herself from the Nazis as the sole party (the Communists had already been banned and in July Germany became a one-party dictatorship) that rejected 'women's cooperation in public life', especially as parliamentary representatives. At the same time she tried to find positions on the Nazi platform that women could support.[27] But she was deceiving herself. The male-centred and racist Nazis immediately carried out what the even more masculinity-oriented fascists had needed over a decade to implement. In February 1933 Bäumer was put on leave from her position in the Ministry of the Interior for political reasons and in February she was removed from her post. She did not become the Labriola or the

Kollontai of National Socialism, though she attempted to continue her work through her journal *Die Frau*, lecture tours, historical novels and by embracing a mystical Christianity. When Nazification was initiated in 1933, by which Nazi women were placed in the leading positions and Jews were excluded, there was an abrupt break with the women's movement. This is why the Federation of German Women's Associations chose to disband themselves in May, followed in September by the German League of Female Citizens, successor organization to the long-established General German Women's Association.

As soon as the Nazis came to power, they worked for mass mobilization of women. There were already some small nationalist (*völkisch*) women's groups. Some of them misunderstood the message; they thought women were also included in the '*völkisch*' mission and soon afterwards the groups were dissolved. In contrast to the situation in Italy, Jewish women were banned from joining Nazi organizations. The hard core of the mass organizations, which strictly followed the Party line, was the National Socialist Women's League (Nationalsozialistische Frauenschaft, NSF) with almost two million members in 1935, 320,000 of whom comprised the active, ideological elite cadre. The German Women's Organization (Deutsches Frauenwerk) had six million members in 1939, of whom one million lived in Austria and the Sudetenland. This organization was under the control not of the Nazi Party but the Reich Ministry of the Interior. It had a less ideo-logical orientation, devoted primarily to domestic and child-related education for women. In the 1930s, over five million women had gone through training programmes of the Reich Service for Mothers (Reichmütterdienst), one-third of whom were working class. The NSF also started promoting women's university education in 1937, reclaiming the history of the women's movement though cleansing it of what was denounced as the 'liberalistic idea of humanity'. This idea was attributed to Helene Lange (who had died in 1930), whom Nazi women claimed had 'opened the door of the German women's movement to the decaying influences of Judaism'.[28] 'Reich Women's Leader' Gertrud Scholtz-Klink was also no Labriola or Kollontai of Nazism; instead she was conventional, scheming and obedient to the Party. Scholtz-Klink emphasized that cooperation between the sexes was more important than 'for the woman to stand out as something special among the people'. Her principle, with due modification, could apply to the mobilization of women in any dictatorship; she argued that women 'should not ask what National Socialism could do for us but what we could do for National Socialism'. As in Soviet Russia – and to a lesser extent in other dictatorships – women in Germany were organized not only separately but also together with men. Women physicians and teachers who previously had had their own professional organizations were now combined with their male counterparts and placed under male leadership. Their mixed-sex organizations were branches of the Party and of all occupational groups they had the highest proportion of loyal regime supporters. Eight million rural women, including both peasants and workers, were integrated into the Reich Food Estate (Reichsnährstand) and four million female factory workers into the German Labour Front. Much to their dismay, strictly female organizations were prohibited from organizing young girls; presumably women were not considered qualified or capable of educating them for the 'higher', gender-neutral goals. The League of German Girls (Bund Deutscher Mädel, BDM) was joined to the boys in the Hitler Youth (Hitlerjugend). As of 1936 membership was compulsory; almost all girls between ten and fourteen years of age were members, since they were registered through their school, as well as a large proportion of older girls. In Italy, too, girls were taken out of the *fasci femminili* in 1929 and organized alongside the boys. In Italy and Germany alike, activities for organized young girls and boys resembled each other more than did those of the purely women's organizations and the mixed-gender associations. Millions of German women were mobilized for the annual Party conventions.

The Second Spanish Republic provided reforms for women, only 13 per cent of whom worked outside agriculture in 1930. Previously only a very small women's movement had fought for these reforms, including suffrage, civil marriage, divorce, maternity insurance and, in industrialized Catalonia, abortion, which was permitted by the anarchist government as of 1936. Since initially only passive suffrage had been granted, in 1931 there was an impressive parliamentary women's debate – unique in Europe – on active suffrage. The Socialist Margarita Nelken opposed it (since women supported the Church); Radical Socialist lawyer Victoria Kent warned against premature reforms, and Radical lawyer Clara Campoamor was an ardent advocate of immediate active suffrage. The republic had only two years to consolidate its reforms before the right wing – army, Church, monarchists, conservatives, large landholders and a fascist group – started recruiting women to support tradition, Church and fatherland, especially in the battle against secularization of schools. In the 1933 elections, those opposed to the republic welcomed women's suffrage as an unexpected 'gift from the state' and sought to mobilize women. The elections went in their favour (it is not known how the women voted). A Women's Falange was formed in 1934. Like the men's Falange – and in contrast to Franco's course, which would prevail – the Women's Falange demanded the separation of Church and state. Like many other rightist groups, the Women's Falange got caught in the paradox of, on the one hand, proclaiming to women that 'action is no longer your province; let man act' (according to their charter), and on the other hand, of mobilizing women for the struggle against the republic. Women were involved on both sides in the murderous civil war (the outcome of which was determined by German and Italian intervention culminating in the bombing of Guernica), though far more were on the Republican side. Women in the militia and the anarcho-feminist *Mujeres libres* became a – controversial – symbol of the republic. Starting in 1939, 30,000 women were arrested and roughly a thousand executed. When Franco's victory was celebrated in 1939, 10,000 Women's Falange members were publicly addressed and told that 'the only mission assigned to women by the Fatherland is at home'.[29] The Women's Falange was then merged with the welfare organization Auxilio Social (Social Aid) and had over half a million members. Their main responsibilities were social welfare and restoration of Church authority. In Spain, too, women experienced the contradictions of political and social modernization and reaction; what extended over a long period in other European countries took place in Spain in the short span of a decade.

The mass women's organizations were a paradox, especially those in the dictatorships where official rhetoric declared women's most important national task to be in the private sphere of the family. As earlier, some women overstepped these bounds by turning to charitable activities, either encouraged from above or on their own (albeit limited) initiative. A smaller yet highly significant share became involved in political activities in the interest of the regime, especially in Soviet Russia and in Germany, as demonstrated by the NSF and Scholtz-Klink, who proclaimed in 1937 that women should learn to 'think politically'. This type of politics implied an attack on the family and the private sphere. A popular joke told in whispers concerned a girl who said: 'My father is an SA member, my older brother is in the SS. My younger brother is in the Hitler Youth, my mother is in the NSF and I am a member of the BDM.' 'Do you ever get to see each other with all this service?' 'Oh yes, we meet each other every year at the national Party convention in Nuremberg.' Nazism in particular attempted to eliminate the traditional separation of political and private spheres. The only function of the private, including the family, was to serve the political as its tool, its extended arm. The head of the German Labour Front announced: 'No, in Germany there are no private matters anymore. When you sleep, that is your private matter', but not 'once you wake up and come into contact with another person'. In fascism, the elimination of that separation was symbolized through the ten commandments that the 450,000 girls in the Giovani italiane were taught: 'You are also serving the Fatherland when you sweep your own house.' Conversely, defence of private space could become a form of resistance to totalitarian demands. An 'oppositional familism', which emerged in fascist Italy and Vichy France, in a way corresponded to Hegel's statement that the state, which 'in its efficient operation in general is the manhood', on the one hand needs 'families which are under the management of womankind'; on the other hand, the state could get 'itself subsistence only breaking in upon family happiness' and therefore it created 'it's enemy for itself. . . – womankind in general': the 'everlasting irony in the life of the community'.[30]

The Metaxas dictatorship mobilized Greek girls and women between the ages of seven and twenty-five, and the co-ed youth organization EON promised integration across class and gender lines. Metaxas praised the organization in 1936 for mothers as well as non-mothers; it aimed to 'convey the feeling of solidarity, clarify the concept of companion, and give you a sense of consolidating your strength. What holds for men, holds for you too'.[31] The authoritarian regime in Portugal had come to power not through a mass movement but from above; and it eliminated both liberalism and fascism. It was exceptional in that women were mobilized only to a modest extent. Women's suffrage was granted in 1931, under the dictatorship, though a higher level of education was required for women than for men. Three women were elected to the parliament in 1934, a teacher, a lawyer and a physician; they were active primarily for Catholic-national school reform (76 per cent of elementary school teachers were women, 36 per cent in secondary schools). Even later there were always roughly a dozen female parliamentarians, elected within the framework of the State Party. The only Salazarist women's organization was one for girls; it was compulsory for seven- to fourteen-year-olds and optional for older girls. It was founded in 1937 based on the Italian model, and in 1940 about 38,000 girls over fourteen were members. While the boys, whose association was considerably larger, were trained in nationalist ideas, the girls were trained in Catholic values such as humility, obedience, love of family and Christianity. The feminist National Council of Women (founded in 1914) was not disbanded until 1947. It had welcomed the election of women to the parliament and advocated the extension of suffrage. Salazar answered their wishes in 1946, extending the franchise to women who were married or paid taxes. Motherhood and family were at the centre of the Salazar regime's image of women. Maria Guardiola, a member of parliament, founded the Organization for the Protection of Mothers and Children (OMEN) in 1936. Like its Italian model ONMI, it was hardly a mass organization, but its annual 'mothers' week' and medals for mothers with large families helped it reach a relatively large number of women (in other dictatorships, the distribution of such medals was not in women's hands). OMEN's hopes to have a state allowance for mothers approved proved futile, as did the government's hopes of raising the birth rate (which dropped from 30 per thousand in 1930 to 20 around 1970).

However, in Portugal – as well as Spain, Italy and Vichy France – there was a different kind of mass mobilization of women, namely, within the context of Catholicism. Whereas the Orthodox Church had been eliminated in Soviet Russia and some of the Catholic women's organizations banned in Nazi Germany, Church and religious belief were a point of departure for women's organizations in southern Europe. They were oriented towards social Catholicism and – irrespective of the clerical hierarchy – were able to maintain a certain autonomy with regard to the dictatorship. In all three countries the Church was anti-liberal, anti-modern and a constitutive element of authoritarianism (a concordat was concluded with Italy in 1929, with Portugal in 1940 and with Spain in 1953). At the same time the Church functioned as an alternative to the totalitarian tendency of the state organizations, especially the fascist ones. Catholic women believed in higher values than nation or state, in the inner motivation of the individual and in the strength of the personality; for them, the ideal of motherhood stood side by side with that of virginity. The Marianist movements and organizations in particular expanded in all three of these countries. In the restructured Catholic Action, Portuguese women (22,000 in number) comprised three-quarters of the membership in 1934; 72,000 Portuguese women were members in 1957.[32] In Italy the Catholic women's groups offered a clear alternative to the fascist ones. In 1931, when the *fasci femminili* had only 150,000 members, the Unione femminile cattolica italiana had 250,000. Women in Catholic organizations exercised considerable influence on Italy's political culture through neighbourhood networks, groups across class lines, schools, orphanages and organizations for girls of all ages – not only the *beniamine* from six to twelve years old but also the *piccolissime* from four to six years old and even the *angiolette* under four. In view of the new times, Catholic women also took advantage of modernization, using radio, cinema and the press. They were not politically in the opposition but in the 1930s they openly competed with the growing ambition of the fascists to control Italian youth; consequently, they were occasionally attacked by fascist gangs.

Elections had only minor importance along the road to dictatorship, and the voting behaviour of women carried even less weight, such as in the 1933 Spanish elections or the 1917 soviet elections in Russia. Only in Germany (and Austria) had it been legal to count male and female votes separately since 1919 (this is why the voting behaviour of German women became one of the major areas for the study of electoral behaviour and statistical methods developed in the 1930s in the United States). In Germany separate counting was optional and actually happened for a fifth of the electorate at most during the 1920s. As elsewhere, women in the 1920s voted to a vast extent for the political centre and refused the extremism of either the left or right wings. This still applied to the Reichstag elections on 14 September 1930, from which the Nazi Party emerged as the second largest parliamentary party. About 15 per cent of female voters had voted for the Nazis, which was somewhat less than half the 6.5 million Nazi Party votes (18 per cent of all voters). However, when the 'Hitler Movement' claimed exactly one-third of all ballots cast in the Reichstag elections in November 1932 (4 per cent less than in the Reichstag elections in July 1932), women, with the exception of the Catholics, seem to have aligned their voting behaviour with that of the men. But this time the votes that were counted separately according to gender were only a minimal fraction of those counted separately in the 1920s, since expenditure was no longer allowed for such luxuries (for example, ballots in different colours) owing to the Depression. Certainly National Socialism's rise to power could not have been prevented if German women had *not* been made 'active voters' in 1918, to once again take up Hippel's hypothetical speculation of 1792. Moreover, the last free elections in Germany were more an indicator of public opinion than the sole deciding factor for Hitler's coming to power. Hitler was named chancellor by Reich president Paul von Hindenburg, and women voters were indeed partly responsible for Hindenburg's presidency, since the female vote in the 1932 presidential election was more clearly for Hindenburg – and against Hitler – than the male vote was.

One woman who not only voted for the Nazis but made her vote public – an uncommon occurrence – was Margarete Adam. She was also unusual in yet another respect. Adam was a devout Catholic and democrat and had published articles in the 1920s in the feminist journal *Die Frau*. She demanded that women be allowed to enter the priesthood; and she studied philosophy, receiving her doctorate in Hamburg under Ernst Cassirer, who was then dismissed in 1933 because he was Jewish. In December 1930 the Central Association of German Citizens of Jewish Faith (Centralverein deutscher Staatsbürger jüdischen Glaubens) published a brochure with an essay by Adam, together with a riposte by Eva Reichmann, editor of the Jewish journal *Der Morgen*; after she was forced to leave Germany, Reichmann wrote *Hostages of Civilization* (1950), an analysis of anti-Semitism. Adam in 1930 identified herself as a philo-Semite and condemned Nazi anti-Semitism; she believed that anti-Semitism would no longer find a public consensus and that a 'state disenfranchisement' of the Jews was inconceivable. 'The path of anti-Semitism runs downhill; that of philo-Semitism is looking up. In spite of everything!' Reichmann, too, suggested not 'tired resignation, but hopeful optimism'.[33] Two epilogues followed. Adam explained that she had written her text before the 14 September elections; she admitted having voted for the Nazi Party – not *because of* but *despite* their anti-Semitism and after much soul-searching. What convinced her was that the Nazi Party was fighting against the Versailles Treaty, general corruption and Bolshevism. On this point Adam was by no means unusual, since most women – and men – who voted for Hitler did so for just these reasons. Reichmann was laconic in her epilogue; she criticized Adam's political judgement and sent her a signed copy of the brochure. Soon Hamburg Nazis started confronting Adam with polemics, accusing her of having voted insincerely. In 1933 she lost her teaching position in Hamburg. Adam decided to join the resistance and tried to have the murderers in the Röhm Affair of 1934 brought to trial and to convince officers and other public figures to resist. She single-handedly typed countless flyers on her typewriter, always with seventeen carbon copies, which she distributed in officers' cafeterias, at employment offices and other public places. Adam now put her hopes in a monarchy. In 1937 – at a time when most non-Jewish Germans, both men and women, were more or less dedicated supporters of the regime – Adam was charged with high treason. She was found guilty and sentenced to eight years in prison. Her co-prisoners admired her inner strength, compassion and willingness to take responsibility. She died in 1946 as a result of her incarceration.

National Socialism and Race Policy

> The German race question is first and foremost defined by the Jewish question. Far from this, but of no less significance, is the Gypsy question. . . . The German national body can be subverted not only from the outside by foreign races, but also from within by unrestrained breeding of inferior hereditary material.
>
> Government official, 1943[34]

The 'race question' was the core of National Socialism. It was at the centre from the outset, despite the fact that it was played down in election propaganda in 1932 and the regime initially concentrated on eliminating political opponents. Nazi race policy was complex but inherently consistent; it became more and more radical – albeit without a clearly laid-out plan – up to the very end of the regime. The real or alleged problems of the majority were to be 'solved' by discriminating against and persecuting 'inferior' minorities. The Nazis used ethnic ('racial') and eugenic ('race-hygienic') criteria to classify people as 'hereditarily' or 'biologically inferior'. Discrimination, persecution and ultimately the murder of Jews, Romany (Gypsies) and Slavs, sterilization of the 'hereditarily diseased', marriage bans and the murder of handicapped people were intended to serve the 'regeneration of the German people'. The Nazi 'protection of heredity and race' (*Erb- und Rassenpflege*), affected both men and women, and women comprised about half of its victims. Approximately 150,000 women were subjected to forced sterilization by 1939, including hundreds of black and Romany women. From 1939 on, about 100,000 Jewish and non-Jewish women were killed within the scope of murder of the hospitalized handicapped ('euthanasia'). More than two million foreign women were forced to work in Germany during the war, and hundreds of thousands of them, especially Poles and Soviets, were forced to undergo abortions or sterilization. After 1933 about 150,000 Jewish women were forced to leave Germany and starting in 1941, roughly 100,000 German and three million non-German Jewish women were murdered, as well as around 100,000 Romany women and an unknown number of Slavic women. On the one hand, the race policy hit both sexes equally hard; on the other hand, it was by no means gender-neutral, just as the gender policy was not 'race'-neutral.

Some aspects of Nazi race policy were neither new nor limited to Germany or Nazism; they emerged from a number of different traditions. The 'Nordic' or 'white race' was glorified internationally. Anti-Semitism was widespread in many countries, albeit to varying degrees. Mussolini enacted anti-Jewish legislation in 1938 based on the German model (the Italian variant was somewhat milder), though he did not find the necessary support among the Italian population to enforce the laws consistently. That same year, anti-Jewish laws were passed in Romania and Hungary, and the German laws also became applicable in Austria after it was annexed. In most of the countries conquered by Germany, individuals and institutions collaborated with the German occupiers in their persecution of the Jews. Eugenics, with its major tool, the sterilization of people classified as 'inferior' in the interest of the 'people' or the 'race', was an international movement. Its organizations initially helped German race policy gain an international reputation. Laws for – more or less forced – sterilization of individuals whose progeny were considered 'undesirable' had long since existed in some states of the United States, and in 1930s Europe such legislation was also introduced in Sweden, Norway, Finland, Estonia, Iceland and Denmark. Dictatorships in southern Europe rejected eugenics and sterilization policies; Catholicism (and the pope, in 1930) spoke out against it, and Mussolini viewed the children of all Italians, not just some of them, as guarantors of the quality of the 'race'. Among democratic countries where eugenic movements existed, Britain and Holland rejected sterilization legislation because individual rights and liberties were given more weight than state control of reproduction. Despite the international nature of racism, however, and despite the international use of the ambiguous concept of 'race', Nazism was unique. For only Nazism raised 'race' to a political category, which

it placed at its very centre and implemented through institutionalized and violent race policy, taking all forms of racism to the extreme.
Only Nazism consistently enforced the sterilization laws; only Nazism
inextricably linked ethnic and eugenic racism; and only in Nazism
did eugenics become a preliminary stage leading to mass murder and
genocide.

National Socialism attempted to penetrate all aspects of society with
its race policy. Germans, according to the head of the Office for Race
Policy within the Nazi Party, had to learn to 'think in racial terms'. Along
with the general mass mobilization, the race policy undermined the traditional relationship between the private and the political. This would
have serious consequences for the sexes and gender relations. The sole
function of the private sphere was to serve the political sphere, but the
political had come to mean 'people and race', which is where the Nazi
slogan 'common good before personal good' diverged from its traditional
meaning. The sterilization law of July 1933 (the first population policy
law of the Nazis) was based – according to the official commentary – on
the 'primacy of the state over the sphere of life, marriage and the family'
and on the fact that where the line was drawn between political and
non-political was viewed not as a personal matter but as a political one.
Intervention into the private sphere was most grievous with respect to
the Jews; it affected family, career, friendships, community and neighbourhood. Whereas all dictatorships shared the aim of 'emancipation
from women's emancipation', the German dictatorship was unique in its
aim, at least until 1935, to actively seek emancipation from the rich tradition of the emancipation of the Jews by systematically removing all its
achievements and ultimately threatening the life and limb of the Jews
themselves.

National Socialist policy regarding women was neither uniform nor
consistent; instead, it corresponded above all to the current priorities of
race policy. Praise of motherhood was reserved for the rhetoric of Sundays, Party conventions or Mother's Day. In contrast to the rest of Europe, in Germany it never referred to all women but only the 'German
and hereditarily healthy' ones. Nazis never propagated the slogan of
'*Kinder, Küche, Kirche*' as women's domain, and they clearly opposed
the biblical dictate to 'be fruitful and multiply'. Even before he came to
power, Hitler announced that the prevention of procreation of 'millions'
of people would avoid 'unnecessary suffering'. His future minister of
agriculture Darré divided women into four categories according to their
'worth'. Only for the 'most worthy' of these was maternity to be promoted. As of 1933 the Reich Ministry of the Interior prepared measures
banning 'marriages harmful to the people' wishing thereby to prevent
'undesirable' births. The result was the two marriage prohibition laws of

1935. The Law for the Protection of German Blood and Honour, which was part of the anti-Jewish Nuremberg Laws, banned Jews (later extended to blacks and Romany) from marrying or having extramarital sexual relations ('race defilement') with those of 'German blood'. Its authors saw this as a 'mild' alternative to sterilization. The Marriage Health Law was passed one month later, prohibiting marriage between those considered 'hereditarily healthy' and those considered 'hereditarily diseased'. Whereas the 'blood protection' law was strictly enforced, the second law could only be applied in a limited number of cases. Here the decision whether or not a marriage was judged 'undesirable for the national community' was made by registrars, who were therefore instructed in the 'protection of heredity and race'. If the decision was made against the marriage, the couple would be sent to the sterilization agency for review. From the perspective of the Ministry of the Interior, both marriage prohibitions also had 'educational value'; they were to 'force the entire German population to deal with these issues', with the goal of avoiding 'some births which until recently were taking place unscrupulously'. Everyone classified as ethnically and eugenically 'inferior' was excluded from all marriage and family benefits.

Propaganda accompanied these laws. From 1933 on, flyers, brochures, newspapers and films were circulated in the millions; and speakers gave hundreds of thousands of instruction classes, all with the message that not childbearing but 'regeneration is the state's aim'. The propaganda conjured up 'women who must not become mothers', while the propaganda ministry declared guidelines: 'The order of the day is not "Children at any price", but "As many children as possible within the hereditarily healthy German family."' Minister of the Interior Wilhelm Frick announced in 1933 that children were undesirable in 20 per cent of the population. Himmler drilled into his SS group leaders in 1937, the phrase 'let us never fall victim to the delusion of numbers!' According to the race policy propaganda and practice, the 'quality' of the births was more important than the quantity. This is why plans were dropped for a law making any abortion subject to penalties; instead, abortion in cases where eugenic criteria were satisfied was anchored in the sterilization law of 1935. According to the justification for the law, it was 'in line with the logical thought process' that had led to the sterilization law. A total of roughly 30,000 women were given abortions on eugenic grounds (they were always also subjected to forced sterilization). An equal number of women were sentenced between 1933 and 1942 for voluntary and illegal abortions (as were around 12,000 men). The different treatment of women with respect to abortion corresponded to a principle of the eugenically and ethnically motivated race policy: 'Unequal worth, unequal rights.'[35]

The regime was quite flexible regarding 'German and hereditarily healthy' women, and certainly did not reflect the picture of 'Children, Kitchen, Church' or 'home and hearth' as women's domains that regime opponents had painted. In the election campaigns of the early 1930s in particular, the Nazis had been accused of wanting to turn all women into 'submissive birth machines'. Until 1939 women's level of employment was influenced primarily by the economic situation. Although many Nazis, especially the 'old fighters', had wanted to exclude women from wage-earning during the Great Depression (as did many non-Nazis in and outside Germany), there was no mass layoff of women. Their contribution to the economy, especially at this time of autarky and increasing armament production, was far too great and many families were all too dependent on the woman's income. From 1933 to 1936 the number of female industrial workers rose 29 per cent, and in the following two years it rose another 19 per cent. The trend towards lifetime wage-earning persisted; the share of the married among all female blue-collar workers doubled from 1933 to 1939; and there was a distinct rise in the share of twenty-five- to forty-year-olds in the workforce and even in women over forty. In 1939, 52 per cent of women worked outside the home (in 'Greater Germany', that is, including Austria and the Sudetenland); 24 per cent of employed women had children under fourteen, and women made up 36 per cent of the labour force, far more than the countries of western Europe (except for France) and the United States. A majority of women certainly did not regard their employment as emancipation; a 1936 survey of the women's office of the German Labour Front – similar to the surveys carried out in several western countries in the first three decades of the century – revealed the strain on the women: 'We have no free time, especially those of us with children. Sometimes the work is so hard that I feel like throwing in the towel.'[36]

At the highly professional level there was a break in the trend; first of all, however, it was temporary and, second, it was more about race policy than about gender policy. The law of 7 April 1933 to 'restore professional civil service' led to the dismissal of female school principals in particular. Especially hard hit were Jewish teachers, both female and male, who were all dismissed. The termination of the Jewish teachers was permanent, whereas the number of secondary school teachers who were non-Jewish and female increased again after 1938 (though the number of female school principals did not). The same applied to the medical profession. Jewish women – and men – were definitively excluded from being physicians; they were pressured out of the profession in stages, until their licences were finally withdrawn in 1938, at which time they were only permitted to treat Jewish patients. Conversely, the number of non-Jewish female doctors doubled between 1930 and 1939 and then continued to increase. One of their main tasks became medical service for the mass women's organizations. The only academic career from which non-Jewish women were also systematically excluded was that of judge. With respect to women studying at the universities, there was no lasting intervention by the regime; enrolment was limited for women in 1934, but restrictions were lifted only a year later. A temporary decrease in the number of female students (which also took place in other countries affected by the Great Depression) was almost the same as the decrease in male students; it was caused by the economic situation, the decreasing desire to study and temporary bottlenecks in the labour market. Nazi propaganda started trying to recruit women for university studies in 1937, and the number and share of women grew (to 20,000, or 39 per cent, by 1942). The only group of female students that decreased and ultimately disappeared as a result of intervention by the regime was the Jews. Their exclusion, which included the men as well, was for reasons of race policy, not gender policy.[37] The basis for this was the law against the 'overcrowding' of German schools and universities of 25 April 1933. This cosmetic euphemism replaced the original title of 'over-alienization', which had triggered negative reactions from abroad.

The race policy had been conceived and largely carried out by men, but many women participated in it. Some women in academia assisted their male supervisors in designing the genetic and racial foundations for the persecution of 'undesirables'. Women made up 15 per cent of the newly installed 'state medical officers', who were on the lookout for, and initiated sterilization proceedings against, 'hereditarily diseased' individuals before the 250 sterilization courts, staffed entirely by men. Female doctors and roughly two thousand Nazi or Protestant female social workers (Catholics refused to participate) had reported about 10 per cent of the 400,000 people referred to the sterilization authorities by 1935. Most of the women sterilized between 1934 and 1945 had been diagnosed as 'feeble-minded' (the second most frequent reason for sterilization was 'schizophrenia'). This diagnosis was used for all kinds of deviations from 'normality'. With respect to women, but not men, it was used for 'abnormal sexuality', the alleged risk of being raped (because it could lead to pregnancy and 'undesirable' offspring), 'disorderly' housekeeping and inability to care for children (this also applied to childless women). Agnes Bluhm of Berlin was the first physician who had enthusiastically welcomed 'racial hygiene' even before 1933, and she was among its most important propagandists. In 1934 Bluhm praised sterilization in the journal *Die Frau* as 'a race-hygienic panacea'. Female as well as male doctors were among the professional groups that most actively supported the Nazi race policy. The League of German Women Doctors was one of the first women's associations to expel its Jewish members. The Jewish physician Hertha Nathorff documented the story of the Berlin branch in her autobiography. She had attended a meeting of the League in April 1933. A man had also been invited and he demanded the Nazification of the organization. A female physician then requested that 'the German colleagues go into the next room for discussion'. A Catholic woman protested, 'What does that mean, German colleagues?' The reply was: 'All who are not Jews, of course.' Subsequently, the League sent a telegram to Hitler reporting its commitment to 'responsibility for the people and race'.[38] It was not only the female Jewish physicians who were expelled but also the – very few – non-Jews who refused to support the expulsion of their Jewish colleagues. Hertha Nathorff did not emigrate until 1939, since her Jewish husband had been unresolved about leaving Germany. At this time Gentile female physicians, some of whom had assumed the positions of their former Jewish colleagues, successfully fought to improve their professional status, although they never fought for their Jewish colleagues, some of whom had already emigrated in 1933. Rahel Straus, Zionist and member of the League of Jewish Women, went to Palestine; Käte Frankenthal, who was persecuted not on race policy grounds but for political reasons, went to Czechoslovakia; and Charlotte Wolf went first to France and then to England, after having been fired in February on account of being Jewish.

The leaders of the elite women's organizations and writers for the women's press also participated in the race policy. They promoted the ban against marrying Jews, Gypsies and others with 'inferior hereditary material' and pressured women to report potential candidates for sterilization, even their own children. This made it necessary to revamp traditional images of motherhood and femaleness. 'Motherliness' became a target of racist polemics and was considered 'sentimental humanitarianism', alongside Christian charity and Marxism. Nazi women polemicized about the 'danger' that would 'ensue from the woman precisely as a result of her motherliness', since a 'strong sense of motherliness' served the 'inborn drive to care for the needy' and the 'natural altruism' of women worked 'against the race, as does every egoism'. There was 'hardly a worse sin against nature' than the situation that 'the woman feels especially close and has a special inclination to all living beings through her physical and psychological peculiarity'.[39] The Nazi newspaper *Völkischer Beobachter* stressed in 1934 that the sterilization law marked 'the beginning of a new age', especially for women.

Although animosity towards Jews had already been widespread before 1933, that year marked a major turn for the worse for Jewish women (and men). Before 1933 the lives and activities of Jewish women were largely determined by the fact that they were women; from 1933 on they were defined largely by their being Jewish or defined as Jewish. At this time, one-third of the half million members of the Jewish faith in Germany lived in Berlin (there were also roughly 200,000 who were defined by the Nazis as Jews and another 200,000 once Austria was annexed by Germany). Almost 30 per cent of adult Jewish women were employed around 1933 (20 per cent less than their non-Jewish counterparts). Of these, one-third worked as clerks (saleswomen, secretaries, accountants), and these were the women whom Hitler referred to in his diatribes in *Mein Kampf* as 'department store Jewesses' whose children – especially in mixed marriages – were undesirable. Twenty per cent of employed Jewish women worked in family businesses and another 20 per cent were self-employed in a number of fields. Jewish women had been – in Germany as elsewhere – strongly represented in the women's movement, and they were among the pioneers on the long and rocky road leading to women's access to universities. In 1929 they comprised 7 per cent of women studying at universities in Germany (all together, Jews made up almost 1 per cent of the total German population). Unlike non-Jewish women, 44 per cent of whom studied languages and cultural studies, Jewish women preferred law, economics and medicine, and in 1925 more than 20 per cent of the roughly 1,500 female German physicians were Jewish. The race policy measures of the 1930s thus struck at the core of Jewish women's lives and their recently begun social mobility. What Gershom Scholem wrote from Palestine to his mother Betty in Berlin in 1933 also applied to many Jewish women: exclusion from the liberal professions showed that the Jews 'can be destroyed through other means than physical attacks', and that the Nazis now 'eliminate them in a bloodless way'.[40]

The changes in everyday Jewish life were just as dramatic, and women were particularly affected by virtue of their presence in the family and neighbourhood and their role as mothers: 'Neighbours became Jews.' Marta Appel, wife of the Dortmund rabbi, reported that at first many Gentile friends, neighbours and even people they had scarcely known came to assure them of their friendship and to tell them 'that the horrors could not last long'. But 'after some months of a regime of terror, fidelity and friendship had lost their meaning, and fear and treachery had replaced them'. Now it was up to the Jews to express their friendship for their Gentile friends by not greeting them in the streets, 'for we did not want to bring upon them the danger of imprisonment for being considered a friend of Jews. With each day of the Nazi regime, the abyss between us and our fellow citizens grew larger. Friends whom we had loved for years did not know us anymore. They suddenly saw that we were different from themselves. Of course we were different, since we were bearing the stigma of Nazi hatred, since we were hunted like deer'. Marta Appel did not attend the meetings of a group of old girlfriends in order not to endanger them. Her former teacher had pleaded with her – 'we miss you' – to come again. But when she stepped into the café after a sleepless night, the table they usually sat at was empty; someone had called to cancel. 'I could not blame them. Why should they have risked losing a position only to prove to me that we still had friends in Germany?' The risk was in fact rather small, and Betty Scholem had good reason to write in April 1933: 'I cannot understand why 10,000 or even just 1,000 upright Christians do not refuse to go along with it and voice their protest loudly.' Jewish children were increasingly perceived, insulted and ostracized as Jews; some of them had not even been aware of their Jewish heritage. 'Race studies' or 'protection of heredity and race' was introduced at all levels of school instruction (as well as in the medicine and biology departments of the universities). Erika Mann, who had emigrated to the United States, analysed the effects of this education in her 1938 book *School for Barbarians*. Marta Appel told a story about her daughters coming home from school one day, giggling. An official from the Race Policy Office came to talk about 'high and low races' and demonstrated the theories on a girl with long braids. 'Look here, the narrow head of this girl, her high forehead, her very blue eyes, and blond hair' and 'her slender figure': 'These are the unequivocal marks of a pure and unmixed Germanic race.' The class broke into laughter: 'But she's Jewish!'[41] It was a shock to the children when they finally had to leave their school for good.

Pressure was put on people in 'mixed-race marriages' to get divorced. Starting in June 1933, no one married to a Jew was allowed to enter the civil service, and in the same year divorce law was interpreted by the courts to the disadvantage of the Jewish partner, who enjoyed some protection in a marriage with a Gentile. The fact that a large proportion of mixed marriages were maintained was no consolation for those for whom that was not the case. In 1938 Erika Mann said that 'Aryan' men tended to divorce their Jewish wives more often than 'Aryan' women divorced Jewish husbands. Around the same time Betty Scholem told of her sister Käthe, who had received a letter from her husband who had been travelling: 'He had to divorce her on racial grounds and if she did not consent he would lose his livelihood and would no longer be able to support her. Besides that, he had been having an affair for several years already and now he wanted to have children and start a new life.' Käthe Schiepan later died in Theresienstadt. Two months before that letter was written a new divorce law came into effect. Though it allowed divorce for 'eugenic' reasons but not yet on 'racial' grounds (that would be discussed as of 1942 but never implemented), divorce was made easier if the marriage did not correspond to the 'nature of marriage'; this served to destabilize mixed marriages further. A leading jurist explained that 'the racial drive of our times will increase the conflicts in some mixed marriages to such an extent that existing divorce law is sufficient in solving the problem'. In view of the 'racial drive' Jewish couples chose less and less often to have children; thus the birth rate dropped dramatically. 'Who wanted to have children at such a time?'[42]

The 'racial drive' also became clear with respect to 'race defilement'. Trials provided a forum – in court as well as in the press and in public in general – for sexual fantasies, which were supposedly based on 'basic life experience' but were in reality male fantasies and were also significant in the sterilization trials against women. Racist discourse was always a breeding ground for such fantasies. Jewish women were often presented as prostitutes and Jewish men as pimps or as rapists of German women; and 'inferior beings' of all varieties were accused of being 'wanton and uninhibited'. The Supreme Court defined criminal sexual relations between Jews and non-Jews in 1935: 'It is not limited to coition. It includes all forms of natural and unnatural sexual intercourse – that is, coition as well as those sexual activities with the person of the opposite sex which are designed, in the manner in which they are performed, to serve in place of coition to satisfy the sex drive of at least one of the partners.' Alfred Rapp, a 'full Jew', was sentenced in 1936 to two years' imprisonment; his 'full-blooded German' partner Margarete Lehmann received a nine-month sentence. 'Aryan' women who had in fact or allegedly slept with a Jewish man had their heads shaved and were dragged through the town. In the reverse case, Jewish women were put in 'preventive detention'. Sixty-nine-year-old Leo Katzenberger and his thirty-one-year-old friend Irene Scheffler-Seiler, whose families had been friends since the 1920s, had kissed each other in a manner appropriate to their father-daughter-type relationship. In 1942 Katzenberger was sentenced to death by guillotine in Nuremberg and Scheffler-Seiler to two years in prison. When the trial was reopened in 1967, the former judges in the case were convicted of manslaughter but never had to serve their sentences. One of them said that the judicial murder 'was not all that bad, since the final solution followed anyway'. Scheffler-Seiler, who had once been a member of the Nazi Party and later lived in East Germany, was not recognized as a 'victim of fascism' until 1973, since her conviction was considered to be 'not of a political, but a private nature'.[43]

Most 'race defilement' cases were brought to court through denunciations. Katzenberger and Scheffler-Seiler – 'the Jew-whore' or 'Jew-lover' – had already been the subject of gossip in their Nuremberg neighbourhood in 1933, by women and men, whether Nazi Party members or not. Hundreds of thousands of non-Jews denounced both Jews and Gentiles (for example, as 'Jew-friends'). The regime had a foundation not only of terror and coercion but of consensus and complicity. About one in five denouncers and one in six of those denounced were women. The motives of denouncers, whether male or female, were generally the same; usually it was an attempt to solve personal conflicts with the help of the state, an individual need for revenge or attention. A Gentile businessman named Paasch had been married for a long time to a Jewish woman. Their relationship worsened over the course of the 1930s and became increasingly difficult in 1943, when Herr Paasch's sister, Frau Kempfer, moved in with them. The two women often quarrelled, as did the husband and wife. In 1944 Herr Paasch and his sister filed a denunciation report with the 'Jewish Question Department' of the Gestapo. It was filed against the 'Jewess Paasch' and signed by Frau Kempfer. In it Kempfer accused her sister-in-law of having said that the Jews would be avenged, that German soldiers were murderers, that children who died in air raids had been killed by Hitler and that Germany would lose the war. Herr Paasch included a petition for divorce, which was then approved. In July 1944 Frau Paasch was deported to Auschwitz where she was killed in the gas chamber.

From 1933 to 1939 German Jews were increasingly segregated from their surroundings; starting in 1938 Austrian and Czech Jews faced the same conditions. Thousands of directives at Reich, protectorate and local levels forced them into a new ghetto. They had to close their shops and dismiss their non-Jewish employees; they were excluded from professional careers and stripped of civil and political rights by the Nuremberg Laws. They became impoverished and left to their own resources to manage their economic survival. Now even Jewish women who had previously not been employed, especially married women, worked in factories, stores, their husbands' law or medical practices or as domestic servants in Jewish households. The 'blood protection law' prohibited non-Jewish domestic servants under forty-five from working for Jewish families (in order to prevent sexual contact with Jewish men and the possible pregnancies that could result). More and more women, earning pitiful wages, were responsible for supporting entire families, often leading to a role reversal between the men and women. Women also worked in the Jewish Welfare Organization (Jews were banned from the non-Jewish counterpart). The League of Jewish Women was involved here as well as in job referrals for women, though only unskilled jobs were available. In addition to poorly paid positions, work in the family expanded, especially with respect to caring for – and worrying about – the children. The *Israelische Familienblatt* newspaper appealed to them: 'Jewish mothers: You must, yes, you must' and 'She must be there; she simply must be there'.[44]

The main subject of family conversations and in the Jewish press was the question of emigration. Often the women favoured emigration earlier and more strongly than the men, who held on to their jobs and only very reluctantly let go of hopes for a political turn. Marta Appel and Peter Wyden recalled the debates: '"Isn't the future of our children more important than a completely senseless holding out . . .?" All the women shared this opinion . . . while the men, more or less passionately, spoke against it.' And: 'It was not a bit unusual in these go-or-no-go family dilemmas for the women to display more energy and enterprise than the men. . . . Almost no women had a business, a law office, or a medical practice to lose. They were less status-conscious, less money-oriented than the men.' On the other hand, the willingness of women to emigrate in order to save their children was confounded by another family responsibility, care for elderly family members who had trouble deciding to emigrate. Leading women in the Jewish Women's League, such as Cora Berliner and Hannah Karminski, assisted others in emigration and remained in Germany for this purpose until they themselves were deported. The gender role reversal often persisted as émigrés (up to 1937 most emigrated to western Europe, where many were again caught by Nazi occupiers and deported). A conference on 'Women in Emigration' was held in 1940 in New York; according to the *Aufbau* newspaper report, 'The load on the shoulders of the emigrant family . . . is not always equally distributed and very often the heaviest share falls on the shoulders of the women. . . . The fate of a family that has emigrated often depends more on the woman . . . than on the man. If she succeeds in overcoming the obstacles, then the family will move forward; if she stumbles, she'll take the rest of the family with her'; she can 'earn a few dollars in the household and in unskilled labour more easily than the man, . . . who seeks more specific work and – no matter what he wants to do – requires a higher weekly wage (which makes it more difficult to find work)'. Hertha Nathorff, who made it possible for her husband to become a doctor again while she had to give up the idea for herself, gave lectures even after a hard day's work: 'Charwoman during the day, Chairwoman at night', as *Aufbau* affectionately put it.[45] In this situation the women played an important role in helping the family become acculturated in exile, and they were often better capable of adapting to the new living conditions than the men were.

The 1938 November Pogrom in Germany turned concern to despair. Men were the first to experience physical violence. Thirty thousand were put in concentration camps and physically abused. About a hundred men and women died during the pogrom. Having been told that their husbands would only be released if they emigrated immediately, countless women fought for emigration papers, which were difficult to obtain, and for the release of their husbands. Shortly afterwards, the Security Service reported 'that an incredible hysteria has broken out among Jewish women and men', and they illustrated it with the words of a Jewish woman from Ludwigsburg, who had said 'that she would have long since taken her life if she didn't have children'. Suicide by Jews had been increasing since 1933, parallel to the anti-Jewish measures; it became more frequent after the November Pogrom and the annexation of Austria, and then again with the mass deportations from late 1941 on. These Jews preferred a 'death of their own' to humiliation and imminent death. Two sisters who lived with their mother decided that 'When we get the eviction notice then we will sit down in the kitchen with our mother and turn on the gas. That is the only love we can still prove to our mother'.[46] Before taking poison, Käthe Mugdan gathered her family around her; they read from Schiller and the Bible and she put on her burial dress. The historian Hedwig Hintze-Guggenheimer had written about women's suffrage during the French Revolution; in 1936 she was expelled from the staff of the historical journal *Historische Zeitschrift*, which prompted her Gentile husband Otto Hintze to stop working there as well. After 1934 she lived partly in France before emigrating in 1939 to the Netherlands, where she committed suicide in 1942. Thirty-two-year-old Elisabeth 'Sara' Alexander (as of January 1939 Jewish women had to take the name 'Sara' and Jewish men the name 'Israel') of Berlin, 'very sad' and full of 'anxious fears', made a futile attempt to take her life in 1936. She had been in an institution since 1935 for 'depression'; the medical officer had filed for her to be sterilized on the grounds of 'schizophrenia'. Jews were also subject to the sterilization law. Alexander was sentenced to forced sterilization in June 1941 because of her 'depressive condition'. In 1942, two months after the Wannsee Conference, a decree was issued to discontinue the sterilization of Jews. Instead of preventing them from having children, they would be murdered.

War and Genocide in Europe

Different horrors, same hell.[47]

With the start of World War II women once again moved into the war industry or took on other jobs that were declared essential for the war effort, both women who had been working in other areas and those who had not previously been employed at all. The number and proportion of employed women grew most in those countries where the level had been previously low and where there was female unemployment. The rise was smallest in Germany, where the female employment rate had been higher than in other western countries in 1939 and where there was no longer any female unemployment. In 1943, at the height of the war, the proportion of employed women among all women over fourteen years of age was 42 per cent in Britain, 37 in the United States and 45 in Germany. This does not include women working in agriculture but does include those hired by the respective armies – in Britain and Germany about half a million. In France the proportion of women employed outside agriculture among all women in paid employment rose from 14 per cent in 1940 to 23 per cent in 1944. In Britain the share of women among all industrial workers rose from 10 per cent in 1939 to 34 per cent in 1943. In France as well as Germany, the proportion of women working in agriculture was traditionally very high (in Germany there were six million women in agriculture in 1939, four times as many as in Britain). Many of the 4.7 million French and 11.5 million German soldiers left behind their wives as the main worker on their farms. In both France and Germany, women's work was essential in order to feed the population (even though Germany also plundered the conquered territories for this purpose); despite – or because of – this, the share of women working in agriculture as compared with the total number of employed women went down in the course of the war in both countries (in Germany it dropped from 40 to 14 per cent). Like thirty years earlier, women became more visible in the public sphere. They became streetcar conductors, worked at the counters in post offices and train stations or as Red Cross nurses (in Germany there were also 'Brown Nurses'). Many women took on volunteer work that was particularly important during the war. In Germany this included the Nazi social welfare organization (Nationalsozialistische Volkswohlfahrt) and the Winter Relief Works, and in Germany, France and Britain women worked in the evacuation of children from cities under bombardment (for Germany, the number of workers lost to the war industry through bombings was estimated in 1945 at half a million).

Britain and Germany sought to recruit women for war jobs through propaganda. At first they relied on voluntarism, but that proved insufficient in both countries. After heated debates, both within the government and in public, other measures were taken. In Britain women were required to register from 1941 on; compulsory conscription was intensified up to 1943. At first it applied only to nineteen- to forty-year-olds, but it was then extended to forty-five- and fifty-year-olds, although protest to the 'conscription of grandmothers' was at times very vocal. Mothers of children under fourteen were exempted from the outset, and from 1942 on this exemption also applied to married women (though that remained disputed). In Germany women were prohibited from quitting their jobs as of 1939 and compulsory registration was introduced in 1943. This applied to all women between seventeen and forty-five, with the exception of pregnant women and mothers of small children or at least two children under the age of fourteen (which triggered an immediate baby boom). In 1944 the age limit was extended to fifty, and mothers of small children also had to register at the employment office if alternative childcare could be arranged. The Vichy regime yielded to German pressure in 1942 and declared compulsory registration, which was successively intensified until 1944. Initially applying only to unmarried women between twenty-one and thirty-five, it was later extended to those between eighteen and forty-five, though it never applied to mothers. In all three countries mothers, wives and housewives were at the heart of conflicts on the use of women in the labour force and the 'exceptions'. Everywhere women's domestic labour, which especially during the war was more extensive than otherwise, was weighed against compulsory work outside the home and attempts were made to reconcile the two. On top of this, the problem of mobility was raised regarding cases that required work outside one's own town or residence. So while war was raging there was a debate on women's domestic labour. It took place at the government level and within the agencies where women had to go to register. It received considerable attention in the press; in Britain female members of parliament and the major women's organizations also got involved, whether to push for women's employment or to prevent hardship. Workers in Germany, mostly men but also women – in familiar class-struggle manner, as the Security Service liked to claim – attacked the women from 'better circles' who tried to avoid service for the fatherland. In fact, however, 58 per cent of married women who were not employed as of 1939 were married to working-class men. According to a British survey, many women who supported the compulsory registration expected that they themselves would be among the 'exceptions'. Like German women, they argued that 'I've got enough to do at home', or they rejected being called 'shirkers' on the grounds that the housework they did was useful.[48]

Nonetheless, one-third of married, employed British women had children under fourteen at the height of the war. In German cities with a population over 200,000, the figure was 38 per cent. In 1944 day-care services were available for one in four pre-school children of British women working in the armaments industry; the figure was higher in Germany, whether consequent to the law to protect employed mothers (1942), which provided for kindergartens to be established, or because numerous businesses, local districts and women's and welfare organizations set them up on their own initiative. In virtually all belligerent countries, the respective governments guaranteed the wives of drafted soldiers a separation allowance, a compensation for the lost wages of the husband. The regulations varied considerably, but non-married couples living together in common-law marriage and children born out of wedlock were often also taken into consideration, as well as unmarried female relatives. Only British soldiers had to contribute a portion of their pay, and only in the Soviet Union was disability or neediness a prerequisite for receiving the benefits. Wives in France received the main support, with supplemental allowances for the children; this was combined with an increase in the traditional *allocations familiales*. The allowances were essential in securing the livelihood of the women and children, especially since 1.5 million French men were German prisoners of war in 1940. One million of them remained in Germany for five years, and as of 1942 there were 700,000 French men working in Germany as forced labourers. Only in Germany was the amount of the allowance based on the former wage level of the man and, in an international comparison, it was the highest. A mother of two received 73 per cent of the previous income (71 per cent in Canada, 38 per cent in Britain, 37 per cent in the United States). There was a political reason for this generosity on the part of the Nazis. They wanted to avoid a similar experience to World War I, when women in particular, torn between duties within and outside the home and without sufficient income, challenged the government and the war on the 'home front'. In fact this situation was not repeated during World War II, not even when there was little available to buy with money. The separation allowances were consistent with the core of Nazi policies; all those defined as 'inferior' who were forced to work in Germany were excluded from that generosity and from the 1942 Maternity Protection Act.

Neither in England nor in Germany did the conscription for war-work run smoothly. On the one hand, the industries were not always satisfied with the women sent to them to work, and on the other hand, the women were not always pleased with their assigned place of employment. In fact, only a modest proportion of the women who registered in Britain and in Germany could be referred to industry. In both countries, as well as in France, women preferred working as employees in the private sector or public service, partly in new positions and partly in those freed up by men who had gone into military service. In England, as elsewhere, they found factory work to be monotonous and believed it brought a greater risk of sexual harassment. The previous 'feminization of office work' continued its course. There were also women working as war correspondents in Britain (though not in Germany). Erika Mann worked temporarily for the BBC, and the Austrian émigré Hilde Spiel for *New Statesman*. In Germany there was even a female ship captain, Anneliese Teetz, who started in 1943, having been referred by Hitler. But in Germany it was primarily the SS who trained women as of 1942 for highly qualified positions in the 'female intelligence corps of the SS' or as 'SS auxiliaries'; they were supposed to 'hold outstanding positions' during the war as well as after the 'final victory'. After being carefully selected, the women were instructed in race ideology and trained to be radio or teleprinter operators, staff assistants, drivers of heavy equipment, and so on, and – as was said in 1944 – 'they would also have to bear arms if necessary'.[49] About 10,000 such 'helpers' were trained up to 1945. Many of them worked in concentration camps and for the SS special units (*Einsatzgruppen*) in Poland and the Soviet Union.

Only in Germany was women's labour during the war marked by race policy. A total of almost 2.5 million foreign women were forced to work in Germany under conditions not of employment but of slavery. In 1944 'non-German' women (this also included German and non-German Jews) made up 5 per cent of all civilian positions (36 million), German women made up 41 per cent, non-German men (including Jews and prisoners of war) 16 per cent and German men 38 per cent. The degree of coercion corresponded precisely to the 'racial value' within Nazi thought. In occupied France and northern Europe women had been recruited since 1941 for the war effort primarily through German propaganda, and in fact tens of thousands went to Germany. However, when an additional 250,000 men and (unmarried) women were to be recruited in 1943 in Vichy France, open protest ensued. Cardinals and bishops as well as the French Resistance proclaimed: 'Not a single French woman for the Reich!' Nevertheless, as a result of pressure from Germany and through deportations, almost 50,000 French women were working in Germany in 1944.[50] Open force was used against workers from eastern Europe. Gender relations, too, were based on the respective 'racial value'; the lower the value, the more women were used. Accordingly, 85 per cent of all foreign women came from Poland and the Soviet Union. The female 'East workers' (as the Nazis referred to labourers from the Soviet Union), numbering more than one million, made up more than half of all civilian 'East workers' in 1944. The average 'East worker' was female, approximately twenty years old and from Kiev. Among foreign workers from western and northern Europe, women comprised only 5 to 15 per cent. Whereas Polish women (and men) worked largely in agriculture, replacing German men, the female 'East workers' were usually placed in the most difficult and hazardous departments of the armaments industry. Here they were above all intended to relieve the male workers who remained in Germany and had been moved up to skilled and foreman positions. Pregnant Poles and 'East workers' were often forced to perform such heavy labour to encourage miscarriages. Himmler told his SS leaders in 1943 that they should 'never be savage or heartless' to 'these human animals', but 'whether 10,000 Russian females keel over from exhaustion in the construction of an anti-tank ditch interests me only insofar as the ditch for Germany gets finished'.[51]

The shifting of major population groups throughout Europe brought additional problems with respect to sexual gender relations and new 'solutions'. From the very beginning prostitution had attracted the attention of the new rulers in fascist Italy and Nazi Germany. The fifty years of struggle by social reformers, including the international women's movement, for the elimination of state regulation of prostitution had come to an abrupt end. The liberal prostitution law of 1927 was a '*lex judaica*' to the Nazis. The new state control was coupled with intensified health checks. In Italy independent street prostitution was combated through police raids. As early as 1926, according to a contemporary, there was a 'pogrom of the prostitutes' and state brothels, *case chiuse*, were opened. In Germany thousands of prostitutes were arrested after 1933 and put into workhouses and camps; instead of street prostitution, local brothels were established. Many prostitutes were declared legally incompetent on the grounds of 'feeble-mindedness' and then sterilized. Himmler saw the regulation of prostitution as a way to combat male homosexuality: 'We cannot aim to prevent the youth from all drifting to homosexuality, on the one hand, and then block all alternatives, on the other. That is insanity.'[52]

The German state intensified its role as pimp once the war started. The ban against brothels was officially lifted and prostitutes working on their own were threatened with being sent to concentration camps; indeed, many were deported to the camps. A four-tiered system of controlled and often compulsory prostitution was set up during the war. The Wehrmacht high command arranged to have the military's sexual needs satisfied. In occupied France brothels were established in 1940 (the same was true under the Vichy government). The occupiers acquired French women – at first only from the northern zone, but later also in the south – through raids and in the detention camps and forced them to serve the German soldiers, separated according to officers and enlisted men.[53] The German medical service thoroughly examined the thousands of women, thereby cooperating with the French authorities. As a result of rumours that French women intentionally infected German soldiers with venereal disease to put them out of action (similar rumours circulated about Romanian and Polish women), the Wehrmacht ordered such women to perform additional forced labour. Soldiers also had sex with German staff assistants, who were sarcastically referred to as 'Wehrmacht mattresses'.

The second level concerned the concentration camps. Auschwitz commandant Rudolf Höss worked together with the IG-Farben company to design a 'primitive piecework system' called FFF – Freedom (within the camp), Food and *Frauen* – in order to raise the productivity of the prisoners. After visiting the Buchenwald concentration camp, Himmler ordered that a piecework system be instituted there 'in an ingenious and virtually artistic manner'. The first step was cigarettes, the second was 'a small wage' and the third was 'that the man visit the camp brothel once or twice a week'.[54] Women from the Ravensbrück and Auschwitz camps were forced to work in such camp brothels, which guards also visited. The third level applied to the work camps. Starting in 1941, brothels for foreign forced labourers were set up in many work camps (of which there were over 30,000) in almost all larger cities and all large concerns. Foreign women, often French, Polish and Czech, worked in these brothels. In disputes over the financing of these 'B barracks' (brothel barracks) the companies were reassured that the 'investment would soon pay for itself'. On the other hand, it was stressed that this was not a matter of private industry but was 'a political' and 'even an ideological matter', and thus the responsibility of the state. In the case of a Polish woman 'brought in' from Lodz who was forced to work as a prostitute and soon contracted gonorrhoea, the respective sides argued over who should cover the costs of treatment, resolving that prostitutes could not be regarded 'as workers in the true sense'.[55] The brothels staffed by foreign women were intended to prevent 'German blood' from being 'threatened' by German women having sex with foreign workers (in 1942 the number of out-of-wedlock children of foreign workers was estimated at 20,000). Especially with respect to Poles, an effort was made to bring equal numbers of men and women to Germany so that Polish men would have sexual relations with Polish women rather than Germans. French and Belgian men were considered almost as 'dangerous' as Polish or Russian men. Tens of thousands were charged and convicted. If a German woman had an affair with a French man, the man received a sentence of two to six years and the woman up to four years. If the man was Polish, he was publicly hanged and the woman was sent to jail or a concentration camp.

It was also feared that SS men stationed in the occupied eastern territories could 'endanger German blood' by having relationships (so-called 'East marriages') with Polish or Russian women, much to the dismay of their commanders. Thus the fourth tier involved the establishment of brothels for the SS (in Auschwitz alone there were a total of 6,800 SS men). This was Himmler's attempt to ensure that under no circumstances would 'any kind of inner bonds' develop between SS men and Polish women.[56] The SS men were also periodically given leave to visit their wives. For the SS leadership, however, especially the commandants of the concentration camps and ghettos, a 'private' solution was found. They were permitted or even encouraged to bring their wives (and children) with them. Affairs with and marriages to SS women (there were 200 in Auschwitz) were also common. There were about fifty families living around the Auschwitz concentration camp. The wives were aware of the murderous activities of their husbands; they supported them and took advantage of the labour of the imprisoned men and women, enjoyed personal gain from the property of those imprisoned and those killed, tortured prisoners and occasionally shot them. Thirty years after the fact, the wife of the Austrian Franz Stangl, former commandant of the Sobibór and Treblinka death camps, reported that for a short time she refused to have sex with her husband after she heard about the killing (though this did not apply on his home leaves). If she had seriously confronted him with the alternative 'Treblinka or me', he might have – so she thought – chosen her. But there was no sex strike by the SS wives; and Frau Stangl perhaps overestimated her sexual power and needed Herr Stangl more than he needed her. In any event, he answered the question why he continued his murderous job with 'I don't know', 'perhaps . . . love for my wife?' But 'in the end, the only way to deal with it was to drink'. Countless documents indicate that sex was less important for committing the murders than was alcohol (brandy for the higher ranks, schnapps and vodka for the rank and file). An immense volume was consumed day and night, and before, during and after the killing. Many SS men refrained from having their wives join them – as the Security Service complained in Galicia in 1943 – 'in order not to get into trouble with their Polish lovers'.[57]

In all occupied countries where Jews were persecuted and deported by the Germans, women had comprised somewhat more than half the local Jewish population. The asymmetry was greatest in Germany; of the roughly 167,000 people of Jewish faith still living in Germany in 1941, almost all of whom were killed, about 100,000 were women and 60,000 were over sixty years old. More young than old had been able to leave Germany, and more men than women. Many men left alone in hopes of arranging for their families to join them later. Also the men seemed in more immediate danger, since more men than women had lost their jobs. Particularly since the November Pogrom in 1938, men were more threatened by physical violence than were the Jewish women. Alice Nauen of Hamburg recalled: 'Should we send the men out first? This had been the dilemma all along. . . . If you have two tickets, do you take one man out of the concentration camp and his wife who is at this moment safe? Or do you take your two men out of the concentration camp? They took two men out . . . because they said we cannot play God, but these are in immediate danger.' Anti-Semitic tradition – especially the *Protocols of the Elders of Zion* and the theory of the 'conspiracy of world Jewry' – also seemed to suggest that Jewish women would only secondarily become targets of racist polemics and persecution, at the side of their men. In the early 1940s many Jews throughout Europe still believed that the Germans were a civilized people and would therefore respect the traditional gender standards, at least sparing women and children from suffering. Before the 'Black Thursday' raid on 16 July 1942, when 13,000 Jews were rounded up in Paris and brought to the Vélodrôme d'hiver cycling stadium (Vél d'hiv), Jews had been warned. Men went into hiding while the women stayed home, assuming they were not in danger; in the end 6,000 women were arrested, along with 4,000 children and 3,000 men. In eastern Europe as well, Jews often assumed that men faced a greater risk. It was true that they were easier to identify than the women because of their beards, haircuts, clothing and especially the fact that they were circumcised. When Germany invaded Poland many Jewish men fled to the Soviet Union, and so women made up the majority of the populations in the newly formed ghettos. With respect to Italy, Alberta Levi reported that until the day the SS attempted to arrest all the Jews in Rome (on 16 October 1943), 'Jews feared only for the men', and Signora Mortara had said, 'I am over eighty; what do they want with me?' It was then mostly women and children who were arrested, and they were transported to Auschwitz. In places where the persecution was implemented less thoroughly and not by the Germans, such as in the Italian-occupied zone of southern France, in 1942 it was still the norm, as issued by the Italian Minister of Foreign Affairs, for imprisonment to 'spare the elderly, children, women and the sick'.[58]

The Nazis had other norms. When in 1941 it was made compulsory for Jews to wear the yellow star, some thought it applied only to the men. Goebbels cleared up the misunderstanding in a radio broadcast: the Jewish woman, too, must wear the yellow star because she is not to be classified any differently from the man in the 'conspiracy of world Jewry', 'no matter how frail and pitiful she makes out to be'.[59] Mass shootings began in Poland and the conquered part of the Soviet Union in late June 1941; the deportations from Germany – and soon from other countries – began in October, destined for the concentration and death camps in the Generalgouvernement (once part of Poland). At the same time the gas chambers were brought from Germany to the Generalgouvernement along with the male gas chamber personnel to carry out systematic killing. Until then the gas chambers had been used to kill 70,000 handicapped people, starting with children, as a logical next step to the sterilization policy. Among the handicapped killed in Germany were all the Jewish residents of psychiatric institutions (up to 5,000), the first systematic mass murder of Jewish women and men. A Jewish mother whose son had been living in one of the Bethel hospitals for years was informed in 1943 by the hospital's pastor that her son had been deported. She wrote to the pastor: 'He was really the only tie I still had to this world. . . . I did the only thing I could do for him, I stayed with him and for him. And I will never regret that, even if it means my own destruction. Now I am less afraid than before of what lies ahead.'[60]

In the operations of the SS special units, the killing was at first select-ive. Most of the victims were adult men, the Jewish leadership and real or alleged partisans. Starting in August and especially from September 1941, the share of murdered women and children increased dramatically and soon far outweighed that of men. These massacres reached a peak when thirty-four thousand Jewish men, women and children were shot in the ravine of Babi Yar near Kiev. For the perpetrators as well as many victims, this elimination of all differences of gender (and age) marked the transition from unsystematic and selective killing to the systematic mur-der of all Jews. One of the SS chiefs stated, 'All Jews, that is, including women and children', and another, 'in principle, that is, including the women and children'. The SS Special Unit C was told that measures against the Jews had to be intensified, which was why Jewish women and chil-dren also had to be executed 'so no one would survive to avenge the killing'.[61] 'Jewish men, women and children' was the generalized termi-nology used from this point on in most of the special unit reports on those shot.

SS men often had to overcome certain inhibitions, especially when women and children were to be shot; the killing of men appeared to be psychologically easier. Thus Himmler gave orders for a new method of killing to be developed that would avoid obvious bloodshed and free the SS men of their largely gender-related scruples. The first gas vans were used in Serbia and Russia to kill women and children. In Auschwitz Jew-ish women, especially Jewish mothers with their children, were usually sent directly to the gas chambers upon their arrival, whereas most able-bodied men were subjected to 'annihilation through work'; one survivor said that 'every Jewish child automatically condemned his mother to death'.[62] The scruples of the SS men did not lead to an end to the killing but to a more effective method of murdering anonymously. 'Men, women and children' was also the description of the victims of mass murder using gas. But the 'technical' problem was an expression of the more comprehensive race policy, as Himmler defined it in 1943 to his political and military leaders. In an inhumane manner he inverted the old ques-tion, 'What is human?' – Primo Levi would later reformulate it as *If This is a Man* – by defining what he considered 'subhuman' with respect to the female sex: 'I ask you only to listen to what I have to say within this circle and never to speak about it.' He wanted 'to answer a question that is certainly in the air. The question is: yes, you know, you are killing adult male Jews, I understand that, but the women and children . . . ? – Well, I must tell you something, the children will one day be grown'. And 'a question has reached us: what about the women and children? – I have decided, here too, to find a clear solution. I do not think I am justified in exterminating the men – that is, to kill them or have them killed – and to let the avengers in the form of the children grow up to face our sons and grandsons. The difficult decision had to be made to wipe this people off the face of the earth'.[63] Finally, Himmler put women in the centre of his own definition of genocide: 'Whenever I was forced to take action against partisans and against Jewish commissars in a village . . . , as a principle I gave the order to have the wives and children of these partisans and commissars killed as well. . . . And believe me, this command was not given lightly nor is it carried out as easily as it is logically thought out and announced in this auditorium. But we have to acknowledge more and more what a primitive, primordial, natural race struggle we find ourselves in.' In this 'race struggle' Jewish women and children became a symbol of Jewry as a whole (and thus, as Hannah Arendt would say, of humanity).

The 'race struggle' was to be fought on the entire continent. In France, where approximately 300,000 Jews were living on the eve of World War II (half of whom had fled from Germany or Austria), most of them were quickly stripped of their means of survival after the French capitulated to Hitler in June 1940. In the occupied part of France this was accomplished through 'Aryanization', under the Vichy regime through French legislation, especially the 'Statut des Juifs' of 3 October 1940 and 2 June 1941, which built upon traditional anti-Semitism and excluded Jews from public service, the army, the liberal professions and the school system. In March 1942 transports from the northern zone began bringing Jews interned in the Drancy and Compiègne camps to Auschwitz. At first only men were deported, hardly any of whom survived. Soon flyers announced 'Deportation means death'. Jewish women and children wrote moving letters to the Vichy government and its diplomatic mission in Paris – often supported by the Resistance – pleading on behalf of their husbands and fathers and to request permission to visit them. 'Our husbands and sons, who have done nothing but work honestly, are being held prisoner under despicable conditions', and 'in the Drancy camp a large number of them have already been shot. And the killing continues. There are already numerous widows and orphans'. From the third transport on 22 June, women were included. It started with young women ('All Jewesses between eighteen and twenty-two report to the collection point!' was the order), but the age limit was soon lifted. On the way to Drancy some of them started singing the *Marseillaise*. At this point children were still being spared; separated from their parents, they often wandered around, lost and homeless. On 6 July 1942 Theodor Dannecker, fanatic anti-Semite and head of the Gestapo department for Jewish matters in Paris (and later in Italy), reported the order given by Pierre Laval, president of the Vichy government and also a rabid anti-Semite: 'Not a single Jewish child shall remain in France', and that 'when Jewish families are evacuated from the non-occupied zone, all children under sixteen shall also be transported out'. Several weeks later, Eichmann agreed that 'the children of stateless Jews should be deported in adequate numbers'.[64] On 'Black Thursday' it was mostly women and children who were locked in the Vél d'hiv, where they remained for three to six days, after which they were taken to other camps and finally to Auschwitz. Marie-Louise Blondeau, a young social worker, reported with horror: 'There was unimaginable chaos, a pitiful sight that tore your heart out: so many babies on the straw; so many babies confused. . . . The shattered women tried to manage in this confusion of screaming and crying children. Some clashed with all kinds of people, arguing, trying to grab everything they could get hold of, while others cried silently. . . . There were very small children, two-and-a-half or three years old, who ran into the large stone blocks around the camp and fell down with contorted expressions, being too serious and tragic for anyone to comfort them. And so they went on. Some were alone, others clung desperately to their mothers, afraid of losing them. They arrived in the Vél d'hiv with distraught looks on their drawn and aged faces, nicely dressed girls and boys from the 20th district, cherubs of sixteen months and lads of eight years.' In later transports as well, children were separated from their mothers. Léon Reinach – descendant of Joseph Reinach, indefatigable fighter in the Dreyfus affair – was deported with his children Fanny and Bertrand to Auschwitz in 1943. Their mother, Béatrice de Camondo, the last surviving member of her long-established Sephardic family, was deported in March 1944.

But in France there was also a public outcry against Himmler's 'natural race struggle' and here, too, there was the question what were women, men, human beings? Jewish fates had previously not received much public attention, but with the horror at the Vél d'hiv outrage surged throughout France over the treatment of 'hommes, femmes, bébés'. A woman resident of Saint Girons who had observed the buses driving by filled with pregnant women, children, entire families wrote to Marshal Pétain: 'Even the people who had loudly shouted "Down with the Jews! Death to the Jews!" were now shaken to tears. . . . We are ashamed of being French, Christians, human beings.' Cardinal Suhard protested in late July in the name of the cardinals and bishops. Monsignor Saliège, bishop of Toulouse, wrote a pastoral expressing the public opinion as well as he influenced it: 'That children, women, men, fathers and mothers are treated as animals, that the members of one and the same family are torn apart and carted away to an unknown destination – it has been left to our times to experience such a tragic spectacle. . . . Shocking scenes have taken place. . . . Jews are men and women; foreigners are men and women. Not everything is permitted against them, against these men, against these women, against these fathers and mothers of families. They are part of the human race.' Reformed Pastor Boegner declared: 'Divine law does not permit the destruction of families willed by God, the separation of children from their mothers, the denial of the right to asylum and compassion.' In view of the misery and death, women and children again came to symbolize all Jews, and the protest against their persecution became a protest against the murder of Jews in general.

The horror at the Vél d'hiv caused the Resistance to take up the issue of the persecution of the Jews. Their press, including the Communist press, printed the bishop's pastorals; for months the voice of the Resistance coincided with that of the clergy, even though most of them were otherwise loyalist, and public opinion in protesting against the separation of children from mothers and parents, and their being put on transports, whether separately or together. At some point protest against the persecution of the Jews quietened down again; the Jewish-Communist resistance continued to focus on it virtually single-handedly, as the non-Jewish population was more concerned with men being channelled into forced labour. But that spontaneous, mass human reaction had laid the groundwork for a large segment of the population to refuse to support the racist atrocities. Saving and hiding Jewish children ('You won't get the children!') became an essential form of resistance by Jews and Gentiles alike. In France, as at the same time in Italy, women's convents were particularly active in this respect. Here children often had to adapt to the Christian faith, such as the Czech Jew Saul (then Paul-Henri) Friedländer. But they were often met with respect for their Jewish identity, as in the case of the strictly Catholic Aide aux mères de famille in Chamonix. In all, three-quarters of the French Jews were saved; however, two-thirds of the 76,000 Jews who were deported from France and then murdered were stateless Jews who had fled Poland, Germany, Austria or Romania. After liberation in 1945 the Committee of the Associations to Protect the Victims of Persecution organized an event to commemorate the 'separation of mothers from their children on 16 July 1942 in Paris' and the event in the Vél d'hiv as 'one of the most barbaric deeds committed by the Germans during the occupation'.[65]

In Germany there was no public outcry – neither by men nor by women, neither against the deportation of the Jews as a whole nor that of Jewish women and children. Would more women than men in Germany have considered themselves friendly to Jews if there had been a poll such as the one in late 1942 in the southern zone of France had shown? In any case, the wife of the former commandant at Sobibór and Treblinka denied ever having known that 'there were children too, or even women' among those murdered. She said she believed that 'women and children were being left at home' and, regarding the Jewish men, she believed that 'we were at war and that they were killing the men; men, you know:

enemies'. Only few women were ashamed 'of being German', such as Frau Angermeier, who had helped save Jews.[66] Some concentration camp prisoners who had been treated with brutality by the women guards were ashamed of sharing the same sex. Lucia Schmidt-Fels, a German-Jewish prisoner in the women's camp of Ravensbrück, described the guards: 'To the shame of my sex I must admit that women can be more cruel and evil, more hateful and petty than men, as soon as they are in a position of power.' But it seems her image of men might have been a bit too chivalrous. Auschwitz survivor Ruth Klüger argued that on average the women guards were less brutal than the men; she presumed that the overall picture of the women guards had been influenced by the cruelties of some of them. Margarete Buber-Neumann, a former prisoner in the Soviet Union who had been handed over to the Nazis in 1941 and then imprisoned in Ravensbrück, stressed that female guards behaved very differently with respect to abuse of power. The testimony of Claude Vaillant-Couturier (who had been imprisoned in Ravensbrück and Auschwitz) before the Nuremberg tribunal might apply as a general appraisal: there 'was no difference' between the male and female guards. The Italian Lidia Beccaria Rolfi, who had been in Ravensbrück, saw the matter in a similar way: 'They copied the men and tried to outdo them in violence and brutality.'[67]

For many prisoners, the loss of their femininity was the same as losing their humanity. 'We are no longer women, no longer human', wrote one woman. Survivors and other authors frequently summed up the camp with the image of hell. Reports by French survivors were called *Descente aux enfers* (Descent into hell) or *L'enfer existe* (Hell exists). Primo Levi referred to hell as 'like being already dead', and Hannah Arendt, too, said it was 'as if they were already dead'. The image stands for 'life after death' or dying before death. A Jewish survivor felt hell was nothing in comparison with Ravensbrück; women and men 'suffered in different ways' and 'We were waiting for death, but God did not want us to die'. Lucia Schmidt-Fels saw herself confronted with a 'horrendous image' after she passed through 'the gates of hell' in Ravensbrück: 'their heads were shaved'. Judith Isaacson recalled the agonizing procedure of being stripped, having all bodily openings searched for valuables and having all body hair shaved, which was an abominable humiliation, especially for devout Jews. 'We wanted to cover our nakedness. . . . The going rate for a ragged kerchief soon rose to a day's ration of bread. My family was spared the cost: Magda's gypsy gown sufficed for two, and I ripped a band from the hem of my dress.' She borrowed a needle, paid for by a small piece of her bread ration, and hemmed her kerchief with some unravelled thread. 'We women were a strange sex, I decided: we sustain our sanity with mere trifles. Even in hell. Yes, even in hell'.[68] Many

imprisoned women – both Jews and Gentiles – appear to have coped
with the terrible everyday routine of the camps better than the men. But
for the Jewish women, their survival was not a consequence of their behaviour but merely one of chance. And it was rare. The Berlin Jew Grete
Bloch, mother of Franz Kafka's son who died at an early age, was arrested in 1944 near the Italian Montecassino front and died in Auschwitz.
Milena Jesenská of Prague planned to write a piece on 'the age of the
concentration camp' together with Buber-Neumann while they were in
Ravensbrück; Jesenská died in May 1944. Rosa Manus of the Netherlands had been active since 1908 in the international women's suffrage
and peace movements; she was brought to Ravensbrück in 1942 and all
that is known about her after that time is that she died in April 1943.
Thirty years earlier she had confided to a friend in London: 'It is a thing
I find so difficult to accept: nothing will ever change the world's attitude
towards our race.'[69]

6

Civil, Political and Social Rights:
A New Gender Debate

All human beings are born free and equal in dignity and rights.
United Nations, 1948

The second half of the twentieth century stood in the shadow of the horrors of the first half; and the more time had passed, the longer the shadow became. Most perpetrators, male and female alike, did not talk about the events, defended themselves or lied outright; German parents were silent to their children. Irrespective of significant earlier studies and major trials, the Holocaust, as well as collaboration outside Germany, did not enter the public consciousness and become general knowledge in its full dimensions until a generation had passed. The question has been raised with respect to Germany as well as other war-waging countries: why did women, who were left largely to their own resources during the war and the hardship of the post-war period, who supported their families on their own and took over many other 'male' responsibilities, let themselves be pushed back into the 'private sphere'? Yet against the background of what had happened, the question basically answers itself. For it was precisely the private sphere whose civil autonomy had been destroyed, or at least questioned, through dictatorship, war and the Holocaust. A change in gender relations, if it is to be fundamental and lasting, does not arise out of misery and certainly not in the wake of years of terror in which the female perpetrators resembled the male and, similarly, the female victims were persecuted and murdered as were the men. It is no coincidence that after World War II there was no time of renewal comparable to the Roaring Twenties that followed World War I. And it is no surprise that a new departure in gender relations would not emerge until the direct war memories and consequences seemed to recede into the background, when the 'economic miracle' of the 1950s and 1960s took place and democracy was stabilized.

Yet there were early signs of change. In addition to the condemnation of discrimination on the basis of race, a clause guaranteeing equal rights of men and women was adopted into the United Nations Charter in 1945 on the pressure of the few female delegates, especially those from the United States. Equal rights within marriage, protection of the family and equal pay for equal work were also anchored in the 1948 Universal Declaration of Human Rights. (Eleanor Roosevelt and Bodil Begtrup, Danish delegate to the United Nations, were especially active in this regard.) The original wording of the first article ('all men . . .') was changed to clearly reflect the fact that not only men but all of human-kind was meant: 'All human beings are born free and equal in dignity and rights' (although the 'right to . . . an existence worthy of dignity' was granted only for 'him and his family').[1] In English the 'rights of man' became 'human rights', and in Italian the *diritti dell'uomo* became *diritti umani*. In French the *droits de l'homme* remained unchanged in the title, but the first article referred to *êtres humains*, and in German and Dutch no change was necessary since these languages have a gen-der-neutral term (*Mensch*, *mens*). Equal rights were incorporated into the French (1946, 1958) and Italian (1947) constitutions. For those of East and West Germany (1949), an example had already been set by the Weimar Republic constitution. Nonetheless, the untiring efforts of So-cial Democrat representative Elisabeth Selbert and an extra-parliamen-tary storm of protests by women were necessary in West Germany to push through the equal rights clause. In many countries former wom-en's organizations were revived or new ones were founded in their tradi-tion to attempt to influence post-war political and social life. American women supported the process of democratization in Germany, often bringing up the role that German women had played. Chase Woodhouse, a Democratic Congresswoman, made the appraisal in 1948 that 'psy-chologically women are better oriented to reconstruction on a demo-cratic basis than are the men. They have no "face" to save. Since 1933 they had no status. . . . They were not a part of policy making in Nazi Germany'. Male domination and '*Kinder, Küche, Kirche*' were assumed to have determined the lives of German women.[2] Women's actual con-tribution to Nazi evil – which had nothing to do with the kitchen or children, and women had not been encouraged to go to church – had been just as forgotten or repressed as that of many men and would not come to light until the 1980s, after the second-wave women's move-ment in western countries, the form and goals of which also shaped its German counterpart, had contributed to rewriting history. But in the beginnings of this movement – which in Germany was carried by the first generation that had not personally experienced the Nazi period – the present seemed more important than the past.

Liberty and Equality

A new way of being, loving, and living.[3]

In contrast to the first-wave women's movement, the second-wave movement took the stage suddenly and provocatively in the late 1960s. By 1975 it was a mass movement and had had an international communication network from the outset. In 1968 American women crowned a sheep on the occasion of the Miss America beauty pageant, threw their bras, curlers and cosmetics into a 'freedom trashcan' and buried traditional womanhood in Arlington National Cemetery. The Jeanette Rankin Brigade took part in the peace march on Washington, named after the first woman elected to Congress in 1919. Provocative groups chose names such as Bitch and WITCH (Women's International Terrorist Conspiracy from Hell). A Danish group borrowed their name from the New York Redstockings (reminiscent of the Bluestockings, who had been defamed for centuries). Danish women stormed public buses, paying only 80 per cent of the fare, corresponding to the share of women's wages as compared with men's. In Britain women protested against the Miss Universe pageant, supported striking blue-collar women and launched the debate on women's liberation within the Left. Women in Paris laid a wreath at the tomb of the unknown soldier at the Arc de Triomphe, dedicated to the 'unknown wife of the unknown soldier'; others stormed the editorial offices of the long-established women's magazine *Elle*. In the Netherlands the *Dolle Minas* (the 'Great Minas', named after Wilhelmina Drucker, a pioneer of the early women's movement) drew attention to themselves through spectacular actions. In West Germany tomatoes were thrown at the male comrades of the Socialist German Student Union, who refused to take women's liberation seriously. The Berlin Action Council (Aktionsrat) for Women's Liberation and the Frankfurt Women's Council (Weiberrat) were the first women's groups to break from the not-so-new New Left. Around that time autonomous women's groups started forming; *brot & rosen*, Bread and Roses, was named after the slogan attributed to the women involved in the 1912 textile strike in Lawrence, Massachusetts, which had substituted the traditional union slogan 'bread and butter'. Private day-care centres were started, beginning in Berlin, as a mothers' self-help initiative and an alternative to the authoritarian educational methods of the state-run kindergartens and in the family. Within a short period of time, women's centres were established everywhere, serving as a meeting place and point of departure for many groups, alternative projects and a counterculture. Battered women's shelters provided refuge for victims of sexual, especially domestic, violence (in Britain there were already 200 by 1980), and rape crisis centres and hotlines supported rape survivors. Women in Rome, Turin and Milan marched at night demonstrating against being threatened by men when walking the streets at night. 'Take back the night' became an international battle cry. Impatience was the order of the day; *The Power of Men is the Patience of Women* (Cristina Perincioli) was the title of the first 'women's film' in Berlin. All over, small groups and their networks were the heart and soul of the movement.

Three innovations throughout Europe had been greatly influenced by forerunners in the United States. First, women examined and discovered their individual situations and the common roots in consciousness-raising groups. Second, a new form of self-help group emerged, often inspired by *Our Bodies, Ourselves* (1970), a book published by the Boston Women's Health Collective which revealed the inextricable connections between body and subjectivity. The handbook was translated into many languages; by 1995, over three million copies had been sold worldwide. Third, lesbians began to make themselves heard (women had used the term 'lesbian' from the 1920s, though love among women has existed since time immemorial). Many lesbians abandoned mixed gay and lesbian groups and joined or were even a driving force in the women's movement from the very beginning. The attack on discrimination against lesbians also implied a vision of love and community among women as an alternative to male domination. Sharp criticism was voiced against Freud's image of the woman as an imperfect man. *The Myth of the Vaginal Orgasm* by New Yorker Anne Koedt (1970) gained inter-national acclaim (some of its contents could already have been read back in the 1920s). Women in Italy and Britain started a campaign in 1972 for the state to pay for women's domestic labour, and it was taken up in Germany, the United States and Canada as well. They argued that work outside the home had not served to liberate women and demonstrated that so-called non-working women did indeed perform work; in fact all paid labour was dependent on the non-paid work that women performed for home and family. Giving women access to money would also support their independence within marriage, and child-rearing and housework needed to be taken into consideration with respect to child allowances, old-age pensions and divorce. The slogan was 'wages against housework'. If housework were no longer performed without a reward, so it was argued, it would be transformed and reduced through labour-saving devices, collectivization and having men assume more domestic responsibility. Like the women's movement as a whole, this campaign rejected the role of woman as housewife, the traditional domestic drudgery as well as its modernized variant, the 'problem without a name' that Betty Friedan denounced in her international best-seller *The Feminine Mystique* (1963). Around 1975, prostitutes started speaking out against police repression, state-regulated brothels and exploitation through pimps. The movement started in Lyon, moved on to Berlin and became especially active in Italy and Britain, where prostitution was decriminalized in 1978. Black German women, largely daughters of US or French soldiers who had been stationed in Germany after the war, became active as feminists against racism. The International Tribunal of Crimes Against Women that convened in 1976 in Brussels represented a peak in these developments.

The abortion issue accompanied the entire decade of the 1970s. First, because it was the only issue on the diverse agenda of grievances voiced by the women's movement that was facing legislative reform at that time; second, because abortion, although feminists generally agreed that more liberal abortion laws were necessary, was controversial even within their ranks. In contrast to other issues, many men also participated in the abortion debate. The thrust of the campaigns coincided with the legislation; public speak-outs started in 1971 in France and followed in Germany, in which women (and some men) publicly admitted having had (or performed) an abortion. The British law was liberalized in 1967 and women successfully fought against its revision in 1975. In 1973 the US Supreme Court defended first-trimester abortions on the grounds of the right to privacy, but in 1989 jurisdiction was transferred to the individual states. The entire Italian movement mobilized in protest of a mass trial in 1974 against 263 Trento women who had had abortions. Abortion was decriminalized in Italy in 1978 within limits set to prevent the use of abortion as a means of birth control. The abortion law was liberalized in France in 1975. The West German parliament passed a law in 1974 allowing first-trimester abortions, but on appeal to the Federal Constitution Court it was modified into a law allowing abortions only on medical or several other grounds. Negotiations for German unification threatened to fail in the final stages in 1990 due to the contrast between West German abortion law and the full freedom of abortion guaranteed in East Germany. The campaign in West Germany was led under the slogan 'My womb belongs to me' (which was at least a significant improvement on 'Your womb belongs to you', the slogan with which the Communist Party had pushed for freedom of abortion around 1930). Feminist groups and publications quickly expanded the debate beyond the narrow issue of formal legalization of abortion to the question of voluntary or involuntary pregnancy and thus of sexual power relations. There was discussion on the fact that fathers were often not willing to accept the responsibility connected with becoming a father. Many Italian women feared (as the earlier women's movement had) that full freedom of abortion could reinforce masculine privilege: 'The woman asks herself: for whose pleasure did I become pregnant? For whose pleasure am I aborting? This question contains the seeds of our liberation.'[4] *Our Bodies, Ourselves* warned against diverse instances of abortion abuse, such as women all too quickly being given abortions if they or their children were considered 'undesirable', especially ethnic minorities. Some feminists considered abortion the epitome of women's freedom; others saw it as an emergency measure, rejecting it as a means of birth control (as was common in the Soviet Union) and instead propagating dissemination of contraceptives, including the birth control pill, which became widespread despite criticism in the late 1960s. Even though abortion, and even the glorification of it, would later often become identified with feminism, the issue was really a different one, namely, that of freedom of choice. 'Kids, yes or no; it's our choice alone' (*Kinder oder keine, entscheiden wir alleine*) was a slogan of the West German movement. In Italy, it only seemed to be a paradox: 'We want abortion, so we will no longer have to have abortions.'

The women's movement of the late 1960s and 1970s was deliberately eccentric and the expression of their *doléances*, their grievances, was imaginative, emblematic and utopian – yet without a blueprint for a future society – often employing irony and sarcasm, in words and images, prose and poetry. It was about the freedom to speak publicly (as in Article 11 of Olympe de Gouges's *Déclaration*, but also in keeping with the female *doléances* of the nineteenth century). The new women's press, including numerous translations, as well as other media served to publicize the provocations. Modern mass and consumer culture, though despised by the new movement, helped spread news of its spectacular actions. Feminists relied on spontaneity and direct actions and (with the exception of many French women) not so much on theories designed to integrate their experiences into the 'greater whole'. They laid claim to autonomy, dissociated themselves increasingly from the parallel 'sexual revolution', which privileged male freedom and heterosexuality, and believed their insights lacked any historical models. Many of them broke with the New Left, which was not always easy, although – or because – they had been greatly influenced by that movement, the protests against the Vietnam War and, in the United States, the black civil rights movement. They dissociated themselves from the traditional women's organizations of the present and those of the older women's movement, about which they knew very little. They thought that that movement had been merely 'liberal' and had not carried out any fundamental revolt; that it had striven at most for legal reforms that did not question the system as a whole and merely for 'equality' with men (Italian women called it *emancipazionismo*), which could be considered neither a model for the future nor autonomous. The time-honoured achievement of women's suffrage was treated with disrespect (as was the case in all extra-parliamentary movements). Simone de Beauvoir, whose *The Second Sex* (1949) became a best-seller in the early 1970s and who identified herself at that time as a feminist, declared in 1978: 'I don't have a very clear idea of what the elections mean.' Feminists broke with the old (also feminist) tradition of combining rights with duties, and 'common good' was lacking in their vocabulary, as was citizenship, *citoyenneté*, *cittadinanza*, *Bürgerschaft*. In Germany the notion that 'hardly any woman today still associates citizenship with any emancipatory hopes' retained validity for a long time.[5] That would fundamentally change in the 1990s.

But tradition was not abandoned to the same degree everywhere. In Ireland the issues of sexuality and male domination remained in the background and the new movement cooperated with the older women's associations. Women in Norway could take advantage of the relatively strong presence of women in the political parties. The same was true in Sweden, where women successfully fought within the social democracy for a social policy favourable to women. Consequently, the autonomous women's movement was less pronounced there and the subject of citizenship was given priority in both countries early on. In Spain and Portugal, women's activities were closely connected to the end of the authoritarian regime and the building of a democracy. American feminism had little influence in Spain; more important was the International Women's Year, declared by the United Nations in 1975. In Portugal, and then internationally, the 'Three Marias' – who wrote *New Portuguese Letters*, which were published in 1973 (English 1975) and then banned – were a strong mobilizing force.

Within the autonomous women's movements the term 'feminism' was initially treated with scepticism and as burdened with tradition. Some even adopted the heritage of the Left, calling it 'bourgeois'. The new motto was not equality but liberation. Everywhere, the message was 'women's lib'. The French called it simply MLF (Mouvement de Libération des Femmes) and the German-speaking among the Swiss called it FBB (Frauenbefreiungsbewegung). In Britain the term 'women's liberation movement' marked the break with an allegedly restricted feminism that was thought to strive solely for 'formal' rights; distinctions were made between 'radical feminists', who felt affiliated with the Left, and 'women's liberationists'. The earliest American anthology on the subject was entitled *From Feminism to Liberation* (1971). What liberation was supposed to look like, however – this hadn't changed since the earlier women's movement – was disputed. No wonder, considering the different and often colliding priorities of a movement that claimed to speak for all women (*Sisterhood is powerful*, or *Frauen gemeinsam sind stark* [Women united are strong]), on the one hand, and insisted on individualization, self-realization, subjectivity and personal space to develop oneself, on the other. Virginia Woolf's book title *A Room of One's Own* (1929) became a common metaphor. In Paris, where women's liberation was also discussed theoretically from the very beginning, an open conflict developed between representatives of a 'materialist' theory and the Psychanalyse et Politique group; it even led to a spectacular and (much lamented) court suit over the monopoly on the term 'mouvement de libération des femmes'. 'Feminism' gained popularity only gradually, and in 1988 a corresponding title appeared in Great Britain: *From Women's Liberation to Feminism*. This neo-feminism was immediately modified with differentiating epithets, such as radical, liberal, libertarian, materialist, socialist, social, individualistic, relational, cultural, French or American. The protest by African American women in the United States against the predominance of white feminists led internationally to increasing awareness for national, ethnic and religious differences in the situation and needs of the female gender (though class differences had been discussed from the outset); black women suggested replacing 'feminism' with 'womanism'.

Yet diversity and conflicts are not only obstacles; they are also a source of enrichment. Their territory is liberty and a new gender debate had commenced, at first among women, though men soon joined in. Mothers and non-mothers, wage-earners and students took part. For those activists who had come from the student movements, study and revolt against outdated university structures had a different meaning for the female students than for the male since this was the first generation of women who comprised a large, and growing, percentage of the total student body. The new impetuses spread within a decade from the metropolises, where they first emerged, to provincial regions. Irrespective of the divergences there was a shared international slogan: 'The personal is political.' Dichotomies such as woman/man, private/political, nature/culture were to be dismantled. Feminists – and soon others as well – charged that power was exercised not only in the public and political sphere but especially in the private sphere as well. In this respect the women's movement found itself caught in a paradox. On the one hand, women claimed a politicization of the problem of private power relations, thus changing the concept of the political; on the other hand, they rejected politics in an institutional sense (and were consequently accused of being 'non-political' by their adversaries, and sometimes even their friends).[6] They opposed institutions, power, elites and competition, causing problems on two fronts. First, more and more feminist projects were themselves becoming institutionalized, especially once they started receiving subsidies (from the state or from other women), usually after hard-won battles. Second, it revealed the contradiction in the complaint that women were absent from traditional institutions and, where that was not the case or was beginning to change, the complaint about 'token women'.

But mostly the issue was about the old question with which Simone de Beauvoir had opened *The Second Sex* in 1949: 'What is a woman?' One of her answers modified the older wisdom of Erasmus of Rotterdam ('Homines non nascuntur, sed finguntur') or Kant's ('Man is nothing but what education makes of him'): 'One is not born a woman; one becomes one.' Since 'transcendence' was open to the man, according to her theory, and to the woman only 'immanence', what was required for women was 'assimilation' to men;[7] this was something that many who stressed the value and dignity of womanhood chose not to accept. *Donna è bello* or 'Woman is beautiful' was the slogan, borrowed from the Black Power Movement's 'Black is beautiful'. In Berlin, the first women's rock festival took place in 1974. A party without men, where more than a thousand dancing participants shouted *Frau-en*, *Frau-en*, for minutes on end; it was one of many symbols of women's identification with their own gender, as well as their refusal to accept firmly defined labels. The relationship between the consciousness of a deeply rooted and often internalized sense of inferiority of the female sex, going far beyond mere discrimination, and the consciousness of women's own strength, dignity and desire to break out remained an inevitable contradiction that would be expressed in many forms and with increasing intensity. In the early 1970s this emerged in a controversy that could be seen as a foreshadowing of future conflicts over identity and self-realization. A feminist who felt excitement at the idea that she did not only have to be a woman said: 'Why would anyone who likes being a woman need to be a feminist?' Her feminist conversation partner retorted: 'How can someone who doesn't like being a woman be a feminist?'[8] Was Rousseau's claim correct (though it was rejected by Olympe de Gouges and Mary Wollstonecraft) that a woman is always a woman, but a man is only sometimes a man? Ultimately the issue was not whether or not someone wanted to be a woman but what being a woman meant.

In some places early on and in other places not until later, an issue emerged that in classical political terminology would be called the relationship (or contrast) between liberty and equality; this was a heated, ongoing, international debate on the relationship (or contrast) between 'difference' and 'equality'. The Italian movement and parts of the French in particular insisted on the right to be 'different' – not in a traditional sense, which would indeed be nothing other than assimilating with male society, but in a new, not yet created sense ('The difference between woman and man is the basic difference of humanity'). In France 'difference' was viewed more in a psychoanalytical sense, while in Italy it was understood more politically and included a transformation of the mother-daughter relationship. In the United States it dealt more with morality and justice and in many places involved a new appreciation for women's caring work for others. African-American women questioned early on the concept of equality, asking 'equal to whom?' 'Since men are not equals in white supremacist, capitalist, patriarchal class structure, which men do women want to be equal to?' And: 'We're fighting for the right to be different and not be punished for it. Equal means sameness. I don't want to be equal with the white community, because I don't think it's very groovy.'[9] Other feminists rejected the vision of improving the status of mothers by valuing child-rearing more, viewing it sceptically as a variant of pro-natalist misogyny. To many, 'equality' implied liberation from mother-hood by having test-tube babies (Shulamith Firestone); by having childcare centres and kindergartens open all day and even nights, in order to en-able mothers to take up full-time employment; or by not having children or shifting domestic work to outside institutions. Feminism often had a decidedly anti-natalist tone (even though the idea of extended day-care services also had clear pro-natalist qualities). Compared with the early women's movement, which had put so much energy into improv-ing the status of mothers, the new motto was often 'Motherhood – from springboard to obstacle'.[10] The debate joined forces with other related questions; the front by no means simply divided mothers from non-mothers. How could the sexual division of labour (this term first became a central theme in the second-wave women's movement) be elim-inated? How could women's and men's work histories be made more similar, thus bringing about a gender-neutral society? Did paid employ-ment truly lead to liberation? The question 'What is a woman?' led to the question 'What is feminism?' and, ultimately, since the 1980s, 'What is a man?'

The debate was as lively as it was lasting. It became clear that differ-ence did not necessarily mean hierarchy and that equality did not neces-sarily mean sameness but – in keeping with a venerable tradition – equal freedom. The dynamic battle cry 'Women unite!' did not suffice when it came to real change. Radical women's liberation's claim to speak for the entire female sex was sorely tried. In 1974 Betty Friedan was worried that the hopeful movement would end up in a dead end – especially with slogans such as 'Down with men, childbearing and motherhood' – and that a majority of women would reject it. She sought advice from an-other authority, Simone de Beauvoir. They met in de Beauvoir's elegant Paris salon amidst treasures from the many countries she had visited with

Sartre. How was it possible, Friedan asked, to support women getting into better positions? In France, de Beauvoir replied, they had already accomplished that. But they were only ambitious elitist, token and career women. Feminists should refuse something that simply served to stabilize the system; they should aspire to become 'simple' schoolteachers, for example, not the president of a university. Change would not come from the top, but from the bottom, she stressed, and it was not about getting an elite position in society but destroying that society. But, Friedan countered, what about de Beauvoir's own elite position, from which her voice reached millions? De Beauvoir took up the new language of difference in her own way, saying she was herself from an older generation that did not know feminism, and 'the idea was for women to be the equal of men!' Feminists, on the other hand, did not want to be 'the equal of men'.[11] The main task, she thought, was solidarity among women of all classes, and that was the idea behind the abortion rights campaign. Unfortunately, non-employed wives of workers thought nothing of the feminist criticism of housework as 'exploitation of women by men', since housework was their reason for being. Wouldn't it be best, Friedan commented, with reference to American considerations, to acknowledge the value of housework in the form of a minimum wage value and by taking it into account for social security, pensions and in the case of divorce? De Beauvoir sharply rejected that idea. Housework should be eliminated, shared with men, collectivized, but in any case it should not be given material recognition since that would tie women to the home. But what if women chose to raise their children themselves? 'No, we don't believe that any woman should have this choice. No woman should be authorized to stay at home to raise her children. Women should not have that choice, precisely because if there is such a choice, too many women will make that one.' The important thing was 'forcing women in a certain direction'. Friedan insisted on the American tradition of individual freedom, pluralism and appreciation of motherhood. As pressing as was the need for childcare, a woman should not be forced to put her child in a childcare centre. De Beauvoir insisted on the 'Chinese' model: 'Every individual, woman as well as man, should work outside', and as long as 'the myth of maternity and the maternal instinct are not destroyed' women remain oppressed. Friedan was disappointed; de Beauvoir had no sense of 'those mundane questions that real women have to confront in their personal lives'.

German sociologist Helge Pross tackled those mundane questions in a cogent survey on women who were 'just housewives', *Nur-Hausfrauen* (this term had been used by Max Weber to distinguish such women from wage-earning housewives, and both kinds of homemakers were diagnosed in the 1970s by economist John Kenneth Galbraith as 'a crypto-servant class'). The six million 'just housewives' in West Germany made up less than half the female population between the ages of eighteen and fifty-four in 1974. Pross's findings instantiated the 'problem without a name', further specified Friedan's more recent suggestions and put de Beauvoir's Chinese model in its place. Glorification of marital and maternal domesticity was a thing of the past, 'just housewives' had become a contemptuous label, and women in paid employment enjoyed greater prestige. The roughly fifty thousand million hours spent annually on domestic labour corresponded almost exactly to the amount of time spent in labour outside the home; now it had to be performed 'without metaphysical glory' and was, in both western and eastern Europe, almost entirely women's business. It was not considered work, though industrial society was dependent upon it.[12] Pross's findings continued that men were at best part-time fathers; nevertheless, they had the last word in major decisions, the women only in routine matters. Housewives lived largely isolated from society and politics, though on that point they hardly differed from women in factories and offices and many men. Housewives were clearly aware of, and resented, the social superiority of men; this was especially pronounced among the lower classes. Precisely this awareness and resentment showed that a partnership marriage was, among women, more the norm than a hierarchical marriage. Housewives fluctuated between feeling satisfied and dissatisfied with their family duties. Their status and their name were derived only from the husband and they had to give more than they received. Having more than three children almost always meant living in poverty. The three-phase scheme (education and paid employment, fifteen years of family and housework, resumed employment) that Viola Klein and Alva Myrdal had once envisioned as the model of the future was not found to correspond to reality. While lower-class women workers would have preferred to be just housewives, interest in having a career had generally become widespread and female employment an irreversible trend. This led to a 'growing dual orientation among an increasing number of women', which meant a precarious balance of family and employment. Women's demands for independence and social security, especially in old age, had increased, whereas this had hitherto depended solely on the husband. Housewives expressed wishes for more day-care facilities and full day schools, their own old-age pensions, the repeal of the prohibition on abortion, career support measures, part-time employment and wages for mothers of small children. But most of all, Pross found that housewives, like women in general, were not a homogeneous collective and they demanded the right to individuality and to make their own decisions. These *doléances* and hopes would mark the coming decades.

The Longest Revolution

Women: the longest revolution.

Juliet Mitchell, 1966[13]

A majority of western European women had long since stopped living the life in which conservative ideologues preferred to see them. They continued to be responsible for the family (in 1989/90 Norway, for example, women performed two-thirds of unpaid housework, the value of which was estimated at 45 per cent of the gross domestic product), but at the same time their level of employment increased steadily everywhere. One major reason for this was that working conditions had improved considerably as compared with the early twentieth (and especially the nineteenth) century, and incomes started rising in the 1950s. Men earned a family wage far more often than previously, and the familiar gap between male and female wages remained intact, though it decreased in some branches or countries (among industrial workers, women earned 62 per cent of male earnings in Britain and 83 per cent in Portugal in 1989; among all those employed, women in West Germany earned 86 per cent of male earnings, in France 79 per cent and in the Netherlands 77 per cent). Women's income now comes closest to men's in Sweden, where there is a high degree of segregation between women's employment in the public sector and men's in private industry (some feel the virtual equality of salaries is a result of this segregation). This has led to a reversal of the traditional 'public man, private woman' into the dictum 'private man, public woman'. Women's employment in the service sector has grown since the post-war period, while female industrial labour has gone down (together with the significance of the textile industry as a former domain of women's employment). Economic growth and new needs awakened by mass culture and consumerism – far beyond the large cities and towns, now extending into the rural regions – not only made women's paid employment possible and necessary, it also made it profitable. Among the lower classes, it often remained as essential as it was (in France, for instance) unpopular. Since the 1960s – after modest beginnings in the 1920s and 1930s, and generally twenty years later than in the United States – households have had labour-saving equipment, which usually required saving for them for a long time. Many housewives with whom Helge Pross spoke claimed tax exemptions for such purchases, similar to exemptions for investments in the area of paid employment. It was not necessary to coerce women to work for pay, as de Beauvoir had envisioned; but, in contrast to de Beauvoir's hopes, they sought new ways of combining family and career.

One of the most important innovations to this end was part-time work. The International Labour Organization and the United Nations defined it in 1953 as a contractually protected position of twenty-five to thirty-five hours per week. Today non-insured positions are usually also included and those with even fewer hours, as well as annual part-time positions in the form of seasonal work. Throughout Europe (though not in the United States) part-time employment expanded, ultimately serving largely to nullify the three-phase model. Part-time employment became the work of mothers and wives. Few men, but many women, chose to work part-time. In most European countries jobs involving thirty-five or fewer hours per week are considered part-time; distinctions are also made between long part-time and short part-time (fewer than about sixteen hours). Long part-time includes entitlement to social security, whereas short does not. Denmark has a high level of women in part-time employment (in 1989, 78 per cent of women were employed, 42 per cent of whom were part-time), where they have relatively good social insurance coverage. In Britain (65 per cent of women are employed, 44 per cent of whom part-time) they have less social security than in France (38 per cent, of which 24 per cent part-time). Thirty-five per cent of employed women in Sweden worked part-time in 1988 (at a female employment rate of 81 per cent); in 1991 in Germany it was 30 per cent (at an employment rate of 62 per cent), and in France it was 24 per cent (employment rate 58 per cent). In southern Europe public service work was often only six hours per day anyway, which was favourable for women with families. Elsewhere as well, conditions for employed mothers are better in public service (whether part- or full-time) than in private industry, since public service often gives more weight to political concerns than economic efficiency (as can be surmised from the extent of paid absence from the workplace). Especially but not only in southern Europe, new forms of 'flexitime' are also emerging, including homework (e.g., telecommuting), temporary contracts, occasional and seasonal work and informal jobs without a contract (including private childcare and domestic service). All in all, with the exception of long part-time that includes social insurance, this diversity resembles a modernized variant of the early modern economy of expedients. While these forms of employment are typically female, a different concept of 'typical' and 'atypical' work was developed, especially at the European Community level since the late 1980s. Primarily male full-time employment is considered 'typical' and female part-time, 'atypical' (and this at a time when male-dominated trade unions are negotiating for a regular thirty-five-hour working week, which for women represents the upper limit of part-time employment). Again, this is one of many levels where – in centuries-old tradition – the standard 'universal' is what is considered male, and the deviant 'special case' applies to women.

In East Germany as well, women retained responsibility for household and family; yet here the social ideal was that of the women's full-time employment (with or without family), due to economic demands, low wages and the ideology of emancipation through employment. This was supported through the gradual establishment of full-day state-run facilities for children (often from eight weeks old). Debate started in the 1990s whether education in childcare facilities, the goal of which was integration into the collective, led to social competence and solidarity (resulting in praise of the regime) or to obedience of authority and conformity (resulting in criticism of the mothers, albeit not the fathers). In any case, all sides agreed that the education was not geared to development of individuality and the personality. The official female rate of employment was 91 per cent (1989), which profoundly impressed many western feminists, though this was a statistical illusion. East German statistics also included women in training; according to western European statistics, the employment level was 80 per cent (compared with 55 in West Germany). With respect to the relationship between freedom and coercion, which Friedan, de Beauvoir and Pross (and many others) discussed, a comparison between the two Germanys is insightful. Labour shortages in the 1950s led both countries to push strongly for housewives to work part-time. In the West the increase in female employment was seen as an irreversible trend of modern industrial societies and an attempt was made to take women's employment needs into account without threatening the family. The 'right to part-time employment' was a concession to women who would have otherwise devoted themselves entirely to their families and it paved the way to a new image of wives. While part-time employment could barely gain a foothold in private industry, since here there was unwillingness to adapt to family needs, it spread quickly in other areas, especially in trade and office jobs as well as the public service. In East Germany, on the other hand, the increasing legitimacy of part-time work, which was achieved only after fierce debate, was intended to introduce women to the new standard of wage-earning, leading up gradually to full-time employment. Contrary to plans, however, it was not only housewives but women who had been working full-time who largely used the part-time option to reduce their workload. Here, the 'right to part-time employment' became a concession to women who could not or did not wish to work full-time because they had a family. It became the 'secret model' of mothers' wage-earning in East Germany. Many East German as well as Russian women who had heard that 'the' western feminism had preached nothing but abortion and not having children set against it 'the uniqueness of the mothering experience'.[14]

Even more revolutionary than the developments in women's employment was that of civil law. The old hope of equal rights for men and women within marriage was now finally achieved. Efforts had been started several times in the period between the wars. The process in Britain had been concluded, but elsewhere dictatorships blocked progress. It was still a stepwise revolution. Women in France were freed from having their husbands serve as their legal guardian in 1965, but the concept of the *chef de famille* was not removed from the law until 1970. In addition, parental authority now replaced paternal authority. In 1975 divorce was permitted if both parties consented; adultery was decriminalized, the obligation of the wife to perform the housework was removed and in 1985 the husband and wife were declared fully equal in administering the family assets. The West German 'equal rights' law of 1957 was a balancing act. Both spouses equally shared ownership of assets acquired during the marriage. The law broke with male supremacy and defined matrimonial duties of both sexes as having equal worth, but they remained gender-specific. The man was the breadwinner and the woman was responsible for the family (that was also laid down in the Irish constitution in 1937). Women, in contrast to men, could only work outside the home if it did not conflict, in the eyes of the husband, with their family duties. This served to maintain not only male domination but the female double burden. Child custody was to be shared, but the father alone was the legal guardian. The age-old principle of the man having the last word in conflict cases prevailed. The German Supreme Court intervened here in 1959 and declared paternal privilege to be unconstitutional (not until 1979 did joint custody rights become law). Meanwhile, the family code was restructured in East Germany (1965) in an egalitarian sense, which was celebrated as the end of the 'imperialistic system of domination'.[15] The West German marital law reform of 1976 was finally a breakthrough. The division of labour within and outside the family was left up to the spouses (the same liberty and equality was incorporated into the Portuguese constitution in 1976) and the spouses could choose either the man's or the woman's last name to be their married name. On this point the German Supreme Court replaced equality with liberty (or 'difference') in 1991. Spouses could now retain their different names (elsewhere, especially in southern Europe, this had a long tradition). Wives received autonomy in matters of civil law in the late 1950s in the Netherlands, Ireland and Belgium; and in the 1970s in Italy, Luxembourg, Spain and Portugal. At the same time civil marriage was introduced in Portugal, Spain and Greece. The Italian referendum of 1974 to rescind divorce rights (which had just been introduced in 1970) mobilized not only feminists but the entire country. Proponents of divorce rights won out. Finally, a number of countries passed laws making rape within marriage a criminal offence; in Austria the authorities can initiate legal proceedings against a violent husband.

The third innovation dealt with the European welfare state in a more narrow sense, that of state benefits to families: the flip side of women's work between employment and family. Traditional maternity protection for employed women (pre- and postnatal leave with wage compensation) was expanded or introduced everywhere. It became a guideline of the European Community in 1992. In addition, France pressed ahead in the 1970s; its innovations corresponded to the French tradition of child and maternal benefits, coupled with a high rate of female employment (the agricultural share of which had meanwhile dropped dramatically). In 1968, 44 per cent of all women were employed and 34 per cent of those who were married. The rate of employment among mothers rose to 56 per cent by 1982 (it was only 20 per cent for mothers of three) and the parallel decline in birth rate was due to the decrease in families of three or more children. Under the aegis of Simone Veil, the first woman in France to hold a ministerial position (Minister for Health and Population Matters) and under-secretary for the *condition féminine*, and in the awareness that an openly pro-natalist policy would be unpopular, families of three or more children started receiving support in addition to the usual child allowances. According to Simone Veil, it was necessary to recognize 'that demography is a national imperative' and under no circumstances should 'we capitulate on this issue and assume that the French were correct on this matter, even though French public opinion as indicated in certain surveys must be brought to bear'. Hardly a year went by in the 1970s in France in which there was not some new family law, as ministers groped around for the proper path. Initial experiments coupled family policy with anti-poverty policy, and transfer payments were made to needy families and those with three or more children. Only the child allowance remained independent of income and increased with the number of children. Simone Veil strove to implement the old feminist dream of state recognition of a 'social status of motherhood'. 'The social protection of mothers and mothers-to-be must be given highest priority. The goal must be to create a veritable social status of mothers.' The new social citizenship of mothers should bring them their own rights, independent of their husbands and including old-age pensions. The focus was on the compatibility of family and employment. In 1977 the former wage for mothers was eliminated and a family bonus was introduced (340 francs; for single parents it was 510 francs), regardless of the employment status of the mother. It was intended to allow mothers 'to choose between the option of either giving up their outside employment and instead being paid a certain amount, or of continuing to work outside the home, in which case the family bonus would satisfactorily cover the costs of childcare.'[16] The upper income limit was increased, making 80 per cent of families with children under three years of age or with three or more children eligible; in 1978, almost 2.5 million families received the bonus. Work in the family, independent of wage-earning, was recognized as a basis for social rights in health insurance and old-age pensions. Family benefits were in principle to be paid to the mother (though she could pass them to the father). The income-independent child allowance – which remained the main transfer payment within the scope of family policy – and the birth bonus were increased, especially from the third child onwards (in 1980 the bonus was 2,500 francs each for the first and second children, and 8,000 for the third). Third and later children were also given priority for a place in public childcare. Around 1990, 20 per cent of children under three and 90 per cent of three-year-olds received care in public facilities, far more than in Germany and many other European countries.

Similar social rights were also instituted elsewhere. Sweden pioneered a forward-looking innovation; the parent insurance scheme of 1974 served to make 'mothers' into 'parents' and raise the status of paternity. The insurance entitled either the father or the mother (if previously wage-earning) to a six-month (fifteen as of 1989) parental leave with a parent allowance of 90 per cent of the last gross income (this was lowered in 1996 due to the economic crisis to 75 per cent, but raised again in 1998 to 80 per cent). Mothers who had not previously worked for wages received a six-month basic allowance that was higher than the benefits of the former maternity insurance. In addition, a pregnancy allowance was introduced (in 1980); child allowances also still existed as well as paid leave to care for sick children, and as of 1979 parents had a right to work reduced hours per day. At the same time, public childcare was expanded. The labour market was expected to make concessions to families and double-income families became the predominant model. France followed in 1986 with a similar child-rearing leave, but it was limited to parents of three or more children. Payment, amounting to roughly 2,900 francs monthly, was made to the parent who took the leave. Whereas East Germany had a birth bonus for third and additional children and offered a paid one-year 'baby leave' for women with two or more children (similar to the Soviet Union), West Germany followed the new western model of revaluing paternity. In 1986 it became possible for the mother or the father, or both in alternation (if they had previously been employed), to take a paid child-rearing leave (initially ten months, it was soon extended to three years). For the first time in German history (aside from the maternity benefit paid to employed women), mothers in general became eligible to receive benefits. Here, as in Sweden, but unlike the situation in France, parents are entitled to receive payments starting with the first child (France has a birth bonus instead), and independent of previous income. The number of parents entitled to child-rearing allowances is thus higher in Germany than in France, but the benefit itself is lower, 600 marks monthly, and only applies below a certain income level. Benefits can be combined with part-time work up to nineteen hours per week and are also payable to unmarried parents and to foreign nationals working in Germany (who generally have more children than German families). Having children and tending to the family have become a foundation for social rights for mothers and fathers, not only in these three countries but elsewhere as well (though least in southern Europe).

Although this development does not (yet) apply to all of Europe, it does represent a trend towards the partial socialization of childcare (that is, the payment for childcare outside the home, where it has remained almost exclusively women's work) and, parallel to that, the social recognition of such work even if it is performed privately. It has led women from southern Europe to welcome the move to join the European Union (EU), while in northern Europe women fear that membership in the EU would cause them to lose some of their welfare state privileges. This does not exist for the United States. While (northern) Europeans speak in this context of 'state feminism' (Helga Maria Hernes), in the United States the subject is the 'feminization of poverty', which hits mothers and children the hardest. Do European children bring advantages to their parents, or has the 'longest revolution' even put fathers in the place of mothers, making the two interchangeable? Are the old visions of the 'pregnant man' becoming reality, and will children (as has been speculated) be born from a male body instead of a female one and be raised by men, even for payment? Or will it come to pass in Europe, as Hippel ironically wrote in 1792, that 'in the case of some of the so-called primitive tribes it is not the woman but the man who holds a celebration at the time of parturition'? That the mother cares for the new-born alongside her other business, while the father 'lets himself be administered to and receives visits as well as congratulations from his neighbors because he – just think of the effort – has borne a child by his wife'.[17] There is indeed a 'renaissance of paternal rights' going on in Germany, where the lobby of divorced fathers or those with children born out of wedlock are trying to interpret the new parental 'equality' in child custody to favour fathers and disadvantage the mothers.[18] Food for thought in the light of rising divorce statistics and the rate of couples choosing not to marry.

But French and German fathers rarely take advantage of the chance, at least for a short time, to be house-husbands (barely over 1 per cent; slightly more for Swedish fathers) or to take leave to care for sick children (here the level for Swedish men is much higher, at 30 to 50 per cent). There are certainly deep-rooted cultural reasons for this as well as other no less compelling ones. The income differential between men and women and the modest level of the child-rearing allowance make the decision for mothers rather than fathers to take child-rearing leave the rational choice. In an international comparison, an employed spouse in Germany receives the greatest tax deductions for the non-wage-earner. Norwegian feminist Katti Anker Møller had expressed the wish in 1918 that childcare become the best paid of all jobs (for mothers). Perhaps if this were extended to include fathers – if male housework were remunerated the same as an executive – it could lead to an elimination of the sexual division of labour. Of course, men would first have to go through some training. Courses to this end are offered in Sweden and since 1995 there has been a 'papa quota': a portion of the leave must be divided among the parents and, as an incentive to fathers, it is paid at a higher rate. Still, those women who wish to raise their children themselves and do not want merely to give birth should not be totally forgotten, in Sweden as elsewhere in Europe. It is also unclear whether high female and low male employment rates are truly indicators of liberation. That question will be left to the twenty-first century. In any case, childcare has changed considerably from simply being unpaid women's work. In 1996 the 'child supplement package', the total of child-related tax rebates and benefits in cash and in kind for poor families with three school-age children, was highest in France, followed by Sweden, Luxembourg, Britain and Belgium. At the low end of the scale were Greece, Portugal and Spain. Wealthy families with two school-age children enjoyed the highest benefits in Luxembourg, followed by Belgium, France and Finland. The worst conditions were in Greece, Italy and the Netherlands.[19]

Reforms in the second half of the twentieth century came as a result of women having appropriated the political arena in three ways. First and foremost was (and is) the parliamentary presence of women. In 1999, 43 per cent of all members of the Swedish parliament were women, in Denmark 37 per cent, Finland 34 per cent, the Netherlands 31 per cent and Germany 30 per cent. This increase came largely as a result of the competition among the political parties for the women's vote (experts assume that the decisive hurdle for effective influence is reached when women comprise one-third of the representatives). At the end of the scale are France, where women held 9 per cent of parliamentary seats, and Greece and Russia (1992) with 6 per cent. Second, the 'traditional' women's associations exerted increasing influence. Third – though this factor was presumably in first place into the 1980s – the vocal and spontaneous feminist grassroots got involved (with slogans such as 'We are all adulterous wives'). It also inspired the older women's associations, and from the late 1970s on (in the Scandinavian countries almost from the very beginning) there was much cooperation between the two. But almost only in Scandinavia did feminists actively support pay for child-rearing work (other feminists were more interested in achieving state funding for abortions). In contrast to what the population politicians of the 1930s had painstakingly to learn, what today's experts and politicians have long since known and what women's common sense (such as that of Eleanor Rathbone) suggested long ago, some feminists (and some pro-natalists) still believe that women will have children and do housework for the sake of money. In fact, however, children are born and raised for very different reasons (with the exception of surrogate motherhood) and there is no statistical correlation between political measures supporting mothers and the fertility rate.[20]

Three other factors that worked from the top down rather than the bottom up promoted change: first, legal practice, especially that of con-stitutional courts and the European Court of Justice; second, the Euro-pean Community or Union (starting with the Rome treaty, in which French pressure led to the incorporation of the postulate of equal wages for men and women), which had a great impact on, for example, Ireland; and, finally, the United Nations with its World Conferences on Women and the strong presence of non-governmental organizations (Mexico 1975, Copenhagen 1980, Nairobi 1985, Beijing 1995) and the ongoing efforts by the International Labour Organization in Geneva.[21] The crucial fac-tor is that public opinion (of both men and women) has shifted, despite frequent resistance, the blocking of difficult or even costly reforms and various conflicts that surfaced at the World Conferences between women from the East and West, and especially between those from the North and South. A generational change also played an important role, which focused not on big politics but on revolutionizing the private domain from the bottom up.

Independent of the level of maternal or family support, the birth rate declined throughout all of Europe and in 1995 it dropped below the level required to maintain a steady population (2.1 children per woman). This is even the case in Belgium, Greece, Spain, France, Ireland, Italy, Austria, the Netherlands, Portugal and Britain, where in 1970 it was still above the 2.1 level. Accordingly, the total amount of time spent in pregnancy and nursing decreased. Although the network of private, church and public childcare varies greatly depending on the country and the region, it is expanding almost everywhere. People are living longer (it is nothing new that women outlive men). While people got married in greater numbers from the nineteenth to the twentieth centuries, increasing numbers are getting divorced from the twentieth to the twenty-first centuries. Mar-riage rates have gone down and divorce rates have gone up (except in Ireland, where divorce is still not possible), but the rate of second mar-riages has also increased. The number of out-of-wedlock births climbed to an all-time high; in Sweden, Denmark, France and Britain it was 53, 47, 37 and 34 per cent, respectively, of all births in 1995. Yet even in Italy (8) and Greece (3) the number has tripled since 1970. There has not only been an increase in the number of single mothers but also a relative increase in single fathers and especially non-married couples (with and without children), as well as single households. Despite all the support measures, many children live in poverty (defined as households with an annual income after taxes of under 50 per cent of the national average). In 1993 this applied to 32 per cent of the children in Britain, 28 per cent in Ireland and 27 in Portugal. At the other end of the scale were Denmark (5 per cent), France (12) and Germany (13). The European Union average was 20 per cent.[22] Baby booms and marriage booms seem to be a thing of the past, despite minor variations from year to year and country to country.

Will the process of individualization ultimately destroy the classical, European family and gender order? This is unlikely, since it is more a search for new ways with an as yet undetermined goal, a variable balance between tradition and innovation. In the light of increased mobility, family relations are often maintained over long distances, though this cannot be registered statistically. Despite fathers' participation in childcare and the partners' sharing of household duties, more women than men still perform the housework, especially the most tedious and menial of tasks. (The Organization for Economic Cooperation and Development and the United Nations have been supporting internationally comparable measurements of the 'dark side of the moon' of the economy since 1992 and the United Nations World Conference on Women passed a resolution to this effect in 1995.) A recent survey showed that for Germany, a critical factor is cleaning toilets. Almost exclusively women work in childcare and kindergartens. Foreign women are hired to clean private households, often being paid under the table, and they clean private and public companies in teams (usually with male bosses) at night. Indicators for the relationship between employment practices and family life in Europe are almost entirely highly aggregated figures at the national level. If these are broken down according to region, a diversity of highly varied coexisting lifestyles is revealed, rather than a general trend; and the differences can best be explained on the basis of cultural traditions. Perhaps we are dealing with a multiple, bottom-up European integration.[23] The developments expressed by the indicators and civil law reform clearly differ from the gender relations that apply within some immigrant groups from countries outside the European Union. In France and in Berlin clitoral mutilation of young girls is sometimes performed (clitoridectomy has been a central target of the international women's movement for decades). In Europe's mainstream societies and especially among the younger generation, the more general changes in attitudes towards marriage and children have indeed led to a high degree of individualization. It is, however, not necessarily anti-marriage or anti-family. Marriage is now considered a site of personal fulfilment and mutual assistance; according to a Portuguese survey, having children only came second as a reason for marrying. Although adolescents ranked 'family' seventh on a scale of what they valued, it was still above 'love' and 'career contentment'.[24] It seems likely that marriage will gain in value in the future, replacing decades of criticism of and scepticism towards matrimony. Non-married couples would like their partnership to have equal status to marriage, but without getting married. The trend is both understandable and needs to be explained. Partnerships of homosexual couples (especially when they have children) are hardly less stable than those of (divorce-happy) heterosexuals. In Denmark, Sweden, the Netherlands and Germany homosexual partners can commit themselves to each other contractually and under state authority. Explanation seems to be more difficult with respect to heterosexual couples. Marriages today are so secularized, liberalized and non-hierarchical that their being officially registered no longer restricts options for individual development and possible separation. Why, then, do couples wish to 'marry' without getting married? First and foremost, they want the rights guaranteed by marriage, especially child custody, but also concrete financial benefits. Is it perhaps more a matter of rights than of duties? The impending reforms should consider the rise and fall of the early Soviet de facto marriages, whose enormous social costs fell on the shoulders of women and children.

The longest revolution is not yet over. The question as to the greatest possible happiness for the largest possible number (in the Enlightenment sense, but across gender lines instead of androcentrically[25]) may be answered for women in two ways. Compared with their mothers, grandmothers and great-grandmothers, things are certainly better for them than ever before (albeit not in war-torn areas). Compared with the men of their own generation, there is a lot to be desired. Gender relations are indeed shaped by history and culture; this is precisely why they are hard to change, irrespective of isolated exceptions and periods of radical change. Culture and history have deep roots and a *longue durée*. The new forms of women's citizenship, their civil, political and social rights, will only promote a lasting change if it is accompanied by a change in public and private, female and male consciousness, and if the goal is not merely equality but freedom. The *querelle des sexes* is not over yet – and that's a good thing.

History, Mind and Gender

And ar'n't I a woman?

Sojourner Truth, 1851

Since the 1960s in western and eastern countries alike, the number of women studying at universities has risen, as well as their proportion among students at large. Women's age-old battle for admission to higher education and the corresponding careers, which led from 1890 to the Great Depression of the 1930s to considerable numbers of women at the universities for the first time, had entered a new stage. In some places, such as West Germany, women were actively recruited for university study in order to save the country from an 'educational catastrophe' that seemed to be emerging, at least in comparison with other countries. Now even young women from underdeveloped rural Catholic regions – a symbol of backwardness – were making their way to the university towns. Starting in the late 1970s, efforts spread out from the United States to help women through affirmative action measures (including controversial quotas) into positions they less often achieved than men did, even if they were equally or even better qualified. The main reason was that in the republic of letters it was usually the academic staff alone who appointed the new members of their republic. Much has changed in the meanwhile, with some departments or universities boasting of the growing percentage of women (sometimes this even brings them bonuses). As in other areas as well, however, the general pattern has remained the same. The higher the professional level, the fewer women there are. Female employment has not only become commonplace, it is the norm (and 'just housewives' are often considered old-fashioned, no matter how highly qualified they might be in their field, often caring for grandchildren and children of other women in addition to their own, doing volunteer work, providing foreign youths with extra help with homework, or even enjoying some leisure time), despite the fact that this norm, according to surveys, is more recognized by women than by men. Upward social mobility, however, is still largely something reserved for men.

Until long after World War II, university study (and even more the teaching) of history remained a male domain. Today half of history students at many universities are women. But while the history of history professors has been one of men only (the profession started emerging in the late eighteenth century), interest in history has for centuries also been a women's domain, despite manifold obstacles regarding access to education and libraries – from Christine de Pizan's *Vie de Charles V* (his epithet 'the wise' is traced back to her) to *History of England* (1763–83) by Catherine Macaulay, the 'republican Virago'. Mary Wollstonecraft admired Macaulay, because her manner of writing history, Wollstonecraft wrote in her second *Vindication*, was so 'strong and clear' and 'no sex appears'. Starting in the late eighteenth century there was an increase in the number of women – outside the historical profession – who not only read history but were researching and writing historians. Hortense Allart published a history of the Florentine Republic in 1837. A generation later Daniel Stern (Marie Flavigny, Comtesse d'Agoult) wrote a history of the French revolution of 1848 and another about the early Dutch Republic. But even if no sex appears in these books, many other women turned to the history of their own sex. The protagonist in Jane Austen's *Northanger Abbey* (1798) complains about how boring history books are that tell only of the 'quarrels of popes and kings' and of 'hardly any women at all'. Many female historians showed no less interest in the 'second' sex than in the 'first', in any case more than professional male historians did. In the late eighteenth century Louise Keralio Robert wrote a four-volume biography of Queen Elizabeth I of England and a history of the French queens. Feminist Anna Jameson published *Celebrated Female Sovereigns* in 1832, and the sisters Agnes and Elizabeth Strickland wrote many books between 1840 and 1860 about the queens of England and Scotland. Henriette Guizot de Witt (daughter of French historian and premier François Guizot) published *Les Femmes dans l'histoire* (1889). In Germany some of the first female PhDs in history chose subjects dealing with women of the Middle Ages for their dissertations. The classical women's movement, too, showed avid interest in the past in order to understand the origins of gender relations and to place their own goals within a historical perspective. Marya Chéliga published a large part of Olympe de Gouges's *Déclaration* in the *Revue Encyclopédique Larousse* in 1896. A generation later, several French and English works were written by women about women in the French Revolution.[26]

When women's history was discovered in Europe in the mid-1970s (and a decade earlier in the United States), merely the question whether or not women even had a history long demanded special legitimization. Meanwhile the inverse is considered true, that history would be impossible without women. Rather than asking about great men, women started asking about little women, great women or the little mothers, sisters, daughters and wives of great men, about women as a group and women in different groups. At first it was thought that asking these questions was charting new territory. The new historians had virtually no tradition connecting them to the earlier female historians. They also seemed to have hardly any ties to the classical women's movement, especially in Germany, where the Nazi regime had broken the tradition. Here, as far as anything at all was known in the 1970s about this earlier movement, it was regarded as 'bourgeois' or at best 'moderate' – the absolute opposite of how feminists wished to be – or even as paving the way for Nazism (since they wanted to better the situation for mothers and, like other women's movements, used 'motherhood' as a metaphor). The earlier movement did not appear to be anything to identify with. Only the minority of 'radicals' or the socialist women's movement of the turn of the twentieth century seemed familiar. Here the new historians found appeals for abortion rights, free love, unwed motherhood, socialization of housework, and calls for revolt and revolution. But gradually the moderate feminists of the earlier movements were revealed to have been concerned with issues that were still incredibly current: the relationship between equality and liberty, between 'equal' rights and 'women's rights', assimilation and difference, between female minorities and majorities; they had been concerned with the diversity of women's lives, which was hard to fit under the one heading of the 'female sex'. Like the 'women's liberation movement', the earlier movement had opposed the assumption of man being the measure of all things.

It took a while for women to discover that their predecessors had by no means always corresponded to the dominant images of the times. New documents had to be found and familiar ones had to be re-read with different eyes. The topos that 'the mind has no sex' was old and women had access to it. It had been passed down from St Jerome to St Augustine and then on to Thomas Aquinas. In the English Civil War, female prophets who announced God's word gave cause for Samuel Torshell to take up the topos again in 1645. William Wotton found that there were never 'so many very great Women in any one Age, as are to be found between the Years 15 and 1600' in his *Reflections upon Ancient and Modern Learning* (1694).[27] Descartes's radical separation of mind and body afforded the option – which many women quickly adopted – of thinking and practising equality with respect to *ratio*. But Descartes himself and the reception of his works quickly brought that to an end. However, Poullain de la Barre followed Cartesian thought in his *L'Esprit n'a pas de sexe* (1763), as did Mary Wollstonecraft. The notion had considerable consequences in the nineteenth century as articulated by John Stuart Mill, and many feminists insisted that men and women were equal in reason. Hedwig Dohm reworded the sentence in a contemporary context: 'the rights of mankind have no sex'. Even though the phrase was not quoted directly, its substance was indeed taken seriously by female natural scientists of early modern times, such as Margaret Cavendish, Maria Sibylla Merian, Laura Bassi and Maria Winkelmann. They were followed by, for example, the Russian mathematician Sonya Kovalevsky, who studied in the 1870s in Germany and was famous in her time; in 1884 she was appointed professor at the university in Stockholm. There was also Marie Curie, French-Russian Nobel prize laureate (in physics and chemistry), and Lise Meitner, a Jewish Austrian who fled to Sweden in 1938 (Albert Einstein called her 'our Madame Curie'). In historical research, it was also discovered that women had expressed unorthodox views not only with respect to *ratio* but also regarding other aspects of gender re-lations. 'Feminist' voices had indeed also been heard in earlier times. They were certainly only a minority; and only a minority of the minority managed to leave any traces. But they confirm that long ago alternatives were conceivable and indeed conceived, even on a cultural terrain that seemed as fixed and permanent as none other.

Two questions (among many others) ensued. What is 'feminism' and did it exist before the term emerged in the late nineteenth century? If feminism is understood (as is the rule today in English-speaking countries) as a muted or vocal, public or private outcry against the *condition féminine*, then it has existed for centuries (or even from time immemorial). If feminism is understood as a social movement of women (with a feminist worldview), then it is a specifically nineteenth- and twentieth-century phenomenon, and it would be preferable to describe earlier voices in the vocabulary they themselves used. 'Liberty', for instance, was both known and popular in earlier times. Second, why did it take three decades of historical research to make traditions visible that contrast with the earlier assumptions of the second-wave women's movement which considered their revolts and vocabulary to have risen up phoenix-like from the ashes of centuries-long female oppression and silence? One answer is that although there were many 'feminist' voices up to the eighteenth century, there was no real tradition within which later women's voices could have built on the earlier ones. The reason was the general exclusion of women from education and its institutions and tools, from the world of knowledge and libraries, and the fact that women's voices never found any lasting response from male scholars who dominated Europe's intellectual tradition. As a result, women searching for change and thirsting for knowledge had to – up to the present day – continually reinvent the wheel.[28]

The most recent reinvention of the wheel has led to three problems, which opened up new questions, possible solutions and yet another stage in the gender debate, this time largely among female scholars. The first problem concerns men; the second, women; and the third, the sexes. From the very beginning, recent historiography on women was also about men, since the history of one cannot be isolated from that of the other. In addition, however, women's history has ultimately led to a comprehensive gender history, since not only women but men as well are sexual beings; and it would be misleading to perceive the male sex as the embodiment of the universal and the female as something specific (manhood suffrage was long referred to as 'universal', and there is still talk of 'universal manhood suffrage', which is a contradiction in terms since today 'universal' means 'regardless of sex'). What are men, then, and how did they change in the course of history? A search thus began for the 'first' sex.[29]

Second, it was also clear from the outset that not all women have the same history but that it varies from individual to individual and with affiliation to many other groups which include men. In other words, it is never about 'woman' but about 'women'. The female (like the male) sex does not exist in the singular but in the plural. The meaning of 'woman' and what women 'are' varies greatly over time and space; the history of the 'second' sex is no less complex than that of the 'first'. Moreover, however, especially under the influence of postmodernism and deconstructivism, it has been questioned whether the concept of 'women', even in the plural, still makes any sense and whether one can even begin to grasp it clearly. The underlying assumption, in keeping with an impulse of the women's movement, is that the notion of being a woman, and even more so as a form of collective identity, needs to be rejected and dismantled. In a historical sense it has been argued that Sojourner Truth, if she lived today, would have to reword her famous 'And ar'n't I a woman?' to 'Ain't I a fluctuating identity?'[30] The twenty-first century will show whether or not this new spoke will be strong enough to keep the old wheel rolling. Yet women 'are' women (and human beings), and at the same time this state of being is undetermined and open and can vary over time and space and affiliation to other 'imagined communities'; being a woman is neither an 'objective' given nor something 'fictional'; and this tension must be endured. This is precisely today's form of the paradox that Olympe de Gouges and so many others had verbalized. Still, when discussion circles around historical sources, around liberty and equality or their opposites, or affirmative action, then women can usually be recognized with sufficient clarity.

It has been clear ever since the historiographical wheel started rolling again that – and this is the third point – women, as well as gender, are culturally and historically shaped categories, identities, attributes. This assumption implied a rejection of some kinds of 'biology'. Biologists were often enthusiastic participants in the *querelle des femmes*. They have long been trying to explain gender relations, and still today they like to do so on the basis of evolution theories (the leading theories within the discipline of biology) that view men and women as more or less willing executioners of the respective tasks assigned to them by their genes. Genes, however, press for nothing but their own propagation and, in view of the differences of the bodies carrying out the tasks, male genes have infinitely better chances of success than female genes. Therefore, according to a progressive biology textbook, prostitution and rape are an outcome of the male 'desire for reproductive success'. Since one woman can only be available to a limited extent, the man's genes drive him 'to seek out multiple copulatory partners' and 'sometimes lead men to inseminate females against their will' (though his sense of reason allows him to harness himself).[31] Such gene metaphysics has recently posed the question why women even continue to live at all after menopause. One response is that they care for their grandchildren, thus increasing the chances for the parents of the children to propagate their own genes and thus those of the grandmother.

Female historians do not rely on metaphysics, however, but on historical documents and shifts in language and meaning. The English word 'sex' has been replaced or juxtaposed with the word 'gender', and this has also been incorporated into other languages (*genre, género*). The English term has become virtually mainstream in German, and the German use of *gender studies* makes the German word *Geschlecht* seem as outdated as the 'just housewife'. The word 'gender' has a long and rich history in the United States. Once it was strictly a grammatical category. In the early 1960s the distinction between 'sex' and 'gender' was invented in order for transsexuals to differentiate between their 'first' and their 'second' sex. A decade later feminism took up the distinction. It was an attempt, first of all, to avoid the sexual connotation of 'sex' (that is, sexuality) and to free women from being reduced to a sexual being; and second, to distinguish between the social (gender) and the 'biological' (sex). But what does 'biology' mean from the perspective of gender history? This heading has usually been used to refer to (hetero)sexuality, menstruation, pregnancy, motherhood; that is, that which seems to be 'traditional' in a woman's life. And yet all these have been shaped by history, as demonstrated by recent cultural studies of the human body, and their present forms are anything but traditional. On the other hand, gender is of existential significance to human beings (including and especially with respect to changing one's gender, dress or name) and it is just as impossible to draw a clear dividing line between 'sex' and 'gender' as it is with respect to the traditional dichotomy of nature and culture. So what is gender? The most significant of currently circulating definitions is 'Gender is a constitutive element of social relationships based on perceived differences between the sexes, and gender is a primary way of signifying relationships of power'.[32] But above all it is often said today that gender does not 'exist'; instead, it is ('only') a social or mental construction. The assumption that gender 'exists' and, even more so, the assumption that the sexes differ has been characterized or criticized until recently in feminist research as 'biologism', later as 'essentialism'. But in view of human diversity, or in Hannah Arendt's words, plurality, the assumption that the sexes 'are the same' is no less essentialist than the assumption of their difference. Out of fear of supporting the (truly mental) constructions of some biologists, feminists have used the term 'gender' to negate the existence of 'gender'. But first of all, fear should not be a factor in the world of the mind; second, mental constructions are just as deep-rooted as those of what is referred to as biology – or even more so. Third, the debate only reproduces a tradition dating back at least to the medieval debate on nominalism and leading ultimately to metaphysics. On this aspect, too, sources are more important for historians than is metaphysics. Debate on the meaning of what is meant should also be possible using the instruments of non-English languages, especially through shifts in language and meaning, as has occurred in the English language. German-speaking feminists have successfully initiated changes in language and writing conventions that give visibility to both male and female components of apparently gender-neutral nouns. Why shouldn't the German *Geschlecht* (instead of the German *Gender*) become generally accepted as having historical and cultural content? Unless this shift in meaning occurs, *Geschlecht* will be relegated to 'biology' as the 'just housewife' is to the domain of 'non'-work. It is still an open question whether *genre* (French), *genere* (Italian), *género* (Spanish and Portuguese) will replace the respective word derived from the Latin *sexus;* but in the Romance languages those terms have too many other meanings for them to be entirely useful for gender history.

Questions were raised early on regarding the relationship between oppression and agency of women. This question regards individual fates and life histories as well as the measure of continuity and change over time. There is much wrestling with the concept of 'patriarchy' (the earlier women's movement hardly used the term), its differentiation with regard to respective epochs, and with 'gender regimes' and 'gender contracts'. It has long since been agreed that women were not always victims but that they also actively shaped their own lives. It was also found that some women were accomplices in their own oppression (this is assumed especially when they thought and acted differently from what is today regarded as emancipated). This issue assumed a particular form with regard to Germany's history. Were German women victims of National Socialism or not? Were they perpetrators; that is, not accomplices in their own oppression but active participants in crimes against other women and men? Here too the issue was initially raised in the United States. On the one hand, an American author had justly warned back in 1939 against newspaper reports with 'headlines, slogans, atrocity stories and selected anecdotes' according to which women were driven out of their offices 'by Storm Troopers and herded back to the home' to serve as 'mere breeding machines' in a form of 'enforced motherhood'.[33] On the other hand, the image of women as victims of National Socialism was difficult to revise. Kate Millett's internationally acclaimed and influential book *Sexual Politics* (1969) presented Nazism as 'the most deliberate attempt ever made to revive and solidify extreme patriarchal conditions'. She saw women's role as 'strictly confined to utter dedication to motherhood and the family' and the 'flat firing of married and unmarried women alike' relegated women to 'the humble status of server and helper' in the 'great masculine project of the state'. Like the leftist approaches of the 1970s to the study of 'fascism', which presented German workers as victims of Nazism and hardly mentioned the Holocaust (it did not move into the foreground until the 1980s, at least as regards German leftists), early feminist studies (and some later ones) saw the female sex as the victim of a Nazi 'mother cult' and 'forced motherhood', as objects and not as agents of the regime.

Since the 1980s the picture has been redrawn and the real female victims were sought, namely, the victims of Nazi race policy. This revision took place at five levels: women's paid employment was not taboo in Nazism, it was commonplace (if not the norm); sterilization policy was more important to the regime than the nebulous 'motherhood cult'; pronatalist reforms were father-oriented, not mother-oriented, and in an international comparison they were meagre, but they did not produce any female 'victims' and 'enforced motherhood' was comparable to that of earlier and later periods; the persecution and murder of Jewish women is not just part of the history of Jews and their persecutors but also part of women's history; and a considerable number of German women actively participated in carrying out the race policy. 'The women' were not victims; instead they were – like the men – victims, perpetrators, followers, bystanders and they rarely resisted; fewer female actors were directly involved in crimes than were their male counterparts, but they had the same motives. St Augustine once said about Adam and Eve that 'they sinned differently with respect to sex, but the same with respect to hubris' (*De genesi ad litteram* XII, 11); yet the female and male agents of Nazism did not only act the same as regards hubris, but also the same as regards sex. Because, as Hannah Arendt said, 'terror enforces oblivion',[34] Jewish women long remained excluded from this part of women's history. Historians in the United States, Israel as well as Europe have begun to recuperate the heritage of Jewish women of Europe: from the merchant and secret theologian Glikl bas Judah Leib (which was how she referred to herself; she later became known as Glückel of Hameln) around 1700 up to the women of the nineteenth and twentieth centuries.

Women of all European countries and religions have contributed much to the concept and implementation of female citizenship, both in the modern republics and in the republic of letters. Citizenship, human rights and the question of how they will be shaped in the ongoing process of European integration – with its different meanings for women of the respective European countries as well as those from non-European Union countries who live in Europe – are on the agenda of gender studies, as well as the relationship between Europe and the larger world. Especially within a global framework, the relationship between human rights and women's rights has currently taken on renewed significance. The fundamental civil liberties – liberty and security of person, right to life, liberty of movement, physical integrity and protection of privacy – as they are laid down in the European Convention on Human Rights (1950) and the United Nations International Covenant on Civil and Political Rights (1966) and social rights (Council of Europe 1961, United Nations 1966) can have a different meaning for women from that which they have for men. The classical postulate of freedom of religion can – depending on the respective religious doctrine – collide with women's liberty.[35] The relationship between women's rights and human rights will be crucial in the twenty-first century in providing an answer to the question, 'Are women human?'

Notes

1 *Querelle des femmes*: A European Gender Dispute

1 Schnell, p. 12; Bloch, chs 3, 6; Georges Duby, 'The Courtly Model', in Duby and Perrot (eds), vol. 2, pp. 254, 265–6.

2 Howard Adelman, 'Images of Women in Italian Jewish Literature in the Late Middle Ages', in *Proceedings of the Tenth World Congress of Jewish Studies*, Division B, vol. 2 (Jerusalem, 1990), pp. 99–106; Israel Zinberg, *A History of Jewish Literature*, vol. 4 (Cincinatti, OH, 1974), pp. 96–9.

3 Robert Klein and Henri Zerner, *Italian Art 1500–1600: Sources and Documents* (Evanston, IL, 1989), p. 41.

4 Elisabeth Gössmann (ed.), *Archiv für philosophie- und theologiegeschichtliche Frauenforschung* 4 (1988), pp. 107, 110, 121.

5 Mme d'Épinay, *Les Conversations d'Émilie* (Leipzig, 1774), p. 5.

6 Elisabeth Gössmann, 'Religiös-theologische Schriftstellerinnen', in *Geschichte der Frauen*, ed. Duby and Perrot, vol. 2 (Frankfurt a. M., 1993), p. 502, in the German edition only; Danielle Régnier-Bohler, 'Literary and Mystical Voices', in Duby and Perrot (eds), vol. 2, pp. 427–82.

7 Eric Hicks (ed.), *Le Débat sur le Roman de la Rose* (Paris, 1977), pp. 139f., 146, 42, 110; see also ibid., pp. 14f., 17, 19, 53, 128f. and Christine de Pizan, *The Book of the City of Ladies*, rev. ed., intro. and trans. Earl Jeffrey Richards, foreword by Natalie Zemon Davis (New York, 1998); Régnier-Bohler, 'Literary and Mystical Voices', pp. 434–42.

8 Schnell, p. 191; Conor Fahy, 'Three Early Renaissance Treatises on Women', *Italian Studies* 11 (1956), p. 46; *Epistre au Dieu d'Amours*, vv. 417–19, cited in de Pizan, *Book of the City of Ladies*. Introduction, p. xxxvi; *L'Avision Christine*, ed. Marie-Luise Towner (Washington, DC, 1932).

9 Adriana Chemello, 'Weibliche Freiheit und venezianische Freiheit: Moderata Fonte und die Traktatliteratur über Frauen im 16. Jahrhundert', in Bock and Zimmermann (eds), p. 251.

10 Henderson and McManus (eds), pp. 173f., 177, 181, 306, 310–14; Moira

Ferguson (ed.), *First Feminists: British Women Writers 1578–1799* (Bloomington, IN, 1985), pp. 266–72; Karen Offen, 'Reclaiming the European Enlightenment for Feminism', in Akkerman and Stuurman (eds), pp. 89ff.

11 Wolfgang Behringer (ed.), *Hexen und Hexenprozesse* (Munich, 1988), pp. 7, 158; Hufton, *The Prospect Before Her*, p. 345.

12 Gisela Bock and Margarete Zimmermann, 'Die *Querelle des femmes* in Europa', in Bock and Zimmermann (eds), p. 19.

13 Keller, pp. 53, 288; Maclean, *The Renaissance Notion*, pp. 38, 106; Hippel, pp. 75–6; Bell and Offen (eds), vol. 1, pp. 116–19.

14 Wollstonecraft, pp. 47, 74; Hippel, pp. 119, 183; Desiderii Erasmi Roterodami, *Opera omnia*, vol. 1, Lugduni Batavorum (1703) (reprint 1961), col. 842; Maclean, *The Renaissance Notion*, pp. 70f.; Gössmann (ed.), p. 254; Johann Heinrich Zedler, Article: 'Weib', *Grosses vollständiges Universallexikon aller Wissenschaften und Künste*, vol. 54 (Halle, 1747), cols 23, 28, 38f., 106f.

15 Schnell, p. 277.

16 Klapisch-Zuber, 'Les Femmes et la famille', p. 329; Hufton, *The Prospect Before Her*, chs 3–5; Carla Casagrande, 'The Protected Woman', in Duby and Perrot (eds), vol. 2, pp. 70–83; Silvana Vecchio, 'The Good Wife', in Duby and Perrot (eds), vol. 2, pp. 112–25.

17 Klapisch-Zuber, 'Les Femmes et la famille', p. 322; Luisa Ciammitti, 'Quanto costa essere normali: La dote nel conservatorio femminile di Santa Maria del Baraccano (1630–1680)', *Quaderni storici* 53 (1983), p. 470.

18 Wunder, chs 3 and 4; Claudia Opitz, 'Life in the Late Middle Ages', in Duby and Perrot (eds), vol. 2, pp. 271–97.

19 Giovanni Pico della Mirandola, *Über die Würde des Menschen* (Zurich, 1988), p. 80.

20 Giovanni della Casa, *Se si debba prendere moglie. Galateo* (Turin, 1991), pp. 59, 77, 79.

21 Eugenio Garin, *L'umanesimo italiano* (Bari, 1965), pp. 49–51; Volker Hunecke, *Der venezianische Adel am Ende der Republik* (Tübingen, 1995), pp. 141f.; Giannozzo Manetti, *Über die Würde und Erhabenheit des Menschen*, ed. August Buck (Hamburg, 1990), books 1 and 4.

22 Bernd Moeller, 'Die Brautwerbung Martin Bucers für Wolfgang Capito: Zur Sozialgeschichte des evangelischen Pfarrerstandes', in *Philologie als Kulturwissenschaft*, ed. Ludger Grenzmann et al. (Göttingen, 1987), p. 320; Martin Luther, *Ausgewählte Schriften* (Frankfurt a. M., 1982), vol. 3, pp. 202, 206.

23 Luther, *Ausgewählte Schriften*, vol. 3, pp. 186–91; Luther, *Werke*, vol. 10.2 (Weimar, 1907), p. 156.

24 Telle, p. 335; Moeller, pp. 315, 325; Harrington, pp. 82f.

25 Maria E. Müller, 'Schneckengeist im Venusleib: Zur Zoologie des Ehelebens bei Johann Fischart', in Müller (ed.), p. 186; Wiesner, p. 23.

26 Frumentius Renner (ed.), *Die Denkwürdigkeiten der Äbtissin Caritas Pirckheimer* (St Ottilien, 1982), p. 128; Marion Kobelt-Groch, *Aufsässige Töchter Gottes: Frauen im Bauernkrieg und in den Täuferbewegungen*

(Frankfurt a. M., 1993), p. 34; Wunder, p. 74; Luther, *Ausgewählte Schriften*, vol. 3, pp. 202, 210; Moeller, p. 309; Harrington, p. 73.

27 Luther, *Werke*, vol. 42, pp. 51f.; Turner, pp. 120–3; Wunder, p. 266; Michael A. Screech, *The Rabelaisian Marriage* (London, 1958), pp. 87, 135f.

28 Hubertus Fischer, 'Ehe, Eros und das Recht zu reden', in Müller (ed.), pp. 220f.; Mary Lyndon Shanley, 'Marriage Contract and Social Contract in 17th-century English Political Thought', in Elshtain (ed.), p. 89; Ursula Vogel, 'Gleichheit und Herrschaft in der ehelichen Vertragsgesellschaft', in Gerhard (ed.), p. 272.

29 Mary Astell, *Political Writings*, ed. Patricia Springborg (Cambridge, 1996), pp. 50, 75, 9, 17; Albistur and Armogathe, vol. 1, p. 202; Wunder, p. 76; Maclean, *Woman Triumphant*, pp. 114–18.

30 Wollstonecraft, pp. 291, 274, 239, 94, 157, 136, 262, 272, 111, 138, 186.

31 Anderson and Zinsser, vol. 2, pp. 53–61.

2 The French Revolution: The Dispute is Resumed

1 Jean M. Clement (ed.), *Petit Dictionnaire de la cour et de la ville*, 2 vols (Paris, 1788), vol. 1, p. 124; 2nd edn (Paris, 1826), p. 33.

2 Doc. 1, in *Les Femmes dans la Révolution Française* (Paris, 1982).

3 Docs 3 and 7, in ibid.

4 Doc. 5, in ibid.; Paule-Marie Duhet (ed.), *Les Femmes et la Révolution 1789–1794* (Paris, 1971), pp. 35–7.

5 Stéphane Rials (ed.), *La Déclaration des droits de l'homme et du citoyen* (Paris, 1988), pp. 691f.; Suzanne Desan, '"Constitutional Amazons": Jacobin Women's Clubs in the French Revolution', in *Re-creating Authority in Revolutionary France*, ed. Bryant T. Ragan and Elizabeth A. Williams (New Brunswick, NJ, 1992), p. 32.

6 Jean Tulard et al., *Histoire et dictionnaire de la Révolution française 1789–1799* (Paris, 1987), p. 816.

7 Arendt, German edn, p. 454; the second part of the passage does not appear in the English version (p. 291).

8 Doc. 25, in *Femmes dans la Révolution*; Condorcet, *The First Essay on the Political Rights of Women*, trans. Alice Drysdale Vickery (Letchworth, 1912).

9 Abbé Sieyès, *Politische Schriften 1788–1790* (Munich, 1981), p. 251; Rosanvallon, pp. 96, 108f., 136.

10 Rosanvallon, p. 68; Doc. 45, in *Femmes dans la Révolution*; Rials (ed.), pp. 153–87, 211; Marcel Gauchet, *La Révolution des droits de l'homme* (Paris, 1989), pp. 220–6.

11 Gary Kates, '"The Powers of Husband and Wife Must Be Equal and Separate": The Cercle Social and the Rights of Women, 1790–91', in Applewhite and Levy (eds), p. 163.

12 Suzanne Desan, '"War between Brothers and Sisters": Inheritance Law and Gender Politics in Revolutionary France', *French Historical Studies* 20 (1997), pp. 623f.; Elisabeth G. Sledziewski, 'The French Revolution as the Turning Point', in Duby and Perrot (eds), vol. 4, pp. 36–7.

13 Olympe de Gouges, 'Déclaration', in de Gouges, Œuvres, ed. Benoîte Groult (Paris, 1986), p. 109; Scott, 'Only Paradoxes to Offer', pp. 4, 178; Mill and Mill, p. 131; Arendt, see p. 41 above; Blanc, p. 67.
14 Laura S. Strumingher, 'Looking Back: Women of 1848 and the Revolutionary Heritage of 1789', in Applewhite and Levy (eds), p. 279; Karen Offen, 'Women's Memory, Women's History, Women's Political Action: The French Revolution in Retrospect, 1789–1889–1989', Journal of Women's History 1 (1990), pp. 211–30.
15 Schama, pp. 850f.; Duhet (ed.), pp. 205f.; Scott, 'Only Paradoxes to Offer', pp. 22, 52, 191.
16 Blanc, pp. 125, 148, 191; Doc. 66, in Femmes dans la Révolution; Schama, p. 859.
17 Dorinda Outram, 'Le langage mâle de la vertu: Women and the Discourse of the French Revolution', in The Social History of Language, ed. Peter Burke and Roy Porter (Cambridge, MA, 1987), p. 127; Olwen Hufton, 'Women in Revolution, 1789–1796', Past and Present 53 (1971), p. 105.
18 Godineau, 'Mot citoyenne', pp. 96, 104.
19 Outram, pp. 120–35, 127; Desan, 'Constitutional Amazons', pp. 24, 28, 29.
20 Godineau, The Women of Paris, pp. 169–70; Elisabeth Badinter (ed.), Paroles d'hommes (1790–1793) (Paris, 1989), pp. 82, 176, 180f.
21 Hufton, Women and the Limits, pp. 110, 112.
22 Ibid., pp. 102, 172, 116f., 118, 108.
23 Suzanne Desan, 'The Role of Women in Religious Riots during the French Revolution', Eighteenth-century Studies 22 (1989), pp. 459f., 462; Hufton, Women and the Limits, pp. 108f., 118.
24 Jean-Etienne-Marie Portalis, Écrits et discours juridiques et politiques (Marseille, 1988), p. 63; Annarita Buttafuoco, 'Virtù civiche e virtù domestiche: Letture del ruolo femminile nel Triennio rivoluzionario', in L'Italia nella rivoluzione 1789–1799, ed. Giuseppina Genassati and Lauro Rossi (Reno-Bologna, 1990), p. 87.
25 Portalis, pp. 37, 50, 107f.
26 Narcisse-E. Carré, Nouveau Code des femmes (Paris, 1828), p. 37; Werner Schubert, Französisches Recht in Deutschland zu Beginn des 19. Jahrhunderts (Cologne, 1977), pp. 33–5.
27 Rosanvallon, p. 143.
28 Ibid., 144.
29 Gabriele von Koenig-Warthausen, 'Ludovike Simanowiz geb. Reichenbach. Malerin 1759–1827', in Lebensbilder aus Schwaben und Franken, vol. 12 (Stuttgart, 1972), p. 133; Peter Kuhlbrodt, 'Die Französische Revolution und die Frauenrechte in Deutschland', Zeitschrift für Geschichtswissenschaft 38 (1990), pp. 409, 417f.
30 Honegger, pp. 15–17, 45f., 71, 193–5.
31 Journal des Luxus und der Moden 4 (1789), pp. 507–15; 8 (1793), pp. 615–22 (facs. Hanau, 1967); Friedrich Eberle and Theo Stammen (eds), Die Französische Revolution in Deutschland (Stuttgart, 1989), pp. 145–9; Frevert, 'Mann und Weib', pp. 68–70; Kuhlbrodt, p. 412; Anon., 'Über die

politische Würde der Weiber: Gegenstück zu Hippels Versuch über die bürgerliche Verbesserung der Weiber', in *Berlinisches Archiv der Zeit und ihres Geschmackes* (Berlin, 1799), vol. 1, pp. 403–6, vol. 2, p. 65; Honegger, pp. 89, 186.

32 Wilhelm Joseph Behr, *System der angewandten allgemeinen Staatslehre oder der Staatskunst (Politik)* (Frankfurt a. M., 1810), pp. 267f.; Behr, *System der allgemeinen Staatslehre* (Bamberg, 1804), vol. 1, pp. 322f.

33 Michel Berr, *Appel à la justice des nations et des rois* (Strasbourg, 1891), p. 63 (facs. in *La Révolution française et l'émancipation des Juifs* [Paris, 1968], vol. 8).

34 Karin Rudert, 'Die Wiederentdeckung einer "deutschen Wollstonecraft": Esther Gad Bernard Domeier für Gleichberechtigung der Frauen und Juden', *Quaderni. Università degli Studi di Lecce, Dipartimento di lingue e letterature straniere* 10 (1988), pp. 224, 239, 242, 255.

35 Ursula Isselstein, 'Die Titel der Dinge sind das Fürchterlichste! Rahel Levins "Erster Salon"', in Schultz (ed.), p. 212; Stern, pp. 184–6, 191f., 225f., 270; Karl August Varnhagen von Ense, *Vermischte Schriften*, part 3 (Leipzig, 1876), p. 206; Barbara Hahn, *'Antworten Sie mir!' Rahel Levin Varnhagens Briefwechsel* (Basel, 1990), p. 187.

36 Veauvy and Pisano, docs 17, 21; Buttafuoco, 'Virtù civiche', pp. 85, 86, 87.

37 Maria Wollstonecraft, *Rettung der Rechte des Weibes mit Bemerkungen über politische und moralische Gegenstände*, 2 vols, ed. Christian Gotthilf Salzmann (Schnepfenthal, 1793, 1794), vol. 2, pp. 213f.; new (abridged) translation of Bertha Pappenheim (pseud.: P. Berthold), *Eine Verteidigung der Rechte der Frau* (Dresden, 1899), p. 161.

38 Honegger, pp. 100f.

39 Germaine de Staël, *Considérations sur la Révolution française* (1818) (Paris, 1988), p. 604.

40 'De l'influence de la révolution sur les femmes', *Révolutions de Paris* 83 (5–12 February 1791), pp. 233–5.

41 Ozouf, pp. 342, 344.

42 Ibid., p. 346; *Révolutions de Paris* 83 (5–12 February 1791), p. 227; Blanc, p. 191; Veauvy and Pisano, doc. 21.

3 Challenging Boundaries: A Third Gender Dispute

1 Helene Lange and Gertrud Bäumer (eds), *Handbuch der Frauenbewegung*, vol. 1: *Geschichte der Frauenbewegung in den Kulturländern* (Berlin, 1901), pp. 350, 404–5; Theodore Stanton (ed.), *The Woman Question in Europe* (London, 1884), pp. v, 1f., 353; Ray Strachey, *The Cause: A Short History of the Women's Movement in Britain* (London, 1928; reprint 1988), p. 11.

2 Article: 'Frauenfrage', in *Meyers Konversations-Lexikon*, vol. 6 (Mannheim, 1894), p. 822.

3 Lown, p. 1; Peter Gay, *Freud: A Life for Our Time* (New York, 1989), ch. 10.

4 Pyle (ed.), p. 40; Gay, p. 521.

5 Gay, p. 514.
6 Helsinger et al., vol. 2, p. 45; Pyle (ed.), p. 242; John S. Haller and Robin M. Haller, *The Physician and Sexuality in Victorian America* (1974; reprint Urbana, IL, 1995), ch. 2: 'The Lesser Man', p. 51.
7 Karin Hausen, '"... eine Ulme für das schwanke Efeu": Ehepaare im Bildungsbürgertum', in Frevert (ed.), pp. 85–117; Karl Hillebrand, *Frankreich und die Franzosen in der zweiten Hälfte des 19. Jahrhunderts* (Berlin, 1873), p. 47; Stanton (ed.), p. 300; Davidoff and Hall, p. 397; Helsinger et al., vol. 1, p. 108.
8 Rendall, *The Origins of Modern Feminism*, pp. 198, 239; Clark.
9 Purvis, p. 3; Giuseppe Mazzini, *Doveri dell'uomo* (Milan, 1972), pp. 67, 70; Jean-Marie Aubert, *La Femme: Antiféminisme et Christianisme* (Paris, 1975), p. 6.
10 Riot-Sarcey, pp. 87f.; Mesmer, p. 52.
11 Helsinger et al., vol. 1, pp. 6–13, 17, 77f.; Bell and Offen (eds), vol. 1, pp. 164–8, 192–8; Riot-Sarcey, pp. 140f.
12 Riot-Sarcey, p. 48; Pierre Leroux and J. Reynaud (eds), *Encyclopédie Nouvelle*, vol. 5, col. 212 (Paris, 1843; reprint Geneva, 1991).
13 *La Voix des femmes* 20 (11 April 1848), pp. 1f.; Riot-Sarcey, pp. 81, 194; Jenny d'Héricourt, *La Femme affranchie*, 2 vols (Brussels, 1860), vol. 2, p. 209; Moses and Rabine, p. 13.
14 D'Héricourt, ibid., vol. 1, pp. 100, 160f., 175, 211; vol. 2, pp. 108f., 124–6; Moses, ch. 7; Bell and Offen (eds), vol. 1, pp. 325–49.
15 Maria Deraismes, *Eve dans l'humanité* (1868), ed. Laurence Klejman (Paris, 1990), p. 37; Hellerstein et al. (eds), p. 140.
16 Hellerstein et al. (eds), p. 209; Thompson, pp. 43f.
17 Davidoff and Hall, p. 25; Peterson; Habermas.
18 Dora Edinger (ed.), *Bertha Pappenheim: Leben und Schriften* (Frankfurt a. M., 1963), pp. 11f.; Meyer; Kaplan, *The Jewish Feminist Movement.*
19 Fanny Lewald, *Politische Schriften* (Frankfurt a. M., 1989), p. 100; Pyle (ed), pp. 89–140.
20 Helsinger et al., vol. 2, p. 128; Hellerstein et al. (eds), pp. 208f., 234–40.
21 Desbois de Rochefort, Article: 'Enfant-trouvé', in *Encyclopédie méthodique*, vol. 2 (Paris, 1786), p. 283.
22 Hunecke, p. 192; Caroline B. Brettell and Rui Feijó, 'Foundlings in Nineteenth-century Northwestern Portugal: Public Welfare and Family Strategies', in *Enfance abandonnée*, pp. 273–300.
23 Helsinger et al., vol. 2, p. 129.
24 Maxine Berg and Pat Hudson, 'Rehabilitating the Industrial Revolution', *Economic History Review* 45 (1992), p. 26; Michelle Perrot, intro. to 'Travaux des femmes', *Le Mouvement social* 105 (1978).
25 Maxine Berg, 'What Difference did Women's Work Make to the Industrial Revolution?' *History Workshop Journal* 35 (1993), p. 23.
26 Joan W. Scott, 'The Woman Worker', in Duby and Perrot (eds), vol. 4, pp. 411, 414; Max Weber, 'Zur Psycho-Physik der industriellen Arbeit', *Archiv für Sozialwissenschaft und Sozialpolitik* 28 (1909), pp. 268, 722.
27 Judith Coffin, 'Social Science Meets Sweated Labor: Reinterpreting Wom-

en's Work in Late Nineteenth-century France', *Journal of Modern History* 63 (1991), p. 251; Canning, ch. 1 and pp. 255ff.

28 Helsinger et al., vol. 2, p. 119; Christina Vanja, 'Bergarbeiterinnen', *Der Anschnitt* 39 (1987), pp. 2–15; 40 (1988), pp. 128–43.

29 Bell and Offen (eds), p. 198; Buttafuoco, *Le Mariuccine*.

30 Rendall, *Women in an Industrializing Society*, p. 37; Michel Frey, 'Du mariage et du concubinage dans les classes populaires à Paris 1846–1847', *Annales* 33 (1978), pp. 803–25; Dirk Blasius, *Ehescheidung in Deutschland 1794–1945* (Göttingen, 1987), pp. 82–5.

31 Berg, 'Difference', p. 39.

32 Coffin, pp. 266f.

33 Helsinger et al., vol. 2, pp. 115–17, 124; Adelheid Popp, *Jugend einer Arbeiterin* (Berlin, 1983), pp. 64, 99–103.

34 Käthe Schirmacher, 'Die Stimmrechtsfrage auf dem Internationalen Frauenkongreß in London', *Die Frauenbewegung* 5 (1899), p. 138; *Die Gleichheit* 14 (1904), p. 108; Henriette Fürth, *Die Hausfrau* (Munich, 1914), pp. 35–42; Mary Beard, 'The Legislative Influence of Unenfranchised Women', *Annals of the American Association for Political and Social Science* 56 (1914), p. 61.

35 Strachey, p. 6.

36 Johanna Goldschmidt, *Rebekka und Amalia: Briefwechsel zwischen einer Israelitin und einer Adligen über Zeit- und Lebensfragen* (Leipzig, 1847), pp. 21–3, 25f.

37 Bettina von Arnim, *Dies Buch gehört dem König*, ed. Ilse Staff (Frankfurt a. M., 1982), p. 56; Michelle Perrot, 'Stepping Out', in Duby and Perrot (eds), vol. 4, p. 472; Louise Otto-Peters, *Schloß und Fabrik* (1846) (Leipzig, 1996).

38 Helsinger et al., vol. 3, p. 4.

39 Ruth-Ellen Boetcher Joeres (ed.), *Die Anfänge der deutschen Frauenbewegung: Louise Otto-Peters* (Frankfurt a. M., 1983), p. 81; Grace Aguilar, *The Vale of Cedars, or The Martyr* (1850) (London, 1895), pp. 172, 228.

40 Gerlinde Hummel-Haasis (ed.), *Schwestern zerreißt eure Ketten: Zeugnisse zur Geschichte der Frauen in der Revolution von 1848/49* (Munich, 1982), p. 150.

41 Sand, pp. 527–42.

42 Nell Irvin Painter, 'Difference, Slavery, and Memory: Sojourner Truth in Feminist Abolitionism', in *The Abolitionist Sisterhood: Women's Political Culture in Antebellum America*, ed. Jean Fagan Yellin and John C. Van Home (Ithaca, 1994), pp. 141f.; Scott, 'The Woman Worker', p. 400; Midgley, *Women Against Slavery*.

43 Prochaska, pp. 172, 224.

44 Ursula Röper, *Mariane von Rantzau und die Kunst der Demut: Frömmigkeitsbewegung und Frauenpolitik in Preußen unter Friedrich Wilhelm IV.* (Stuttgart, 1997), pp. 148f.; Bertha Pappenheim, *Prayers – Gebete* (New York, 1946); Prochaska, p. 126; Rendall, *The Origins of Modern Feminism*, p. 265.

45 Julie Daubié, *La Femme pauvre au XIXe siècle* (Paris, 1866), pp. 222f., 233; Lipp (ed.), pp. 218, 297; Rendall, *The Origins of Modern Feminism*,

p. 267; Paletschek, *Frauen und Dissens*.

46   Annarita Buttafuoco, 'La filantropia come politica', in Ferrante et al. (ed.), p. 166.

47   Bosch, p. 117.

48   D'Héricourt, vol. 1, p. 185.

49   Stanton (ed.), p. 167; Martha Vicinus (ed.), *A Widening Sphere: Changing Roles of Victorian Women* (Bloomington, IN, 1977).

50   Perrot, 'Stepping Out', p. 537; Lange and Bäumer (eds), *Handbuch der Frauenbewegung*, vol. 1, pp. 40f.; Lily Braun, *Die Frauenfrage* (Berlin, 1901).

51   Alice Salomon, 'Protective Legislation in Germany', in *International Council of Women, Report of the Transactions of Second Quinquennial Meeting Held in London July 1899*, ed. Countess of Aberdeen, 7 vols (London, 1900), vol.: 'Women in Industrial Life', p. 37; Clara Zetkin, in *Die Gleichheit 5* (1895), pp. 6, 55; 6 (1896), pp. 16, 19; Lange and Bäumer (eds), *Handbuch der Frauenbewegung*, vol. 1, pp. 3, 108–19.

52   Aura Korppi-Tommalo, 'Education – the Road to Work and Equality', in Manninen and Setälä (eds), pp. 31–41; Bosch; Braun.

53   Taylor, p. 391; Millicent Garrett Fawcett, 'The Women's Suffrage Movement', in Stanton (ed.), p. 6; Helene Lange, *Kampfzeiten*, 2 vols (Berlin, 1928), vol. 1, p. 77; Lange, 'Altes und Neues zur Frauenfrage', *Die Frau 2* (1895), p. 539; Hedwig Dohm, *Die wissenschaftliche Emanzipation der Frau* (1874) (Zürich, 1982), p. 40.

4   From the Social to the Political

1   Helene Lange, *Lebenserinnerungen* (Berlin, 1921), p. 241.

2   Patricia Grimshaw, *Women's Suffrage in New Zealand* (Auckland, 1987), p. 116; Helene Lange, 'Frauenwahlrecht' (1896), in Lange, *Kampfzeiten*, 2 vols (Berlin, 1928), vol. 1, pp. 180–96.

3   Heinrich von Treitschke, *Politik: Vorlesungen*, vol. 1 (Leipzig, 1897), p. 252.

4   Rendall, *The Origins of Modern Feminism*, pp. 237–42, 307ff.; Constance Rover, *Women's Suffrage and Party Politics in Britain 1866–1914* (London, 1967), pp. 1–7.

5   Holton, *Suffrage Days*, p. 23; Bock, 'Frauenwahlrecht'. Trans. note: Dohm's text appeared in Italian as *I diritti donne* and in English as *Women's Nature and Privilege* (1896, repr. 1976). The latter title is misleading, as the book discusses rights, not privilege.

6   Anne Verjus, 'Le suffrage universel, le chef de famille et la question de l'exclusion des femmes en 1848', in Corbin et al. (eds), pp. 401–13; Gunnar Hering, *Die politischen Parteien in Griechenland 1821–1936*, 2 vols (Munich, 1992), vol. 1, p. 387.

7   Mill, vol. 19, pp. 334, 492; J. A. Kay et al., 'The Franchise Factor in the Rise of the Labour Party', *English Historical Review* 91 (1976), p. 726; Camera dei Deputati (ed.), *Il voto alle donne: Le donne dall'elettorato alla partecipazione politica* (Rome, 1965), pp. 27ff.; Clark.

8   Mesmer, p. 247; Frevert, '*Mann und Weib*', pp. 61, 115; Lange, 'Frauenwahlrecht', p. 187.
9   Bogna Lorence-Kot and Adam Winiarz, 'The Polish Women's Movement up to 1914', in Paletschek and Pietrow-Ennker (eds).
10   Birgitta Zaar, 'Dem Mann die Politik, der Frau die Familie', *Österreichische Zeitschrift für Politikwissenschaft* 86/4 (1987), p. 357; Harrison; Planert.
11   Treitschke, p. 253.
12   Jane Lewis (ed.), *Before the Vote Was Won* (London, 1987), p. 419.
13   Louise Otto, *Das erste Vierteljahrhundert des Allgemeinen Deutschen Frauenvereins* (Leipzig, 1890), p. 29; Rendall, *Origins of Modern Feminism*, p. 316; Lange, 'Frauenwahlrecht', p. 187; Lewis (ed.), *Before the Vote*, p. 420.
14   Mill, vol. 28, pp. 158f.; Terence Ball, 'Utilitarianism, Feminism, and the Franchise: James Mill and his Critics', *History of Political Thought* 1 (1980), pp. 91–115.
15   Rosanvallon, p. 152; Lewis (ed.), *Before the Vote*, pp. 101f.; Cova, pp. 197f.; Lange, 'Frauenwahlrecht', pp. 182–4; Vellacott, p. 137.
16   Lewis (ed.), *Before the Vote*, p. 419; Annarita Buttafuoco, 'Libertà, fraternità, uguaglianza: per chi?' in Crispino (ed.), p. 118.
17   Bacchi, pp. 19f.; Laurence Klejman and Florence Rochefort, '"Au nom du droit et de la spécificité féminine": Ambiguïté des discours et diversité des tactiques dans le mouvement suffragiste avant la première guerre mondiale', in Viennot (ed.), pp. 223–32; Jane Rendall, 'Citizenship, Culture and Civilisation: The Languages of British Suffragists, 1866–1874', in Daley and Nolan (eds), pp. 127–50; Holton, *Feminism and Democracy*.
18   Clara Zetkin, *Zur Frage des Frauenwahlrechts* (Berlin, 1907), pp. 3, 10. (Trans. note: *Woman Suffrage*, trans. J. B. Askew [London, 1907]); *Die Gleichheit* 5 (6 March 1895), p. 55.
19   Françoise Thébaud, 'The Great War and the Triumph of Sexual Division', in Duby and Perrot (eds), vol. 5, pp. 27, 58, 63; Rupp, p. 115.
20   Rossi-Doria, pp. 83f.; Buttafuoco, *Cronache femminili*, pp. 208f.
21   Mill, vol. 17, p. 1728.
22   Bock, 'Frauenwahlrecht', pp. 122, 135f.
23   Lange, 'Frauenwahlrecht', p. 190; Klejman and Rochefort, p. 189.
24   Hardmeier, pp. 205, 227, 233f., 345f.
25   Rosanvallon, pp. 411f.; Hause and Kenney, pp. 237–43; Christine Bard, 'L'Étrange défaite des suffragistes (1919–1939)', in Viennot (ed.), pp. 233–40.
26   Hause and Kenney, p. 248; Mariette Sineau, 'Law and Democracy', in Duby and Perrot (eds), vol. 5, p. 504; Voegeli, pp. 321, 402.
27   Annarita Buttafuoco, 'Motherhood as a Political Strategy', in Bock and Thane (eds), p. 181; Buttafuoco, *Questioni di cittadinanza*, p. 162.
28   Rosemary Feurer, 'The Meaning of "Sisterhood": The British Women's Movement and Protective Labor Legislation, 1870–1900', *Victorian Studies* 31 (1988), pp. 241, 248.
29   Kulawik, ch. 3; Clara Zetkin, in *Die Gleichheit* 13 (6 May 1903), pp. 73–5.

30 Katherine Anthony, *Feminism in Germany and Scandinavia* (New York, 1915), p. 53.
31 Adele Schreiber (ed.), *Mutterschaft* (Leipzig, 1912), pp. 487–94, 688–703; Cova, p. 78; Gisela Bock, 'Poverty and Mothers' Rights in the Emerging Welfare States', in Duby and Perrot (eds), vol. 5, pp. 405–11.
32 Cova, p. 79.
33 Bock, 'Poverty and Mothers' Rights', p. 411; Karen Offen, 'Body Politics: Women, Work and the Politics of Motherhood in France, 1920–1950', in Bock and Thane (eds), p. 148.
34 Holton, *Feminism and Democracy*, p. 26; Bock, 'Poverty and Mothers' Rights', p. 412.
35 Introduction to Henry J. Harris, *Maternity Benefit Systems in Certain Foreign Countries*, Publ. No. 57, US Department of Labor, Children's Bureau (ed.) (Washington, DC, 1917).
36 Cova, pp. 57, 61; Kulawik, ch. 4.

5   Between Extremes

1 Eric Hobsbawm, *Age of Extremes: The Short 20th Century 1914–1991* (London, 1994), p. 1.
2 Gabriele Tergit, 'Die Einspännerin' (1927), in Tergit, *Atem einer anderen Welt: Berliner Reportagen* (Frankfurt a. M., 1994), p. 75.
3 Regina Schulte, 'The Sick Warrior's Sister', in Abrams and Harvey (eds), pp. 121–42; Margaret H. Darrow, 'French Volunteer Nursing and the Myth of War Experience in World War I', *American Historical Review* 191 (1996), pp. 80–106; Miriam Koerner, 'Central Park West, New York', in Benz (ed.), p. 219.
4 Rupp, p. 52.
5 Pugh, p. 158.
6 Gertrud Bäumer, '1919–1929', *Die Frau* 36 (1929), p. 197; Schaser, ch. 3.
7 De Haan, p. 86; von der Lühe, p. 129.
8 Colette, *Le Voyage égoiste suivi de Quatre-saisons* (Paris, 1986), p. 40; Roberts, p. 3; Lydia Gottschewski, 'Männerbund und Gemeinschaft', *Nordische Blätter* 7/9–10 (1931), p. 16; Richard Huelsenbeck, 'Bejahung der modernen Frau', in *Die Frau von morgen wie wir sie wünschen* (1929), ed. Friedrich M. Huebner (Frankfurt a. M., 1990), p. 36.
9 John Stuart Mill, *Autobiography* (1873), quoted in Mary Stocks, *The Case for Family Endowment* (London, 1927), p. 1; and in Pedersen, p. 1.
10 Kundrus, pp. 120, 170; Gisela Bock, 'Poverty and Mothers' Rights in the Emerging Welfare States', in Duby and Perrot (eds), vol. 5, p. 421.
11 *Journal Officiel*, 11 April 1941, p. 1554.
12 Pedersen, p. 414.
13 De Grazia, *Fascism*, p. 43.
14 Bock, *Zwangssterilisation*, pp. 141, 173, 175.
15 Victoria de Grazia, '"Femminismo latino": Italia, 1922–1945', in Gagliani and Salvati (eds), p. 137.

16 Marisa Saracinelli and Nilde Totti, 'L'Almanacco della donna italiana: dai movimenti femminili ai fasci (1920–1945)', in Saba (ed.), p. 105; Stites, pp. 303, 307.
17 Stites, pp. 294f.; Laura L. Phillips, 'In Defense of Their Families: Working-class Women, Alcohol, and Politics in Revolutionary Russia', *Journal of Women's History* 11 (1999), pp. 97–120.
18 Fannina W. Halle, *Woman in Soviet Russia*, trans. Margaret M. Green (New York, 1933), pp. 137, 144, 148–50 (trans. note), originally published in German as *Die Frau in Sowjetrußland* (Berlin, 1932); Stites, pp. 354–6, 378; Edmondson, pp. 94–7.
19 Halle, pp. 128, 137–9, 178; Stites, pp. 360, 364–71.
20 Stites, pp. 355, 360, 383; Halle, pp. 117–26; Barbara Alpern Engel, 'Les Femmes dans la Russie des révolutions 1861–1926', in Fauré (ed.), p. 466.
21 Stites, p. 382.
22 Ibid., p. 386.
23 Françoise Navailh, 'The Soviet Model', in Duby and Perrot (eds), vol. 5, pp. 251.
24 Halle, p. 93.
25 Marina Addis Saba, 'La donna "muliebre"', in Saba (ed.), pp. 30, 212.
26 Fiorenza Taricone, 'La Federazione nazionale laureate e diplomate e l'associazionismo femminile (1920–1935)', in Saba (ed.), pp. 156f.; de Grazia, *Fascism*, pp. 227, 242f.; Kaplan, *Jewish Feminist Movement*, pp. 204f.
27 'Erklärung des Bundes Deutscher Frauenvereine zu den Wahlen am 5. März 1933', *Die Frau* 40 (March 1933), pp. 380f.; Gertrud Bäumer, 'Lage und Aufgabe der Frauenbewegung in der deutschen Umwälzung', *Die Frau* 40 (April 1933), pp. 385, 390–2; Angelika Schaser, 'Gertrud Bäumer', in Heinsohn et al. (eds), pp. 24–39.
28 Ruth Köhler-Irrgang, *Die Sendung der Frau in der deutschen Geschichte* (Leipzig, 1940), p. 216; Gisela Bock, 'Nazi Gender Policies and Women's History', in Duby and Perrot (eds), vol. 5, pp. 170–3.
29 Danièle Bussy Genevois, 'The Women of Spain from the Republic to Franco', in Duby and Perrot (eds), vol. 5, pp. 190–1.
30 Georg Wilhelm Friedrich Hegel, *The Phenomenology of Mind*, trans. and intro. J. B. Baillie (London and New York, 1910; rev. ed. 1931), p. 496; de Grazia, *Fascism*, pp. 77, 79, 112–15; Hélène Eck, 'French Women under Vichy', in Duby and Perrot (eds), vol. 5, pp. 201ff., 206–9; Gisela Bock, 'Ganz normale Frauen', in Heinsohn et al. (eds), p. 257.
31 Ioannis Metaxas, *Logoi kai Skepseis*, 2 vols (Athens, 1969), vol. 1, p. 72. I would like to thank Susanne-Sophia Spiliotis for this reference.
32 Anne Cova and António Costa Pinto, 'Le salazarisme', in Fauré (ed.), pp. 685–99; de Grazia, *Fascism*, pp. 243–6; Genevois, 'Women of Spain', pp. 189–91; Eck, 'French Women', pp. 202–6.
33 Bock, 'Ganz normale Frauen', pp. 247f.
34 Werner Feldscher, *Rassen- und Erbpflege im deutschen Recht* (Berlin, 1943), pp. 26, 118.
35 Bock, *Zwangssterilisation*, pp. 23–5, 63, 85, 98f., 100–3, 121f., 160f., 193f., 388.

36 Alice Rilke and Dorothea Goedicke, *Die Freizeit der erwerbstätigen Frau*; Bundesarchiv (German Federal Archives): NS 5 I, 3–4; Bock, 'Nazi Gender Policies', pp. 158–63.
37 Huerkamp, *Bildungsbürgerinnen*, pp. 30f., 80–90, 161f., 182–8, 236–43, 287–307.
38 Ibid., p. 258; Kaplan, *Between Dignity and Despair*, pp. 17–29.
39 Bock, *Zwangssterilisation*, pp. 130f.
40 *Betty Scholem – Gershom Scholem: Mutter und Sohn im Briefwechsel 1917–1946*, ed. Itta Shedletzky and Thomas Sparr (Munich, 1989), pp. 290f.; Claudia Huerkamp, 'Jüdische Akademikerinnen in Deutschland 1900–1938', *Geschichte und Gesellschaft* 19 (1993), p. 318; Friedländer, pp. 151, 241.
41 *Betty Scholem – Gershom Scholem*, p. 319; Richarz (ed.), *Jüdisches Leben*, vol. 3, pp. 232f., 236; Kaplan, *Between Dignity and Despair*, pp. 40–6.
42 Ruth Klüger, *weiter leben: Eine Jugend* (Göttingen, 1992), p. 28; *Betty Scholem – Gershom Scholem*, p. 449; von der Lühe, p. 161; Kaplan, *Between Dignity and Despair*, pp. 89, 91; Merith Niehuss, 'Eheschließung im Nationalsozialismus', in Gerhard (ed.), p. 864.
43 Christiane Kohl, *Der Jude und das Mädchen: Eine verbotene Freundschaft in Nazideutschland* (Hamburg, 1997), pp. 54, 256, 260, 318, 320, 327f., 345; Friedländer, pp. 159f.; Bock, *Zwangssterilisation*, pp. 397f.
44 Quack, p. 45.
45 Richarz (ed.), *Jüdisches Leben*, vol. 3, p. 237; Kaplan, *Between Dignity and Despair*, pp. 63, 66; Irmela von der Lühe, '"Und der Mann war oft eine schwere, undankbare Last": Frauen im Exil – Frauen in der Exilforschung', *Exilforschung* 14 (1996), p. 48; Koerner, 'Central Park West', in Benz (ed.), p. 227; Quack, pp. 118ff.; Quack (ed.), p. 9.
46 Friedländer, p. 318; Kaplan, *Between Dignity and Despair*, p. 181; Richarz (ed.), *Jüdisches Leben*, vol. 3, pp. 385, 399; Bock, *Zwangssterilisation*, p. 360.
47 Myrna Rosenberg, 'Different Horrors, Same Hell', in *Thinking the Unthinkable: Human Meanings of the Holocaust*, ed. Roger Gottlieb (New York, 1990), pp. 150–66.
48 Summerfield, pp. 40, 29; Schupetta, pp. 147, 56, 74, 72; Eck, 'French Women', pp. 209–13; Tilla Siegel, *Leistung und Lohn in der nationalsozialistischen 'Ordnung der Arbeit'* (Opladen, 1989), pp. 170–4.
49 Gudrun Schwarz, 'Frauen in der SS', in Heinsohn et al. (eds), pp. 231, 236, 238; Schwarz, 'Frauen in Konzentrationslagern: Täterinnen und Zuschauerinnen', in Herbert et al. (eds), pp. 800–21; Robert G. Moeller, *Protecting Motherhood: Women and the Family in the Politics of Postwar West Germany* (Los Angeles, 1993), pp. 142–5.
50 Eck, 'French Women', pp. 209–13; US Strategic Bombing Survey (Washington, DC, 1945), pp. 204–7.
51 Schwarz, *Eine Frau an seiner Seite*, p. 106; Herbert, pp. 272, 297; Schupetta, pp. 95f., 100.
52 Bradley F. Smith and Agnes F. Peterson (eds), *Heinrich Himmler: Geheimreden 1933–1945 und andere Ansprachen* (Frankfurt a. M., 1974), p. 98; de Grazia, *Fascism*, p. 44.

53 Corbin, pp. 345–6; Christa Paul, *Zwangsprostitution: Staatlich errichtete Bordelle im Nationalsozialismus* (Berlin, 1994).

54 Dietrich Eichholtz and Wolfgang Schumann, *Anatomie des Krieges* (Berlin, 1969), p. 402; Institut für Zeitgeschichte (Munich): MA 304/2590812–4 (Himmler, 5 March 1943).

55 Herbert, pp. 124–9, 203; Bundesarchiv (German Federal Archives): R 1501 (alt 18)/3002 (31 May 1943).

56 Bundesarchiv (German Federal Archives): NS 19/1913 (Himmler, 30 June 1942).

57 Sereny, pp. 361f., 200, 209, 45, 137, 170f., 205; Schwarz, *Eine Frau an seiner Seite*, pp. 187, 112–19, 188f.

58 Kaplan, *Between Dignity and Despair*, pp. 140, 143; Rosetta Loy, *La parola ebreo* (Turin, 1997), pp. 139, 142; Klaus Voigt, *Zuflucht auf Widerruf: Exil in Italien 1933–1945*, vol. 2 (Stuttgart, 1993), p. 245; Poznanski, pp. 316–19; Ofer and Weitzman (eds), p. 5; Richarz (ed.), *Jüdisches Leben*, vol. 3, p. 61; Raul Hilberg, *Perpetrators, Victims, Bystanders: The Jewish Catastrophe 1933–1945* (New York, 1992), ch. 11.

59 H. G. Adler, *Der verwaltete Mensch: Studien zur Deportation der Juden aus Deutschland* (Tübingen, 1974), pp. 63f.

60 I would like to thank Eva and Michael Werner for this letter. Henry Friedlander, *The Origins of Nazi Genocide: From Euthanasia to the Final Solution* (Chapel Hill, NC, 1995), ch. 13.

61 Gisela Bock, 'Gleichheit und Differenz in der nationalsozialistischen Rassenpolitik', *Geschichte und Gesellschaft* 19 (1993), pp. 300f.

62 Lucie Adelsberger, *Auschwitz: A Doctor's Story*, trans. Susan Ray (Boston, 1995), p. 100; originally published in German as *Auschwitz: Ein Tatsachenbericht* (Berlin, 1953).

63 Smith and Peterson (eds), pp. 169, 204, 201; Primo Levi, *If This is a Man*, trans. Stuart Woolf (New York, 1959), originally published in Italian as *Se questo è un uomo* (Turin, 1947).

64 Poznanski, pp. 288f., 304, 311f., 321–3.

65 Ibid., pp. 356–62, 390ff., 473–80, 504, 528, 555–65, 571–3, 582.

66 Sereny, p. 234; Sybil Oldfield, 'German Women in the Resistance to Hitler', in *Women, State and Revolution*, ed. Sian Reynolds (Amherst, MA, 1987), p. 95; Poznanski, pp. 454f.

67 Bock, 'Ganz normale Frauen', pp. 252f.

68 Antonia Bruha, *Ich war keine Heldin* (Vienna, 1984), p. 92; Lucia Schmidt-Fels, *Deportiert nach Ravensbrück* (Düsseldorf, 1981), p. 41; Judith Magyar Isaacson, *Seed of Sarah: Memoirs of a Survivor* (Chicago, 1990), p. 77; Levi, p. 16; Arendt, p. 445; Arendt, 'The Image of Hell', *Commentary* 2 (1946), pp. 291–5. My thanks to Irith Knebel for one of the descriptions of 'hell' from her oral history project.

69 Bosch and Kloosterman, pp. 219, 264; Voigt, p. 384; Gabriele Pfingsten and Claus Füllberg-Stolberg, 'Frauen in Konzentrationslagern: Geschlechtsspezifische Bedingungen des Überlebens', in Herbert et al. (eds), pp. 911–38.

6 Civil, Political and Social Rights: A New Gender Debate

1 Johannes Morsink, *The Universal Declaration of Human Rights: Origins, Drafting, and Intent* (Philadelphia, PA, 1999), pp. 116–29.
2 Hermann-Josef Rupieper, '"Bringing Democracy to the Frauleins": Frauen als Zielgruppe der amerikanischen Demokratisierungspolitik in Deutschland 1945–1952', *Geschichte und Gesellschaft* 17 (1991), pp. 61, 70.
3 Mariette Sineau, 'Law and Democracy', in Duby and Perrot (eds), vol. 5, p. 510.
4 Yasmine Ergas, 'Feminism of the 1970s', in Duby and Perrot (eds), vol. 5, p. 544; Ribero, pp. 277–80.
5 Sineau, 'Law and Democracy', p. 518; Viktoria Schmidt-Linsenhoff (ed.), *Sklavin oder Bürgerin? Französische Revolution und neue Weiblichkeit 1760–1830* (Frankfurt a. M., 1989), p. 9.
6 Dominique Fougeyrollas-Schwebel, 'Le Féminisme des années 1970', in Fauré (ed.), p. 731.
7 Marcelle Marini, 'The Creators of Culture in France', in Duby and Perrot (eds), vol. 5, p. 314.
8 Ann Snitow, 'A Gender Diary', in Hirsch and Keller (eds), p. 33.
9 Bell Hooks, 'Feminism: A Movement to End Sexist Oppression', in Phillips (ed.), p. 62; Margaret Wright, 'I Want the Right to be Black and Me' (1970), in *Black Women in White America*, ed. Gerda Lerner (New York, 1973), p. 608; Ergas, 'Feminism of the 1970s', p. 539.
10 Marjan Schwegman and Jolande Withuis, 'Moederschap: van springplank tot obstakel. Vrouwen, natie en burgerschap in twintigste-eeuws Nederland', in *Geschiedenis van de vrouw*, ed. Georges Duby and Michelle Perrot, vol. 5 (Amsterdam, 1993), pp. 557–83. (This article appears only in the Dutch edition of Duby and Perrot.)
11 'Sex, Society, and the Female Dilemma: A Dialogue between Simone de Beauvoir and Betty Friedan', *Saturday Review* (14 June 1975), pp. 14–16, 56.
12 Helge Pross, *Die Wirklichkeit der Hausfrau* (Reinbek, 1975), pp. 17, 131, 197f., 200–19, 237–9, 243–52.
13 Juliet Mitchell, 'Women: The Longest Revolution', *New Left Review* 40 (1966), pp. 11–37.
14 Ilona Ostner, 'Slow Motion: Women, Work and the Family in Germany', in Lewis (ed.), p. 115; Christine von Oertzen and Almut Rietzschel, 'Comparing the Post-war Germanies: Breadwinner Ideology and Women's Employment in the Divided Nation, 1948–1970', *International Review of Social History*, Supplement 5 (1997), pp. 175–96.
15 Dieter Schwab, 'Gleichberechtigung und Familienrecht im 20. Jahrhundert', in Gerhard (ed.), p. 809.
16 Simone Veil, in *Journal Officiel. Débats*, 18–19 May 1976, pp. 3211, 3142, 3145f.
17 Roberto Zapperi, *L'uomo incinto* (Rome, 1979); Elisabeth Badinter, *L'Un est l'autre: Des relations entre hommes et femmes* (Paris, 1986), pp. 343–7; Hippel, p. 71.

18 Schwab, 'Gleichberechtigung', pp. 817–25.
19 Ditch et al., pp. 60f.
20 Ibid., p. VII.
21 Elizabeth Meehan, 'Women's Rights in the European Community', in Lewis (ed.), pp. 194–205; Christine Pintat, 'Les Femmes dans les Parlements et dans les partis politiques en Europe et en Amérique du Nord', in Fauré (ed.), pp. 793–824; Giovanna Procacci and Maria Grazia Rossilli, 'La construction de l'égalité dans l'action des organisations internationales', in Fauré (ed.), pp. 827–60; Berkovitch.
22 Ditch et al.; Nadine Lefaucheur, 'Maternity, Family, and the State', in Duby and Perrot (eds), vol. 5, pp. 433–52.
23 Simon Duncan, 'The Diverse Worlds of European Patriarchy', in Garcio-Ramon et al. (eds), pp. 74–110.
24 Neubauer et al., p. 332.
25 Jan Lewis, 'Happiness', in *Blackwell Encyclopedia of the American Revolution* (Cambridge, MA, 1991), pp. 641–7.
26 Smith; Karen Offen, 'Women's Memory, Women's History, Women's Political Action: The French Revolution in Retrospect, 1789–1889–1989', *Journal of Women's History* 1 (1990), pp. 211–30.
27 Lloyd, pp. 28–37, 107f.; Maclean, *The Renaissance Notion of Woman*, p. 43; Keller, p. 62; William Wotton, *Reflections upon Ancient and Modern Learning* (reprint Hildesheim, 1968), p. 350; Harth, pp. 3, 8, 81, 116, 121, 159, 162.
28 Lerner, p. 166.
29 Ute Frevert, 'Männergeschichte oder die Suche nach dem "ersten" Geschlecht', in *Was ist Gesellschaftsgeschichte?*, ed. Manfred Hettling (Munich, 1991), pp. 31–43; Christiane Eifert et al. (eds), *Was sind Frauen? Was sind Männer? Geschlechterkonstruktionen im historischen Wandel* (Frankfurt a. M., 1996); John Tosh, 'What Should Historians Do with Masculinity?', *History Workshop Journal* 38 (1994), pp. 179–202.
30 Denise Riley, *'Am I That Name?' Feminism and the Category of 'Women' in History* (London, 1988), p. 1; see above p. 111.
31 John Alcock, *Animal Behavior: An Evolutionary Approach* (Sunderland, MA, 1989), ch. 16.
32 Scott, *Gender and the Politics of History*, p. 42.
33 Clifford Kirkpatrick, *Woman in Nazi Germany* (London, 1939), pp. 33f., 160.
34 Arendt, p. 443.
35 Susan Moller Okin, 'Konflikte zwischen Grundrechten: Frauenrechte und die Probleme religiöser und kultureller Unterschiede', in *Philosophie der Menschenrechte*, ed. Stefan Gosepath and Georg Lohmann (Frankfurt a. M., 1998), pp. 310–42.

Bibliography

This book owes much to many people, friends and other scholars, close or distant. They are too numerous to mention individually here, but their names appear in the bibliography and the notes. I am also greatly indebted to the Wissenschaftskolleg zu Berlin, which allowed me to lay the groundwork for the book in the year 1995–6. The German original was published in 2000.

European, International, Comparative

Akkerman, Tjitske and Stuurman, Siep (eds), *Perspectives on Feminist Political Thought in European History: From the Middle Ages to the Present* (London, 1998).

Anderson, Bonnie S. and Zinsser, Judith P., *A History of Their Own: Women in Europe from Prehistory to the Present*, 2 vols (New York, 1988).

Andreasen, Tayo et al. (eds), *Moving On: New Perspectives on the Women's Movement* (Aarhus, 1991).

Applewhite, Harriet B. and Levy, Darline G. (eds), *Women and Politics in the Age of the Democratic Revolution* (Ann Arbor, MI, 1990).

Arendt, Hannah, *Elemente und Ursprünge totaler Herrschaft* (1955) (Munich, 1986); *Origins of Totalitarianism* (Cleveland and New York, 1966).

Bacchi, Carol Lee, *Same Difference: Feminism and Sexual Difference* (St Leonards, Australia, 1990).

Bader-Zaar, Birgitta, *Das Frauenwahlrecht: Vergleichende Aspekte seiner Geschichte in Großbritannien, den Vereinigten Staaten, Österreich, Deutschland und Belgien 1860–1920* (Vienna, 2001).

Bell, Susan Groag and Offen, Karen M. (eds), *Women, the Family and Freedom: The Debate in Documents, 1750–1950*, 2 vols (Stanford, CA, 1983).

Benson, Pamela J., *The Invention of the Renaissance Woman: The Challenge of Female Independence in the Literature and Thought of Italy and England* (University Park, PA, 1992).

Benz, Wolfgang (ed.), *Das Exil der kleinen Leute: Alltagserfahrung deutscher Juden in der Emigration* (Munich, 1991).

Berkovitch, Nitza, *From Motherhood to Citizenship: Women's Rights and International Organizations* (Baltimore, MD, 1999).

Blom, Ida (ed.), *Cappelens Kvinnehistorie*, 3 vols (Oslo, 1992–3).

Bock, Gisela, 'Frauenwahlrecht: Deutschland um 1900 in vergleichender Perspektive', in *Geschichte und Emanzipation: Festschrift für Reinhard Rürup*, ed. Michael Grüttner et al. (Frankfurt a. M., 1999), pp. 95–136.

Bock, Gisela and Thane, Pat (eds), *Maternity and Gender Policies: Women and the Rise of the European Welfare States, 1880s-1950s* (London, 1991).

Bock, Gisela and Zimmermann, Margarete (eds), *Die europäische Querelle des Femmes: Geschlechterdebatten seit dem 15. Jahrhundert* (= Quer*elles*. Jahrbuch für Frauenforschung, vol. 2) (Stuttgart, 1997).

Bosch, Mineke and Kloosterman, Annemarie, *Politics and Friendship: Letters from the International Woman Suffrage Alliance, 1902–1942* (Columbus, OH, 1990).

Calame, André and Fiedler, Maria, *Maßnahmen zugunsten einer besseren Vereinbarkeit von Familie und Beruf: Erfahrungen aus der DDR, Frankreich, Großbritannien und Schweden sowie Empfehlungen für die BRD* (Berlin, 1982).

Daley, Caroline and Nolan, Melanie (eds), *Suffrage and Beyond: International Feminist Perspectives* (New York, 1994).

Davis, Natalie Zemon, *Women on the Margins: Three Seventeenth-century Lives* (Cambridge, MA, 1995).

Ditch, J., Bradshaw, J. and Barnes, H. (European Commission Observatory on Family Policy), *A Synthesis of National Family Policies 1996*, also in French and German (Brussels, 1998).

Duby, Georges and Perrot, Michelle (eds), *A History of Women in the West*, 5 vols, ed. vol. 1: Pauline Schmitt-Pantel, vol. 2: Christiane Klapisch-Zuber, vol. 3: Arlette Farge and Natalie Zemon Davis, vol. 4: Geneviève Fraisse and Michelle Perrot, vol. 5: Françoise Thébaud; trans. Arthur Goldhammer, Clarissa Botsford, Deborah Lucas Schneider (Cambridge, MA, 1992–4).

Dwork, Deborah, *Children with a Star: Jewish Youth in Nazi Europe, 1933–1945* (New Haven, CT, 1991).

Enfance abandonnée et société en Europe XIVe–XXe siècle (Rome, 1991).

Fauré, Christine (ed.), *Encyclopédie politique et historique des femmes: Europe, Amérique du Nord* (Paris 1997); forthcoming in English: *Political and Historical Encyclopedia of Women* (London and Chicago, 2001).

Garcio-Ramon, Maria Dolors and Monk, Janice (eds), *Women of the European Union* (London, 1996).

Gardiner, Frances (ed.), *Sex Equality Policy in Western Europe* (London, 1997).

Gerhard, Ute (ed.), *Frauen in der Geschichte des Rechts* (Munich, 1997).

Hellerstein, Erna Olafson et al. (eds), *Victorian Women: A Documentary Account of Women's Lives in 19th-century England, France, and the United States* (Stanford, CA, 1981).

Helsinger, Elizabeth K. et al., *The Woman Question: Society and Literature in Britain and America, 1837–1883*, 3 vols (Chicago, 1983).

Higonnet, Margaret R. et al. (eds), *Behind the Lines: Gender and the Two World Wars* (New Haven, CT, 1987).

Hufton, Olwen, *The Prospect Before Her: A History of Women in Western Europe*, vol. 1: *1500–1800* (Cambridge, MA, 1995).

Jordan, Constance, *Renaissance Feminism* (Ithaca, NY, 1990).

Jost, Hans-Ulrich et al. (eds), *La Politique des droits: Citoyenneté et construction des genres aux 19e et 20e siècles* (Paris, 1994).

Klapisch-Zuber, Christiane, 'Les Femmes et la famille', in *L'Homme médiéval*, ed. Jacques Le Goff (Paris, 1989).

Kolbe, Wiebke, *Wie aus Müttern Eltern wurden: Konstruktionen von Mutter-, Vater- und Elternschaft in der wohlfahrtsstaatlichen Politik Schwedens und der Bundesrepublik Deutschland 1945–1995* (Frankfurt a. M., forthcoming 2002).

Kulawik, Teresa, *Wohlfahrtsstaat und Mutterschaft: Schweden und Deutschland 1870–1912* (Frankfurt a. M., 1999).

Kuzmack, Linda Gordon, *Woman's Cause: The Jewish Woman's Movement in England and the United States, 1881–1933* (Columbus, OH, 1990).

Labalme, Patricia H. (ed.), *Beyond Their Sex: Learned Women of the European Past* (New York, 1980).

Lerner, Gerda, *The Creation of Feminist Consciousness: From the Middle Ages to Eighteen-seventy* (New York, 1993).

Lewis, Jane (ed.), *Women and Social Policies in Europe* (Aldershot, 1993).

Lloyd, Geneviève, *The Man of Reason: 'Male' and 'Female' in Western Philosophy* (London, 1993).

Maclean, Ian, *The Renaissance Notion of Woman* (Cambridge, 1980).

Maruani, Margaret and Nicole-Drancourt, Chantal (eds), *La Flexibilité à temps partiel* (Paris, 1989).

Melhuish, Edward C. and Moss, Peter, *Day Care for Young Children: International Perspectives* (London, 1991).

Neubauer, Erika et al., *Zwölf Wege der Familienpolitik in der Europäischen Gemeinschaft* (Schriftenreihe des Bundesministeriums für Familie und Senioren, vol. 22.2) (Stuttgart, 1993).

OECD (Organization for Economic Cooperation and Development) (ed.), *Labour Force Statistics 1973–1993* (Paris, 1995).

Ofer, Dalia and Weitzman, Lenore J. (eds), *Women in the Holocaust* (New Haven, CT, 1998).

Offen, Karen et al. (eds), *Writing Women's History: International Perspectives* (Bloomington, IN, 1991).

Paletschek, Sylvia and Pietrow-Ennker, Bianka (eds), *The European Women's Emancipation Movements in the 19th Century: A Comparative Perspective* (Stanford, CA, forthcoming 2002).

Pedersen, Susan, *Family, Dependence, and the Origins of the Welfare State: Britain and France, 1914–1945* (Cambridge, 1993).

Quack, Sibylle, *Zuflucht Amerika: Zur Sozialgeschichte der Emigration deutsch-jüdischer Frauen in die USA 1933–1945* (Bonn, 1995).

Quack, Sibylle (ed.), *Between Sorrow and Strength: Women Refugees of the Nazi Period* (Cambridge, 1995).

Rendall, Jane, *The Origins of Modern Feminism: Women in Britain, France and the United States, 1780–1860* (Houndmills, 1985).

Rupp, Leila, *Worlds of Women: The Making of an International Women's Move-

ment (Princeton, NJ, 1997).

Sangolt, Linda, 'To Count or Not to Count: Increasing the Visibility of Household Labour in National Accounting', *Nora: Nordic Journal of Women's Studies* 7/1 (1999), pp. 63–77.

Schiebinger, Londa, *The Mind Has No Sex? Women in the Origins of Modern Science* (Cambridge, MA, 1989).

Schnell, Rüdiger, *Frauendiskurs, Männerdiskurs, Ehediskurs: Textsorten und Geschlechterkonzepte in Mittelalter und Früher Neuzeit* (Frankfurt a. M., 1998).

Scott, Joan W., *Gender and the Politics of History* (New York, 1988).

Smith, Bonnie G., *The Gender of History: Men, Women, and Historical Practice* (Cambridge, MA, 1998).

Torstendahl, Rolf (ed.), *State Policy and Gender System in the two German States and Sweden 1945–1989* (Uppsala, 1999).

Veauvy, Christiane and Pisano, Laura, *Paroles oubliées: Les femmes et la construction de État-nation en France et en Italie (1789–1860)* (Paris, 1995).

Wiesner, Merry E., *Women and Gender in Early Modern Europe* (Cambridge, 1993).

Wikander, Ulla et al. (eds), *Protecting Women: Labor Legislation in Europe, the United States, and Australia, 1880–1920* (Urbana, IL, 1995).

Yuval-Davis, Nira, *Gender and Nation* (London, 1997).

Other Works

Abrams, Lynn and Harvey, Elizabeth (eds), *Gender Relations in German History* (London, 1997).

Anderson, Harriet, *Utopian Feminism: Women's Movements in Fin-de-Siècle Vienna* (New Haven, CT, 1992).

Albistur, Maïté and Armogathe, Daniel, *Histoire du féminisme français*, 2 vols (Paris, 1977).

Allen, Ann Taylor, *Feminism and Motherhood in Germany, 1800–1914* (New Brunswick, NJ, 1991).

Avdela, Efi, 'Between Duties and Rights: Gender and Citizenship in Greece, 1864–1952', *Journal of Greco-Turkish Studies in Society and History* 1 (2001).

Bard, Christine, *Les Filles de Marianne: Histoire des féminismes 1914–1940* (Paris, 1995).

Blanc, Olivier, *Olympe de Gouges* (Paris, 1981).

Bloch, R. Howard, *Medieval Misogyny and the Invention of Western Romantic Love* (Chicago, 1991).

Blom, Ida, 'Nation – Class – Gender: Scandinavia at the Turn of the Century', *Scandinavian Journal of History* 21 (1996), pp. 1–16.

Bock, Gisela, *Zwangssterilisation im Nationalsozialismus* (Opladen, 1986).

Bock, Petra and Koblitz, Katja (eds), *Neue Frauen zwischen den Zeiten* (Berlin, 1995).

Bonacchi, Gabriella and Groppi, Angela (eds), *Il dilemma della cittadinanza: Diritti e doveri delle donne* (Bari, 1993).

Bosch, Mineke, *Het geslacht van de wetenschap: Vrouwen en hoger onderwijs in Nederland 1878–1948* (Amsterdam, 1994).

Braun, Marianne, *De prijs van de liefde: De eerste feministische golf het huwelijksrecht en de vaderlandse geschiedenis* (Amsterdam, 1992).

Bubenik-Bauer, Iris and Schalz-Laurenze, Ute (eds), '. . . ihr werten Frauenzimmer, auf!' *Frauen in der Aufklärung* (Frankfurt a. M., 1995).

Budde, Gunilla-Friederike (ed.), *Frauen arbeiten: Weibliche Erwerbstätigkeit in Ost- und Westdeutschland nach 1945* (Göttingen, 1997).

Buttafuoco, Annarita, *Cronache femminili* (Arezzo, 1988).

Buttafuoco, Annarita, *Le Mariuccine. Storia di un'istituzione laica: L'Asilo Mariuccia* (Milan, 1985).

Buttafuoco, Annarita, *Questioni di cittadinanza: Donne e diritti sociali nell'Italia liberale* (Siena, 1997).

Calvi, Giulia (ed.), *Barocco al femminile* (Bari and Rome, 1992).

Canning, Kathleen, *Languages of Labor and Gender: Female Factory Work in Germany, 1850–1914* (Ithaca, NY, 1996).

Ceranski, Beate, '*Und sie fürchtet sich vor niemandem*': *Die Physikerin Laura Bassi (1711–1778)* (Frankfurt a. M., 1996).

Clark, Anna, *The Struggle for the Breeches: Gender and the Making of the British Working Class* (Berkeley, CA, 1995).

Clements, Barbara Evans, *Daughters of Revolution: A History of Women in the USSR* (Arlington Heights, IL, 1994).

Conrad, Anne, *Zwischen Kloster und Welt: Ursulinen und Jesuitinnen in der katholischen Reformbewegung des 16. und 17. Jahrhunderts* (Mainz, 1991).

Corbin, Alain, *Women for Hire: Prostitution and Sexuality in France after 1950*, trans. Alan Sheridan (Cambridge, MA, 1990); originally published in French as *Les filles de noce: Misère sexuelle et prostitution aux 19e et 20e siècles* (Paris, 1978).

Corbin, Alain et al. (eds), *Femmes dans la Cité 1815–1871* (Grâne, 1997).

Cori, Paola di, 'Culture del femminismo: Il caso della storia delle donne', in *Storia dell'Italia repubblicana*, vol. III-2 (Turin, 1997), pp. 802–61.

Cova, Anne, *Maternité et droits des femmes en France (XIXe–XXe siècles)* (Paris, 1997).

Crispino, Anna Maria (ed.), *Esperienza storica femminile nell'età moderna e contemporanea* (Rome, 1988).

Daskalova, Krassimira, 'Bulgarian Women in Movements, Laws, Discourses (1840s-1940s)', *Bulgarian Historical Review* 1–2 (1999), pp. 184–200.

Davidoff, Leonore and Hall, Catherine, *Family Fortunes: Men and Women of the English Middle Class 1780–1850* (London, 1987).

De Giorgio, Michela, *Le Italiane dall'Unità ad oggi* (Rome and Bari, 1992).

De Giorgio, Michela and Klapisch-Zuber, Christiane (eds), *Storia del matrimonio* (Bari, 1996).

Dekker, Rudolf Michel, 'Women in the Medieval and Early Modern Netherlands', *Journal of Women's History* 10 (1998), pp. 165–88.

Desan, Suzanne, *Reclaiming the Sacred: Lay Religion and Popular Politics in Revolutionary France* (Ithaca, NY, 1990).

Dick, Jutta and Hahn, Barbara (eds), *Von einer Welt in die andere: Jüdinnen im*

19. und 20. Jahrhundert (Vienna, 1993).

Dubosc, Danielle Haase and Viennot, Eliane (eds), *Femmes et pouvoirs sous l'Ancien Régime* (Paris, 1991).

Duchen, Claire, *Women's Rights and Women's Lives in France 1944–1968* (London, 1994).

Edmondson, Linda Harriet, *Feminism in Russia 1900–1917* (London, 1984).

Edmondson, Linda (ed.), *Women and Society in Russia and the Soviet Union* (Cambridge, 1992).

Elshtain, Jean B. (ed.), *The Family in Political Thought* (Brighton, 1982).

Enders, Lorée et al. (eds), *Constructing Spanish Womanhood: Female Identity in Modern Spain* (New York, 1999).

Esteves, João, *As origens do sufragismo português: A primeira organização sufragista portuguesa* (Lisbon, 1998).

Fagoaga, Concha, *La voz y el voto de las mujeres: El sufragismo en España 1877–1931* (Barcelona, 1985).

Faßmann, Irmgard Maya, *Jüdinnen in der deutschen Frauenbewegung 1865–1919* (Hildesheim, 1996).

Fayet-Scribe, Sylvie, *Associations féminines et catholicisme: De la charité à l'action sociale (XIXe–XXe siècles)* (Paris, 1990).

Ferrante, Lucia et al. (eds), *Ragnatele di rapporti: Patronage e reti di relazione nella storia delle donne* (Turin, 1988).

Frevert, Ute (ed.), *Bürgerinnen und Bürger* (Göttingen, 1988).

Frevert, Ute, *'Mann und Weib, und Weib und Mann': Geschlechterdifferenzen in der Moderne* (Munich, 1995).

Friedländer, Saul, *Nazi Germany and the Jews*, vol. 1: *The Years of Persecution, 1933–1939* (New York, 1997).

Frigo, Daniela, *Il Padre di famiglia: Governo della casa e governo civile nella tradizione dell' 'economica' tra cinque e seicento* (Rome, 1985).

Gagliani, Daniella and Salvati, Mariuccia (eds), *La sfera pubblica femminile* (Bologna, 1992).

Gilfoyle, Timothy J., 'Prostitutes in History: From Parables of Pornography to Metaphors of Modernity', *American Historical Review* 104 (1999), pp. 117–41.

Godineau, Dominique, 'Autour du mot *citoyenne*', *Mots* 16 (1988), pp. 91–110.

Godineau, Dominique, *The Women of Paris and their French Revolution*, trans. Katherine Streip (Berkeley, CA, 1998); originally published in French as *Citoyennes tricoteuses: Les femmes du peuple pendant la Révolution française* (Aix-en-Provence, 1988).

Goodman, Dena, *The Republic of Letters: A Cultural History of the French Enlightenment* (Ithaca, NY, 1994).

Gorjão, Vanda, *A reivindicação do voto no programa do Conselho Nacional das Mulheres Portuguesas (1914–1947)* (Lisbon, 1994).

Grazia, Victoria de, *How Fascism Ruled Women: Italy, 1922–1945* (Berkeley, CA, 1992).

Haan, Francisca de, *Gender and the Politics of Office Work: The Netherlands, 1860–1940* (Amsterdam, 1998).

Habermas, Rebekka, *Frauen und Männer des Bürgertums: Eine Familiengeschichte, 1750–1850* (Göttingen, 1999).

Hahn, Barbara (ed.), *Frauen in den Kulturwissenschaften* (Munich, 1994).

Hanley, Sarah, 'Social Sites of Political Practice in France: Lawsuits, Civil Rights, and the Separation of Powers in Domestic and State Government, 1500–1800', *American Historical Review* 102 (1997), pp. 27–52.

Hardach-Pinke, Irene, *Die Gouvernante: Geschichte eines Frauenberufs* (Frankfurt a. M., 1993).

Hardmeier, Sybille, *Die frühe Frauenstimmrechtsbewegung in der Schweiz (1890–1930)* (Zürich, 1997).

Harrington, Joel F., *Reordering Marriage and Society in Reformation Germany* (Cambridge, 1985).

Harrison, Brian, *Separate Spheres: The Opposition to Women's Suffrage in Britain* (London, 1978).

Harth, Erica, *Cartesian Women: Versions and Subversions of Rational Discourse in the Old Regime* (Ithaca, NY, 1992).

Hause, Steven C. and Kenney, Anne R., *Women's Suffrage and Social Politics in the French Third Republic* (Princeton, NJ, 1984).

Hausen, Karin and Wunder, Heide (eds), *Frauengeschichte – Geschlechtergeschichte* (Frankfurt a. M., 1992).

Heinsohn, Kirsten et al. (eds), *Zwischen Karriere und Verfolgung: Handlungsräume von Frauen im nationalsozialistischen Deutschland* (Frankfurt a. M., 1997).

Henderson, Katherine U. and McManus, Barbara F. (eds), *Half Humankind: Contexts and Texts of the Controversy about Women in England, 1540–1640* (Urbana, IL, 1985).

Herbert, Ulrich, *Fremdarbeiter: Politik und Praxis des 'Ausländer-Einsatzes' in der Kriegswirtschaft des Dritten Reiches* (Berlin, 1985).

Herbert, Ulrich et al. (eds), *Die nationalsozialistischen Konzentrationslager*, 2 vols (Göttingen, 1998).

Hernes, Helga Maria, *Welfare State and Woman Power: Essays in State Feminism* (Oslo, 1987).

Hippel, Theodor Gottlieb von, *On Improving the Status of Women*, trans. and ed. Timothy F. Sellner (Detroit, 1979); facs. of the original edition (1792): *Über die bürgerliche Verbesserung der Weiber*, ed. Juliane Jacobi-Dittrich (Vaduz, 1981).

Hirsch, Marianne and Keller, Evelyn Fox (eds), *Conflicts in Feminism* (New York and London, 1990).

Holton, Sandra Stanley, *Feminism and Democracy: Women's Suffrage and Reform Politics in Britain 1900–1918* (Cambridge, 1986).

Holton, Sandra Stanley, *Suffrage Days: Stories from the Women's Suffrage Movement* (London, 1996).

Honegger, Claudia, *Die Ordnung der Geschlechter* (Frankfurt a. M., 1991).

Honegger, Claudia and Wobbe, Theresa (eds), *Frauen in der Soziologie: Neun Porträts* (Munich, 1998).

Huerkamp, Claudia, *Bildungsbürgerinnen: Frauen im Studium und in akademischen Berufen 1900–1945* (Göttingen, 1996).

Hufton, Olwen, *Women and the Limits of Citizenship in the French Revolution* (Toronto, 1992).

Hunecke, Volker, *Die Findelkinder von Mailand: Kindsaussetzung und aussetzende Eltern vom 17. bis zum 19. Jahrhundert* (Stuttgart, 1987).

Hunt, Lynn, *The Family Romance of the French Revolution* (London, 1992).

Jaworski, Rudolf and Pietrow-Ennker, Bianka (eds), *Women in Polish Society* (New York, 1992).

John, Angela V. and Eustance, Claire (eds), *The Men's Share? Masculinities, Male Support and Women's Suffrage in Britain, 1890–1920* (London, 1997).

Kaplan, Marion A., *Between Dignity and Despair: Jewish Life in Nazi Germany* (New York, 1998).

Kaplan, Marion A., *The Making of the Jewish Middle Class: Women, Family, and Identity in Imperial Germany* (New York, 1991).

Kaplan, Marion A., *The Jewish Feminist Movement in Germany: The Campaigns of the Jüdischer Frauenbund, 1904–1938* (Westport, CT, 1979).

Keller, Evelyn Fox, *Reflections on Gender and Science* (New Haven, CT, 1985).

Kemlein, Sophia (ed.), *Geschlecht und Nationalismus in Mittel- und Osteuropa 1848–1918* (Osnabrück, 2000).

Klapisch-Zuber, Christiane, *La Maison et le nom: Stratégies et rituels dans l'Italie de la Renaissance* (Paris, 1990).

Klejman, Laurence and Rochefort, Florence, *L'Égalité en marche: Le féminisme sous la Troisième République* (Paris, 1989).

Kundrus, Birthe, *Kriegerfrauen: Familienpolitik und Geschlechterverhältnisse im Ersten und Zweiten Weltkrieg* (Hamburg, 1995).

Ladd-Taylor, Molly, *Mother-Work: Woman, Child Welfare, and the State, 1890–1930* (Urbana, IL, 1995).

Lejeune-Resnick, Evelyne, *Femmes et Associations (1830/1880): Vraies démocrates ou dames patronesses?* (Paris, 1991).

Leo, Mimma de and Taricone, Fiorenza, *Le donne in Italia: Diritti civili e politici* (Naples, 1992).

Liljeström, Marianne et al. (eds), *Gender Restructuring in Russian Studies* (Tampere, Finland, 1993).

Lipp, Carola (ed.), *Schimpfende Weiber und patriotische Jungfrauen: Frauen im Vormärz und in der Revolution 1848/49* (Moos, 1986).

Lühe, Irmela von der, *Erika Mann: Eine Biographie* (Frankfurt a. M., 1993).

Lown, Judy, *Women and Industrialization: Gender at Work in Nineteenth-century England* (Cambridge, 1990).

Maclean, Ian, *Woman Triumphant: Feminism in French Literature 1610–1652* (Oxford, 1977).

Manninen, Merja and Setälä, Päivi (eds), *The Lady with the Bow: The Story of Finnish Women* (Helsinki, 1990).

Matthews Grieco, Sara F., *Ange ou Diablesse: La représentation de la femme au XVIe siècle* (Paris, 1991).

Maura, Juan Francisco, *Women in the Conquest of the Americas* (New York, 1997).

Meiwes, Relinde, *'Arbeiterinnen des Herrn': Katholische Frauenkongregationen in Preußen im 19. Jahrhundert* (Frankfurt a. M., 2000).

Melman, Billie, *Women and the Popular Imagination: Flappers and Nymphs* (London, 1988).

Mesmer, Beatrix, *Ausgeklammert – eingeklammert: Frauen und Frauen- organisationen in der Schweiz des 19. Jahrhunderts* (Basel, 1988).

Meyer, Sibylle, *Das Theater mit der Hausarbeit: Bürgerliche Repräsentation in der Familie der wilhelminischen Zeit* (Frankfurt a. M., 1982).

Midgley, Clare, *Women Against Slavery: The British Campaigns 1780–1870* (London, 1992).

Midgley, Clare (ed.), *Gender and Imperialism* (Manchester, 1998).

Mill, John Stuart, *Collected Works*, ed. John M. Robson, 33 vols (Toronto, 1981–91).

Mill, John Stuart and Mill, Harriet Taylor, *Essays on Sex Equality*, ed. Alice S. Rossi (Chicago, 1970).

Moses, Claire Goldberg, *French Feminism in the Nineteenth Century* (New York, 1984).

Moses, Claire Goldberg and Rabine, Leslie Wahl, *Feminism, Socialism, and French Romanticism* (Bloomington, IN, 1993).

Müller, Maria E. (ed.), *Eheglück und Liebesjoch: Bilder von Liebe, Ehe und Familie in der Literatur des 15. und 16. Jahrhunderts* (Berlin, 1988).

Murphy, Ciona, *The Women's Suffrage Movement and Irish Society in the Early 20th Century* (New York, 1989).

Nash, Mary, *Defying Male Civilization: Women in the Spanish Civil War* (Denver, 1995).

Ozouf, Mona, *Les Mots des femmes: Essai sur la singularité française* (Paris, 1995).

Paletschek, Sylvia, *Frauen und Dissens: Frauen im Deutschkatholizismus und in den freien Gemeinden 1841–1852* (Göttingen, 1990).

Pateman, Carole, *The Sexual Contract* (Oxford, 1988).

Pateman, Carole, *The Disorder of Women: Democracy, Feminism and Political Theory* (Cambridge, 1989).

Petersen, Susanne (ed.), *Marktweiber und Amazonen: Frauen in der Französischen Revolution* (Cologne, 1978).

Peterson, M. Jeanne, 'No Angels in the House: The Victorian Myth and the Paget Women', *American Historical Review* 89 (1984), pp. 677–708.

Phillips, Anne, *Democracy and Difference* (Cambridge, 1993).

Phillips, Anne (ed.), *Feminism and Equality* (New York, 1987).

Pietrow-Ennker, Bianka, *Rußlands 'Neue Menschen': Die Entwicklung der Frauen- bewegung von den Anfängen bis zur Oktoberrevolution* (Frankfurt a. M., 1999).

Pimentel, Irene Flunser, *História das Organizações Femininas no Estado Novo* (Lisbon, 2000).

Planert, Ute, *Antifeminismus im Kaiserreich* (Göttingen, 1998).

Poznanski, Renée, *Les Juifs en France pendant la Seconde Guerre mondiale* (Paris, 1994).

Prochaska, Frank, *Women and Philanthropy in 19th-century England* (Oxford, 1980).

Pugh, Martin, *Women and the Women's Movements in Britain 1914–1959* (Houndmills, 1992).

Purvis, June (ed.), *Women's History: Britain, 1850–1945* (London, 1995).

Pyle, Andrew (ed.), *The Subjection of Women: Contemporary Responses to John*

Stuart Mill (Bristol, 1995).

Rendall, Jane, *Women in an Industrializing Society: England 1750–1880* (Oxford, 1990).

Ribberink, Johanna, *Leidsvrouwen en zaakwaarneemsters: Eeen geschiedenis van de Aktiegroep Man Vrouw Maatschappik (MVM), 1968–1973* (Hilversum, 1998).

Ribero, Aida, *Una questione di libertà: Il femminismo degli anni Settanta* (Turin, 1999).

Richarz, Monika (ed.), *Jüdisches Leben in Deutschland: Selbstzeugnisse zur Sozialgeschichte*, 3 vols (Stuttgart, 1976–82); abridged English edition: *Jewish Life in Germany: Memoirs from Three Centuries*, trans. Stella P. Rosenfeld and Sidney Rosenfeld (Bloomington, IN, 1991).

Richarz, Monika (ed.), *Die Hamburger Kauffrau Glikl: Jüdische Existenz in der Frühen Neuzeit* (Hamburg, 2001).

Riot-Sarcey, Michèle, *La Démocratie à l'épreuve des femmes: Trois figures critiques du pouvoir, 1830–1848* (Paris, 1994).

Roberts, Mary Louise, *Civilization Without Sexes: Reconstructing Gender in Postwar France, 1917–1927* (Chicago, 1994).

Roper, Lyndal, *The Holy Household: Women and Morals in Reformation Augsburg* (Oxford, 1989).

Rosanvallon, Pierre, *Le Sacre du citoyen: Histoire du suffrage universel en France* (Paris, 1992).

Rose, Sonya O., *Limited Livelihoods: Gender and Class in Nineteenth-century England* (London, 1992).

Rossi-Doria, Anna, *Diventare Cittadine: Il voto alle donne in Italia* (Florence, 1996).

Saba, Marina Addis (ed.), *La corporazione delle donne: Ricerche e studi sui modelli femminili nel ventennio* (Florence, 1988).

Sand, George, *Politique et polémiques (1843–1850)*, ed. Michelle Perrot (Paris, 1997).

Scaraffia, Lucetta and Zarri, Gabriella (eds), *Donne e fede: Santità e vita religiosa in Italia* (Bari, 1994).

Schama, Simon, *Citizens: A Chronicle of the French Revolution* (London, 1989).

Schaser, Angelika, *Helene Lange und Gertrud Bäumer: Eine politische Lebensgemeinschaft* (Cologne, 2000).

Schochet, Gordon, *The Authoritarian Family and Political Attitudes in 17th-century England: Patriarchalism in Political Thought* (New Brunswick, NJ, 1988).

Schröder, Iris, *Arbeiten für eine bessere Welt: Frauenbewegung und Sozialreform 1890–1914* (Frankfurt a. M., 2001).

Schultz, Hartwig (ed.), *Salons der Romantik* (Berlin, 1997).

Schupetta, Ingrid, *Frauen- und Ausländererwerbstätigkeit in Deutschland 1933–1945* (Cologne, 1983).

Schwarz, Gudrun, *Eine Frau an seiner Seite: Ehefrauen der 'SS-Sippengemeinschaft'* (Hamburg, 1997).

Scott, Joan W., *'Only Paradoxes to Offer': French Feminists and the Rights of Man* (Cambridge, MA, 1996).

Sereny, Gitta, *Into That Darkness* (New York, 1983).

Bibliography

Shanley, Mary Lyndon and Pateman, Carole (eds), *Feminist Interpretations and Political Theory* (Oxford, 1991).

Smyth, Ailbhe (ed.), *Irish Women's Studies Reader* (Dublin, 1993).

Sohn, Anne-Marie and Thélamon, Françoise (eds), *L'Histoire sans les femmes est-elle possible?* (Rouen, 1998).

Stern, Carola, *Der Text meines Herzens: Das Leben der Rahel Varnhagen* (Reinbek, 1994).

Stetson, Dorothy McBride, *Women's Rights in France* (New York, 1987).

Stites, Richard, *The Women's Liberation Movement in Russia: Feminism, Nihilism, and Bolshevism, 1860–1930* (Princeton, NJ, 1990).

Summerfield, Penny, *Women Workers in the Second World War* (London, 1984).

Taylor, Barbara, *Eve and the New Jerusalem: Socialism and Feminism in the Nineteenth Century* (London, 1983).

Telle, Émile, *L'Œuvre de Marguerite d'Angoulême, Reine de Navarre, et la Querelle des femmes* (Geneva, 1969).

Thane, Pat, *Old Age in English History* (Oxford, 2000).

Thompson, Dorothy, *Queen Victoria: Gender and Power* (London, 1990).

Turner, James Grantham, *One Flesh: Paradisal Marriage and Sexual Relations in the Age of Milton* (Oxford, 1987).

Vellacott, Jo, *From Liberal to Labour with Women's Suffrage: The Story of Catherine Marshall* (Montreal, 1993).

Vickery, Amanda, 'Golden Age to Separate Spheres? A Review of the Categories and Chronology of English Women's History', *Historical Journal* 36 (1993), pp. 383–414.

Viennot, Éliane (ed.), *La Démocratie 'à la française' ou les femmes indésirables* (Paris, 1996).

Voegeli, Yvonne, *Zwischen Hausrat und Rathaus: Auseinandersetzungen um die politische Gleichberechtigung der Frauen in der Schweiz 1945–1971* (Zürich, 1997).

Walkowitz, Judith R., *Prostitution and Victorian Society* (Cambridge, MA, 1980).

Willms, Angelika, 'Grundzüge der Entwicklung der Frauenarbeit von 1880 bis 1980', in *Strukturwandel der Frauenarbeit 1880–1980*, ed. Walter Müller et al. (Frankfurt a. M., 1983).

Willson, Perry R., *The Clockwork Factory: Women and Work in Fascist Italy* (Oxford, 1993).

Wollstonecraft, Mary, *A Vindication of the Rights of Men, with A Vindication of the Rights of Woman and Hints*, ed. Sylvana Tomaselli (Cambridge, 1995).

Wunder, Heide, *'Er ist die Sonn', sie ist der Mond': Frauen in der Frühen Neuzeit* (Munich, 1992).

Zancan, Marina (ed.), *Nel cerchio della luna: Figure di donna in alcuni testi del XVI secolo* (Venice, 1983).

Zimmerman, Susan, *Die bessere Hälfte? Frauenbewegungen und Frauenbestrebungen im Ungarn der Habsburgermonarchie 1848 bis 1918* (Budapest, 1999).

Index

CPSIA information can be obtained
at www.ICGtesting.com
Printed in the USA
LVHW050839030721
691496LV00011B/70